Gulf
of
Carpentaria

hem
nd

Cape
York
Peninsula

G   C   O

Great Barrier Reef

S   E   A

Cairns

ERN

ORY

Townsville

20°

Springs

QUEENSLAND

Rockhampton

U T H

Coopers Cr.

Grey Range

Brisbane

L. Eyre

Flinders Range

30°

t Augusta

RALIA

Darling R.

NEW
SOUTH
WALES

Great Dividing Range

Newcastle

Murray R.

Mildura

Murrumbidgee R.

Sydney

T

A

Adelaide

Canberra

Port Kembla

S

VICTORIA

Murray
Great Alps

M

Melbourne

A

N

Bass
Strait

S

E

A

40°

TASMANIA

140°

150°

Hobart

140°

150°

Their Shining Eldorado:

A JOURNEY THROUGH

AUSTRALIA

THE EDGE OF THE RIFT (Memories of Kenya)
THE FLAME TREES OF THIKA (Memories of an African Childhood)
BACK STREET NEW WORLDS (A Look at Immigrants in Britain)
WITH FORKS AND HOPE: An African Notebook
A NEW EARTH
FOUR GUINEAS (A Journey through West Africa)
THE SORCERER'S APPRENTICE (A Journey through East Africa)
RACE AND POLITICS IN KENYA (with Margery Perham)
EAST AFRICA (Commonwealth in Pictures)
WHITE MAN'S COUNTRY (Lord Delamere and the Making of Kenya)
BRAVE NEW VICTUALS (An Inquiry into Modern Food Production)
SUKI: A Little Tiger (with photographs by Laelia Goehr)

Novels

A MAN FROM NOWHERE
THE INCIDENT AT THE MERRY HIPPO
THE RED ROCK WILDERNESS
A THING TO LOVE
I DON'T MIND IF I DO
THE WALLED CITY
RED STRANGERS (A Story of Kenya)
DEATH OF AN ARYAN
MURDER ON SAFARI
MURDER AT GOVERNMENT HOUSE

Their Shining Eldorado:

A JOURNEY THROUGH

AUSTRALIA

by Elspeth Huxley

WILLIAM MORROW
& COMPANY, INC.
NEW YORK 1967

1-15-73

To Isla and Nevil Stuart
Canberra, 1965

A Note About the Author

Though born in England, Elspeth Huxley
spent her childhood in Kenya, where her
parents were pioneers. She returned to
England to attend college, received an
agricultural degree from Reading University,
and thereafter completed a year of graduate
study at Cornell University in Ithaca, New
York. In 1931, she married Gervas Huxley,
a first cousin of Julian and Aldous Huxley.
Mrs. Huxley is the author of twenty-one
previous books including *Back Street New
Worlds, With Forks and Hope: An African
Notebook,* and *The Flame Trees of Thika:
Memories of an African Childhood.* Mr. and
Mrs. Huxley live on a dairy farm in Wiltshire, England.

List of Maps
and Illustrations

General Map of Australia   end paper

New South Wales   61

South Australia   141

Victoria and Tasmania   159

Western Australia   209

Northern Territory   279

Queensland   351

Photographs appear between pages 48-49, 176-177, and 272-273.

Contents

	List of Maps and Illustrations	9
	Foreword	13
1	Sydney	17
2	Canberra and Tidbinbilla	41
3	Snowy and Kosciosko	59
4	The Golden Fleece	71
5	Broken Hill	92
6	Kangaroos	107
7	The Murray, Fruit and Wine	126
8	Adelaide	139
9	Melbourne	157
10	Tasmania	184
11	Goldmines in the West	208
12	Perth	234
13	The Northwest	254
14	Northern Territory	277
15	Aborigines	303
16	Alice Springs	326
17	Tropical Queensland	350
18	The Great Barrier Reef	368
19	South of Capricorn	381
20	Birds and Beasts	396
	Glossary	413
	Bibliography	416
	Index	421

Foreword

It is customary to preface a book of this kind with a note of thanks to those whose help and advice enabled the author to write it. Were I to attempt this, the list of names would read like a telephone directory and even then be incomplete. Australian hospitality is legendary, and in my case the legend was true. All I can do is to thank with very genuine sincerity the very large number of kind and generous people who went to so much trouble to advise me where to go, help me to get there, and invite into their homes a complete stranger, whom they treated with the utmost good humour, patience and benevolence. This blanket acknowledgment is indeed a poor return for so much, but I can only ask my benefactors to accept it with my grateful thanks and if possible to forgive any abuses and misuses to which they may think any of the help they gave me has been subjected.

There is, I need hardly say, far too much to be seen and heard and guessed about in Australia for any itinerant—and we all seem to be in a perpetual White Rabbit sort of hurry, continually looking at watches and muttering about being late—to do more than skim the surface, and a very small part of the surface at that. There are whole areas of Australian life I did not even try to sample, very important areas, too, such as those concerned with education and with law and justice, with politics and organized labour, with social security and health, with religion and the churches; with aspects of the economy such as manufacturing and industry, such as banking and commerce and the great financial flywheels that keep the economy revolving at such a remarkable pace; with the colonial empire in Southeast Asia, the armed forces and military policy, and rocketry and nuclear research, and with many other pregnant things.

13

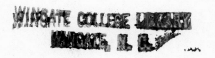

Roughly three out of every four Australians live in cities, work in shops and offices and factories, and have scarcely ever seen a sheep, except in bits when oven-ready, or a mustering yard, except on TV. I know that, to give a balanced picture, I have said too little about the daily lives of these three city dwellers and too much about the fourth concerned with livestock and tillage—too much about the animals and outback and too little about the men and women of Australia's heart, which is worn, in the geographical sense, on a sea-washed sleeve instead of in a manly chest. But then I have not tried to give a balanced picture—merely some personal observations about some of the people, places and things that interested me most and came my way; and I suspect this is about all any traveller can hope to do who does not set out to compile an encyclopedia, a deep thesis, or a wide anthology.

I have used the word "Commonwealth" in its Australian sense, to mean the central government in Canberra which spreads its umbrella over six federated states and eleven territories (two internal and nine external), and not in the sense used outside Australia, to mean that loose league of independent nations that has inherited certain links, practices and associations from the defunct British Empire. Sums of money in this book are stated in Australian dollars. The Australian dollar is equal to roughly an eighth more than the American. I am more than grateful to the officers of the Australian News and Information Bureau of the Department of the Interior, both in Canberra and London, for answering factual queries with such efficiency and dispatch and for supplying photographs, and to the invariably kind and courteous staff of the libraries both at Australia House and in Canberra, where Mrs. Dawson gave me so much valuable help.

Their Shining Eldorado:

A JOURNEY THROUGH

AUSTRALIA

Their shining Eldorado
Beneath the southern skies . . .

The Roaring Days
by Henry Lawson

ONE

Sydney

You reach Australia when they serve you chops for breakfast in your Qantas aircraft, 30,000 feet above the central desert. At this hour, if you are British, eating pig is orthodox and eating lamb is not. So you know you have come to a strange land, a trifle heathenish as all strange lands are, with outlandish practices. Chops for breakfast! You have to guess at country that you cannot see, smell, or feel; far below, it lies in blackness, silent and empty. I was reading *Voss*. It was odd to sit immersed in that somber tale of exploration, and the destruction of its principals in the cruel emptiness beneath us, while sealed in this cocoon of luxury and ease, and to know that somewhere down below, in the indifferent dark, lay the bones of Ludwig Leichhardt, the prototype of Voss, and his six companions—bones that even the aborigines, whose powers of observation the explorer Ernest Giles considered to be "unsurpassed among mankind," failed to discover.

In the next seat was a girl from Melbourne returning from a lengthy exploration of the British Isles, which she had partly spent as an Exmoor midwife, cycling through rain to deliver babies at remote farms. In her leisure hours she had taken to staghunting, travelling with the harbourer in his Land Rover and getting to know the haunts and habits of the deer, or striding on foot through bog and heather. She was a slight, fragile-seeming individual, more like a ballet dancer than a huntress. Australian enterprise.

Then we were in Sydney, and in Sydney was the sun. That must surely be your first, last and most abiding impression of this shining continent: the sun. From it springs the whole Australian temperament—or perhaps from the union of sun with sea. This country is a rim containing people round a withered hub and fringed by over 12,000 miles of coast lapped or pounded by oceans.

As for Sydney, throughout the year it enjoys an average of nearly seven daily hours of sunshine, a fact that, to a British Islander, equates it with paradise. (Brisbane, Adelaide and Perth have even more.) Nearly everyone is nut-brown, well-nourished and informally clad—on the famous beaches scarcely clad at all except in muscular plumpness. Hair is bleached, children marvellously blond and healthy. In essence it is Mediterranean; Sir Joseph Banks thought the climate about the same as that of Toulouse.

Here, on a day in January, 1788, when the First Fleet anchored near the present Circular Quay, was the nation born. Captain Arthur Phillip, who sailed through Sydney Heads on a reconnaissance from Botany Bay, was not far out when he called this "the finest harbour in the world." Inlets, bays, creeks, peninsulas and promentories are everywhere; there is scarcely a flat stretch or a dull square yard. The sea is all about you. It sparkles, it is blue. The wind is salt, the buildings white, the trees green.

Men have spoiled the situation but have not been able to subdue it, although what the architect Robin Boyd has called "the Australian Ugliness" is rampant. Poles and pylons, cables and TV masts, roads and hoardings, shops and signs, straggle up and down this rugged, indented, wooded coastline for twenty miles and more in most directions; but the sea remains, the cliffs, the foam-creamed beaches and the grey-green gums. Ferryboats, tankers, tugs and liners weave about the waters of Port Jackson, which deals with over four thousand ships a year. In the old quarter of the city survive a few of the graceful buildings put up by Governor Lachlan Macquarie between 1810 and 1821, lost now amid encrusted Victorian edifices and modern concrete towers, but for the most part Sydney is an amorphous, undistinguished sprawl of corrugated iron, brick and concrete interspersed by rivers of traffic. Streets are thronged, shops packed, parking spaces chockablock; everyone is going somewhere, everyone has cash to spend. "And at my feet success," Kipling wrote of the city at the time of the Jubilee. Sydney has kicked the ball squarely into fortune's net.

[2]

A golden fountain lifting into the soft summer night a fine golden spray that holds aloft a spinning golden ball; electric signs ablaze, taxis honking, people in white shirt sleeves and black jeans sauntering, smoking, window-shopping; girls laughing, light streaming from the open doors of pubs; smells of roasting coffee and frying steak; empty cartons trampled underfoot; the turkey-gobbling, syphon-bubbling sound of close-packed humans; a syrupy pop song from a jukebox, the twang of an electric guitar; narrow-fronted, squashed-up little shops that offer cigarettes and sweets and fizzy drinks; noise, lights and people, people crowding everywhere—such is the imprint of King's Cross of an evening, any summer evening after dark. And, in particular, that spinning golden ball above the spun-gold fountain: that is the King's Cross signature.

"Sydney's Chelsea," people call it, but it did not remind me of Chelsea. The nearest comparison might be Greenwich Village on a smaller scale. They say King's Cross is one of the most densely packed bits of city in the world; yet a few minutes' walk will take you into quiet, decorous streets quite devoid of flashing signs and Greek restaurants, espresso bars and pubs brimming over with people. But you can feel it humming there like an embedded dynamo. It is what you think of when you think of a city. Noise from its pubs rises like steam from a kettle. How people talk! Or shout, above the din of others shouting, of transistors and jukeboxes, of televisions chattering about sport, and shilling-in-the-slot movie machines.

King's Cross is in the old part of Sydney, but the New Australians have made it by staying up late, eating at all hours and drinking wine. Before World War II, to want to eat out after seven o'clock was practically impossible and morally wrong, and beer was the only drink for honest men. Honest women stuck to tea. Now you can get a nicely grilled steak, a glass of wine and good fresh coffee late into the night.

This is a part of the new Australia, yet there is something about it, impossible to pin down, that is old-fashioned. The feel of leisure, possibly, the lack of bustle, an Edwardian expansiveness, vulgarity and self-confidence? There are pubs along the waterfront that might have been in Wapping before the days when pubs were tarted up. They have the old kind of beer machines, frosted glass, underpowered and fly-spotted light bulbs, spittoons; you almost look for sanded floors and listen for hoof-beats on cobblestones. Half the customers at one I visited were aborigines: amiable, smiling, sweaty men with stained teeth, and their mountainous, jelly-flopping, wispy-haired women. When time was called, one of them in a striped vest and bare feet went round kissing everyone good night.

[3]

My companion was explaining that everyone in Sydney gambles on everything and that the latest craze is art. Dealers are on the prowl to sign up every promising young painter, pre-empt his work and hold it for a rise—not passively, however; they do not wait for time to ripen their investment. The name of their exciting new discovery is dropped, insinuated and spread around in the right quarters by ingenious means known to art dealers the world over and in Sydney carried to a fever pitch. Private galleries proliferate, and in a single week I think six one-man shows were opened. And a Sydney opening is memorable.

One that I attended was in Paddington, whose narrow, winding streets, lanes almost, divide rows of tiny houses built, it would appear, for a race of dwarfs; not bungalows for once, but miniature terraced dwellings, one room thick, often equipped with cast-iron balconies, and having stubby little bull-nosed roofs. They exude charm, and I longed to own one, possibly more to keep as a pet than to live in. For years they were neglected and, indeed, despised as out-of-date, inconvenient and slummy, and a great many were demolished. All would have gone had it not been for the birth, since World War II, of a new interest in old things, a respect for tradition and a reversal of judgment about the creations of the Victorian age. The John Betjeman, as it were, of Australia is Robin Boyd, trenchantly supported by the brilliant camera work of Dr. Graeme Robertson. Both are Melbourne men but they have not neglected Sydney; for Sydney possesses, in addition to its Victorian heritage, a few late Georgian buildings lacking in Melbourne, which was not founded until 1835.

Now these little Paddington dollhouses have become fashionable, and the middle classes, especially members of its more intellectual branches, have moved in, done them up with care and skill and painted them in bright colours. Cast-iron balconies, formerly thrown on scrap heaps, are hunted like truffles. It is a tragedy that the fashion came twenty years too late to save most of the terraces.

Delightful as the surviving houses are, they are not really suitable for art galleries, especially now that so few Australians are dwarfs. Approaching a house in which a one-man show was in the throes of opening, we found cars ravelled into an apparently inextricable tangle in the street and a mob of teen-agers jiving and twisting among vehicles and doorways to pop music emanating from bandsmen dressed as Ruritanian soldiers, blowing like maniacs into their trumpets and horns. Inside, above a layer of jam-packed, shouting faces, a bottle of champagne waved to and fro. We squeezed close enough to see that it was brandished by a young man dressed as a French sailor who was trying to serve drinks. Dozens of empty glasses were being thrust towards him by thirsty guests. He looked round with a hunted expression and then broke into a seraphic smile, put the bottle to his lips, and drained the lot.

The walls, in so far as you could see them, were hung with the kind of paintings you make with watering cans, besoms and garden trowels. No one was looking at them—no one could—but nearly all had red tabs and had probably fetched many hundreds of dollars apiece. By European standards prices for the works of unproven painters seemed to me enormous, if not absurd. Not all the pictures might have been paid for, however. When we battled our way out, the Ruritanian soldiery were trumpeting louder than ever and even more people, young and old, drunk and sober, were jiving in the street. Next morning's newspapers reported the opening to have been so successful that half the guests had been unable to force an entry, so a second opening had been arranged for the following day. This, I believe, was even more successful than the first. I am afraid I cannot remember the painter's name.

[4]

Once an opening is over, you can look at the pictures. In Sydney you will find most of them to be non-figurative—in the international modern idiom. Like airports, highways, flats, clothes, food—in fact, pretty well everything—the regional and national accent is blending into a universal speech.

This was not so among the previous generation of painters, of whom Sydney Nolan and Russell Drysdale are probably the best known outside Australia. Their work speaks in an accent unmistakably and authentically Australian. The stark, harsh contours of ring-barked trees and gibber rocks; the spare, whittled, undefeated men and women standing defiantly amid bitter deserts and dejected shacks; the droughted dying animals and upside-down birds; the myths an folklore of the nation's history—all that is there. A strange and at times bizarre imagery haunts these older, figurative painters, such as Arthur Boyd, Clifton Pugh, Charles Blackman, Albert Tucker, John Perceval and others.

Then the abstract movement came with its new and now fashionable exponents: John Olsen, John Passmore, Stanislaus Raportec, John

Coburn, Frank Hodgekinson, Laurence Daws, Michael .Kmit, William
Rose, Thomas Cleghorn. Although a good many of these painters have
exhibited outside Australia, few are as yet widely known; but the vigour
of their work, their hard-hitting use of colour and their inventiveness
will no doubt win for some of them positions in the world league of art.
The question is, for which? Everyone is backing his fancy; hence the
publicized openings, the ballyhoo and the inflated prices.

A generalization you often hear is that Melbourne painters tend to be
figurative, Sydney painters abstract in their art. In 1959 seven painters,
all but one of whom were Melbourne men (Blackman, Arthur and
David Boyd, Brack, Perceval, Pugh and Dickerson—the only Sydneysider) formed a group they called Antipodeans, held an exhibition, and
published a manifesto in which they defended figurative painting and
lashed out at abstract expressionists who "claimed to have invented a
new language." That was nonsense, said the Antipodeans; for the artist
"the image, the recognizable shape, the meaningful symbol, is the basic
unit of his language." To members of this group the image represented
"acceptance of, and involvement in, life"; whereas, through doctrinaire
pursuit of theory—or possibly a somewhat cynical pursuit of fashion—
abstract painters had detached themselves from the vulgar passions of
humanity. Sydney painters promptly hit back with an exhibition called
Muffled Drums which parodied and mocked the Melbourne practitioners, whom they considered pompous and stuffy.

This sorting of artists into geographical compartments is, of course,
very rough-and-ready. The oldest and—most critics consider—greatest
of the abstract painters dwelled for years in a shack on an island off the
coast of Queensland, patiently perfecting his lyrical, fluent and intricate
patterns of light and colour; this was Ian Fairweather, who is getting on
for eighty. One of the most original of the younger abstract artists,
Leonard French, whose somber-coloured, monumental patterns derive
in part from Russian iconography, is a Melbourne man. And the most
illustrious of them all stands above and beyond these schools and categories and fashions. Is there a finer portrait painter alive in the world
today than William Dobell? He paints most of his contemporaries off the
map. "In seeking to depict men and women as they really are," Dr.
Bernard Smith has written of Dobell, "the quality of his vision is Australian as Rembrandt's is Dutch, Goya's Spanish, and Hogarth's English. He has done for Australian art what Hogarth did long ago for the
art of England; he has shown that it is possible to achieve mastery of his

craft and pursue it . . . without abasing himself before the false prophets of culture."

Is there, can there be, a specifically Australian vision behind non-figurative art? More or less by definition, abstract art is universal; you cannot tie a national label to a rhomboid, a circle or a line of dots. Or, on second thoughts, can you? What about Persian ceramics, Hispano-Moresque pottery, and most Islamic art? But this argument would take us a long way from Sydney, and most Sydney painters, I think, would hold that abstract expressionism excludes a regional approach. "The thing which I always endeavour to express," John Olsen has written, "is an animistic quality—a certain mystical throbbing throughout nature." Another Sydney painter hopes "to unlink the false visual appearances and to portray the universal life beneath"; yet another is "concerned to say something about the vitality and pulse of life in people"; a third, to "make the non-visual visual." These are, I take it, among the universal aims of modern art, whether its practitioners work in Paris or in London, in Sydney or Melbourne or New York.

So I do not think that you could point to any peculiarly Australian style, school or idiom among the younger and non-figurative painters, each of whom is following a line of his own and trying to make the non-visual visual. But only an expert could pronounce on this. All the layman can be sure of is that the art world of Sydney, as of all urban Australia, is very much alive and frothing with confidence; and that Ruritanian bands, traffic jams, jiving juveniles and double openings suggest that painters and the public do not eat at separate tables, as in older countries they are apt to do.

[5]

Australians are said to consume more meat, beer and tea per capita than anyone else in the world; surely they must also produce more paintings, man for man? Who buys all these canvases, collages, and bits of pasteboard decorated with polyvinyl acetate? The rich, of course—imbursed both by the many secondary industries that have sprung up since the war, and are still mushrooming upwards and outwards, and by those older industries that have made Australia: the empires of the pastoralist and banker, shipper and merchant, publisher and chain-store owner, mining magnate and property dealer. The families who form this solid, prosperous and, by and large, respectable upper crust bought the output of the nineteenth- and early-twentieth-century painters such as

Arthur Streeton, Tom Roberts, Frederick McCubbin, Hans Heysen and Sir John Longstaff, moved on to the Dobell-Nolan-Drysdale-Boyd-Tucker-Pugh-Blackman generation, and now support the Olsens and Passmores, the Coburns and French's, Molvigs and Laycocks of today. Sydney is full of them, occupying comfortable, modern, but unpretentious houses—while to *be* rich is socially acceptable, to *act* rich is not—with a fine view over the harbour.

The justly famous modern art collection of Mr. Warwick Fairfax, for example, is catholic and exciting. For over a century the Fairfax family owned the Sydney *Morning Herald,* the oldest newspaper in Australia with a birthday going back to 1831. While a public company now controls this solid newspaper, together with several others including the Sydney *Sun* and the Canberra *Times* (into which Mr. John Pringle instilled new editorial life), two Fairfax brothers, Warwick and Vincent, remain its principal directors. The *Herald* has been a patron. It sent Sydney Nolan to record the effects of drought on man, beast and landscape in western New South Wales in 1944; eight years later the same painter was sent to the Northern Territory for the same purpose by the Brisbane *Courier-Mail.*

Although it is the oldest of the dailies and certainly, now under the vigorous editorship of Mr. Pringle, one of the most influential, in terms of circulation the *Herald* is by no means the largest. Two Melbourne papers beat it, the *Sun News-Pictorial* and another *Herald,* and in Sydney both the *Daily Telegraph*—which employs on its staff one of the country's foremost poets, Kenneth Slessor—and its own stable mate, the *Sun.* By American or British standards, circulations naturally are small. The largest—Melbourne's *Sun News-Pictorial*—prints a little over 600,000 copies, and the three main Sydney dailies around half this number. But Australians' per capita consumption of newspapers, as of meat, beer and tea, is one of the highest in the world. Fewer than twelve million people support some 650 newspapers—not all dailies, of course; the combined circulation of the dailies is little short of four millions, or one copy to every three inhabitants. The British ratio is one to two.

Although Australians, especially in Sydney, often tell you how Americanized they are, on the whole their press steers clear of the frenetic approach of so many popular American journals. There has never been a William Randolph Hearst in Australia, or even a Beaverbrook. By comparison the headlines appeared to me to be sober, informative and pedestrian, the general appearance rather smudgy and congested, and writers have a generous amount of elbow room. Reviews of books, films and plays, for example, are sometimes long enough to allow the reviewer to treat the entertainment seriously, instead of having to manufacture in a few sentences, or even in a single phrase, a pithy pseudo-judgment on a five-hundred-page novel, a three-hour film, or an important dramatic experiment.

The severest critics of the press are, as you would expect, its own members. Donald Horne, a former editor of the Sydney *Bulletin,* has accused it, in his hard-hitting attack on his countrymens' complacency, *The Lucky Country,* of sticking in a rut, of lacking punch and skepticism, of treating public affairs too solemnly and failing to send reporters out to get original stories—in brief, of self-satisfied mediocrity. The status of the journalist, he thinks, has declined; the lively minded and creative are no longer attracted; intellectually there is no cutting edge. If all this is true—and no itinerant can give a useful opinion—the Australian press is not the only culprit; much the same could be said about many newspapers all over the world.

The ratio of advertisements to news must surely fall into another "highest in the world" category. It seems incredible that anyone can do quite as much shopping as the citizens of the six major cities must accomplish if they are to keep afloat on an ocean of soap powders and groceries, beds and blankets, clothes and furniture, garden tools and paints and plumbing, that must threaten to submerge them. These advertisements bear out the reputation of Australians as the greatest do-it-yourself people in the world; there is nothing they cannot buy the wherewithal to do or make, from boats to bathrooms, stuffed birds to stained glass, home movies to engravings and telescopes and windmills, knitwear and cake stands and children's toys.

[6]

While, in general, the press reflects a British rather than an American image, in one respect geography has imposed upon it an American and not a British shape. It is a regional, and not a national, press. Perth is more than 2,000 air miles from Sydney, Adelaide over 700, and 1,000 by rail, Darwin just on 2,000. Distance, if not culture, has made each state a world on its own. The cost and time needed to distribute copies from a single center has prevented the emergence of a national newspaper—or, rather, did prevent this until mid-1964, when Mr. Rupert Murdoch, the son of Sir Keith Murdoch who ran the Melbourne *Herald,* launched the first national daily newspaper. *The Australian* is printed simultaneously in Canberra, Sydney and Melbourne and distributed to the other main cities by air.

It remains to be seen whether so ambitious and expensive a project can succeed. In type, make-up and general appearance *The Australian* has a clean, modern look that is matched by a crisp presentation, and it has attracted some of the best Australian writers. It was by no means meeting with general approbation, however. I at first gained an impression that it was an organ, if not quite of revolution, at least of subversive left-wing, *avant-garde* opinion, and was surprised, when I had a chance to read it, to find what seemed to be a good, sound, balanced newspaper, with an article reprinted from Britain's *Guardian* as possibly its boldest gesture in the direction of revolt, and a better coverage of foreign news than most of its fellows. Whether this will attract circulation is another matter; most Australians, like most people everywhere, take more interest in local racing results and bargains in hardware than in coups in Africa and the future of NATO. But while I was in Sydney the first Australian soldiers left for Vietnam, and as a disordered world closes in upon the lucky continent, perhaps Ibsen's dictum, ". . . that man is in the right who is most closely in league with the future," will prove to apply to Mr. Rupert Murdoch's venture; although it will remain expensive to fly newspapers two thousand miles and to print them simultaneously in three places at once. Even the United States still lacks a national daily newspaper.

Weeklies, of course, have always had a national circulation. The *Australian Women's Weekly* heads the list with some 835,000 subscribers, which implies a readership of perhaps three-quarters of all the women in Australia. The oldest, and possibly most famous, of the weeklies is the Sydney *Bulletin*. Between its birth in 1880 and the death in 1919 of its most famous editor, J. F. Archibald, this then trenchant and irreverend weekly at once expressed and shaped the spirit of a young, brash, cocky and expanding nation; it mocked the politicians, sniped at the mother country, scandalized the rich and beat the drum for a free, white and federated Australia, and it commanded a great constellation of talent. The verse and stories of Henry Lawson, archprophet of Aussie mateship, first appeared in the *Bulletin,* and masters of the black and white incisively delivered political and social judgments. Phil May and David Low worked for it, as did able artists less well-known overseas such as Norman Lindsay and D. H. Souter.

Hardening of the arteries overtook the *Bulletin,* however, and talent forsook it; after World War II it became virtually moribund. In 1961 the owners of the Sydney *Daily Telegraph,* the Australian Consolidated Press, reconstructed it somewhat on the lines of a less ambitious *Time.* I found it informative, well written and neatly produced, a useful guide to the issues of the day and to current books, films, plays and art. But its circulation is modest. There is also the *Nation,* generally held to be more independent and critical. It is hard for an outsider to judge; local politics are seldom exciting to the unconcerned. For this Australians pay the penalty of world neglect. They operate a system of democracy that really functions and stays democratic, and so they do not murder their rulers, stage military coups, wage civil wars, or lead sit-downs, walk-outs or diatribes at the United Nations. Therefore they stay out of the world news and do not get presented with enormous sums of money by the taxpayers of nations more industrious and law-abiding, and less corrupt and bloodthirsty, who are ridden by guilt because their citizens have, on the whole, too much to eat, instead of too little.

When interviewing overseas visitors, most newspaper reporters open with the query, "What are your impressions of Australia?" Sometimes they ask him this before he has disembarked from his ship or while waiting to claim his bags at the airport. Obviously there is little a visitor can say, except how nice it all looks, how bright the sunshine and how friendly the inhabitants, and you might think readers would get bored with that. Is not this hypersensitive concern with what the neighbours are saying a sort of hangover from colonial days, when people were unsure of themselves and of the status of their country? As citizens of a free, thriving, adult and remarkably successful nation, Aussies surely do not need to bother about what visitors think of them; they are presumably content to be taken as they are found.

The question may, of course, be intended as a test of the visitor's resourcefulness. I heard of one, a commercial rose grower, who replied, "This country would look better if it grew more of my roses." I wish now that I had thought of answering, "You would do better if you read more of my books."

[7]

Ten or fifteen miles south of Sydney you come to forests that look very much as they must have looked to Captain Cook when he sailed into Botany Bay. It was a surprise to see this thickly wooded virgin country so close to a city of over two million people, most of whom have motorcars and all of whom like to live in suburbs and have spread out in every other direction. The explanation seems to be that, when land was parcelled out for settlement, these hills were too stony, barren and waterless to be exploited; in due course they became forest reserves held by the state and so remain inviolate.

Ridge after ridge rolls away, tree-clad, a little hazy in morning air with a touch of autumn in it, a faint fuzziness as soft as pollen. The pale olive of the eucalypt foliage is touched here and there with a sober red. No houses, no villages, no development; Sydneysiders are lucky to have all this at their door. Later I looked up D. H. Lawrence's description of this stretch of country, flanking Botany Bay, in *Kangaroo:* of "the dark old rocks, and sombre bush with its different pale-stemmed dull-leaved gum-trees standing graceful, and various healthy-looking undergrowth, and great spiky things like zuccas." Like many others who have struggled to distill the essence of this ancient and elusive landscape, he groped for words to convey "the strange, as it were, *invisible* beauty of Australia, which seems to lurk just beyond the range of our white vision. You feel you can't *see*—as if your eyes hadn't the vision in them to correspond with the outside landscape." This does not torment the native-born who, in the words of the poet James McAuley, are "fitted to that land as the soul is to the body"; the flowers, he writes, "are wide-awake; the air gives ease," and "the magpies call you Jack and whistle like larikins at you from the trees."

We were headed for Wollongong and Port Kembla, home of the largest steel works in the British Commonwealth. This complex of smoke-belching blast furnaces and rolling mills, of mines and new houses and new towns, is one of the major suction points in Australia. It is sucking in capital and labour as a sea anemone sucks in plankton and, in the absorptive sense, sucking in migrants, though not as many as it needs. The steel company could put on another thousand men tomorrow if it could get them, so the personnel manager shouted above the pounding of one of the largest blast furnaces in the world.

People are still apt to think of Australia as a land of sheep, wheat and cattle, and so it is—wool remains the greatest *single* export and money spinner (and nowadays goes mostly to Japan). But for years the output of mines and factories has, in value, exceeded that of the land; it is now roughly two to one, and it is growing faster. The appetite for steel grows with it, and nearly half the men employed in manufacturing now work, directly or indirectly, in iron and steel.

This Port Kembla plant belongs to the largest company in Australia, the Broken Hill Proprietary, known to everyone as B.H.P., which since World War II has spent some $600,000,000 on development; all this money was raised in Australia. Soon this huge Port Kembla plant is to be eclipsed by an even bigger one going up at Whyalla in South Australia, where the largest ship hitherto built in Australia, an ore carrier of 47,500 tons, has lately been launched.

Like the mountains of Morne, the hills of Illawarra run down to the sea, or close to it, and they are stuffed with coal. To get at it, all you need do is to punch shafts into the hillside, and down it proceeds to the blast furnaces just below. This is one of the simplest and cheapest mining operations in the world. Most of the pig iron, however, comes all the way from Yampi Sound in Western Australia, a sea haul of over three thousand miles.

Migrants, as immigrants are incorrectly but conveniently called, make up about half the labour force at Port Kembla. They are drawn from thirty-three different nations. Yugoslavs top the list; next come Italians, whose numbers are dwindling, then the British. Most of the British migrants I spoke to, or who shouted at me above the din, were Welsh. "If I could put the clock back," one of them said, "I'd never have come. Not enough money." Wages look good on paper, but these men had failed to understand that at home their housing is subsidized and here it is not. Another disappointment is a lack of work for women. Migrants' troubles are the same from Wollongong to Whyalla, from Brisbane to Perth. So are their satisfactions. "Best lot of mates you could hope to find. When I came, I hadn't five bob in my pocket. I never said nothing, but they must have rumbled. Teatime, I found a ten-pound note in my tucker box." Another said, "I can have a drink here off-shift and we're all out of one basket. Back home, there's still the old school tie."

In one of the dozen hostels for migrants maintained by the Commonwealth Government in and around Sydney, I met an Austrian woman who had lived for five years in the hostel. Her family numbered seven, and she said that they could not afford to rent or buy a house. For her seven children she was drawing about $30 a month in family allowances, and all were living in the hostel at heavily subsidized rates. Financially, therefore, they were in clover, and the woman, knitting in the sunshine, seemed contented with her lot. In theory she should have left the hostel within two years, but all government departments are sensitive about their images, and that of the landlord kicking a family with seven little ones into the street is nowhere admired. And only about half the hostel accommodation available in Sydney was taken up.

An official told me that, after twenty years' experience in helping migrants to find their feet, three precepts had emerged. Emigrate young; expect both man and wife to work, and work hard; and bring some savings. "Nest-eggers" seldom fail, mainly because they can find or build a house, and possibly their prudence makes them better settlers. There are, of course, exceptions to all these rules.

[8]

"I dreamt that I dwelt in marble halls," sang Alfred Bunn. Had he visited the St. George League's club in Sydney he would have woken up to find his dream come true.

You enter through portals instead of going in by the door—the phrases spring unbidden to your lips, with others like "lavishly appointed," "spacious foyer,", "tasteful décor." They are really true. I have before me an everyday menu, in a plastic cover, measuring fourteen inches by ten. You may start with caviar, smoked salmon, or a lobster cocktail, continue if you wish with oysters—a choice of four kinds—or lobster Newburg, Thermidor, or Mornay; on to a whole spring chicken, or chicken Maryland, or roast duckling, or of course a steak, whether *tournedos,* filet mignon, T-bone, or Diane; or you might prefer a lobster or a chicken salad; naturally a sweet, perhaps a *bombe* or a *tartufi* or meringue; and then there are the chef's specials which include sweet and sour duck in Chinese style, fillets of snapper with oyster sauce, or chicken Maréschal.

For wine the choice is equally enticing: Chablis, Riesling, Leibfraumilch; Hermitage, Nuits St. George, St. Emilion; champagne naturally (imported at $6 a bottle), and sparkling Australian hock; liqueurs of thirteen varieties, old brandy and port. The diners sit at damask-covered tables with folded linen napkins, flowers, and a wine stand at the elbow; they are cosseted by thick carpets, indirect lighting, illuminated curtains and uniformed waiters in droves. There is of course an orchestra and a nightly floor show. Next door there is a ballroom that holds one thousand revellers, with an electrically operated mobile stage. Downstairs are snack bars, espresso bars, ordinary bars, games rooms, hairdressers, a gymnasium and a bowling alley.

And what, you may ask, is so wonderful about all that? We know it of old in the *Queens,* at the Hiltons, at all those Mediterranean and Caribbean resorts where the rich spend their leisure and directors their expense accounts; but not—or at any rate not until quite recently—in a working men's club.

Clearly there is no reason whatsoever why the surroundings in which Bill Bloggs and Jim Jones, the wage earners, eat their meals and enjoy their leisure should not be every bit as lavish as those provided for the Onassises and Gettys of this world. It is merely that ordinary wage earners cannot as a rule afford gracious living on quite such a scale. In Sydney they can. This is not because wages, good as they are, have soared into a sphere that would enable them to live, literally, on caviar and champagne. To join the St. George League's club costs each member about $5 annually. He can get a slap-up dinner for $2 and snacks at café prices; everything but food and drink is free. There are clubs like this in all the major cities and in a few of the minor ones, but this is probably the king of them all.

Just as, beneath the saloons of the *Queen Mary,* hum engines to drive the vessel through the seas, so at the foot of a stairway with Italian marble walls click and whirr the motivating forces of the St. George League's club—poker machines. Before each one stands a silent and devoted acolyte feeding coins into the mouth of his god. Sounds of clicking handles and rattling coins blend into a kind of mechanized prayer. Long rows of white-shirted backs reinforce an impression that you have stumbled upon the observance of some religious rite. Now and again a ping and a rattle signify that one of the idols has regurgitated a mouthful of coins. Has the offering been rejected? The acolyte scoops up his tokens and starts patiently to feed his god again. An incense of tobacco smoke enfolds the scene. The atmosphere is reverend, devoted and absorbed. There is no levity.

Thanks to these serried ranks of slot machines, the club, which has a membership of 20,000 and a waiting list of applicants much, much longer than that of the Union League or the Athenaeum, made a profit of nearly $500,000 last year. That was after it had given $100,000 to charities and financed many sporting activities. For it originated as a rugby league club and has since extended its range to cover many other sports and pastimes: cricket, of course; bowls and boxing; swimming and table tennis; darts, squash, snooker, golf, tennis; there is even a Prawn Club, presided over by a King Prawn.

The social side followed after, and now such clubs as these are part of the Australian way of life. With increased affluence has come increased decorum. You cannot roam about these marble halls in a singlet or a bikini, and there is rather a elaborate set of rules. Jackets, collars and ties are compulsory in dining room and ballroom, and slacks for women are banned. Elsewhere women may wear slacks until seven o'clock, but not thereafter, and expose their midriffs at no time; in the men's bar the patrons may wear shorts or working clothes until the same hour but after that must change into trousers and jackets.

Here you may see into the very workings of a social sausage machine. In at one end go rough workingmen, cloth caps and horny hands and collarless shirts and four-letter words and all; out at the other come strings of middle-class sausages, neat and smooth, all alike and all gentlemen. Profanities and reeling drunks would be as out of place as weevils in a wedding cake. Here is the great leveller-upper of our day. Concerts of classical music are inserted between pop singers and television personalities, Christmas entertainments laid on for senior citizens (the Australian euphemism for old-age pensioners), university scholarships provided for members' young. "We gave more money to the Churchill fund," the secretary proudly told me, "than Leeds and Bradford combined."

In the basement is a cellar full of enormous barrels, each attached to a plastic pipe that conducts the beer into one or other of the bars. Rivers of beer are consumed. (But, in the dining room, more table wines are drunk then beer.) The kitchens are more wonderful even than the marble halls, replete with gleaming metal units, electrical devices, thermostatically controlled cooking cabinets and machinery for doing practically everything, all under the control of a chef aged twenty-four, trained at the East Sydney Tech. Lobsters are ordered in lots of 10,000 pounds at a time.

It was all so impressive that perhaps I have been carried away, so I will end with a small *winge* (Australian for complaint). The brochure I was given referred to a lounge whose "spacious carpeted comfort includes a large library and reading room." I asked if I might see the library. Without enthusiasm my guide led me to a door labelled Reading Room that opened into a bare, uncarpeted cubbyhole, furnished with a few chairs and a table at which sat three senior citizens sticking newspaper cuttings into a scrapbook. Attached to a wall were two empty shelves. Books? "No demand," my companion said brusquely. Not even paperbacks, James Bond? "Those get taken." Clearly a dilemma—a demand either too weak or too strong.

I was wrong about the shelves being empty. Lying on its side at the back there was one book: a volume of the *Official History of the Great War of 1914–18*.

I wished I had been able to see the club of an evening, when things really hum. They were getting ready for Mother's Day: two sittings in the dining room, a souvenir menu and special wine list, an organ recital; bookings limited to one thousand which had all been taken up weeks ago. That was on the Sunday. On Monday there is always Old Tyme dancing; there was to be boxing on the Tuesday, wrestling on the Wednesday, a comedy show on Thursday, and then *Iolanthe* with a full orchestra on the electrically operated mobile stage.

At the foot of the Italian marble stairway the one-armed bandits clicked and whirred to pay for it all. The club has 150 of them, and I doubt if one is ever idle for a minute of the day.

[9]

The zoo in Sydney is a zoo and not a nature sanctuary, and it was interesting to contrast the two approaches to keeping animals in captivity. A sanctuary's aim is to imitate as closely as possible the natural habitat; iron bars and concrete floors are anathema. In Sir Edward Hallstrom's zoo there are no bones made about concrete or the status of the animals. They are captives, and it is useless, on seventy acres in a Sydney suburb, to attempt to deceive them into thinking otherwise.

"You can breed anything in captivity if you know how," Sir Edward Hallstrom said. His formula is simple: cleanliness plus feeding, which add up to perfect health. Two strict rules are observed: concrete floors, hosed down every day and hosed thoroughly, and no food unfit for human consumption to be given to any animal. And the food must be fresh. Sir Edward has a farm just outside Sydney where lucerne is cut every morning at seven o'clock and is in the cages by ten.

Strictly speaking, it is not "Sir Edward's zoo"; it is called Taronga Park and belongs to Sydney. But he shaped and made and now directs it with the love of a progenitor and the drive, at over seventy, of a man in his prime. When I met him he had just returned from New Guinea and was dispatching to Chester a planeload of birds of paradise he had brought with him. Having made a fortune out of refrigerators, he has spent most of it on the zoo.

Everything is spick and span. Through trees and flowering shrubs and creepers, and over beds of flowers, glimpses of the ocean beguile the eye. In their cages and exercise yards the animals nibble fresh lucerne and carrots. I have never seen captives with more bloom on their coats, an many gave evidence of fertility; we saw a tubby little rhino born the day before, and many joeys hopping in and out of pouches. Most of the marsupials breed freely in captivity, and indeed almost anywhere; there are, I believe, even wallabies breeding in Derbyshire.

Most animals have food preferences, just as humans do, and these are sometimes unexpected. Gorillas, it seems, have a weakness for sweet potatoes, rhinos for the fruit of Moreton Bay figs. At the other extreme are the koalas, so conservative that they will eat the leaves of only about twelve species of eucalyptus out of several hundred and perish rather than change their diet. What is more, they eat the leaf tips only and must get through enormous quantities, since each koala consumes between two and three pounds a day. To deal with all this roughage, they pack into a modest abdomen—a koala is no larger than a medium poodle and weighs about thirty pounds—an appendix six to eight feet long and have pouches in their cheeks for storing herbage.

I had supposed koalas to be almost extinct outside zoos and nature sanctuaries and was surprised to be shown scratches on the trunk of a tall blue gum in a garden at Clareville Beach, on the outskirts of Sydney, made by these entrancing little animals who could often be heard, my host assured me, squawking in the branches; this was one of the approved trees. At night we shone a torch into the foliage, but there was no one at home.

The numbers of wild koalas are, it seems, building up satisfactorily, after the near-extermination of the species about a generation ago. It is a dreadful story. Once countless millions of koalas placidly digested gum leaves all over the eastern and southern portion of the continent; the aborigines left them in peace. Then came the white man with his weapons and his greed. Koala pelts had value; in the first quarter of our bloody century an estimated ten million were sold. In South Australia the last koala perished soon after World War I. In Queensland, where the creatures had enjoyed some measure of protection after an epidemic had seriously depleted their numbers in the early 1900's, traders and trappers lobbied the state government so successfully that, in 1927, licenses were issued to 10,000 trappers. In that year alone 600,000 koalas were massacred.

And so for years the species tottered on the brink of extinction. What threatens it now is not direct slaughter—koalas are protected, and I think effectively protected, everywhere—but the shrinkage of the food supply. If people have stopped trapping and shooting, in order to grow more food and build more houses for their own swelling numbers every year they cut down more and more trees.

Rather surprisingly, koalas have discarded their tails and substituted calloused pads, on which they sit for hours in forks of trees, wearing an expression of sagacity utterly at variance with their natures; they are, I am afraid, stupid animals—certainly too stupid to defend themselves or to learn the first law of survival in the wilds, fear of man. They are, however, very endearing, with their black-button noses, their soft and guileless eyes, their furriness and childlike arms that clasp the branches and with which they will enfold your neck. They do not bite; they move sedately and very seldom drink: model citizens. They are powerful tourist attractions. It is reassuring to know that those countless tea cozies with koala faces on sale at every notion counter and in every curio shop are not made of the pelts of these harmless creatures but of kangaroos.

[10]

Koalas were not the only form of wildlife in my host's garden at Clareville Beach. Just outside the door, beside a paved terrace, was a tree harbouring a kind of loose, untidy nest in which dwelt a phalanger, or possum. I did not discover which of the many species of the *Phalangeridae* family it belonged to; it was one of the larger gliders, or flying squirrels. (No relation to European squirrels, any more than koalas are to bears.) Gliders have evolved folding membranes between their legs and bodies which enable them, like the young man on the flying trapeze, to fly through the air with the greatest of ease and to make graceful landings on branches as much as twenty-five or thirty feet away. Like most marsupials, they sleep by day and emerge by night only, to feed on insects, nectar, or the flowers of trees. They have strong, prehensile tails by which some species hang upside down to feed, and they range in size from creatures as large as foxes to pygmies of such dimensions that, according to the naturalist John Gould, "an ordinary sized pill-box forms a convenient domicile" for them. These tiny phalangers can rear four young ones at a time in a minute pouch; their newborn babies must surely be the smallest mammals on earth and need a magnifying glass to be seen.

I have called the domicile of the koalas and phalangers a garden, but this is inexact; it is a stretch of steep hillside, more or less a cliff, clothed in its native vegetation, and with its feet washed by an inlet of the Pacific. Yachts and dinghies come and go with gaily coloured sails. Across the water lies a natural forest, safe from development; at the rear, a precipice with caves once dwelt in by some long-forgotten tribe of aborigines. From the terrace steps wind down to a boathouse and a small, home-built swimming pool. Papaws and bananas bear fruit among the gums. I had no idea that Sydney was so subtropical, but this is a particularly sheltered spot.

The center of the city is only twenty miles away and my host commutes daily to his office by car, leaving his wife Elaine to paint in rich colours Mediterranean-looking canvases, or to design the sets and costumes for stage and ballet for which she is renowned. At weekends there is sailing and bathing and fishing—spearfishing has become a major Sydney sport. The less energetic sit in the sun, prune fruit trees, weed terraces, or enjoy long, leisurely visits with long, cool drinks and good-natured, relaxed and gossipy conversations that seldom decline, as their British counterparts do rather too often, into complaints, criticisms and winges, if only about the weather. And if they do not perhaps—or seldom—probe very deeply into the world's great issues, in view of all the horrors that such probes must touch on, what a relief! You can fix a meal when you feel like it, go to the beach if you want to; people drop in. Wine, if bought in bulk, works out at little more than ten cents a bottle.

Lest all this should seem impossibly idyllic, I must mention a prevalence of midges and some nasty-looking spiders with fat, striped bodies and long, hairy legs. These, I was assured, are quite harmless. But the Sydney funnel-web, which is far from harmless, has been seen. This is one of the only two species, out of over 1,500, dangerous to man. There are spiders in Australia that catch birds. I am glad to say I did not see a giant Gippsland earthworm, which can grow up to twelve feet long, and gurgles as it writhes through the ground.

On Sunday morning we watched a yawl cast off from a nearby jetty, hoist her sail, and head towards the open sea. I asked where she was going. "Round the world," someone said. I thought this was a joke, but it was not. On board were two young men just finished with the university who had spent a couple of years in fitting up the vessel; now they were off to follow tides and winds and the inclinations of their hearts. They expected to be away at least a year. Half a dozen people waved good-by from the jetty; their first landfall would be Auckland. They had a red sail. I have often wondered how they fared.

[11]

There was a craze for Strine when I was in Sydney—or Sinny, as it is rendered in this ear-teasing tongue. The moment of its birth was when Monica Dickens, autographing copies of her books in a department store, inscribed in one: "To Emma Chissit," which she thought to be the name given by a customer who proffered a copy to be signed. The customer was furious, and after a confused conversation it emerged that her actual phrase had been: "How much is it?"

Professor Afferbeck Lauder of the University of Sinny then contributed to the *Herald* series of articles about Strine. He soon compiled a dictionary and phrase book. Bake necks, for instance, he identified as a popular breakfast dish, semmitch as two slices of bread with a filling, laze and gem as the opening words of any public speech. Flares are blooms or blossoms—wile flares, for example; air dress is your place of residence; and if you are an ass prad woman, you will keep it clean and tidy, which should give you a keen ebb tide, or desire for food.

Everyone was busy translating everyday speech into Strine. "Arm, arm, I bin bimbye errs nile. [Mum, mum, I've been bitten by a snail.]" "Ear, lemmy's ee. Dough bees illy, sniles dough bite. Cummin iran aveyer brekfuss—ice baked necks. [Here, let me see. Don't be silly, snails don't bite. Come in here and have your breakfast—nice bacon and eggs.]" "Dough wan baked necks. Ides oona avver hop eye. [I don't want bacon and eggs. I'd sooner have a hot pie.]" "Hop eyes aunt fur brekfuss, emenit imes die affter telyer hope eyes erfurt ee. [Hot pies aren't for breakfast, how many times do I have to tell you hot pies are for tea.]"

On a somewhat higher social level, a resident of Sinny's Naw Shaw (North Shore) might inform a friend: "Mervyn Bevvuv jess borta gloria soame. Airsply fair billis rilly. Its gotten egg mishner, wart-wall carps, pay show anna luvly rumps rum further kitties. [Merv and Bev have just bought a glorious home. Absolutely fabulous really. It's got an air conditioner, wall-to-wall carpets, patio and a lovely rumpus room for the kiddies.]" Strine is not, at first, an easy language and can get the native-born as well as visiting pommies into trouble. A shopper who asked for fly swatters in what she thought to be an appropriate part of a department store was directed to the toiletries. She failed there. Eventually a supervisor, acting as interpreter, led her back to her starting point. "I thought she said fice washers," the salesgirl explained.

A lively interest in the new tongue prompted Professor Lauder to write a simple guide and phrase book, *Let Stalk Strine,* and the vocabulary grew. There is garment, meaning an invitation to visit, as in "garment seemy snile seward icon do"; harps, meaning thirty minutes past the hour, as in harps tait; jans, an opportunity, as in "he neffrader jans"; furry tiles, defined as sick humour for children; garbler mince, which has a double meaning: either in a little while, as in "I'll beewiv ewe garbler mince," or as a form of greeting, as in "with the garbler mince of the gem of directors." It took me some time even to interpret the professor's name. (Afferbeck Lauder: alphabetical order.) The secret of his identity was at first closely guarded—or should I write "known new hooey wars"?—but subsequently Mr. Alistair Morrison, a commercial artist, revealed himself to be the philologist. He has had the satisfaction of seeing *Let Stalk Strine* go through ten editions and a Strine Association formed whose members are translating into the new tongue *The Merchant of Venice.*

[12]

Every visitor to Sydney has to see the Opera House, emerging like some fabulous creature from a gigantic steel and concrete egg in the heart of the harbour. Everywhere except in Sydney it has become a joke. The first estimate of its cost was, I think, $8,000,000, which seemed quite a lot for a city of two million inhabitants without an operatic company or even an operatic tradition; that belonged to Melbourne, in so far as there was one. However, Sydneysiders decided to have an Opera House, raised $800,000 by public subscription, and held an international competition. This was won by the Danish architect Joern Utzon, with one of the boldest and most imaginative designs to emerge in recent times from any European architectural office.*

To have a bold, original idea and be precise about the details of its execution is perhaps impossible; the eight million dollars can have been little more than a guess. It did not prove to be a good guess. Very soon

---

* Mr. Utzon has since resigned, following a dispute with the New South Wales Government.

it was revised upwards, and it has been revised upwards continually ever since. By 1965 it had got as far as $46,000,000, and no one supposed that this would be the last word. The building was not half completed; by the time it is, costs may have doubled again. Few people mind. No one has to pay taxes towards it; no one has to go to rich Foundations with a begging bowl; no one has to get into debt or worry himself into ulcers. Construction, I was told, was costing less than $6,000,000 a year, and there was a good $10,000,000 on hand.

It is all financed by lotteries. A draw takes place every few months with a first prize of $200,000 and a great many smaller prizes. The money rolls in and the Opera House slowly rises from its massive foundations to float like some white, serene sea kraken, with wide cocked ears or batlike wings, on the sparkling blue surface of the harbour, facing out to sea. All round are ships, and the famous bridge arches across the water humped like a whale. Tugs hoot, horns blow, gulls cry, ferries chug to and fro; it is all a kaleidoscope of life and movement. This is Bennelong Point, called after Captain Phillip's favourite aborigine whose camp was there, who used to dine with the governor and was sent to England as a kind of exhibit.

This will be an enormous opera house; already you feel dwarfed by those great arching ribs, those oceans of cement, those massive concrete walls. Its construction presented engineering problems that had never before been posed, let alone solved: such, for example, as how to construct those huge, arching ribs that sweep upwards and outwards to support the precast concrete shells that will form the roof, or roofs, of the Opera House. It is the roof that is so original—ten roofs, to be precise, that will rise above the harbour like sails, it is commonly said, but they put me in mind of the curved wings of white bats or of cocked ears. A vast number of segments of varying weights and sizes had to be made and then fitted together with a kind of glue. The necessary calculations have been worked out by computers, and without computers they could not have been made. Up to date the sums have occupied over 2,000 computer hours, and one computer hour, roughly speaking, equals forty-five working years of a man's life; so a lot of men with a lot of working lives would have been needed. All of the ten united and yet separate, sprouting roofs are to be faced with white ceramic tiles especially made in Sweden, and the computers say there are to be 1,555,-941 of these. How they will shine and glitter in the brilliant sunshine, high above the blue sea!

Several opera halls are planned, the largest to hold nearly three thousand people; an experimental theater; forty-eight dressing rooms and nineteen rehearsal rooms. Everywhere are balconies and decklike spaces where you can survey the harbour and cool your forehead in a sea breeze. Inside, every foot of wall—and there is to be wall after wall after wall—will be panelled in plywood. Opposite stands a tallish skyscraper, but the bats' wings—or could they be sea elephants' ears?—will rise considerably higher. Some of the more down-to-earth details have been brushed aside. With all those thousands of people coming to imbibe culture, or possibly to attend conferences, the restaurant will hold a mere 250, and there appears to be nowhere to park the car. But Sydneysiders do not mind; a few office blocks and shops and flats beside the harbour can be bulldozed out to make way for parking spaces when the time comes. No one knows when the structure will be completed—certainly not before 1970; the pace lags. It was begun on March 2, 1959.

I would like to be able to report that my ears were deafened by the screech of drills, the pounding of hammers and rattle of cranes as eager workers, inspired by the grandeur of their task, set to with a will, like the builders of medieval cathedrals, to complete the Opera House on schedule; but just as I arrived a whistle blew, the workers laid aside their tools or climbed off their machines, and a restful silence reigned. Another strike. Scarcely a day has passed without a strike somewhere or other on the site. So Sydney's Opera House rises very slowly from the harbour. Still, gradually it does rise, that great sea kraken, and when completed it will be among the finest and the gayest buildings not only in the Southern Hemisphere but in the world.

On my last morning in Sydney I hailed a taxi whose driver was checking the sum put into his hand by the previous fare. He had been paid six cents too little. Anticipating a London taxi driver's usual reaction to such a misfortune—I had just read of one fined the equivalent of $150 for endangering the life of a fare who only tipped him threepence —I climbed nervously into the seat beside the driver. This burly Australian merely thrust the coins into his pocket and remarked, "Poor bloke needs it more'n I do. Where to, missis?" And we were on our way.

TWO 〰️

Canberra and Tidbinbilla

In Canberra the first home I entered had a Japanese flower arrangement on a Japanese mat: the owner had not long returned from a Tokyo posting. Canberra has become cosmopolitan. It is also probably the most middle-class city in the world. One-third of the breadwinners are public servants and there are scarcely any factories, but there are three million trees.

Fifty years ago there was little here beyond dry, brown scrub, coarse grass and gum trees. There was a church, St. John's, built by the former owners of these limestone plains, a family of Campbells. In the middle of Canberra there is a mound and on the mound a slab of stone to mark the spot where, in 1913, the governor-general's wife, Lady Denman, unfolded a slip of paper bearing the name, until then kept secret, of the still nonexistent capital; in reading it out, she settled the pronunciation. No one really wanted a federal capital, and it remained a capital in name only until, in World War II, Victorians and New South Welshmen temporarily ceased their feuding and the Commonwealth Government stepped in to centralize the income tax and so secured the key of the coffers.

Thenceforward Canberra swelled like a balloon and it is still swelling; it has reached the size of Portland, the largest city in the state of Maine. Its kernel is not a group of buildings but an artificial lake that has cost millions and enraged many citizens who do not live in Canberra and think the money would have been better spent on some less ornamental and more productive project such as a dam or irrigation scheme. But Canberra dwellers are very proud of their lake, which attracts birds, and envisage future lakeside esplanades, parks, concert halls and restaurants.

41

Water fascinates Australians, so often made or broken by its lack or excess. A belief that in the arid center lay a great inland sea drew on many of the first explorers. "Tomorrow we start for the ranges," wrote Charles Sturt, "and then for the waters—the strange waters on which boat never swam and over which flag never floated; but both shall, ere long." This is the driest continent in the world. People douse you in statistics: if all the rivers were made to flow inland, they would spread over the surface to a depth of one and one-third inches of water annually, compared with nine inches in the United States; the average rainfall is only sixteen inches against twenty-six for the rest of the world; six times as much water flows into the Danube as down all the rivers of Australia lumped together, and so on.

I never heard Canberra's lake called by its official name, which is Lake Burley Griffin, after the unfortunate Chicago architect who, with his wife, won the competition for a new capital and city beautiful in 1912. Unfortunate because of the many frustrations he met with after he arrived in 1913 to carry out a grand design that, in the meanwhile, had been mangled by a government board which substituted a travesty of its own. The competition had been boycotted by Australian and British architects on the grounds that the prize money, $3,500, was too meager and lay judges unfit to adjudicate.

[2]

For seven years Walter Burley Griffin battled with bureaucracy and then resigned in despair to practice privately in Melbourne and Sydney. He won a reputation for boldness and originality—in Chicago he had worked with Frank Lloyd Wright—combined with a disregard for practical detail which modern admirers ascribe less to professional incompetence than to a gentleness of character that did not fit him to deal with unscrupulous contractors: to faults of execution rather than design.

Griffin was a romantic idealist, disciplined by the doctrine of functionalism which then ruled the architectural world. His aim, he wrote, was "to treat architecture as a democratic language of everyday life, not a language of an aristocratic, especially educated cult, as it has been since the year 1500, when architecture as a natural expression and a creative art died with the Renaissance."

He wanted to build homes for ordinary people, but not ordinary homes; he wanted to give each family the dignity of space, harmony and, above all, contact with nature. He was a lover of light, air, water and trees. "We need a common basis," he wrote, "running through all our buildings—the architect is taught too much. The basis of our study is nature itself—beauty is where nature is allowed to work itself out."

In Sydney, in 1921, he designed a garden suburb called Castlecrag in which he expressed his architectural beliefs. "I want Castlecrag to be built so that each individual can feel that the whole of the landscape is his. No fences, no red roofs to spoil the Australian landscape." Each house was to have the outlook of a castle; one-fifth of the whole area was to be kept *au naturel* as reserves; houses were to have flat roofs, courtyards, cloisters, light, space and air. Every Australian home needs "a terrace for outlook, for secure and airy sleep-outs and for promenades and gardens." The vein of romanticism expressed itself in crenellated parapets and embossed wall designs. In his opinion, "civilised men has never had a greater opportunity to find his home in the middle of a natural paradise than that offered him in the Australian city." As with so much of Griffin's work, most of Castlecrag remained on paper. Only fifteen houses took shape.

In technique, as well as in his vision, Griffin was an innovator. In his invention of a cheap, machine-made standard concrete block that needed no plastering or bedding he was a pioneer in prefabrication, and he patented an arrangement of small white tiles which enabled him to reduce the pitch of Melbourne roofs. Why pitch roofs so high when there is no snow? His were almost flat and got him into trouble: some leaked. A goldfish tank built into a ceiling so as to allow the shadows of sportive fish to flicker across a polished dining-room table dripped disastrously onto a grand inaugural dinner. The wife of another rich client found bitumen oozing from above into her bath. Some of his wrought-iron drainpipes rotted away. But his legacy to Australians, Robin Boyd has written, was "a gallery of buildings which could have been their greatest inspiration." Most of these have been altered beyond recognition or demolished altogether.

By 1930 his practice had so fallen away that he was thankful to accept a commission to design some municipal incinerators. With his native optimism he took this not as a comedown but as a challenge to create beauty out of industrial ugliness. In 1937 he went to India to design a university library in Lucknow, fell off a scaffolding, and died of peritonitis at the age of fifty-one. Photographs depict a sensitive, intelligent countenance with an air of gentleness but not of weakness. He has been described as a small, shy, modest non-smoker and vegetarian, who seemed to make most of his meals off dates munched from a bag in suburban trains.

[3]

Griffin was not invited to design a single one of Canberra's buildings. After his resignation its growth proceeded spasmodically and piecemeal until the mid-fifties. Its heart remained a vacuum, but all around suburbs proliferated, each bungalow separately designed without the unity that Griffin had again and again returned to as the essential—a unity of over-all design. Like Washington, Canberra became a tragedy of a high aim and a single, creative vision frustrated by timidity, narrow-mindedness and petty jealousies. Parallels between the fate of the two cities are close; the plan drawn for a grand federal capital after 1790 by the French engineer Major Pierre L'Enfant also foundered, and Washington degenerated into a muddle of unrelated structures until after the Civil War.

Canberra's turning point came in 1955, when a select committee of the Senate put the Griffin plan back into the center of the picture, and Sir William Holford was summoned from London to bring it up to date. No fundamental changes were needed. On the contrary, Griffin had anticipated most of the ideas by then in fashion, such as those which have inspired Britain's New Towns. Canberra, Griffin had explained, was planned on the British model as a federation of small and independent groups, in contrast to the Continental plan of a unified whole which had arisen, he suggested, from needs of defense, the concept of the walled city. For walls Griffin had substituted space and trees. He fell in love with Australian trees. "The gum tree instead of being one continual monotony has strongly appealed to me. It is a poet's tree and ought to have a more dignified name. Gum tree! That does not fit at all. It's a wonderful tree—a decorator's tree." The tree-mindedness of modern Canberra would delight him.

Now the city's growth is controlled by the National Capital Development Commission set up in 1957 with wide powers, with funds that are at last adequate, and an enlightened professional commissioner. Stylistically it cannot but remain a hotchpotch. Everyone has put up the kind of building he liked and, on top of that, foreign missions have added a musical-comedy touch with embassies in national costume, like peasants dressed to pose for tourists: for the United States, a miniature Williamsburg; for South Africa, an old Dutch colonial farmstead complete with curly gables; for France, what Robin Boyd has called a ranch-style Petit Trianon, and so forth.

Politically Canberra has always been a hot potato, but two men have grasped it boldly. They could hardly have been more different men. The first was King O'Malley, American by origin, a swashbuckler who had prospered as a real estate salesman in Kansas by founding religious sects with such names as the Redskin Temple of the Cayuse Nation. In Australia he became Secretary for Home Affairs in the Commonwealth Government at the time the capital was planned and started, and a strong supporter of his compatriot Griffin. The second was Sir Robert Menzies, who in recent times has taken a personal pride in the metamorphosis of the capital from a dry, dusty, shabby and improvised suburban sprawl into a spacious garden city with an annual population growth of 12 per cent, one of the highest in the world. Most of the accouterments of a capital are in being or in building, and it has a superb climate: cold enough in winter to invigorate, warm enough in summer to send people to beaches only two hours' drive away. In its lambent, half-hazy autumn sunshine the foliage is as gold and crimson and magnificent as any in New Hampshire and Vermont. Teen-agers, however, find it dull: no niteries or pop orchestras, few coffee bars and, one would think, a low drug-addiction rate—respectability all round.

Most of the tourists who flock these days to Canberra make a pilgrimage to a memorial more like a temple dedicated to war itself as a technique than to the men wars have killed. In it are weapons of all kinds, from muskets to mines, pikes to field guns and fighter aircraft; diaramas of great episodes like the Gallipoli landings; relics—the actual tin hats and camouflage nets, water bottles and hand grenades, colours and tattered uniforms; and then portraits, dozens and dozens of generals and brigadiers, with a sprinkling of admirals and air marshals, mostly as wooden as only dead-and-gone, mediocre military commanders painted by bad artists can be. But half a dozen superb portraits and sketches by William Dobell shine like beacons in the night. This is a memorial not to the dead merely, although their names are here, or to the glories of war, but to its necessity. This is what Australians did and caused and saw, it seems to say, and did efficiently. Here is one of man's activities, like mining coal or raising sheep. Men will fight, and Australians will fight better than any of them; they will make a tidy job of it and use the right tools.

In a chapel sacred to the dead, adorned with bronze figures of great sincerity, immense size and overemphatic art, are stained-glass windows, each of which depicts a separate virtue of the warrior—Courage, Endurance, Loyalty, Fortitude, Valour, all those noble qualities with resounding names we revere and usually lack. Among them, enshrined like the others in a stained-glass window, is the quality of Curiosity. This I have never known before to be extolled as a *noble* virtue; one associates it more with children and journalists than with warriors. I found it heartening to see among the sterner Roman virtues this frivolous interloper, so traditionally feminine.

[4]

As water and trees have attracted birds to Canberra, so has the National University drawn professors. This is a prestige university, started in 1947 as an attempt to halt the brain drain, and expanded in 1960 by incorporating a University College which had existed since the 'thirties. Now the National University has a student body multiplying like starlings, as indeed are student bodies all over Australia; in every state capital either new universities are going up or existing ones are doubling, even trebling, their enrollments, and more than ten thousand students come from overseas. Canberra is still weighted with scholars of distinction, including seven Fellows of the Royal Society; the School of Physical Sciences has at Mount Stromlo the largest observatory in the Southern Hemisphere; the John Curtin School of Medical Research has a winner of the Nobel Prize, Sir John Eccles, on its staff. The Institute of Advanced Studies attracts postgraduate scholars from all over the world. The brain drain has been not merely halted but reversed.

And no wonder. Here visiting scholars can find some of the most up-to-date, best-equipped laboratories in the world. Here is good pay, excellent study leave, academic freedom. Far from being cut off at the end of the line, here is an academic hub. Some three hundred graduates from over thirty countries enjoy its sunshine, seminars and relaxed atmosphere and bring to it an intellectual yeastiness resulting from the interaction of minds from many different nations, cultures, outlooks and disciplines. The lake sparkles, birds sing, everyone looks healthy. Offered a choice between Canberra and, say, Leeds or Manchester, who would hesitate?

Yet apparently many do, and this at once pains and baffles the professors. "Look at the opportunities!" one exclaimed. "In Europe everything's been worked over and over and sifted with a fine-meshed sieve. To find a subject for a postgraduate thesis can be a desperate affair— almost ludicrous, the trivialities they have to resort to; a laundry list, possibly, left by a minor poet; an aspect of the life cycle of a barnacle that's already been thrashed out half a dozen times. Here whole subjects are untouched. In biology there are species that have not even been recorded, let alone studied. Why don't more of your people come? The young, postgraduate researchers with a name to make? What's become of the spirit of enterprise?"

I heard the same complaint in all the universities I visited and came across many instances that justified it, especially, as the professor had said, in biology. "Very little," I have just read, "is known about the breeding of the dugong . . . and *nothing* [my italics] is known about the age of maturity, length of gestation, period of suckling or rate of growth."* And the dugong is a mammal nine or ten feet long and weighing half a ton, known to the ancients (possibly the prototype of mermaids), relished as a human food and widely distributed!

British indifference to things Australian saddens everyone. Professor Manning Clark, one of the country's outstanding historians, regretfully remarked that he had met no one at the University of Birmingham who seemed to have heard of Sir Henry Parkes, although Parkes was a local man, born at Stoneleigh and apprenticed to an ivory and bone turner in Birmingham, where he imbided the radical politics that were to carry him, a penniless immigrant and subsequent bankrupt, three times to the premiership of New South Wales. It was Parkes who presided over the convention that framed the federal constitution and became known as the Father of the Commonwealth. He was also the father of a great many children and was survived by six sons and six daughters. "Even on the grounds of manly vigour," said the professor, "you'd have expected him to have aroused *some* interest; he begat a child when his eldest son was over sixty, and he himself eighty-six. Although he wrote a number of books, including half a dozen volumes of pretty dreadful poetry, all they could dig up in the university library in Birmingham was one speech he made before he emigrated in his early twenties."

This insularity extends to contemporary affairs. "In Britain," observed another professor, "there's an almost total neglect of Pacific studies. But we are a Pacific power. You ignore our strategic position.

* Bertram, C. & K., *Dugongs in Australian Waters, Oryx*, April, 1966.

Yet our task may now be to save European civilization, of which we're a part, from the forces of disintegration. You're putting your heads in the sand. And pouring away your money and, even more important, your limited pool of skilled and professional men, in an effort to prop up the corrupt and decomposing regimes of Africa, or trying to feed the starving millions of Asia—both impossible tasks."

Australia, added this professor, has one of the few governments in the world that is both stable and democratic and one of the few peoples in the world who still believe in and support the British. "We've never defaulted on a debt. We don't use threats and blackmail, by and large we keep our word. The African states do none of these things but you pour in your money, you send our your bright young men. Try to raise money for a reasonable project here and we get a dusty answer and have to turn to the Americans. What's gone wrong?"

This British unconcern, as they see it, creates in some Australian minds a feeling of embattlement, of pressure, of abandonment by the West. Australians can be almost hagridden by the pressure of time which is against them and by the emptiness of their continent. Four hundred miles from their shores the anti-Western camp begins: one hundred and twenty million brown people who, while they have bloodily renounced Chinese communism, certainly have not yet replaced it by European democracy. So the contemporary Australian mind is like a rosy, sweet and healthy-looking apple concealing in its core a worm of insecurity. "Although," added the professor, "I wouldn't say this feeling has yet penetrated to the ordinary man—even to most of our undergraduates."

Canberra's student body seemed, from the little I could see and hear, to be a well-balanced and reasonably contented cross section of the young. They live de luxe, each with a separate study-bedroom, and enjoy excellent common rooms, good food, conscientious teachers and the perpetual sunshine. Beatnik types are rare. A professor just back from a year at Oxford contrasted their outlook with that of their British counterparts. "Too many of the Oxford undergraduates are cynical, sloppy, purposeless and superficial—their minds lack a cutting edge— third-rate material. At least our students *want* to learn, they take their responsibilities seriously. One doesn't want solemnity in students, but one does hope for curiosity and some mental discipline. I didn't find it at Oxford." Perhaps the designers of Canberra's war memorial were right to canonize Curiosity?

Australian News and Information Bureau

City Square at Civic Centre, Canberra.

The erection of new buildings, reaching ever higher, is continually changing the face of the business area of Sydney. On the left is the Opera House under construction; in the distance, Botany Bay.

Qantas Airways

Qantas Airways

Brisbane sits astride the Brisbane River, overlooked by mountains to the West and faces the island-studded Moreton Bay.

Perth; The Narrows Bridge across the Swan River links the city with its southern suburbs.

Country Road Board, Victoria

Adelaide; the winding Torrens River forms the northern boundary of the city, which is framed by parks, while away in the distance the suburbs extend out to the Mount Lofty Ranges.

Melbourne; the city centre with the Yarra River in the background.

Mildura on the Murray River, Victoria.

Windsor Court House, New South Wales. Architect Francis Greenway, completed in 1822.

Typical 19th century small town corner building in Charters Town, Queensland.

Ornate cast-iron railings decorate these 19th century terrace houses in Paddington, an old inner suburb of Sydney.

G. Bottomley

Country town house with a good example of the cast-iron railing and pillars of veranda and balcony, in this case well preserved. Thousands more have been demolished.

The ruined church at Port Arthur, Tasmania. Convict designed and convict built, the church was begun in 1836, but was gutted by fire and abandoned in 1878.

Australian News and Information Bureau

The ore shaft at Mount Isa overlooks Black Rock copper open cut.

The plant buildings at Mount Tom Price in the Hammersley Range, Western Australia.

New South Wales Government Office, London

The interior of T1 power station at Tumut in the Snowy Mountains.

Hydro electric scheme, under construction and completed.

Australian News and Information Bureau

The National University has one of the lowest suicide rates in the world. An unexpected reason was advanced for this: the kindness of the dailies. "They're a motherly lot. If one of the students falls sick, his daily will look after him. They take a personal interest in their students and treat them like son or daughter. We've had the same dailies for years."

Architecturally the campus disappoints. The opportunity was great, the site promising; there was a plan drawn by one of Australia's best architects, Professor Brian Lewis of Melbourne University. Like Griffin's larger plan, it was first mangled and then abandoned. Now the university is a hotchpotch like the city, studded with buildings of every shape and style unrelated to their neighbours; there is no visible attempt to achieve architectural unity. Australians have never taken kindly to discipline, whether architectural or otherwise, so no doubt this cannot be helped. But when you build from scratch a National University in the national capital, it is perhaps a pity.

[5]

All capital cities have zoos, and Canberra has made provision for one in its master plan. About $4 million is needed to establish it. If the money can be found, it will be a new kind of zoo altogether and set a pattern for the world. It is not even to be called a zoo, but a Biological Center, and it is the brain child of a brilliant young pathologist at the John Curtin School of Medical Research.

Dr. Stephen Boyden envisages his Biological Center not as a place where you look at animals but where you see how nature works: how it is all knit together, the delicate and marvellous system by which man and beast, bird and reptile, insect and microorganism, tree and plant and fungus, together with the elements of earth and sun and water, sustain and regulate each other. It is to be a place where you can apprehend the wholeness of nature and the oneness of man with his environment. Its exhibits, some permanent, others changeable, will illustrate such major biological themes as the food chains that mount from ultra-microscopic organisms through species that prey upon each other to the major predators such as eagles and man. The art of conserving soil fertility; population dynamics and the balance of nature; how the numbers of all living creatures fluctuate according to such factors as the food supply; how insects spread disease and what diseases and how these can be kept in check; the migration of birds; how animals communicate, whether by sound, smell, or by such device as the dances used by bees to tell each other where to look for honey; the principles of hierarchy, rank, order and degree among so many living species—these are among the many themes Dr. Boyden has suggested.

Everything that can be will be alive—living insects and bacteria, living plants and algae, viruses and cells. You will be able to watch certain kinds of ant milking "herds" of aphids; certain kinds of wasp thrusting a rapier-like ovipositor into a grub within a tree trunk, or into the buried egg of its host. You will be able to listen to tape recordings of bird song or of frogs; at night to watch by infrared rays the small, shy nocturnal mammals such as marsupial mice; to learn how plants and creatures adapt themselves to the extreme dryness of deserts, like those grasshoppers whose ovaries start to develop four days before it rains. And Dr. Boyden sees his center as a place people will visit not only to learn but to enjoy; a place where children come to gape, young couples to hold hands while they gaze at wallabies mating or crayfish laying eggs, and the more sedentary to watch films on bird migration, aboriginal dances and territorial display. Two hundred acres have been allocated for a project that will offer to the world something new, creative and significant.

Dr. Boyden himself might almost model for the boffin of current mythology; bearded, gentle, unassuming, but now inspired by a cause that is said by his friends to have changed his personality, giving him strength to address Lions Clubs and speak at public dinners, where, before, the whiff of a single Rotarian would have routed him. I watched the emergence from his pocket of a sugar glider (*Petaurus breviceps*), an entrancing grey-and-black-striped little possum no more than six inches long, not counting its bushy tail. With astonishing agility it leaped about the room, landing on curtains in which it tried to disappear and on people's shoulders—or rather on the shoulders of men, not women. Possibly it chose men, Dr. Boyden thought, because the roughness of the male coat bears some resemblance to the bark of trees.

These gliders live in trees, curled up in hollows, and on trees, sucking sap and chewing blossoms to get at the nectar. They have been said to be able to glide for fifty yards, but the naturalist Harry Frauca of Queensland found that twenty feet was as much as his specimen could be persuaded to manage—even so, a sizable leap for so small a creature. In the air they are supported by a membrane stretched, like a bat's, between wrists and ankles, and they steer by a long, rudder-like tail.

Their feet have claws especially adapted for digging into trees and for combing their fur. The newborn joey of a six-foot-high kangaroo is less than one inch long. A newborn sugar glider can be no larger than a pin's head.

[6]

Canberra lies on the foothills of the Great Dividing Range, which runs from north Queensland into Victoria and is the only mountain mass of any size; its highest peak, Mount Kosciusko, is only 7,316 feet. What Australians, generally speaking, call a mountain, we should call a hill, and their hills are mounds to most people. The reason lies in the continent's immense antiquity; its face has been ground by aeons of erosion.

So the mountains near Canberra are pleasing rather than impressive. In them a small national park has lately been established in which land that has been deforested and flogged is to be restored to a state where, its restorers hope, wildlife will return and flourish. Here, at the head of the Tidbinbilla Valley, the Wildlife Division of the Commonwealth Scientific and Industrial Research Organization, universally known as the C.S.I.R.O., has a field station devoted, at the time of my visit, mainly to the study of lyrebirds. Here one of their officers, Norman Robinson, has festooned 12,000 yards of wire over eucalypts and undergrowth and staked out six acres in rectangles, with posts twenty-five yards apart. To some of these posts are fixed thermometers wired to a little wooden hut among the trees, in which, at fixed intervals, temperatures are automatically recorded. So are the forest sounds, including the songs of lyrebirds, picked up by hidden microphones.

Norman Robinson is a highly mechanized ornithologist, who was trained not in biology but in linguistics, and it is the means of communication between birds that engages him. He has compiled one of the most thorough documentations ever made of the sound behaviour of a single avian species. But it was bowerbirds that I was hoping to see. This was in summer, and lyrebirds do not start their mating displays until the autumn; they breed in winter, and there have been occasions when their egg—the hen lays only one—has been covered in snow.

We left Canberra before dawn and were soon into hilly, tree-clad country that reminded me of parts of highland Africa: hills with rounded, swelling shoulders slashed by dark gulleys, and long sunrise shadows lying across tawny slopes. Here was the crisp, clean air of hilltops, the bright song of birds, the brown and spike-awned grasses. We came upon a fox struggling in a steel trap and released it, which we should not have done, since foxes are a pest nowadays as serious as rabbits. It galloped off, carrying a mangled pad and leaving a rancid smell.

The track grew steeper and the trees larger. We passed a tumble-down shack and the remnants of an old still. A pair of elderly Yugoslav brothers had lived there, gathering eucalypt leaves from dawn till dark and distilling from them essential oils which they sold to support their sons at a Yugoslavian university. Now they had vanished—no one knew where.

At the center of the web of wires stands a little wooden hut beside a mountain rill. The air is cold, even in summer, and smells of leaf mould, moss, ferns and purity. Norman Robinson made tea and fried eggs and bacon, and I retreated into a hide beside a bower, which consisted of two tufts of dried grass, each about a foot high and the same distance apart, and a rough sort of platform made of grass and sticks. A dozen blue and yellow feathers, laid there by the male bowerbird, were strewn about the platform. He collects objects of these two colours only, blue and yellow, preferably blue. On a log outside his hut Norman Robinson lays the cap of a blue pen, and this the bird regularly takes to his bower. Mr. Robinson retrieves it, and the game starts over again. "Anything blue and portable will do." So compulsive is the need to secure blue objects that a mature male kept in captivity killed a blue Cuban finch and laid the body on his display ground.

After I had sat an hour or so in the hide, a male appeared. This bowerbird is about the size of a large pigeon and, when mature, of a metallic blue all over like an African starling; immature males have green plumage. This is the satin bowerbird (*Ptilonorhynchus violaceus*); there are several species, distantly related to birds of paradise. The male does not get his blue plumage until he is between five and seven years old. Before that, although sexually mature, he seldom breeds, because he has seldom acquired a territory.

[7]

The satin bowerbird's mania for collecting blue and, to a lesser extent, yellow objects used to be ascribed to a desire to please the female. (Other species fancy different objects—the spotted bowerbird, for instance, prefers to collect shells.) Students of bird behaviour now believe the defense of his territory to be the prime reason and the feathers to be a symbol of ownership and a warning to rivals that the owner is around. Just as we used to suppose that songbirds sang, peacocks spread their tails, turkeys gobbled and raised their wattles, and birds of paradise grew splendid plumage all to attract mates, it now seems that they do these things mainly to intimidate other males. Their motive is more often hatred than love. I suppose this matches the human parallel. All the plumes and feathers, the scarlet and gold of military uniforms cannot have been intended to please women, not normally present on the battle-field; like the birds' plumes and feathers, their function was to strike fear into the hearts of other males with whom they were contending for possession of territory.

The male bowerbird will sometimes paint his structure with saliva mixed with ash to make a black, glutinous kind of cement that dries to a gritty powder. For this purpose he will grasp in his beak a small wad of bark which Professor Jock Marshall, the leading bowerbird authority, described as "a combination sponge, wedge and stopper"—a tool. Older naturalists suggested that an aesthetic sense underlay this decorative impulse. John Gould, who in 1848 published the first complete Aus-tralian bird book, referred to bowers as sporting places in which the sexes meet. Captain Stokes, who traversed the interior of New South Wales between 1837 and 1843, thought they were some Australian mother's toy to amuse her child, and Sir George Grey believed them to be crèches made by kangaroos.

I watched this particular bowerbird pick up a blue feather, hop about a bit, lay it down, repeat the performance several times and then fly off with a low, whirring noise, almost a chuckle, rather like the subdued purr of a cat or the mechanism of a clockwork toy. He did not reappear. Male bowerbirds have busy, anxious lives. In a territory three or four acres in extent, each will build several bowers and must defend them from the attacks of other males who try to steal the trophies and, if possible, demolish whole structures. "A wrecking rival," Professor Mar-shall has written, "will . . . hop in stealthily, rather than fly boldly through the open timber . . . At the bower the marauder swiftly and silently tears down beakfuls of the walls and strews them about in disorder. A wrecker rarely completes his task before he is disturbed by the swift swish of wings of the owner. Usually he snatches up a beakful of blue feathers or glass as he flees. He never stays to fight." His object is to gain possession of the territory; and the function of territorial behavior appears to be to spread a population of any given species as evenly as possible throughout the habitat, relating the number of young to the food supply, and so controlling the total numbers of the population.

The bowerbird departed, but the forest was full of sound. Parrots of many species flew over. Most were sulphur-crested white cockatoos, who live in flocks and look beautiful but sound horrible. There were also galahs, perhaps the commonest and certainly among the loveliest of the parrots. Their plumage is restrained: a soft dove-grey above and rose-pink breasts and underwings. They also live in flocks, and their name has become synonymous with that of dolts. I never could discover why; they seem neither more nor less stupid than other parrots. I caught a glimpse of the magnificent Eastern rosella which has a breast of pure scarlet, a brilliant green tail and rump, canary-yellow on the abdomen and blue on the shoulder. The colours of these parrots' plumage are as pure, intense and clear as those used by the medieval painters.

Parrots dazzle the eye; more drably plumaged birds beguile the ear. I heard the modest call of several kinds of honey eater, which are legion; of the whipbird, whose sharp, lashlike call is often imitated by mimics, among whom bowerbirds and lyrebirds are pre-eminent; of the grey thrush, which is not a true thrush but whistles like one; tree pipits, wood swallows, the small, unobtrusive, white-browed scrub wren, who scuttles like a mouse, and of many others. On our way home we watched through binoculars a cloud of slender little grass parrots, who run so swiftly that they seem to evaporate into the grass before your eyes. Even the expert found it hard to say which species these belonged to—they do not stand and pose. Green was their colour, with touches of yellow and red on the face—probably the ground parrot, elegant and slim with a long tail, said to have so strong a scent that it can be hunted by dogs.

[8]

Later in the year, in early autumn, I came back to Tidbinbilla, this time to look for lyrebirds (*Menura superba*) which by then had started their display. Once more we saw a soft blue dawn transfuse the dark mountains, where the tall gums had just shed their bark and gleamed white as ivory pillars newly scoured in the fresh, clean light. The air was crisp as a skin of ice on a pool and, as before, the birds were calling. A pair of swamp wallabies bounded into the shadows.

As before, we brewed up in the wooden hut and then set out on the rounds of Norman Robinson's hidden microphones and web of wires. He had under observation at the time six pairs of lyrebirds, each with a territory varying in extent from two to five acres. The size of the territory depends upon its richness, or otherwise, in food supplies, which consist mainly of insects. The remains of twenty-seven different species have been found in a single bird's stomach. The eastern slopes of these hills are wetter than the western slopes and therefore support a somewhat different type of eucalypt and wattle forest and a more dense vegetation, which lyrebirds like. They must have shade and moisture. So, on the western slopes, territories are larger to make up for their relative poverty.

How does a bird win and hold his territory? By aggression, expressed mainly in song. "If the song stops," Mr. Robinson explained, "that is a signal to others that a territory is vulnerable, and the most aggresive bird will move in. Not necessarily the nearest—the next in order of rank. A couple of years ago I had to take out one male lyrebird to send to a zoo. There was a general post. Another pair took over his territory and they all moved on. How this is organized, we don't know. There's a lot we don't know: whether lyrebirds are monogamous, for instance, how long they live, exactly what they eat, and so on." There is a record of a tame bird, Jack of Drouin, caught in 1885, who lived for twenty years on a farm in Victoria. He was a champion mimic, including in his repertoire the creaking of a horse and dray, and orders issued to the horse such as "Gee up, Bess," and sounds made by a violin, cornet, piano and saw, and by a pig being killed, a dog barking, a baby crying and sheep scrambling through a fence. And he could do all this with a beak full of insects.

Every six minutes throughout the day and night the Tidbinbilla microphones switch themselves on to record the forest sounds for eight seconds. This gives 240 recording periods in the twenty-four hours, and from this the time devoted by each bird to song has been calculated. It averages four and a half hours a day. The song of lyrebirds, far from being a spontaneous expression of *joie de vivre,* appears to be an onerous, almost a crushing, duty. "Try going out at seven o'clock," Norman Robinson suggested, "and start singing the *Saint Matthew Passion* at the top of your voice and see how far you get—you won't keep it up for twenty minutes. Even an opera singer couldn't manage four and a half hours at full stretch every day."

Like most of Australia's living creatures, lyrebirds as a species are of great antiquity. Probably they were displaying in these forests before mankind appeared on the planet, and they have retained several biologically primitive features. They can run more efficiently than they can fly—flight is a relatively late development—and they have fewer vocal chords than more sophisticated species. They compensate for this by a more vigorous use of those they have and possibly by taking up positions on a slope where their song is amplified by echo from the opposite bank, like a Swiss yodeller. It has even been suggested that the magnificent peacock-like tail spread of the displaying male may act as an echo chamber to project the sound. The bird is an accomplished ventriloquist and can mimic with astonishing accuracy the calls of many other birds; this he does with a closed beak, like a human performer. But, unlike the human, he does not, mainly by suggestion, project his mimicry onto an object such as a dummy. It is therefore impossible to tell where the sound is coming from, and this no doubt confuses those predators who hunt by sound and in daylight. But few do this.

[9]

A number of Australian birds construct mounds, either, like the mallee fowl and scrub turkey, to lay their eggs in or, like the lyrebird, for display. The quantity of mounds a single bird will make is quite astonishing. Mr. Robinson has counted up to fifty in the territory of one pair of lyrebirds, and thirty is quite common. These mounds are often only a few feet apart. They are not all in use at one time, however; that would be too much even for a lyrebird, since he must visit each mound not once but twice a day. He may have six or seven on the active list at any one time. Most of the mounds are two or three feet in diameter—some are more—and they are between eighteen inches and three feet high. While the bird is no larger than a bantam, his legs are so strong that he can move a log as thick as a man's arm; to construct his mounds, each male must shift several tons of earth in a season.

To man, birds have always been a symbol of freedom. Watching them ride the air so easily, with all their grace and power, we think ruefully of our own fetters: of our chains of duty, of routine, of possessions. Birds, we think, are spared all that; they go where the spirit wills and celebrate in song their joy of living.

The more we find out about bird life, the more false is this idea seen to be. A lyrebird, for instance, appears to be every bit as much a slave to routine as any insurance clerk who catches the eight-fifteen each morning and six-ten back at night. The bird starts on his rounds every morning and works his way downhill, ending with the lowest of his mounds. Each one must be scratched over, perhaps to show the female where he is, certainly to warn off other males. At this stage he does not feed.

In the display season, which lasts about three months—although the hen will mate only for about one month of this period—he performs that extraordinary dance in which he flattens the huge spread of his tail, with its long, lyre-shaped feathers, over his back so that he is peering through its drooping fringes—barely able, you would think, to see out, like a Yorkshire terrier. Then he shakes. No purple-heart addicted teen-ager at the top of his bent, no Egyptian belly dancer, could shake with greater vigour. He quivers all over. His feathers shimmer; he is an oscillating ball of dark brown and silver, and all the while he drums so quickly and energetically with his feet that a thrumming sound accompanies the performance.

No wonder this has provided the Australian ballet with a theme for choreography. This *is* ballet, even to the constantly repeated advances and retreats, the little rushes and darts, the fluidity of movement almost too swift for the eye to chart, like some scuttering water beetle. All this to scare off rival males; the female need not, often does not, look on. There is something formidable and a little frightening and uncanny about this strange object, gyrating and cavorting as if possessed by spirits in the darkness of the forest with that low thrumming sound, like some African witch doctor stamping out the measures of a savage fandango to terrify the initiates of a secret cult. Not that I was fortunate enough to witness a performance. Lyrebirds are shy creatures with acute hearing, and to see their display needs a lot of time, luck and patience. Fortunately there are some superb films. One I saw was made by Mr. Harry Pollock, a naturalist-photographer said to be as elusive and solitary as one of the wild creatures he tracks and photographs, who has found a generous patron in the shape of the Bank of New South Wales.

In one of their offices, high above the Sydney traffic, I watched a female lyrebird feeding a solitary chick in her nest. When the chick wishes to clear his bowels, he passes out a little sealed capsule which the hen receives into her mouth; she then flies off and deposits it in water. Thus not only is the nest kept absolutely clean, but predators are denied any clue to the whereabouts of a nest. The contrast between the lyrebird's standard of hygiene and those of humans can be appreciated by a stroll along the margins of any highway in Britain where every lay-by has become an unofficial outspan for caravans.

Mr. Pollock's remarkable film followed the male lyrebird's routine. After his morning mound inspection he will feed and enjoy a short rest in the heat of the day. Then he works his way uphill again, visiting each mound in turn, carrying out repairs where necessary—storms do a lot of damage—continually pumping out his melodious but exhausting choral repertoire and, in due season, repeating his display. As for the hen, once she has laid her egg she broods for six weeks in an untidy nest that seems to be stuck haphazardly to a rock or tree stump; the male plays no part in this. He has plenty to do. Were the crops of birds susceptible to ulcers, the lyrebird would surely suffer, so arduous is his routine, so many his worries, so unrelenting his need for vigilance.

THREE

Snowy and Kosciusko

To the bowerbird, a blue feather is a symbol of possession; to Australians, "The Snowy" is a symbol of modernity. Imaginatively bold, technically brilliant, economically sound—Americans or Russians could do no better; it has expunged the Australian image of the sweaty bloke in braces swilling beer and substituted that of the engineer in a white boiler suit at the switches of an underground power station.

Statistics flow as forcefully at the Snowy as the waters which engineers are driving in gigantic pipes through mountainsides. Kilowatts, cusecs, acre-feet; diversions, catchments, off-peak loads . . . But the essence is simple. From the peaks and gorges of the Great Dividing Range arise Australia's greatest rivers, the Murray and the Murrumbidgee, which flow westwards and inland to meet on the borders of New South Wales and Victoria and to reach the sea some fifty miles east of Adelaide in South Australia. They flow through country whose soil is fertile but whose rainfall is too low and unevenly distributed to support a reliable agriculture. Irrigation is the answer, and both these rivers already irrigate considerable tracts of land.

On the other hand, the Snowy River irrigates nothing; rising on the eastern side of the range, its course is short before it reaches the sea. So why not drive a tunnel through the mountain, turn the Snowy round and join it to the Murray-Murrumbidgee system, using its waters both to fructify more land and to generate electric power? That is the essence of a project talked about for eighty years. In 1949 the Snowy Mountains Hydro-electric Authority came into being to carry it out.

One man has been in charge since the start and assembled the team that has passed the halfway mark without a single major error, miscalculation, or general strike. This is Sir William Hudson, a New Zealander who gained much of his experience working on the Galloway power

59

scheme in Scotland before World War II. Now he is over seventy—not only an outstanding engineer, but a leader of men. Although pay is good on the Snowy, you get the feeling that the men employed on the scheme are not in it only for the money; they believe they are helping to create something that is big, and useful to their country, and beneficial to the world.

The Snowy Mountains Authority has about the best public relations setup I have come across in any land. By this I do not mean a team of illusionists trying to pull wool over people's eyes; I mean liaison officers trying to explain to the public what the Authority is aiming at and why, and personally convinced of the truth of their message.

It is largely because people are wanted and welcomed, and treated as humans rather than as regrettably necessary sheep, that the Snowy has become Australia's foremost tourist attraction. Coach drivers—at any rate the ones I saw and heard—are polite and well-informed and answer the obvious questions with patience and humour. Canteens are efficient, clean and remarkably well designed. There are plants in tubs, fresh paint, even high chairs for tots, and the food is well-cooked, cheap and ample. And the construction gangs I saw were working, not having tea breaks—although I am sure they do have these—or doing the equivalent, with heavy machinery, of leaning on shovels.

[2]

Outside the headquarters of the Authority at Cooma fly the flags of thirty nations whose ex-nationals are employed on the scheme. Seven out of ten of these are New Australians from non-English-speaking countries, with Italians and Yugoslavs forming the largest groups.

The Yugoslavian flag was currently in trouble. It had been torn down, and then torn up, several times. In hostels accommodating Yugoslavs a tinderbox atmosphere prevailed. Many of the Yugoslav migrants are Croatians who left their native land in the belief that they were being persecuted by Serbs. This presents a dilemma for Old Australians, who believe that men seeking political asylum, especially from Communist regimes, deserve succour; yet to perpetuate old feuds in a new land is wrong, besides being dangerous in a camp full of well-paid, well-fed, single men. So they run up a fresh flag, keep Serbs and Croats apart in hostels, and try to impress upon both sides that the law must be obeyed.

In the canteens you hear a little English spoken with the native drawl and twang; it is the halting English of the Continental that prevails. "Go

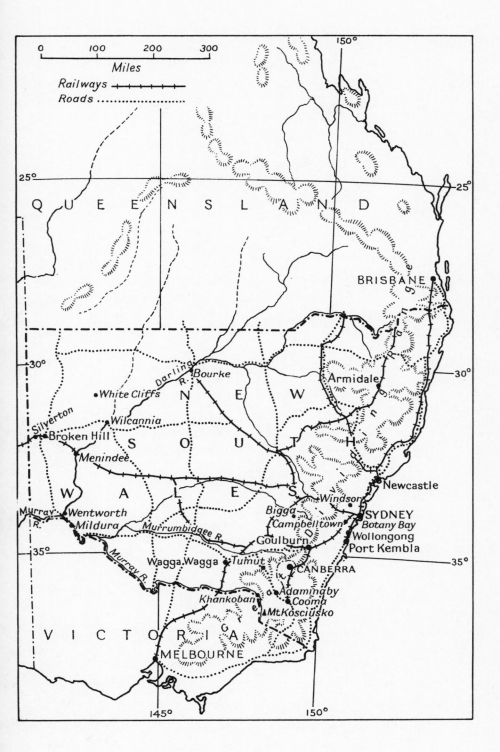

back to Europe?" said a broad-faced, hard-bone, pale-eyed Yugoslav. "Never, no. Australia is an easy country. People here eat meat three times a day! Where else in the world can they do that?" He had arrived, quite penniless and eight years ago, as a political refugee. "I was a clerk. At first it was hard here—a steel foundry, then fireman on the railroad. Too many blowflies—I gave it up." But on the Snowy he had saved money, with which he proposed to start a business in Sydney and then find a wife—an Australian. His eyes twinkled. "Here the money's good, but in the evenings there is no life, no gaiety. It is not like Europe. Here is freedom to say and do what you like. No one stops you. No one is afraid. You say what comes into your head. But to whom do you say it?"

A young German agreed. He was dapper, handsome and chatty, and formerly had been an electrician in Hamburg. "I saw the ships, I got itching feet—nothing political. I had a contract with the Snowy before I sailed. My wife works; we've saved money and bought a block on the coast. I shall build a house and rent it out and have a boat to hire for deep-sea fishing. Anyone who works can get on in Australia. It is the best country in the world."

Most British migrants are also satisfied but apt to be more critical. "Some migrants go home because they don't like the Aussie way of life," one of them said. How can that be defined? "T-bone steaks—beer—shirt sleeves—take-us-as-you-find-us—outspoken. It's a harsh country, yet it's easygoing. Hard to explain." This was a Geordie who had failed to settle back to life in Sunderland after national service in the R.A.F. "Don't come with kids is my advice—the wife must work, too, then you can save and get a start. I've bought a block on the coast. I mean to build a boat and go fishing. Anyone can fish here in the rivers; anyone can shoot a kangaroo—you don't have to ask permission. That's Australia. You can do what you like—there aren't all those traditions. That's what's killing England, traditions—people sitting on your head. An Aussie, he tells you what he thinks straight out. You should hear the politicians, calling each other bloody bastards, and no one minds. But if you make a friend of an Aussie, he's a friend for life."

The common language makes it harder for the British to adapt themselves. An Italian or a Yugoslav knows that he is coming to a foreign country, that customs will be different, that he must make the effort to learn new ways as well as new words and to please his hosts. The Englishman, who finds the words the same, unthinkingly expects to find the ways the same too. The Aussies are British, aren't they? They drive on the left-hand side of the road? Eat fish and chips, have the same movies and portraits of the Queen all over the place? Then why isn't *everything* the same?

"The words muddle us," an English woman migrant told me. "Australians still talk of England as the mother country. Australia's a daughter, in that case. We expect it to be the same, only somehow better, which is why we came—England without the snags. When it isn't, we feel let down. Homesickness is the real enemy. I was homesick for two years and it was awful. If you can stick two years, you're over the hump."

What is so different? "Hard to say. Friendly enough on the surface, but no real effort to get to know you. No curiosity. Take it or leave it. They'll stand you a drink at the pub, but very few ask you into their homes. In their hearts I think they resent us somehow. And then I missed the little things: no Marks and Spencer. I hated the stockings. Silly, but . . ."

"Too many of us pommies expect it to be like home and are put out when it isn't," said a British migrant on the Snowy. "Naturally that annoys the Aussies. We should keep our mouths shut."

The aim of almost every migrant is to save enough to make a down payment on a block of land and then to build a house. If he can save $1,500, the government will give him $500 outright. Italians are the best savers and virtually the only group whose members sometimes take their savings back to their native land. Men on the construction gangs can earn up to $100 a week and live in barracks free, with meat three times a day and nothing to spend their money on but drink, cigarettes and gambling. And yet, "Ours must be one of the highest labour turnovers in the world," said a manager. "Most of the men work for two or three months, stash away a couple of hundred quid* and clear off. They can't stand the isolation. There's nothing for them in the evenings, only grog and cards, no women. They blow the lot and are back in a week or so."

Very few native-born Australians work in the construction gangs. "They don't like the cold. And they've mostly got their homes anyway." That is the great Australian dream, the big incentive—a home of your own. Australia has the highest proportion of homeowners in the world.

* Equal to $400.

[3]

One gulp of morning air—chilly, crisp and clean—and you know that you are in the mountains. Eucalypts exude an aromatic freshness and sunshine falls bright and golden on the tall and tapering boles, whose coat of bark is many-coloured and constantly changing. The air is full of bird song and flashes of colour. Those parrots! They never cease to astonish. With notebook, field glasses and a pocket bird book I peered through foliage and undergrowth, struggling to identify them.

"Grey, speckled or banded all over, brilliant sulphur crest"—probably the cockateel, also called the Quarrion, a link between the cockatoos who sport crests and the parrots who do not. "Scarlet head and breast, green wing coverts, yellow abdomen, touches of blue"—this must be the Eastern rosella. Parties of a smaller but no less brilliant bird with sapphire blue, blood red and lemon yellow in its plumage—lorikeets perhaps—were extracting nectar from tightly clustered flowers of gums. With strong and flexible claws they clung to twigs and seemed to run up and down the slenderest of branches almost like squirrels.

There are fifty-seven species of parrot in Australia, said my bird book, of which over fifty exist nowhere else in the world. No wonder an early explorer wrote on his blank map the words *terra psittacorum,* land of parrots. While it is nonsense to suggest that Australian birds are songless—"From the elfin whispers of tiny wrens," observes my authority, "to the deep-throated clangour of currawongs in company, there is a festival of music in the Australian bush"—one cannot honestly admire the voices of parrots. "When they are not chattering noisily, they are screaming unmelodiously." But their colours are fantastic, and you cannot have everything.

Through silvery and rosy-tinted tree trunks I could see the blue waters of Lake Eucumbene. The tourist circuit takes you by launch over this big reservoir, created by a dam across the Eucumbene River, the main tributary of the Snowy. Now the Eucumbene has been twisted round to flow through a fourteen-mile-long tunnel piercing a mountain into a different river, the Tumut, which in turn joins the Murrumbidgee.

The scheme is complex, and I found it hard, even with all the diagrams and models used to instruct the visitor, to grasp just which river was being made to flow where. On the western side of the range three rivers are being diverted into a storage reservoir and then conducted, as they fall some 2,700 feet, through four power stations. Then they—the combined waters—are to be stored in an enormous reservoir, Lake Blowering, that will fill when the snows melt in spring and be released in the dry summer to irrigate more of the great Murray-Murrumbidgee valley. Under Lake Eucumbene already lies a small town, Adaminaby; a new Adaminaby has arisen a few miles away. Another town, Jindabyne, is due for drowning, and its successor, complete with all amenities, is already occupied.

These rivers and mountains lie partially within the Kosciusko State Park of New South Wales, the largest park in Australia. Generally this, and other areas like it, is called a national park, but the phrase is misleading; there are no true national parks in Australia. All parks, except the small one near Canberra, belong to the states and vary widely in their purposes, policies and sizes. Kosciusko Park covers 1.3 million acres; there are others only a few acres in extent, established to safeguard a rare plant or animal species. In Kosciusko the lakes which are a by-product of manipulating rivers and generating electricity will enrich the park's recreational resources. Fishing, sailing, water skiing will develop, tourist lodges arise, bird watchers and campers converge upon reedy shores even now forming on once dry pastures.

[4]

From Lake Eucumbene the road winds up to the highest township in Australia, Cabramurra, just under 4,900 feet. Here is another excellent tourist resthouse run by the Authority. In the canteen such enormous helpings are dished out that I could scarcely believe even Australian stomachs to have so great a capacity. Nor have they; the canteen manager estimated that one-third of the meals go into the refuse bin. A notice above the serving counter reads: "If you want a larger helping, ask the chef." Quite a lot of the customers do this, I was told, "but they never finish it." Australians think themselves to be heartier trenchermen than they are.

We came to the gorge of the Tumut River which drops steeply down the western face of the range through thick eucalypt forest. There are precipices here which perhaps even now have never been scaled, so thick is the cover and so steep the rock. Here grows the tall splendid Alpine ash and the mountain ash (*E. regnans*), the smaller and straggling snow-gum (*E. niphophila*), and in places the narrow-leaved peppermint (*E. australia*). One of the first lessons you learn in Australia is not to think of gums as monotonous. There are several hundred species and between some of them as much difference, to a nonbotanical eye, as between oak, ash, thorn, or any other deciduous tree. Some, like these mountain ashes, will thrive above the snow line and grow more than three hundred feet tall; others inhabit the central desert as stunted, scruffy little shrubs. Some have magnificent red blooms; others produce flowers so nondescript as to be all but invisible. Some grow in swamps and river beds; others apparently emerge from solid rock. The pointed leaves of many kinds are designed to direct every drop of moisture that falls upon them into the ground; their narrowness cuts down the loss through evaporation. Some produce essential oils, others tannins.

There are eucalypts to suit all tastes and climates. Like the fauna, they were evolved after the continent was cut off from the mainland about fifty million years or so ago and are Australia's special contribution to the arboreal world. (They are a branch of the myrtle family, which includes wattles, tea trees and bottle brushes.) Their colour is often said to be monotonous, and perhaps this at first seems true. But the more you see of them, the more you see *in* them. There is a great deal of red about them—the red that is the colour of Australia, in its soils, its rocks, its trees. Young growth is a darkish, dull red at the tips, and the bark, so often hanging in strips, or banded or striped with colour, is frequently tinged with pink. It is the bark of eucalypts that gives them such variety; their boles can be untidy but are seldom dull.

[5]

Deep down in these gum-clad gorges, about a thousand feet underground, lie the power stations. Everything about them is uncanny, from the moment when one of those invisible rays lets you in by rolling up a steel mesh curtain to enable you to glide through in your car, haunted (in my case) by the fear that you may never get out again. It is like advancing into the enormous, grey, shiny, smooth gut of some sinister mechanized animal. And once inside, you see no movement, no gush of waters, no revolving shafts, or torrents flowing in and out of valves. All that is visible are great panels of dials and gauges, lights like green or white eyes that flick on and off, needles that point at numbers. Time was when mountainsides were opened by a magic password to reveal goblin kings and queens keeping their court; now here are these invisible turbogenerators ruled by silent dials and switches, all totally dehumanized. The whole station is run without the physical presence of a single person. I found it alarming.

In a long, spotless, silent gallery—a fly, a feather, a speck of mud would desecrate this temple—stood a party of black-robed, white-coifed nuns, peering with bewildered Irish smiles at dials and gauges, their rosaries looped at their sides. I hoped they made more than I did of the guide's helpful recitation. The total installed capacity of Tumut 1, Tumut 2 and Tumut 3 will be over a million and a half kilowatts . . . additional water made available in the Murrumbidgee River will amount to over one million acre-feet per annum . . . eight major dams . . . sixty-six miles of tunnel . . . the load to be transmitted at 330,000 volts . . . In at one ear and out at the other. Was this the gorge down which the Man from Snowy River galloped on his legendary little steed? Today the thunder of hoofs would not disturb by the fraction of a kilowatt the underground turbogenerators or be heard against the sound of monster earth scoops crashing down trees.

Aboveground again, we came suddenly on a switching station. All around were black, dead stumps and trunks of blasted trees. Behind rose a hillside spiked by living boles that glistened ivory and pewter and a greyish silver in the hard sunlight, ghostly and monstrous like the writhing limbs of dancers frozen in grotesque positions. The switching station was the colour of a skeleton, all loops and discs festooned on pylons; clusters of insulators threaded on masts were like the beads of an abacus set up vertically. In the sun everything shimmered, sparkled, was ethereally beautiful. Across the mountain loped the pylons, glistening also, each surmounted by a four-pointed star. It all looked queerly fairylike, or like the web of a gigantic mechanized spider spun among the weird-shaped, somber-foliaged gums.

[6]

The name Khancoban carries a suggestion of shaggy Asiatic goats, pack mules, ewes'-milk cheeses and bearded men in astrakhan caps. The reality is another new township with a clean and tidy lodge run by the Authority with car parks, canteens and lawns kept green by sprinklers. Sitting on a balcony in brilliant sunshine, drinking coffee, I watched a party of galahs searching for insects; in the air they look like flights or rose petals. Below the lodge, and in the distance, a fuzz of brown dust arises from a dam site where machinery roars away all night and will roar all round the clock until the dam is finished. Enormous pipes are being anchored to precipices, in order to conduct waters through turbines at the rate of three million gallons every minute. The mountaintops are patched with snow. One is Kosciusko, but unless you know the terrain well you cannot identify it.

The Kosciusko State Park, like most such parks, is both a sanctuary for wildlife and a pleasure ground. The two interests conflict. Few ani- males take kindly to cinecameras, hands thrust into nest to feel the eggs, the din of motorcars and transistor radios. (There are exceptions.) Few plants thrive when trampled on and used as picnic grounds, still less when dug up to take home. Roads and lodges destroy that tranquillity which it is a prime object of a park to preserve.

This is a dilemma which faces national parks and and nature reserves all the world over. Each man kills the thing he loves. Crowds of humans kill the seclusion of the creatures, the silence of forests, the loneliness of hills. People take with them what they are trying to leave behind—their own environment and the incessant company of their fellows. The grove, the dell, the meadow by the waterfall turn into caravan sites. There is no way to avoid this dilemma; all that can be done is to compromise. Here a little less than 100 square miles out of over 2,000—no more than 5 per cent—has been declared a "primitive area" which is to be left just as it is, for nature to take its course. No roads are to be built; people may enter it only on foot. Aqueducts have been buried so as to conceal all traces of the works of man. No one may carry a firearm, pick a flower, or even take away a specimen of rock.

Across the range through Dead Horse Gap lies Thredbo, which is anything but primitive. This is the headquarters of Australia's only win- ter sports ground. Here has arisen an imitation Swiss village, modern as polythene and earth satellites, where a luxury hotel charges each guest $100 a week and chalets have steeply pitched roofs and dark timbers to make them look suitably Alpine. You expect to see yodellers with curly horns and men in leather shorts and Swiss braces, and no doubt you do in winter, when these mountains lie deep in snow. Skiing has become the smart thing to do, status-bearing. But construction work during winter is tough, with heavy snowfalls to contend with, icy gales, and temperatures below freezing point.

Despite this, construction is well ahead of schedule and the scheme should be completed by 1970. Its finances seem to be as well conducted as its engineering side. Of the total cost of $800 million, only $80 million has been borrowed, and that on easy terms from the World Bank. The rest has been provided by the Commonwealth Government, out of annual revenue, in the form of loans. Work was begun in 1950, the first power sold in 1955, and now the sale of power services the loans, which are to be repaid with interest over seventy years. The scheme will add 40 per cent of the present total generating capacity to the country's power resources and enable another $60 million worth of irrigated produce to be grown every year. And not an extra penny of taxation has been called for. It all seems too good to be true.

FOUR

The Golden Fleece

On the road to Gundowringa we passed two fires and saw, through a fog of smoke, people belabouring flames with sticks and sacks. Cars stood empty by the roadside while their owners lent a hand. Now in midsummer, and in mid-drought, a single spark or carelessly jettisoned cigarette end will send a line of fire racing across this open, rolling country. Tongues of flame—a cliché, but how well it describes the way the flames dart out like a snake's tongue, to the accompaniment of an inexorable growl; or like the red breath of an enraged dragon destroying every small creature, the lizards and frogs, mice and beetles, as well as panic-stricken sheep. Where the fire has passed, the ground is black and sooty, fence posts charred, trees blasted.

It was not the best moment to arrive for the weekend. The fires were on our hostess's property.

The house was full of small children eating sandwiches and watching television, while their mothers had joined the fire fighters. One of the houses on the property was threatened and, even more imminently, a shed full of prize rams. Gundowringa breeds Corriedale sheep that win prizes all over Australia and are worth tens of thousands of pounds; not only that, they are the fruits of half a century's endeavour and creatures in their own right.

The property belongs to two maiden aunts and is run by two energetic nephews. One of them was playing cricket twenty miles away when the fire started; a message fetched him back in fifteen minutes. A six-hundred-gallon water tanker had been standing ready for such an emergency, for at times of drought these stations live in an all-round-the-clock state of preparedness. After a while a slim girl in shorts appeared, charcoal-smeared; she and one of the aunts had driven a mob of rams out of the endangered shed and across a creek by a narrow plank bridge: no mean feat, with the panic-engendering flames advancing to the very steps of the ram shed. Next morning we saw just how close the flames had come: the heat had warped some of the barn's timbers. Everything was charred and the grazing destroyed, but all the sheep had been saved.

Last year about 21,000 sheep were sheared at Gundowringa. This is a large flock, but by no means out of the way; there are stations with twice this number. Shearers make good money and they earn it, for the work is very hard. Each man will handle between a hundred and a hundred and fifty sheep a day. He drags one from its pen, clamps it between his knees and grasps it in a particular fashion—only one grip will do— which seems almost to mesmerize it, for you scarcely ever see one kick or struggle as the shears, with a smooth, flowing and continuous motion, never hurried, never jerky—under leg pits, into body crevices, round the eyes—peel off the fleece like a banana skin.

The woolshed is the hub of the station. Some families occupy a dilap- idated shack and possess a substantial woolshed which cost ten times as much. In it there must be room for the mustered sheep awaiting their turn in pens, for the actual shearing, and for the handling of the fleece by skirters, folders, pressers and the highly skilled and paid classers, down to humble roustabouts who sweep floors and carry fleeces. Planks and boards have a smooth bloom on them from grease in the wool, and the shed a sharp, pleasing smell of lanolin.

In days gone by the grazier's wife had to feed the shearers—five square meals a day for possibly a dozen hefty men, or even more. Her work must have been never-ending. Now each team brings its own cook, and he is, people will tell you, the most important man in the team. If he is good, there is contentment, peace and steady work; if he is bad, everyone sulks and winges. No one tires of mutton three times every day so long as it is good mutton, ample mutton and reasonably tender mut- ton. But if it is tough mutton, burned mutton, or not enough mutton, there is hell to pay.

The Prells' prize rams were chewing the cud in peace, unconscious of their narrow escape. They looked absolutely square. The fleece opens to show a creamy, crimpy, clean staple, soft as down. The fineness of each fiber, its crimpiness and its capacity to stretch without breaking mainly determines its quality. Breeders and flockmasters strive for a perfection they never quite attain, blending a score of qualities as other experts blend tobacco, coffee, or wine. They must select for shape and conformation, for strong bone and fine fleece, for thriftiness and economy as feeders, for length of life, fecundity and milk production, for many other qualities.

The time may be coming when a computer will do all this. At present humans still do it, using art, instinct and experience, and using patience, too, and sometimes courage. The work of fifty years can go up in smoke, literally, in an hour. I met a man who, some weeks later, personally shot many of the sheep he had spent a lifetime creating and which had become charred, pitiful creatures bleating for mercy. Then he himself was taken off to hospital.

The homestead at Gundowringa is a large, rambling bungalow with a wide, encircling veranda, a shady garden and sprinkled lawns. Why, when the right kind of house for the climate has been evolved, do modern men build shadeless boxes that confront the sun with no insulating veranda, obliging their owners to live in gloom behind permanently closed shutters?

If, at Gundowringa, you tire of the veranda or of the cool and spacious rooms that open out of it, you can migrate to a large meat safe beside a swimming pool, a sort of grotto encased in fine wire gauze to exclude flies. (So persistent and abundant are these small, non-biting, but maddening insects, which crawl into your ears and will not be driven off, that women wear hats with veils like those of bee keepers to work in their gardens.) The Prells' meat safe is equipped with an electric cooker, running water, a refrigerator, comfortable furniture and a telephone, and here you can spend the day watching children splashing in the pool, or splash there youself, in perpetual sunshine, but only on Sundays. Here everyone works, not apparently at high pressure, but steadily, starting at sunup when the bell magpie, also called the currawong, utters his well-named bell-like call, sweet as honey, clear and soft and melodious. He is a handsome, pied bird about the same size as, but not related to, the English magpie and with similar black-and-white colouring, and as ubiquitous as the sparrow—an inhabitant of gardens. As a rule his rippling cadence is the first sound you hear when a rising sun throws long bars of shadow across lawns and bush outside your window.

[2]

The Bigga section of the local telephone directory has seventy-three names, of whom twenty-seven are Pickers. There are Pickers to right of you, Pickers to left of you, Pickers in front, as you drive along the byways of this closely settled part of New South Wales. All stem from Great-grandfather Picker who came from Yorkshire about a century ago, took up a free section of 640 acres, and had a lot of sons.

From the third year running, fleece from Trevor Picker's merinos had made the top prices in the wool sales in Australia. Other Pickers do not lag far behind. This has been achieved without capital or scientific training but by native wit and father-to-son, word-of-mouth tradition. Trevor Picker's grandfather started to select, by eye, those of his merinos with the longest, softest and finest wool and narrowed down his breeding stock to the progeny of four families. His wool soon won a name for quality but did not fetch higher prices and, in the slump, sold for thirteen cents a pound. This year one of his grandson's bales fetched $18, a world record. It was flown to Yorkshire and supplied the cloth from which twenty-five suits were made, to be sold in New York for about $400 each—a publicity gimmick, of course. And yet, despite these record prices and a world-wide name for the quality of their fleeces, the Pickers had reluctantly concluded that other forms of production yielded more reward and were about to switch to the raising of fat lambs. A young man still, with an attractive wife and four small, brown, scrubbed sons, he runs the place with his father and the help of an uncle who lives beside the woolshed surrounded by kelpies, those intelligent and stubby native dogs said to be partly dingo. The worst enemies are fires. Chemical sprays control the blowflies, foxes can be shot and poisoned, but no one has an answer to the fires.

Bigga is, I suppose, a typical small Australian country town—sprawling, untidy, the streets laid out in rectangles and the site divided into blocks each exactly the same size, each with its boxlike bungalow. There are no terraced houses and none semidetached; each bungalow is on its own, built as a rule by its owner. The gardens are most apt to display empty beer cans and old tires than roses or dahlias—in fact, they are yards, not gardens. It is far too hot, dry and dusty to stoop with fork and barrow or for any other strenuous motion.

> Verandas baked with musky sleep,
> Mulberry faces dozing deep . . .

This might have been the very place in the mind's eye of Kenneth Slessor when he wrote of

> Country towns with your schooner bees,
> And locusts burnt in the pepper-trees,

Drown me with syrups, arch your boughs,
Find me a bench, and let me snore
Till, charged with ale and unconcern
I think it's noon at half past four!

The women are indoors behind the fly screens, solitary or with under-six's, and with torn and thumbed, smudgy magazines, a ticking clock and the droning on of a transistor.

"It's a hard life for women," said my companion. "Nothing but work and what for? Masses of kids, heat, flies, a monthly meeting of the Country Women's Association, or school events that mean yet more cooking. They get too thin or too fat too young."

The men are at the pub. That long line of male backs hunched over a bar, each with a brown, hard fist clasping a glass, each with a cigarette between the lips, each with a foot on the rail—there is country-town Australia. A grubby little cubbyhole at the far side, furnished with a rickety table and half a dozen kitchen chairs, caters if need be for feminine needs. But few women come; indeed, why should they? There is little to come for and, to say the least, an unenthusiastic welcome. Beer gardens are the fashion now, it was said; men take their families and everyone drinks together in the European style. Perhaps this custom will spread, but there is a long road to travel before that shirt-sleeved phalanx, shoulder to shoulder like battery hens, breaks its all-male ranks.

[3]

At Wollongorang, not far from Goulburn, I saw my first kangaroos. Here Mr. John Watson preserves a small mob or two on his property because he likes to see them around, but he has to control their num-bers; most graziers shoot them on sight or get them shot by professional killers. "To ask a sheepman not to destroy kangaroos is equivalent to asking the American wheat farmer of a century ago to allow herds of bison to tramp through his crops," Dr. Harry Frith has pointed out. As head of the Wildlife Division of the C.S.I.R.O., Dr. Frith's concern is to preserve the native fauna; but, in order to preserve it, the numbers of species like the kangaroo which compete with domestic animals must be limited. Kangaroos can exist only on sufferance and only with the graziers' goodwill.

To shoot kangaroos because they can become a pest, like rabbits, is one thing, to pretend it is a sport quite another. Kangaroos are inoffensive, harmless, and quite without guile or any talent for concealment or escape. They stand and look at you with thrown-back heads, sloping ears and long, slender, sensitive faces, a look at once proud and trusting. If you approach, off they go with their queer yet gainly hops, dangling their human-seeming hands in front of them as if in supplication, the little joeys bounding frantically beside their mothers as if on springs. Quite unlike any animal one is accustomed to in other lands, they have an air of innocence about them impossible to describe, that makes their killing a kind of murder. "Her little loose hands, and drooping Victorian shoulders," D. H. Lawrence wrote of a mother kangaroo he fed with peppermint drops while she sat up on "the great muscular python-stretch of her tail," and from her pouch:

> A lean little face comes out, as from a window,
> Peaked and a bit dismayed,
> Only to disappear again quickly away from the
>   sight of the world, to snuggle down in the warmth,
> Leaving the trail of a different paw hanging out.
>   ***   ****   ***
> She watches with unsatiable wistfulness
> Untold centuries of watching for something to come,
> For a new signal from life, in that silent lost land of the
>   South.

Supposedly the kangaroos evolved their long, parabolic leaps and bottom-heaviness the better to clear the bush, just as the pouch protected their young in a spiky environment. The landscape they inhabit is full of the dead, black corpses of trees killed by fires and the white, bleached skeletons of trees killed by ring-barking and the twisted, angular shapes of stumps and fallen logs and broken branches. This is a landscape that has grandeur and a timeless patience and is full of death because it is a vast, almost boundless morgue of dead trees. The numbers of eucalypts that must once have clothed it stuns the mind: as many as grains of sand on all the seacoasts of the world, as many as stars in all the sky's galaxies.

To cut down all those trees and burn them was a task too formidable for any group of humans. Millions have been so felled and burned, but millions more were ring-barked, and these remain like the stumps of rotten teeth sticking up from the jaws of a continent. And their shapes are the shapes of modern sculpture and painting. The whole landscape might have been designed by Graham Sutherland and have inspired Lipschitz, say, or Lynn Chadwick, or Reg Butler, or any others who depict a spiked, harsh, tortured universe. If there is a single word for the shapes you see in an Australian landscape, the shapes of trees dead or alive, it is tortured. You imagine a dance of queer, macabre old men, summoned perhaps from purgatory, lifting their arms, posturing at odd angles, and then at some magic word frozen in their uncouth positions in the hard sunlight, or in moonlight which makes the scene weird and haunted and rather terrifying. You would have to be or to become either brave or unimaginative to live in the bush, or perhaps both.

The honey light of evening was on the hillsides when we saw the kangaroos, dark grey among tawny grasses and among charred stumps and bone-white branches. A tree stump with two jagged protuberances looked just like a kangaroo on its haunches with head thrown back and sloping ears. The country undulates and rolls away to far horizons, neither flat nor hilly. In the creeks are tall, spreading, handsome gums.

[4]

I had been told by other graziers, with varying degrees of disapproval, that at Wollongorang "they starve their sheep." This turned out to be partially true. Not all their sheep all the time, but some of them, some-times, to "train" them to eat thistles and other weeds and unpalatable grasses, and in order to find out just how sheep behave as grazing animals. The strange thing is that, after a century of raising wool from merinos, so much of what is now being found out breaks new ground.

That does not surprise Mr. John Watson, who maintains that little has changed on most sheep stations for the last century because it has been too easy to get by without undue effort. Only one major change has come about in sheep management since the first grants of land were made in these parts in the 1820's, and that is the introduction of super-phosphate and subterranean clovers. And even today many graziers either ignore these methods or dabble with them halfheartedly. Most are content to coast along, making fortunes in good years and losing them in years of drought; and—in Mr. Watson's opinion, by no means generally shared—they grossly understock their land. Average wool production hereabouts is nine pounds an acre; on Wollongorang, after only seven years of treatment, it is eighty pounds, rising on the best paddocks to 135 pounds an acre. Three sheep graze here now for every one main-tained before. In these parts of eastern New South Wales the output of the pastures could, in Mr. Watson's view, be increased tenfold by means of techniques already at the grazier's command, without any new dis-coveries.

The soil is poor initially. Poor and thin. In fact, there are places where there *is* no soil, only quartz rock. Elsewhere it is raw and red, eroded by gulleys, gritty, with no humus to bind it, and so easily destroyed. The natural grasses are coarse and sparse and unnutritious and devoid of those legumes, such as clovers, which extract nitrogen from the air and fix it in their tissues. Nitrogen is an essential ingredient in protein, and protein is the stuff of meat; so, other things being equal, the more a soil can be enriched with nitrogen, the more animals per acre can it support. To make the best use, therefore, of these poor pastures, legumes must somehow be persuaded to grow. And this ultimately depends upon the presence of a class of bacteria, called Rhizobia, which form little nodules on the roots of legumes such as lucerne and clovers and draw nitrogen from the air. If you sow an alien variety of clover, you must inoculate the seed with the right strain of rhizobium. A normal dressing sticks perhaps two thousand rhizobia organisms onto each clover seed, but scientists are experimenting with ways of raising this to *ten million* organisms per seed; each root would then fix ten times as much nitrogen as a normal plant fixes now.

Once you get the clovers going, you must pile on sheep to act as mowing machines and dung spreaders. This builds up the soil fertility, which in turn stimulates the growth of clovers, which produce more nitrogen and so more fertility—a virtuous circle. The whole system rests on the use of sheep to control the pastures, instead of allowing pastures to dictate the use of sheep.

The first graziers fenced their runs into very large paddocks, each paddock several thousand acres in extent, and that is about all a majority did. Now smaller paddocks—much smaller paddocks—are needed. Into a paddock of fifty acres 3,000 sheep may be crowded for a couple of weeks: shock treatment, a mass attack on the composition of the sward. And this is where starvation comes in. Many of the paddocks were formely overrun by thistles, reeds and other poor types of vegetation. Mr. Watson uses the sheep as mowing machines. Sheep will not eat thistles unless they are hungry, but they will then, and what is more, once "trained" to do so, they will prefer thistles and other weeds to most of the grasses. A mob put on to a pasture full of a weed called horehound developed such a taste for it that now they seek it out on pastures containing, in abudance, superior plants with superior names like *phalaris*.

But things are not as simple as that. Sheep can be starved with safety only at certain times. Ewes need good and ample food before and after lambing. One of the discoveries made at Wollogorang, as a result of these experiments, is that, in between lambings, a ewe may eat three times as much food as she needs to keep her weight steady and her health good. So she is wasting food that could and should be conserved. That is what is meant by management.

All this is based on regular weighing. Every day, on some part of the property, a mob of sheep is gathered at a mustering yard, driven through the crush, and about one in ten is weighed. From graphs and charts resulting from these figures, body-weight curves have been compiled. When the body weights are at their peaks, the ewes are turned on to nutritious pastures; when body weights fall, they are fed on thistles. By such means the grazier may husband his pastures, carry more sheep per acre, and so increase his output of wool.

That is all very well, retort the critics, but sooner or later there will be a drought and then the fully stocked—or overstocked?—grazier will have no reserved to fall back on. Understocking is a form of insurance. To this, Mr. Watson's answer is that you must feed your sheep on bought-in grain when drought comes. He believes that everyone must face up to more intensive, and therefore more skilled, methods of production, as mounting populations put more pressure on the land. Wollogorang methods may be right or wrong, but they are part of the wave of the future.

At this moment, however, there appears to be too much wool in the world; prices have slumped, and a tax has been imposed to raise funds for campaigns to persuade people to buy more wool. If every sheep station in Australia were to double its output, let alone raise it tenfold, there would ensue economic disaster. So who is right and who is wrong? Believers in intensification, progress and improvement? Or in traditional methods, *laissez faire* and getting by?

It all depends, presumably, on whether you take a long view or a short one—or perhaps just on your cast of mind. Mr. Watson's mind is one that favours change. Seven years ago, when he took over Wollogorang it carried 12,000 sheep; today 36,000. He intends to double that. He has circulated to fellow graziers a list of 104 questions about sheep management to which he says there are not proven answers; he runs a training scheme for cadets—a sort of one-man agricultural college; as a hobby, he buys up the carcasses of old vehicles from which to build new ones; he allows no shooting on the property, and he hatches in a fertile mind many "projects of importance" which range from adopting a new system of numerals "as far ahead of the Arabic system as the

Arabic is ahead of the Roman," controlling the stomach microflora of sheep, and compelling politicians to retire at fifty, to introducing clover festivals in country towns, setting up a committee "for the promotion of clear thinking," and working out a system for "reporting all experiments which give a negative result."

[5]

For a land dedicated to egalitarianism, there is an oddly feudal flavour about life on many of the country properties. I do not suggest a pulling of forelocks, but that each station is a community in the sense that manors were in the Middle Ages. The manor of Wollogorang supports about thirty families who receive free meat, milk and bread, and free housing. It is like a small village with its resident squire, and in the grange, at a long, polished dining-room table, there seems to be a place for everyone who drifts in. Solid silver adorns the sideboard; there are old-fashioned silver meat dishes with heavy covers. The house has many spacious rooms, but everyone foregathers in a small, cluttered, cozy chamber full of journals, cups of tea and photographs of horses and rams.

People came and went: a young man collecting old horse-drawn buggies who had just discovered a "sociable" lurking in a barn; a girl from the farming college doing her "prac"; a French schoolboy from the New Hebrides; a scientist interested in the pasture experiments; and among the phloxes and dahlias beyond the lawn was a brawny Yugoslav who had abandoned a restaurant in Sydney, drifted in and stayed to garden and to meditate about the price of a suit of clothes in terms of hours of labour in each of the world's countries and the interpretation of the Apocalypse.

In the library I dipped into a book of recollections by an early settler which cast back to convict days when most of these properties were founded. A pair of ticket-of-leave men, the author related, were taking a dip in a creek when a party of officials rode by. As the bathers were naked and there were ladies in the party, they stayed in the water. This was treated as a mark of disrespect; the men were returned to chain gangs and each received a hundred lashes in two installments, fifty to start with and the other fifty when the wounds began to heal. Another man got fifty lashes for running into the servants' quarters one dark night to say that he had seen the devil, which turned out to be a white pony. At the penal settlement near Goulburn a Negro called Black Francis carried out the floggings with such savagery that he won fame throughout the colony and was eventually murdered; one of his victims, after receiving seventy-five lashes, staggered to his feet, spat in the Negro's face and said, "You can't flog hard enough to kill a butterfly." The great-grandsons of such men are among today's Australians.

On this brutal foundation there arose a society of grace and elegance, whose leaders, enriched by the fleece of sheep, built comfortable and comely houses and observed a way of life transplanted, like the convicts, from England. A plain and pleasing Georgian style persisted in the colony for at least a decade after the Victorian coarsening process had set in at home.

The first settlers must have carried in their heads recollections of the country manors and rectories in which so many of them had been reared. Some were regimental officers who had served in the American colonies, and in Australia they drew on memories of a colonial architecture that had evolved in southern plantations and New England country towns. They burned their bricks from local clay and used native timbers for shingle roofs, panelling and furniture. Australia's greatest aesthetic tragedy was the introduction in the 1850's of corrugated iron, whose jagged ugliness has replaced the hand-cut wooden shingles that formerly roofed all these country buildings.

Some of the eucalypt hardwoods, after a century of polishing, are magnificent. Their colour glows. I recall with keen pleasure the wide doors, the dignified stairway with its balustrade, the deep-red knotted planks, smooth as glass and as shiny, and the fine Regency chairs of Wollogorang, whose plain Georgian façade faces on a garden alive with birds; the rambling, nicely proportioned rooms of Wingello and its great tithe barn with an original woolpress that was destroyed by fire only a few weeks after I saw it; and perhaps the finest of all these colonial mansions, Camden Park near Campbelltown, still occupied by direct descendants of John Macarthur, whose architect, John Verge, completed it in 1835.

[6]

Here is a plain, beautifully proportioned Regency house, dignified and comfortable, with nothing about it either ostentatious or shabby—a house of perfect manners and balanced design. It was the final achievement of an honest, sober family man untouched by scandal in an age of debauchery and corruption, when for years the colony was tyrannized by dissolute officers of the Rum Corps, as the New South Wales Corps of the British Army came to be known.

John Macarthur's family revered him, his wife Elizabeth cheerfully endured great hardships for his sake, yet he is remembered chiefly as a touchy, quarrelsome, hot-tempered rebel who, through influence, secured vast acreages of free land and intrigued against the only governor who tried to discipline the Rum Corps, Captain William Bligh, R.N. He was also the founder of Australia's prosperity through establishing the first flock of fine-wooled merino sheep and exporting the first fleeces that competed in quality with those from Spain and Germany.

In the words of his biographer, M. H. Ellis, John Macarthur had "an explosive quality"; he could be haughty and scornful; he could also be affectionate and tender, indulgent as a father and just and generous as a master. He fought a duel with the captain of the ship on which, as an ensign newly commissioned in the 68th Foot and transferred to the New South Wales Corps, he travelled to Sydney Cove in 1790. Eleven years later he wounded his commanding officer in another duel, and so ended his army career. But probably in both cases it was Macarthur who was provoked.

He had the unfortunate knack of making influential enemies. One of these, Governor Philip King, wrote of him: "There are no resources which art, cunning, impudence and a pair of basilisk eyes can afford that he does not put in practice to obtain any point he undertakes." But then, Macarthur had just bought a flock of merinos that Governor King, also a sheep enthusiast, had wanted. After his quarrel with the governor Macarthur was shipped back to London to answer for his conduct, taking with him some botanical specimens for Sir Joseph Banks and a box of "Spanish fleeces."

It was not Macarthur who introduced merinos from Cape Town, but he had bought from the first shipment four ewes and two rams and had had the nous to breed a pure strain from this foundation. A few years later he bought from a fellow officer the much larger flock that Governor King had wanted for the colony. The fleeces he took to London with him in the barque *Hunter* in 1802 did indeed prove to be golden. In New South Wales the coarse hair of Indian crossbred sheep —it was not wool—sold for two cents a pound. Yorkshire manufacturers, cut off from European sources of supply by the Napoleonic wars, offered the equivalent of fifty cents a pound for this fine-stapled wool of Macarthur's.

Fired now with a prophetic vision of what merino wool would mean to Australia, Macarthur presented his ideas to a committee of the Privy Council to such effect that the Secretary of State, Lord Camden, recommended "that a conditional grant of lands of a reasonable extent may be, perhaps, with safety granted to Mr. Macarthur, for the pasturage of sheep only." This led to the award of 5,000 acres of what was then called Cowpastures and is now part of the Camden Park estates, plus the services of thirty ex-convicts. Probably no grant of land to any individual has ever been more fruitful. From this beginning arose the enterprise that made Australia, sustained it, and is still by far its most important industry. Descendants of those first merinos are still living, like descendants of the Macarthurs (now called Stanham), at Camden Park. But the founder never lived to see his mansion completed. He died a month too soon, in the shade of insanity brought on by a lifetime of ill-health that was in part, at least, traceable to a long and devastating sickness, probably rheumatic fever, contracted in the convict ship in which, at the age of twenty-three, he first voyaged to Australia.

[7]

Parramatta is now a Sydney suburb and here, marooned amid modern bungalows and gridironed avenues, can still be seen Elizabeth Farm House, said to be the oldest dwelling in Australia. In 1793, within three years of his arrival in the colony, John Macarthur secured a grant of a hundred acres and established his family there. This was the birthplace of farming in Australia. It was at Parramatta, in 1792, that Governor Phillip made the first grants of land: twenty-five acres for a soldier, thirty for a ticket-of-leave man. The feckless soon gambled or traded away their plots to the prudent, and development hung fire until Phillip's successor, Major Francis Grose, allowed the convicts to be paid in rum for their labour. They had to work nine hours a day for the government, but after that they could strike their own bargains. Few were natural toilers, and nothing short of rum would persuade them to chop with hand hoes at the hard sod of the Place of Eels, as the aborigines had called this region.

The arrival from the United States of the *Hope,* loaded with provisions which the captain refused to sell unless the government also took 7,597 gallons of raw Bengal spirits, was one of those trivial events, often unmarked by historians, that make history. Grose gave way; rum flowed. The *Bellona* followed with five pipes of port. Distilleries sprang up; officers of the New South Wales Corps were allowed both to trade with the masters of incoming vessels and themselves to finance trading and whaling ventures, and the colony's economy began to move. Convicts toiled, officers thrived, harvests ripened, houses went up, and the toes of a few respectable English families began cautiously to test the murky waters of the antipodes. So near to starvation had the colonists been that guests who dined with Governor Phillip were expected to bring their bread rolls with them in their pockets. By 1794 Macarthur was able to write: "From a state of desponding poverty and threatened famine, that this settlement should be raised to its present aspect in so short a time is scarcely credible." All done by free enterprise—and rum.

By this time the Macarthurs had a hundred acres under cultivation at Parramatta, 1,800 bushels of corn in the barn, two mares, two cows, 130 goats, a hundred hogs, and another hundred acres as a reward for being the first settler to cultivate over fifty acres. Ten ex-convicts had been assigned to them, and Macarthur wrote, "With the assistance of one man and half a dozen greyhounds, my table is constantly supplied with wild ducks and kangaroos." And on his land he had built "a most excellent brick house . . . surrounded by a vineyard and garden of about three acres, full of vines and fruit trees and abounding with the most excellent vegetables." His wife liked it all as well as he did. "No two people on earth," she wrote a few years later, "can be happier than we are."

Today the house is in private hands, but the public comes at all hours, with or without warning, and Australian traditions of hospitality, combined with their own good nature, forbid the owners to turn visitors away. In 1904 the house was bought by the late Mr. William Swann, whose three surviving daughters now inhabit and lovingly tend it. No grants of public money are made towards its upkeep. New South Wales has a National Trust whose members make up in enthusiasm what they lack in funds and depend wholly upon private subscriptions.

I paid my visit, under the wing of Miss Rachel Roxburgh, on a Sunday afternoon, and at least half a dozen others had turned up. The Misses Swann gave us all tea in the dining room where the Macarthur family must so often have sat down to their wild duck, kangaroos and home-produced cream and butter, their home-killed pork and excellent vegetables. The low, long and unpretentious house has the wide doors, uneven walls, graceful mouldings and air of rambling informality only to be found in old dwellings that have been added on to several times. When I asked how many rooms it had, the reply was, "That all depends on what you mean by rooms," and I could see the point; the place is full of odd corners and bits of passage which might or might not be classed as rooms. The sunshine is filtered by a low veranda; eyes are rested and heat restrained. Ferns hang from beams in baskets or stand about in pots. It all has dignity and homeliness and charm.

It was here that Elizabeth Macarthur was left to cope with the farm and all its worries and with her growing family, while her husband was in exile overseas. The first of these long absences, after he had wounded his commanding officer, lasted four years; the second, occasioned by the far more serious offense of open rebellion against Governor William Bligh, continued twice as long. Life for Elizabeth was hard, but she had a remarkable skill in detecting silver linings through rose-coloured spectacles that enabled her to endure with almost unflawed cheerfulness everything from a miscarriage in the stinking confines of a particularly odious convict vessel to the last, sad years of her husband's insanity.

Elizabeth Macarthur proved herself to be so able a businesswoman that both the farm at Parramatta and the large estates at Camden Park ran more smoothly under her management than under her husband's, and Governor Lachlan Macquarie rewarded her with a grant of another six hundred acres. She had to contend not merely with droughts, dingoes, bandits and unreliable labour, but with attacks by aborigines, who killed several of her men, and even a rising of Irish "croppies" who advanced upon Elizabeth Farm, intending to burn it down, and forced her to carry off her small children to Sydney in the middle of the night. The portrait of her as an old lady shows a face strong, capable and determined, with clear blue eyes, a firm chin and an air of authority. She raised four exemplary sons, levelheaded and enterprising, sober and industrious. "Indeed my beloved wife," her husband wrote from London, "when I reflect on the many adverse circumstances to which you have been exposed, and the extraordinary trials that you have borne, not only without sinking under the accumulated pressure, but with the most active fortitude and good sense, it is impossible for me to express the admiration that reflection excites—or to repress the pride I feel in having to boast of such a pattern for wives and mothers as my own."

[8]

It was at Elizabeth Farm that the so-called "Rum Rebellion" of 1807 might be said to have started, when the chief constable of Parramatta served on John Macarthur an order to appear before the Court on a criminal charge, arising out of his removal from one of his own vessels of the coppers which had formed part of two stills he had imported. These stills had been impounded on the orders of Governor William Bligh. According to one version, the praiseworthy efforts of the governor to end a scandalous rum monopoly held by dissolute officers of a disreputable corps was the cause of this rebellion; the officers rose in anger, seized the person of the governor and installed their commander, Major George Johnston, as administrator of the colony. Others hold that Bligh's own arrogance, megalomania and stupidity were the underlying causes. Even Elizabeth Macarthur, who saw good in everyone, called him "violent, rash and tyrannical," observed that "the excessive despotism of the ruling power called aloud for a reform," and gaily referred to the act of treason by which the governor was arrested and deposed as "a spirited measure."

Spirited indeed it was, and quite bloodless, taking place after no less spirited celebrations of the twentieth anniversary of Captain Phillip's landing at Botany Bay. A posse of spirited men advanced upon Government House and, after a two-hour search, winkled the portly governor from behind a bed in a servant's cubbyhole. Naturally there were two versions of this also. Bligh had retired there, he said later, "to deliberate on the means to be adopted for the restoration of my authority," and been seized by twelve men with fixed bayonets; Johnston retorted that only three had entered—the room would have held no more —with no fixed bayonets but, on the contrary, "a friendly hand stretched out to help him out of the strange situation in which he was found."

Members of the new class of emancipists, and of independent merchants and farmers, were no less determined than the rum-trading officers to get rid of the despotic, apoplectic Bligh, whose language could be so obscene as to cause his predecessor, Governor King, seated at the gubernatorial breakfast table, to burst into tears.

But however justified they were in getting rid of Bligh, in so doing they had committed an act of high treason and knew that they must answer for it in London. The loneliness of eight years' exile ruined

Macarthur's health and brought on attacks of devastating homesickness. "Dearly beloved beings," came a cry from London, "when shall I see and embrace you all again?"

Macarthur could not be tried in England for an offense committed in New South Wales but knew that Bligh's successor, Governor Macquarie, had been instructed by the Secretary of State to bring a criminal charge against him the moment he set foot in the colony. So there he was, marooned in England with no money, writing frantic letters to Elizabeth to remit to him all she could, learning a great deal about the marketing of fine Spanish wool, and suffering from dreadful bouts of nervous depression. At intervals he vainly importuned Lord Bathurst for an assurance that the charges against him would be dropped if he were to return home. The one bright spot, apart from infrequent letters from Elizabeth —so many packets were wrecked or captured that once he had no word for two years—was the arrival of his fleeces in mounting numbers. By 1817 Elizabeth was looking after some five thousand sheep and exporting more than half the total wool clip of the colony.

This was the year in which Bathurst at last cancelled his instructions to Macquarie and allowed Macarthur to sail for New South Wales, taking his sons James and William, a sectional greenhouse and 120 pots of olives, vines, capers, figs, apples, nuts and rhubarb, as well as various seedling trees and plants like jasmine, cowslips and daisies. He set to work immediately to reconstruct Elizabeth Farm until, in the words of his son James, it was "transformed by our father's fertile genius into an elegant and commodious residence." Within six years of his return his Camden estates were described as the finest agricultural establishment in the colony. They employed 123 ex-convicts, who enjoyed tea and sugar twice a day and were given clothing and tobacco. Macarthur wool consistently topped the market, and James and William had worked out a system of washing the sheep in a river to cleanse the clip that was the prototype of the woolshed and of shearing methods later adopted throughout Australia. By 1830 the Macarthurs were shearing 19,000 sheep.

But the flockmaster was no longer the same man. Bouts of feverish energy alternated with fits of black despair; in the end he could not endure the presence of his wife and children. Their own affection and respect never faltered. They remembered him as "a man of quick and generous impulses" who was "at all times ready to take arms against oppression and injustice"; fond of reading aloud from the classics, modelling his conduct on Coriolanus and Scipio Africanus—and deriving from the former, it was said, the habit of washing his head and feet in cold water every morning—and in his unruffled moments "imbued with a spirit of truly Christian benevolence and calm philosophy." In the year of his death, 1834, Australia exported 4½ million pounds of fine wool. Today the figure is 4½ million bales; each bale weighs about 300 pounds.

[9]

The country town of Windsor in the Hawkesbury valley, the oldest settled district in Australia, has a mellowed, contented, indefinably English feeling. Certain Georgian buildings no doubt contribute towards this, such as the Macquarie Arms, built in the year of Trafalgar, a two-storied edifice combining solidity with elegance and possessing lovely shutters and doors made from local cedar; one of the latter has a knocker carved in the shape of a bunch of grapes. The showpieces are the Courthouse and St. Matthew's Church, both built to the design of Francis Greenway, generally considered to be Australia's greatest architect.

By training Greenway was not an architect at all but a builder, born at Mangotsfield near Bristol, and not even a successful builder; he went bankrupt, forged a document purporting to show that he was owed $500 by a client, and in 1813 found himself transported to the penal settlements for fourteen years. Governor Lachlan Macquarie was by then in charge and had become known as the convict's friend; he entertained emancipists at his table and appointed them to responsible positions, often over the heads of law-abiding colonists. "My principle is," he wrote to Lord Sidmouth, "that when once a man is free, his former state shall be no longer allowed to act against him; let him feel himself eligible for any situation which he has, by a long term of upright conduct, proved himself worthy of filling."

In Greenway's case, even the "long term of upright conduct" was dispensed with. Macquarie had been seized by a vision. He had seen the filthy, sordid, unplanned convict settlement on Sydney Cove transformed into a spacious, dignified and decent capital city, worthy alike of its wonderful natural setting and of England's honour and glory. To translate this vision into reality his only human instruments were his military engineers who, while sympathetic to his ideas of order, to the needs of defense and to the efficient housing of convicts, were scarcely qualified to create the stately mansions, the fine churches, the dignified public buildings and the well-planned squares and parks and boulevards that had beguiled Macquarie's imagination. No wonder that he quickly picked out Greenway, removed him from the chain gang and set him to work, first on a lighthouse, and then on Hyde Park Barracks, to accommodate male convicts.

At the formal opening of the Barracks on the King's birthday in 1819, Macquarie sat down to a meal of beef, plum pudding and punch with 589 felons who "appeared very happy and contented and gave us three cheers on our coming away." So delighted was the governor with this handsome, dignified and practical building that he rewarded Francis Greenway with an absolute pardon.

Three churches were built by Greenway, using convict labour: St. James' in Sydney, St. Luke's in Liverpool, and St. Matthew's in Windsor. All share the same harmonious, simple dignity. There are no frills. Though Greenway's work was not original, it was perfectly successful in what it set out to achieve: to re-create in the antipodes the polite and satisfying Regency style of English architecture derived mainly from Wren and exemplified in the buildings of Nash and Wood. Spiritually Greenway was never out of reach of Bath and the Clifton that was growing up in his youth.

Greenway's career ended when his patron left the colony in 1822 under a cloud, and publicly accused of extravagance, misjudgment and overindulgence to emancipists who had abused his trust. The commissioner who investigated these charges, J. T. Bigge, remarked of Greenway: "Why, if this fellow is suffered to go on, he will make a city superior in architecture to London." This disaster was easily averted. Greenway was a touchy, arrogant, awkward customer who, once he had lost his patron, also lost no time in quarrelling with his superiors, who in turn lost no time in dismissing him from his position as government architect. He went to pieces, badgered everyone with his grievances, and was kept from starvation only by his wife's enterprise in running a small school. Ironically enough, he was sold up on the day on which St. James' Church was consecrated in the heart of Sydney, with full civic pomp. He died in poverty in 1837.

Locally burned sandstone bricks made St. Matthew's in Windsor, consecrated in the year of its architect's downfall. A plain square tower is surmounted by a graceful octagonal belfry whose reconstruction was in hand at the time of my visit. The original belfry was supported by heavy curved beams made of stringybark, blackbutt and tallowwood—three kinds of eucalypt. In 1820 the builders had only to go out and fell the trees close at hand. In 1964 the timbers had to be brought nearly 400 miles. Local shingles simply could not be obtained, so the contractors had to use Canadian redwood. An Irish builder, Mr. Irons, was carrying out the work with enthusiasm and skill. His foreman was a Dane, several of his workmen Italian; all were fascinated by a task calling for craftsmanship and the use of such old materials as lime and mortar instead of cement. In modern times, with modern wages, this craft work is fantastically expensive, and the raising of the needed money by the women's committee of the National Trust of New South Wales was little short of a miracle.

The same mellow brickwork graces Windsor's courthouse which, designed by Greenway, was completed in 1822. Not only justice was dispensed here, but entertainment, including a singlehanded performance of *Othello* when the actor blackened one side of his face to turn towards the audience for the part of the Moor but exposed the untreated half to deliver the lines of Desdemona and Iago. An unappreciative audience chased him from the town, clamouring for the return of their money.

[10]

My own memories of Windsor are more peaceful, culminating in a picnic beside the Hawkesbury River. We sat in the dappled shadow of a casuarina and enjoyed delicious fresh fruit and one of the dry white wines from the nearby Hunter River valley, whose quality is excellent and whose price wonderfully modest. Most of the good things of life in Australia, if not free, are easily come by. Some bad things also: roadside litter can be appalling. The Hawkesbury road, so laced with history, is studded now with roadside shacks dispensing meat pies, repelling synthetic fruit drinks, hot dogs and hamburgers, everything you can imagine that is starchy and horrible, and roast choox; all around lie discarded beer bottles, rusty cans, trampled cartons, torn cigarette packs and all sorts of nameless, sordid objects. Does any other species of animal on the earth's surface void such horrible inorganic excreta, and in such enormous quantities, as man? The feces of the body are quickly rendered inoffensive by the action of air, sunshine, rain and bacteria. These have no effect on beer-bottle tops, broken glass, old boots, rusty cans and the steel framework of abandoned motorcars.

Back from the road stand shaggy little farmsteads which, like the terraces of Sydney's "Paddo," seem to have been designed for pygmies. Odd, when most Australians are so husky and when they have so much space and emptiness to fill. The little shacks look drawn in on themselves, shrunken like withered trophies of head-hunters. The originals were "slab houses," made of roughly sawn planks and roofed by shingles. A few of the older houses still retain their shingles as a sort of petticoat underneath the corrugated iron.

Is there such a thing as an Australian style in architecture? We discussed this as we drove along, and my guides thought yes: traditionally a square bungalow encircled by a veranda, standing alone, built to be seen from all sides; no need here for terraced houses or for semidetached ones, for squashing up together. Therefore no planned zonal architecture has arisen, nothing comparable to the English Nash terraces, for instance, or to the mansions-cum-warehouses that line Amsterdam's canals. What about modern urban architecture? For the most part it is just like everyone else's; there can be no localizing of the steel-and-concrete tower and cube. Concrete is concrete, whether it is mixed in Sydney, Tokyo or Accra, and architectural regionalism, in the cities, is just about dead. My guides, however, took me to see a brand-new church just outside Sydney. Built throughout of Australian hardwoods, unpainted, its roof is steeply pitched and a veranda encircles it. The rafters are exposed; everything is strong and solid, rather dark, sturdy, not elegant, but not mannered either—honest-to-God. "That could be the modern version," my guides suggested, "of the true, native Australian style: and overdue reaction from the international style brought in by Seidler." But no one could put up a building of that kind in the middle of Melbourne or Sydney. In the modern city there can surely be no opting out of the steel-and-concrete tower or cube.

FIVE 〰〰〰

Broken Hill

There cannot be many places in the world in which you are debarred from working in its only industry unless you were born in the locality. Yet this is almost the case in Broken Hill—almost but not quite, because if you can live there for eight consecutive years, and find favour in the right quarters, you may become eligible for employment. This seldom happens. Broken Hill is not just a closed shop but a closed city. In it live 32,000 people entirely dependent on four mines producing lead, zinc and silver. About half the work force is directly employed by the mining companies, and the other half lives by servicing the first half.

This extraordinary mining town in western New South Wales is way out in the desert, 200 miles from its nearest urban neighbour and 700 miles from Sydney. It is parched and, in summer, blisteringly hot. Its average annual rainfall of nine inches means nothing, for in some years not even one inch falls, and the whole of the rainfall may be precipitated in two or three violent storms interspersed by dry spells lasting for six or eight months. Yet a favourite pastime of the workers is water skiing, which takes place on a system of reservoirs about seventy miles away that contain more water, people will tell you, than Sydney harbour.

Gambling is illegal in New South Wales—but not in Broken Hill, where bookies openly conduct a roaring trade. Closing time for pubs is ten o'clock—but not in Broken Hill, where they stay open until midnight and you can get a drink at almost any hour. On the other hand, your freedom just about stops there. If you are the wife of a mineworker, you may not take a paid job, even a part-time one, of any kind. You may trade only with certain shops or firms. If you run a business, you must employ only approved individuals, whom you cannot dismiss, and observe certain practices on pain of being declared black. If you are black, you are finished. Not only will you do no business, but you will be

92

ostracized and find no employment. No one will mend your cooker, deliver your fuel, sell you petrol, or wave to you in the street. You may even get threatening telephone messages, and there have been cases where dentists have got into trouble for attending to *persona non grata*.

It is impossible to winnow the hard truth from all you hear. Some of the instances I was given of trade-union tyranny over private lives may well have been influenced by personal prejudices and by the national habit of grumbling at authority whoever exercises it. Probably there are people who live all their days in Broken Hill without interference. Certainly there are many who either do not mind this interference or who justify it. Allowing for all that, there is no doubt that people who are employed, or whose husbands or fathers are employed, in the mining industry are not on all occasions free to trade with whom they like, to say what they like, take what jobs they like, or buy what they like.

To give three examples: every union member, which means every mine employee, must subscribe to the union newspaper, the *Barrier Daily Truth*. If there are five union members in a family, then five copies of that newspaper must be delivered daily. Then: a retired miner took two part-time jobs. He was summoned before the union authorities, shown an informer's letter, and told to give up one of the two jobs immediately. A union official overheard him giving his week's notice to one of his employers. "A week nothing," he ordered. "You're out to-night." Finally: a firm that reduced the price of its carpets was declared black and forced to close its branch in Broken Hill. Some of its female customers refused to take this lying down and drove several hundred miles to buy the carpets at another branch. Their husbands were warned that if these orders were not cancelled, there would be serious trouble, and the women were threatened by anonymous telephone calls. The orders were cancelled. I was told that even the makes of cakes house-wives could buy or not buy were at one time specified but did not check this.

The fact that I was given these and many other instances suggests a climate of resentment, at least among the women. Most husbands think differently. They are doing very nicely: drawing high wages, playing the slot machines, betting on the horses. They are buttressed by mateship, enriched by the lead bonus, given a whole month's free holiday on full pay at the seaside with their families every year, and safely ensconced in their jobs for the rest of their working days. What do they care if their wives buy one kind of cake rather than another, or pay a couple of collars more for carpets? "It's a man's town," the women said. "If you're born in Broken Hill, a male, and eighteen, everything falls into your lap." One or two miners even play polo. Iced beer never fails; there is a new car in the garage; houses are screened against flies, and you get used to the heat. So what is there to worry about?

If you are a woman, there may be the petty tyrannies I mentioned and also heat, loneliness and monotony. Most of the men are either at work or in the pub and come home merely to roll into bed. On Sundays they will take their families to the sailing club at Menindee. There is nowhere else to go. The ban on paid employment condemns active-minded women to long days of boredom and frustration, relegating them almost to the status of chattels. One confided to me that she had always wanted to be a journalist and could have become a stringer for a metropolitan newspaper, but the rules forbade it and she had to let the chance go by. There is also a lack of employment for school-leaving daughters; many go to Melbourne or Sydney and do not return.

"Jealousy," a woman said. "That's our trouble here in Broken Hill. No one's willing to see another bloke make a few extra dollars or do better than he's doing. Everyone's got to be cut down to size." Another malcontent asked, "Why do you see so much washing out on a Sunday? The men are in bed sleeping off their Saturday beer. My husband never takes me out. Some men don't even tell their wives what they earn. Poker machines, horses, beer, beer, beer. A man's town."

But some women defend the system. "Broken Hill is the best town in Australia," one defiantly said. "People who tell you the bad things are traitors. Everyone is looked after. My husband pays a dollar a week and if anyone in the family is sick we get everything free—hospitals, operations, drugs, anything. We have the best hospital in New South Wales and the best high school. The B.I.C. has done it all."

[2]

B.I.C. stands for Barrier Industrial Council. This is an association of nineteen unions, formed in 1925, which every three years negotiates an agreement with the mining companies. The terms of this agreement must be ratified at a mass meeting attended by delegates from all the unions; if unanimity is not achieved, a new agreement must be negotiated. And once the document is signed, the unions stick to it. There has been no serious stoppage since 1954.

The strength of the B.I.C. lies in the discipline it exercises over its members. There are no wildcat strikes, no union breakaways. Every three months there is a badge show. Every member must wear his union badge, and anyone who fails to do so loses a shift, which means a fine of $14. Suppose a member loses his badge? "No excuse. One man had his house burned down with the badge in it, but he still had to pay." Wasn't that unjust? The union official shrugged his shoulders. "We haven't been able to work out a way round."

All the main objectives of the B.I.C. have been achieved. Its shop is as closed as condemned cells in the Lubyanka prison. There are no backsliders, no rebels. Members of the constituent unions enjoy security, stability, perhaps the highest living standards in Australia. Most of them own their own homes. They have recreations, clubs, medical benefits, scholarships for children, generous paid holidays, many other joys. What next?

"Living standards can always go higher," a B.I.C. official said. "Shorter hours, better pensions, extension of our welfare work. We are working on a project for a dental clinic. Then probably convalescent homes. Help for widows, more university scholarships . . ."

Union officials do not get large salaries, by Broken Hill standards; this would rile the members. They work in an atmosphere of informality and mateship, with open doors, open shirts and an easy tempo, in a rambling Victorian building whose foundation stone was laid by Ben Tillett. The setup suits the unions and they shy away from any suggestion of change. "Our secret is," the general secretary told me, "our members tell *us* what to do." It seems unlikely that the members often tell them anything uncongenial, unorthodox, or unrehearsed. On the whole, it suits the bosses too. The Mine Management Association bargains collectively with the B.I.C. and knows that the B.I.C. has the authority to hold its members to their side of the bargain. The Association speaks for four companies of which the largest, Conzinc Riotinto of Australia, produces about half the ore.

[3]

Beneath a low ridge that traverses this barren sandstone country lies a zinc/silver/lead lode said to be the richest on earth. Like most mines, these began with fossickers, the foot-loose shearers and swagmen who explored these plains and drought-punished ridges with little to sustain them but dreams of sudden fortune. These men were ignorant of geology but keen of eye to catch a sparkle in the rock and peeled of ear to catch a few words dropped indiscreetly in a grogshop.

Broken Hill started when a German immigrant, Charles Rasp, employed as a boundary rider on Gipps Hill Station, chipped a few samples of rock from a long, jagged range that ran across the property and sent them to an assayer in Adelaide. This was in 1883. A disappointing report came back: carbonate of lead, with traces of silver. But silver was booming and it is always part of the dream that a trace may lead to a lode. Rasp and seven of his mates formed a syndicate, each putting up $140, and got a twenty-one-year lease of nearly 300 acres covering what proved to be the richest mineral field in Australia.

Squeezing two dollars a week each from their wages, members of the syndicate—the local storekeeper, the overseer and the jackaroo at Gipps Hill were among them—engaged a miner who sank a shaft and still found silver only in traces. They would have sold everything if they could have recovered their stake but could find no buyers. Two of the members did sell out, for next to nothing, and a cattle dealer called Sidney Kidman took a part share in exchange for some old steer; he resold it to a fellow traveller in a coach for $240. This was one of the few mistakes he made; he became a cattle millionaire but could have become a mining one as well if he had kept his part share. At long last the shaft reached ore that contained enough chloride of silver to justify the sending of a bullock wagonload to be smelted near Melbourne. In 1885 the Broken Hill Proprietary, to become Australia's biggest company, was born. The mining camp followed the usual boom-town pattern: shacks run up from poles and sacking, streets deep in dust or in mud, flies and filth, sly-grog shops and brawls and gambling, typhoid fever. Six years after the first silver was smelted the camp held 20,000 people, the Broken Hill Proprietary paid $2 million in dividends, and one-third of the world's silver was being mined there, and in times of drought water was carted seventeen miles in horse-drawn drays.

Romantic birth, disreputable infancy, checkered adolescence and staid maturity—the usual pattern. Despite all the beer and gambling, today's Broken Hill seems eminently respectable and middle-class. "We're not a shantytown," said one of the mine management executives, "but a stable community. The B.I.C. encourages a civic sense. Our people are proud of their schools, their hospitals, their art school and their parks and playgrounds. We're planting a green belt of trees and shrubs all round, making irrigated gardens, and trying to beautify the city. But of course the setup works both ways. We're very conservative."

Too conservative, he implied, and gave as an example the failure to encourage any industry but mining. Fewer men are being taken on these days, and opportunities for the young are diminishing.

"The answer, of course, lies in starting new industries to get us away from our total dependence on the mines. But high wages and the union strangle hold keep out new enterprises."

Most underground miners work in teams of between two and four men who contract to do a certain job, like hauling timber to a production party or boring a face. Such contractors can earn up to $100 a week, and on top of this they draw the lead bonus, at present over $34 a week. But now the B.I.C. has limited the time a man may work underground to 310 minutes a day for five days a week.

On the surface, sedentary men in self-propelled trucks or trolleys lift everything with grabs. A good-humoured, friendly lot, they greeted a representative of the bosses with a friendly wave and a "How'y'doin', Johnnie?" as he passed by. Most of them seemed to be just looking on. "I got fed up with standing around pretending to have something to do," one of the miners told me. "But I couldn't get into an underground contract party because I'm a ring-tail, or ring-in." That means an outsider, one not born in Broken Hill. After a good deal of fossicking, however, he found a loophole and slipped through it into a well-paid job underground.

Members of the salaried staff, no less than miners, must obey B.I.C. rules. Directors and executives are not allowed to wash their own cars, even on Sundays.

[4]

Committee members of such organizations as the Country Women's Association and the Y.W.C.A. receive their guests in smart frocks, gay hats and white gloves and serve tea from immaculate china, with thin sandwiches and iced cakes on paper doilies. In their largely manless world these women work prodigiously both to keep and improve their homes and to further charitable causes. To raise money they do all the catering at almost every public event, from race meetings, school sports and football matches to church bazaars and weddings. This work can be very gruelling when the thermometer registers over 100° F. on the veranda for weeks on end and joints must still be roasted, cakes and pies baked.

The young wife of a miner told me of a school she had started for mentally retarded children; now she has thirty pupils and several helpers—*Unpaid* work is permitted by the B.I.C. (On the other hand, a Girl Guide organizer who started a bob-a-job project to help the aged transgressed the rules and had to desist.) Members of the Country Women's Association raised in six years, entirely by catering, $36,000 to build a well-equipped hall with kitchens, library and rest rooms, contributed $2,000 towards the Flying Doctor service, started a fund to provide holidays for elderly women and books for country libraries, and are now intent upon a hostel for outback women who come to visit hospitals or schools or to have their babies.

Divested at last of hats and gloves, we relaxed in an impeccably neat, pink-painted, corrugated-iron home built, as so many homes are, by its owner, a tradesman employed on the mines, with his own hands and ingenuity. Broken Hill wives, said my hostess, favour nailed-down, wall-to-wall carpets because these cannot easily be removed for sale by husbands who have met with disaster on a Friday night at the slot machines. In the garden irrigated figs, nectarines and plums were fruiting, and a vine hung with bunches of muscatels covered one wall of the house; in the concrete yard were pens where the son of the house had bred game cocks. From the local school he had won a scholarship in physics, and now he is a space missile research worker overseas.

The owners of these carefully tended, shipshape homes are often to be found at the Musicians' club, whither I was taken furtively, since it is a male sanctuary to which women are admitted only on certain days and into one compartment. Even so, few are normally invited in, and I knew my visit was a privilege. The club has nothing to do with music; membership is open to all who work on the mines for a subscription of $6 a year. It is almost a replica, on a smaller scale, of Sydney's St. George League's Club, with the same handsome veneers and concealed lighting, lofty ceilings and chromium-plated bars and luxurious décor. Batteries of slot machines, so well patronized that after five o'clock you must queue up to get near one, bring in a profit of $6,000 a month. The profits on the bar are even larger.

The B.I.C. official who kindly took me to the club brought his wife. She looked around with interest—it was her first visit. The club had been open for two years. "Men don't bring their wives." Do the wives mind this? "Some do. I've a friend whose husband came here every Friday and as often as not got home without a penny of his wages left.

No one knows how she managed. Time and again she was in tears." The story had a cheerful ending. "They got religion, both of them—turned Baptist. Now he doesn't gamble, drink, or smoke and their home radiates happiness."

"It's a man's town." An English migrant, the wife of a professional man, echoed this phrase. "My husband and I aren't asked out together of an evening or at weekends. My husband goes and I'm supposed to sit quietly at home. The women asked me out to morning tea at first, but I don't like cream buns and they resented this. They resented my keeping my figure when the cream buns ruined theirs. One even said, 'We shan't ask you to morning tea if you turn up your nose at our cakes.' Once a woman really went for me. She shouted at me, 'You're a disgrace, coming out like that, no lipstick on, no make-up,' and she tried to smear my face with lipstick. It's the loneliness and the climate, and a lot of women here don't lead a normal married life." Perhaps she was prejudiced; the heat did not agree with her, gardening as she knew it was impossible, and she was homesick. Broken Hill is indeed a long way from Gerrard's Cross.

[5]

This question of the segregation of the sexes is one that bothers most self-critical Australians; they feel there must be something wrong. Are Australian men really so indifferent to women, compared with men elsewhere? Are they undersexed or even, as has been suggested, homosexual in an unconscious and repressed way? How has it all come about?

"The woolshed tradition." That is one theory. In Australia's formative years people were isolated and scattered; it was an event to gather in someone's woolshed for a Christmas celebration, a wedding party, or a ram sale. On these occasions the men clustered together to discuss the wool clip, the price of sheep and the performance of race horses, while the women exchanged news about babies, the latest fashions and cooking recipes. "Some of them mightn't have seen another woman for six months. They'd heard all they wanted to about the wool clip and sheep prices. They *wanted* to talk to each other." So arose the custom still observed at many an Australian party, even though the wool clip has given way to car models and test match scores.

One man put the blame squarely on the women. "They don't *try* to interest the men," he complained. "If a man approaches them, nine times out of ten they'll snub the poor bloke." To this a woman retorted, "That's because they're afraid of their husbands. Australian men are very jealous. They're possessive. They don't like to see their wives even talking to other men, and when they get home they'll kick up a row about something else and make life impossible."

Several women agreed with this, but one suggested, "It may be true we don't try hard enough to interest the men. But if it comes to that, what *does* interest Australian men? Sport, union politics, performance of cars. Pretty dull subjects, to be honest, but I've found that if I experiment with something else, the bloke takes off to join the other men and get back to safety. No normal Australian man would admit that a woman knows more about a thing than he does."

Perhaps it is six of one and half a dozen of the other. Meanwhile an impasse, and possibly a certain social sterility. But people say that times are changing. Cocktail parties, travel overseas, television, beer gardens, New Australians, the Americanization everyone believes to be taking place—new influences are reshaping Australian society.

"Learning to drive a car has made the whole difference," said a station manager's wife. "We used to be stuck here for months on end and couldn't move unless our husbands took us—we were almost prisoners. Now we can go off for a day's shopping when we want to or visit neighbours. The main thing is we know we *can*. The kids know it too. They grow up to think of their mother as a person in her own right. Boys and girls share things in a way they never did when I was young. That will change everything."

Isolation shaped Australia, first its animals and plants, then its humans. All were cut off by time and distance and obliged to work out their own adaptations to the environment. Archaic forms survived, such as the marsupials, the monotremes, the various plants that continued in their primitive ways of forming seed. Humans continued also in the archaic patriarchal form of society evolved to meet the conditions of northern Europe with its cold winters, its obstinate and heavy soils, its inclement forests and the need for hard and unremitting toil to master the environment. All that is scarcely needed in the easygoing south with no cold winters, no dark forests and no dark forest gods. The long Australian isolation has ended; and soon the customs that it has preserved, like specimens in jars of spirit, must surely end too.

[6]

The playground of Broken Hill is Menindee, one of a chain of lakes now harnessed into reservoirs and formed by the river Darling, which flows into the Murray. On Sunday a mass exodus takes place along the bitumen to reach the water and the beaches, so far from the sea. Everyone looks brown, brawny and well-nourished, and to make quite sure of the nourishment there are frequent stops at roadside pubs and cafés to load up with meat pies, hot dogs, biscuits, cakes, lollies and armfuls of chilled beer cans. No one goes hungry or thirsty at Menindee.

All around is the desert, speckled with sage-green saltbush a foot or so high that seems able to survive without moisture. Because the lakes never quite dried up, Menindee and its surroundings were much frequented by the aborigines, who have left little but their cave paintings at Mootwingie, a number of round stones with which they ground seeds of the nardóo plant, and the strange, attractive names of the lakes on which the water-skiing miners now disport themselves—Cawdilla, Pamamaroo, Tandure, Bijtjie, Balaka.

Formerly these lakes alternately flooded and shrank, but now they form part of a complex irrigation system that sustains the vines and orchards of the Murray basin. Every Sunday their surfaces are gay with the orange-, scarlet-, topaz- and rust-coloured canvas of innumerable sailing boats and crisscrossed by the sweeping tracks of water skiers, while the buzz of speedboats shakes the air. Beaches are lined with caravans equipped with more conveniences and luxuries than many houses offer. Near one of the caravan parks are tethered several light aircraft, whose owners fly out from Broken Hill, or from drought-struck sheep stations, for a couple of hours on the water.

Children scutter about like water beetles. However dark their parents, they all seem to be blond. Are they merely bleached, or is some change occurring in the genes? In countries of strong and perpetual sunshine, natural selection normally seems to favour the dark pigments and to result in "the shadowed livery of the burnished sun." Here the process appears to be reversed and the livery to become shining rather than shadowed. Certainly the number of fair-skinned, towheaded children you see about is remarkable, and apart from those with aboriginal blood, I noticed few that were swarthy.

A vivid patch of scarlet caught my eye in the yard surrounding one of the bedraggled little houses in the township of Menindee. This was the

Sturt pea (*Clianthus formosus*) which, I was told, after rainstorms will spread a blood-red carpet over the desert. It was named after the explorer Charles Sturt, the first white man to trace the course of the Darling. It is a dramatic flower with a jet-black center amid scarlet petals, likened by the aborigines to the black head of a girl in a cloak of red parrot feathers given her by her lover. The young man went off hunting and never returned; the girl pined away, and on the spot where they had parted, this bright flower appeared.

It was Charles Sturt who brought the first sheep to the Darling to feed his men. To everyone's surprise they thrived on saltbush, and this led to a demand for grazing leases. From the early 1850's the land was taken up in very large runs held on long leases and wool sent down the Darling to Adelaide either by camel train—the camels continued into the 1920's —or by paddle steamer. Then in 1862 the land of western New South Wales was thrown open to free selectors, who could take what they wanted in blocks of 340 acres if they could make a small deposit. So all the big runs were broken up, and economic disasters followed; 340 acres of this country would support about fifteen sheep, and it is generally held today that about 5,000 sheep is the minimum economic unit. For these you would need hereabouts at least 100,000 acres, and that would be the next thing to a small holding.

This semi-arid belt between the continent's wet rim and its dry center is dotted with ghost towns. At one such, fourteen miles from Broken Hill, silver was struck in 1882, and within three years some 3,000 people were enjoying there a boom as spectacular as it was brief. Mines sprang up with names like Jo the Marine, Chanticleer, the Hen and Chickens; and a young Irishman who made a fortune on the Day Dream Mine, Harry Meaney, went to his wedding in a dray drawn by four grey horses, with bell ringers fore and aft also mounted on greys, and provided a wedding breakfast at the Nevada Hotel which lasted all night and demolished twenty cases of champagne. Within ten years the mines were closed and the town deserted. The courthouse has become a youth hostel where I came upon a party of lads from Broken Hill taking a course in leadership given by a Methodist minister. The dilapidated, down-at-heel remains of Silverton were sweltering in a savage heat that would have singed bare feet. Three or four part-blood aborigines were squatting on the pub's veranda while goats scrounged in the dust for a stray twig or stolon.

Silverton formerly had thirteen pubs and a flourishing brewery. Now there remains this one small pub, a couple of stores and half a dozen dwellings of unmitigated squalor where part-bloods live like rats in a rubbish dump. The pub is kept by an Italian couple who are putting by their money until they have enough to start a business, probably in Adelaide or Melbourne. "People come out here from Broken Hill at weekends," they said. You wonder why. Then you see part, at least, of the answer in the shape of a young aboriginal girl coming in to buy wine. Slender, smooth-skinned, firm-breasted, she carried off the flagon with a swagger. "They're finished when they're twenty," said the Italian, outlining with his hands a flabby female figure. "You know, go to seed." A bottle of brandy (Australian) is the usual fee for a girl's weekend services.

Among the humpies made from bits of rusty corrugated iron and torn shreds of sacking we found an old, old man with a weather-beaten, parchment-coloured face, rheumy eyes and a big, wide, spreading white mustache. He sat in the dust in a lean-to full of rusted, twisted, broken junk, leaning against an empty oil drum and fiddling with an ancient pipe. He spoke slowly but in clear English. "Had a bit of a party last night, don't feel too good." In the humpy a granddaughter sprawled across a dirty bed, sleeping it off.

The old man had been a drover who took mobs of cattle from Queensland down to South Australia. They used to swim the beasts across the Darling near Wicannia, he recalled; all his life had been spent in the saddle. He was born near Coopers Creek. "My people knew Burke and Wills. They didn't harm them. They looked after them, fed 'em, did what they could." Veined lids as brittle as a snakeskin drooped over his dark eyes. Even in the midst of all the squalor, lying in dust, and dry-mouthed from a hangover, he had a certain dignity.

Poverty is not the reason for the squalor. Wages here are the same for blacks as for whites, and so are pensions; the old man was probably quite well off. The blacks inhabit, at this point of time, a limbo between the conditions of nomads and hunters living on the country and those of twentieth-century city dwellers who live by money tokens. It is the use of money that the aborigines have hitherto failed to master. For them things come, things go. There is drink, tobacco, cards and sunshine. There is food and there is love. Life is easy. As for the women— "They're all prostitutes," said the Silverton publican. This is no sin in their eyes. Men want sex and so do they, most likely—also brandy. They cherish their babies and look after their dogs.

[7]

On the outskirts of Broken Hill I was shown a hillock which is the site of the only battle fought on Australian soil in World War I. Unlikely as it seems, this was against the Turks—to be precise, against two Turks, Gool Mahomet and Mulla Abdulla. They were ice-cream sellers, and on New Year's Day in 1915 they hoisted the Turkish flag over their ice-cream cart and fired a volley at a trainload of Broken Hillers on their way to a picnic at Silverton organized by the Manchester Unity Independent Order of Odd Fellows. The volley killed three picnickers and wounded several more. Then the mad Turks retreated to a rocky outcrop and for two hours kept at bay posses of revengeful citizens and armed police, who finally rushed the position and found Mulla Abdulla dead and Gool Mahomet still alive with sixteen wounds. He died in hospital. The picnickers' casualties numbered four dead and seven wounded, of whom five were women.

This episode has become part of Broken Hill legend. As I was first told it, the holiday-makers going to an Odd Fellows' picnic had become the first trainload of volunteers leaving for Gallipoli; the Turks had shot the engine driver and derailed the train; troops had been called out; after a running fight, and many acts of heroism, the train had blown up. Truth was less dramatic but no less strange. What had come over the Turks? No one will ever know. Mulla Abdulla was a camel butcher recently convicted for killing away from licensed premises. He was unable to pay the fine and threatened with the loss of his livelihood.

This episode has been commemorated by Broken Hill's Grandpa Moses. Like the famous American lady, Sam Byrne started to paint when he was over seventy and then painted primitives in clear, bright, primary colours, each one a meticulous record of a place, a time, an event. On the walls of his trim bungalow they hang frame to frame, their colours glowing. There is the town of Broken Hill laid out like a planner's model, every house exact, detailed and correct, down to the colour of the door and magpie pecking in the garden. There are the surface workings of a mine, each truck, each notice board, each winding shaft in place; there is a pastoral scene packed with a solid mass of rabbits, layer after layer of them, thousands of rabbits, and each one depicted individually.

Sam Byrne's patience is infinite, his eye sharp, his humour lively. "Everything has to be exactly right," said his wife. He is an ex-miner, eighty-two years old. The other day he cycled thirty miles to paint a scene he fancied, slept the night in a barn, and cycled home next morning with the canvas strapped to his carrier; then he gave it to a friend. He does not paint for money. Australians are intrigued by having a genuine primitive among them and now there are others, notably Henri Bastin; he also was a miner, on the South Australian opal fields.

Broken Hill harbours a nest of artists who emerge from their underground stopes and tunnels, discard their boots and tin hats, and hurry home to their easels standing amid the children's toys, and to their canvases propped against washing machines. And there, with furious energy, they paint and paint.

Why should Broken Hill, of all places, have so many artists, and artists of such merit that three have had one-man shows in Adelaide or Melbourne? "Our isolation has a lot to do with it," one suggested. "Even today Broken Hill is a world on its own, so we don't get swamped by fashion. We can paint what we see and not what other people see, which today means copying the international style."

May Harding is another reason: a part-time art teacher attached to an embryonic municipal museum she is also a competent painter, an enthusiastic botanist, a befriender of anyone who needs befriending, and a human catalyst. It is she who has stimulated these Broken Hill miner-artists, given them confidence, and persuaded them that painting is an occupation fit for men and not a diversion for queers. She has managed to make it at once respectable and exciting.

The best-known of the Broken Hill painters is probably Pro Harte, whom we found at work on several canvases at once, each propped against the back of a chair in a garden hut. As he worked away, moving from one painting to another, he talked away with equal energy; the "Pro," he said, is short for Professor, the name given him by his mates. He was working on a series—Australian painters are much given to series—inspired by one of the ballads of Banjo Paterson, before going on night shift to drive an underground locomotive. On the lawn he had trained a telescope on the moon, and in a corner of his shed lay a number of peculiar objects.

"Machine guns," he explained. "I make them. If I didn't paint, I should make things. I made some pictures with those guns—fired them at a sheet of plywood." A tubby, broad-shouldered, blunt-featured, voluble and very friendly man, you could scarcely find a greater contrast to the popular image of a painter. His pictures have a gay, dashing and imaginative quality, the touch of a poet, and they sell.

We visited so many other painters that it seemed as if, when night falls, half the citizens of Broken Hill must reach for their palettes. Les Willis conducted us and displayed a few of his own paintings—not many, because, like Pro Harte and others, he sells them almost before the paint is dry. A dealer from Sydney had just been round the bedrooms, sheds and garages that serve as studios. Les Willis is another who, like Pro Harte with his machine guns, likes to handle machinery when he is not painting. He was an amateur racing driver until he crashed badly in his homemade midget. "So I took up this instead. I really enjoy it."

Then there was Fred Pratt, a battered veteran of World War I who inhabits a small bed-sitter, with paints and brushes as almost his only possessions. In his youth he drove his horse-drawn van from one small country town to another, painting anyone who agreed to be painted for the price of a dinner. He enticed his horse up hills, he told us, by walking backwards in front of it proffering a biscuit; when it halted, he ran round to the back of the van and kicked a stone under the wheel. No one buys his works now, but he goes on painting, with love and care, the scenes of his youth.

It was long after midnight when we returned to May Harding's kitchen, full of cats and tinkling wind vanes, for coffee. Her sitting room was stacked with books and half-completed botanical drawings, her bedroom with half-finished landscapes and portraits in oil. She has little leisure for her own painting. Here, at least, is one Broken Hill woman who is never bored.

By the time we reached our beds, the night-shift artists were deep underground, transformed back into miners like coachmen into mice. I did not meet any who wanted to stop being miners, or whatever job they were being paid to do, and leave Broken Hill for the artist's life in New York or Paris, or even in Melbourne or Sydney. Even painters in Australia—at any rate these painters—seem content; they are not wracked by doubts, mangled by *angst,* or enslaved by trends. They are remarkably sober; our art crawl was refreshed by tea or coffee only, from beginning to end. Painters like Francis Bacon might be living in another universe. In Broken Hill there is competence but no experiment. There is also enjoyment, respect for the image, and a love for what the eye sees.

Kangaroos

Around Tero Creek, nearly two hundred miles north of Broken Hill, last year's rainfall totalled four inches; the year before that, five. Drought continues, heat rages. Seen from the air, these interminable plains are like the hard, red, gritty floor of a clay bake oven. Here and there a square brown eye winks opaquely up at the aircraft—a blob of water hoarded in a clay-walled tank.

This landscape could have been created by an abstract artist; it is all patterns and scrawls. You look down at a skeleton and see no flesh on these elemental bones. Dry gulleys scoured out by storms lie in bold swirls like hair tossed about in long strands. The colouring is subtle and reserved; a fleshlike pink and the pale, blotched green of ripening cheese, pinpricked all over with scrub. You see no sign of life, only now and then a clump of buildings beyond measure isolated and vulnerable, and without trees—a tiny scab on the bare flank of the world. One roof had been painted sky-blue. One homestead had no roof, but all around it lay a litter of planks and sheets of corrugated iron blown off by a cyclone.

We landed on a waste of pebbles. To a fence post was nailed a box into which the pilot stuffed a few letters and a bundle of groceries. This little Cessna that lands here once a week is one life line; you order groceries by radio, and down they come on Saturdays. There is a road of sorts, but it is rough, dusty, tedious and unpredictable, and when rain *does* fall, every creek becomes a torrent several hundred yards wide. The other life line is the Flying Doctor service, providing a radio network on which people chat to each other twice a day.

All the news is handed round—rain, if there should be any, has priority, but mostly it concerns what the children are up to, the health of sheep, the progress of shearing if that is in season, even the cat's accouchement or the outcome of the bake. Nothing is too trivial or too

107

great. On these isolated stations people live publicly and keep little concealed. Is reticence a defensive mechanism of the overcrowded? Here the need is to escape from it, to share. The Flying Doctor service has saved many lives and it has also saved people's sanity, especially women's. It has brought to these isolated folk a feeling of community.

Now, like so many other things, the service has become a tourist attraction. In Broken Hill you are courteously conducted to a seat in an air-conditioned little hall where you watch the doctor, on the dot of the appointed time, start to receive his calls, unflurried by frequent plops from flashlight bulbs let off by visitors. Call signals come in thick and fast; a harsh, cackling voice emerges from nowhere.

Good afternoon, Mrs. Brown.

Good afternoon, Doctor. The baby—he's getting nine drops daily. Is that right or should he have them twice daily? Over.

He should have eighteen drops daily. That is nine twice daily. Over.

Thank you, Doctor. Cheerio.

Cheerio for now.

321 Pinendee. 321 Pinendee. Hello, Doctor.

Good afternoon, Mrs. Ford.

She's still troubled. Wednesday there was at least two inches protruding from the bowel.

Probably threadworm—they're about two inches long—but a close watch should be kept on the stool for roundworm. Carry on with the medicine. It should clear things up in a few days.

Thank you, Doctor. Cheerio.

Cheerio for now.

Then a bee sting on the foot, a medicine disagreeing with a child, an injured back. Finally a conundrum. A woman's voice:

PMQ at Tero Creek. There's a filly four years old, fifteen hands, reared over and hit her head. She was out for ten minutes and now she's gone blind. She's staggery and doesn't get any better.

Can she eat or drink?

I don't know.

A pause. Another station comes in about pills.

No, Doctor, the horse hasn't eaten or drunk.

Sounds as though she's got a fractured skull in which case the outlook isn't very hopeful. There's a chance it might be severe concussion. The treatment's epsom salts to reduce the fluid in the body.

All right, Doctor, what's the dose?

A pause. I'm working out what a fifteen-hand horse weighs.

A hand is four and a half inches, Doctor.

Pause.

Four tablespoons of epsom salts now and more tomorrow morning.

Thanks, Doctor. Four tablespoons of epsom salts in water. Cheerio for now.

Cheerio for now.

All doctors nowadays are glamorized, and Flying Doctors most of all. The service is efficient but the load heavy. This doctor's farthest patient lives more than 500 miles away. The area covered from this single base—one of fourteen—is seven times as large as the entire British Isles, and there are two doctors to patrol it, with over five thousand patients. One of the pair is always on call, and both fly every day of duty. This base has three pilots and two air ambulances. There are plenty of trained pilots about, but doctors have become hard to recruit. The outback no longer appeals as it did; year by year the pull of the cities grows, and one or two Flying Doctor bases have already closed. Yet the purpose they serve is not obsolete.

[2]

At Tero Creek the Wildlife Division of the C.S.I.R.O. has a field station consisting of an aluminum hut dumped on a gritty plain with little shade and no water, where two young men are trapping, marking and observing kangaroos in order to discover how these creatures—the macropods, or large-feet—live, eat, breed, travel and generally conduct their affairs. This is part of a project which Dr. Harry Frith, the divisional chief, told me in Canberra was one of the most thorough scientific studies of a single mammal ever to be undertaken.

It is astonishing how little has been found out, scientifically, until very recently, about the tribe of kangaroos and wallabies in the two centuries since Captain Cook wrote of a strange creature he observed in some abundance: "I should have taken it for a wild dog, but for its walking or running in which it jumped like a hare or deer." Zoologists have since argued lengthily, and still do, about the identity of this animal. Captain Cook's party collected two skulls, one of which probably belonged to a grey kangaroo, *Macropus giganteus,* and the other either to a whip-

tailed wallaby, *Wallabia elegans,* or to a wallaroo, *Macropus robustus.**
Since then kangaroos and wallabies have been shot in millions; they
have become the emblem of Australia, yet many basic facts are still not
fully known: the life span of each species, for instance; precisely what
they eat, how far they travel, how their reproduction is regulated, and so
on. Even now not much really *is* known except that they hop, eat grass
and rear their young in pouches.

The future of the kangaroo tribe has become a matter of urgent and
sometimes acrimonious controversy. Is the animal good—from a human
angle, naturally—or is it bad? A harmless, beautiful and unique creature, quintessentially Australian, to be protected and cherished? Or a
pest comparable with rabbits and dingoes that eats food needed by
sheep and so must be destroyed? A tourist attraction or a 'roo-shooter's
prey? Are preservationists long-sighted or merely sentimental? Anyway,
is the kangaroo being exterminated or is it actually on the increase?

The first thing to be clear about is that "the kangaroo" as a single
kind of animal is a myth. There are between forty-five and fifty separate
species of kangaroo and wallaby, ranging from miniature rat kangaroos
less than a foot long (without the tail) to big species which are what
most people mean by kangaroos, notably the red (*Megaleia rufa*) and
the grey or forester (*Macropus giganteus*); males of both these species
can stand taller than a man and weigh up to two hundred pounds,
although the average weight of the male red is in the region of eighty
pounds. (It is only the males of this species, incidentally, that have
reddish fur; the females are grey, and the female young are called "blue
fliers.") The family includes walleroos, whose pelts are rather more
hairy than those of reds or greys, and which are also known as hill
kangaroos, or as euros. The geographical range of this species is remarkable: a huge crescent embracing most of the continent, and here
and there penetrating some way inland where the chosen habitat, that of
rocky hills, will permit. The grey or forester sticks, as its name suggests,
to timbered country and also has a very wide range. Most experts believe that walleroos and greys are in no immediate danger of a serious
reduction in numbers. (One should remember the words *immediate* and
serious.) It is the red that hops about the dry, open, inland plains, the

---

* T. H. Kirkpatrick, *A Note on the Dental Eruption of some Macropodinae,*
Queensland Department of Primary Industries Bulletin No. 262, 1963.

common kangaroo of New South Wales, around which controversy mainly centers. The red kangaroo *is* in danger, possibly in grave danger since the drought of 1959–66 devastated its main habitat in the western part of New South Wales.

[3]

Both red and grey kangaroos are being mercilessly hunted for their meat and skins. The meat is either exported for human consumption to Hong Kong, Singapore, Japan and other Asian countries or used for pet food. The skins are made into boots, belts, wallets, handbags and other useful articles such as tourist souvenirs in the shape of toy koalas, hot-water-bottle jackets and bottle openers contrived from paws.

How many kangaroos are being annually destroyed? The meat and skin "industry" is a state and not a commonwealth affair, so even when figures are compiled, there is no uniformity. Expert opinion is clouded. Probably the man qualified to make the best guess is Dr. Frith, and he has put the annual "take" of all species at, roughly, two million. Professor Marshall of Monash University has put his guess as high as ten million, which most people think much too high.

In Queensland, whose laws allow an open season all the year round on greys and reds and on six species of wallaby, a total of 1,305,111 macropod skins, most of them greys, passed through the hands of licensed dealers in 1964. This took no account of wounded beasts that died in the bush, of young in the pouch that perished with their mothers, or of those killed by "sportsmen." (The quotation marks really do seem necessary; I do not know how sport is best defined, but to pump lead into an inoffensive, defenseless and semi-tame animal, generally bemused by spotlights in the dark, can scarcely be included in any interpretation of the word.)

The "take" in New South Wales cannot fall far short of that in Queensland and is mainly of the red kangaroo. Until 1965 the State's Fauna Protection Panel, headed by Mr. Allen Strom, had no power to register professional shooters or chillers or to collect statistics of any kind; it is therefore impossible to show statistically whether numbers are going up or down. But lack of statistics does not wholly invalidate common sense.

Dr. Harry Frith has very roughly estimated the state's total population of 'roos to be two million. In less than a year after the state's powers to register professional shooters and record their "crops" came into force, over 800,000 carcasses passed through the chillers. Deaths from other causes—from station owners destroying 'roos as pests, from accidents, and from the death of young deprived of their mothers—must bring the annual "take" to at least a million, and that is half the total population or more. No species could stand up for long to a "cropping" of this order, and drought has given the animals a devastating knock. Scientists have put the infant mortality in some districts at 98 per cent.

In New South Wales, red kangaroos are officially "protected animals," as are all marsupials, and licenses have to be obtained to shoot them. Applications for licenses are scrutinized by the Chief Guardian of Fauna as carefully as his limited staff and intelligence service allow, but in the western division of the state, the red 'roo's stronghold, licenses have been issued virtually for the asking. This is the region in which graziers, beset by drought, have clamoured most loudly against the 'roo and in which officers of the Fauna Protection Panel, who are dedicated men with all too little public support, believe that numbers have declined in the last few years by two-thirds. They are still declining.

Yet it is possible to argue—and so eminent an authority as Dr. Frith has argued—that the total numbers of red kangaroos have increased over the last century. They have built up in the wake of sheep. Graziers who have constructed tanks and sunk bores by the thousand have provided water for 'roos as well as for sheep, and the sheep themselves have influenced their environment in the direction of replacing saltbush by grass, which has been to the red roo's liking. But the crux of the matter is not whether this species or that will survive the destructiveness of man, but whether it will be squeezed out of existence by changes in the habitat resulting from man's economic activities. "An animal," Dr. Frith has pointed out, "must be left with a place in which to live if it is to survive," and "kangaroos cannot be expected to survive on hundred-acre dairy farms from which all native vegetation has been removed and replaced by Mediterranean grasses and clovers." And so "they persist only in areas considered useless for agriculture."*

[4]

The process of bringing into economic use areas previously considered useless for agriculture and for grazing has lately been enormously ac-

* G. B. Sharman & H. J. Frith, "The Kangaroo Situation," *Animals*, Vol. 4, No. 19, September, 1964.

celerated. It is bound to continue at an ever faster rate as population pressure mounts and as techniques are widened and perfected. Every year more bush and forest will be cleared, paddocks will be subdivided, native vegetation changed. The wilderness is going. So in the long run, and except in nature reserves and some state forests, and perhaps on the properties of a few wildlife lovers, most of the kangaroos must go, too, unless they should be bred in commercial herds for meat, as in parts of Africa buffaloes and some of the larger antelopes are being bred. "The animals that are being lost every day," the Chief Guardian of Fauna in New South Wales has written, "because scrublands are burnt, forests cleared or swamps drained, far outnumber the effects of shooting."

The nature reserves hitherto established in Australia are not big enough or numerous enough to safeguard the future of the red kangaroo. Most of the larger macropods have already been eliminated from the relatively well-watered and fertile coastal regions where they once abounded and retreated to the wide belt of dry scrub, saltbush, mallee and mulga that lies between the Dividing Range and the central desert. This is the region where they are now being so relentlessly pursued with spotlight and rifle, and should they be eliminated there as well, they would have lost their last stronghold. Apart from the state forests, which are also fauna sanctuaries, there is no significant residue of publicly owned land fit to support stable populations of the larger macropods, allowing for periodic droughts. There is plenty of desert left, but kangaroos cannot survive without food and water any more than sheep can, even though they make fewer demands than sheep do upon their habitat.

So by and large, and with some exceptions, it looks as if the larger macropods must survive on land in private ownership, if they are to survive at all. This they can do only with the goodwill of the landowners. You cannot, in the long run, force people to keep pets that compete for food with their domestic livestock. That some graziers *do* keep pets—such as Mr. Watson of Wollongorang, and there are many others—is more remarkable than that the majority hunt them down with spotlight, rifle and poison. Optimistic conservationists believe that opinion not only in the cities, where it is easy to think kindly of kangaroos, but among the graziers who have to feed them, is slowly but surely moving in the right direction, but a gloomier expert in New South Wales said, "I personally believe that the death of the last kangaroo will be an occasion for joyful celebration by the great majority of landholders."

One kangaroo, I was told by several graziers, eats as much grass as five sheep. This is the popular belief, and it is quite wrong. Research has lately shown that one red 'roo eats just about the same quantity of grass as one merino and that a grey 'roo eats considerably less. (A grey weighing seventy pounds will eat about 4½ pounds dry weight of vegetable matter daily, against 9¾ pounds needed by a sheep that weighs a hundred pounds.) Another belief widely held among graziers is that 'roos migrate over long distances. As soon as you get a storm of rain, they say, and a flush of young growth in the paddocks, 'roos will converge upon it from many miles around and rob the sheep.

To find the facts about kangaroo movements forms one of the projects which two young biologists at Tero Creek, Peter Bailey and Peter Marteniz, are pursuing. Their inquiry is incomplete, but so far no single marked animal—these are reds—has been "recovered," either as a corpse or by observation, more than twenty miles from its marking place, and the great majority had travelled no more than four or five miles.

[5]

About twice a week the two young men go out trapping. This takes place at night and is centered on one of the tanks, or reservoirs. These are strongly fenced and equipped with a gate through which sheep and 'roos alike come to drink.

We went out at sundown to shut the gates. The sole access to the water then became a narrow wire-mesh funnel at one corner; at another corner the researchers pegged some soft netting to make a little paddock into which the 'roos were to be driven before the actual capture, without risk of injuring themselves. After a blistering day—about 106° F.—it was a wonderfully still evening. The horizon was hard and straight, a line not pencilled but scored against a crimson sky. The sun went down whole like an orange, and there was not a trace of cloud. This is red country: red sand, barred with long shadows of spindly mulga trees and solitary bushes; red sky; a red light, no half tones. Red, hard as granite, ancient and indifferent—not cruel, because not caring. You could not go into partnership with this land. You live on it, not with it. Or so I felt, an alien; Australians who have learned to love it may also have learned to master its indifference. A man who understood it wrote: "This delicate country responds like a piano to whatever touches it."* He also wrote: "Australian disasters are when nothing happens—it simply doesn't rain."

* C. E. W. Bean, *On the Wool Track,* Scribners, New York, 1947.

After tea off chops and pumpkins in the aluminum hut, a great deal of gear was stowed into the Land Rover: weighing scales, sacks, collars, staples, torches, drugs and other things. Nightfall brought a pause until nocturnal creatures were astir. There was a clear half-moon. Our headlights picked out one or two small mobs of kangaroos hopping about among black clumps of dwarf shrubs. These reds tend to live in small family groups, with a joey or two bouncing along beside their mothers.

Only two were in the tank enclosure. Armed with torches and shod in heavy boots, the two biologists tried to drive the two 'roos through the narrow funnel and into the trap. The 'roos refused to be driven. Round and round the big tank they hopped at an astonishing speed: thump, thump, thump with flat feet and thick tail on the loose sand. Round and round after them pounded the two Peters, running like quarter milers and panting like dogs. The 'roos were bashing themselves against the wire in their frenzy. This went on for about half an hour until one of them was cornered with a flying tackle and swiftly netted. It lay in the torch light gasping for breath, with panic-stricken eyes. The biologists were lathered with sweat: a far cry from the popular image of the white-coated boffin peering through thick-lensed spectacles down a microscope. Wildlife researchers must combine a football player's physical fitness, a swagman's indifference to home comforts, the resourcefulness of a born mechanic, and a scholar's mind.

Physical strength was needed even to inject the 'roo with nembutal, so thick was his hide. He passed out, and the second animal was then pursued. He was even wilder and kept hurling his whole weight against the wire. A hunted female will throw out her joey and refuse to take it back. Both of these were males. The second was bleeding from a battered nose when finally they got him, pumped in the drug, and carried both inert forms to the Land Rover to be weighed and measured all over, even down to the teeth. The heavier of this pair weighed 150 pounds. Then a wide yellow plastic collar was stapled round each 'roo's neck. These would be there for life. You would think their fellow 'roos might take alarm at so queer and startling a deformity, but apparently they do not notice anything unusual, or perhaps are too polite to call attention to the matter; collared 'roos are not shunned. Finally the animals received another shot to bring them round. They revived in bursts, rolling over and over, kicking at the ground and looking very miserable, but before the pursuers had finished off a long, cooling drink, both animals had hopped away into the dark.

Human curiosity takes a heavy toll of kangaroos, even if not so heavy as that exacted by human greed. Once a month Peter Bailey shoots about twenty in order that their glands may be dispatched to a physiochemist in the United States who has worked out a technique, said to be superior to any other, for measuring the hormone content. Hormones regulate reproduction, and the reproductive system of kangaroos is complex and remarkable.

[6]

All marsupials expel their young from the womb as very small embryos and rear them in an external pouch instead of wrapped in a placenta, or membrane, safely inside. This is a primitive form of reproduction; later in the evolutionary story animals developed the placenta, which proved a rather more efficient device, so the pouched species declined— not completely, for there are still marsupials in Latin America, and in North America the possum thrives. By this time, between fifty and sixty million years ago, the land bridge formerly linking Australia to the Asiatic mainland had been submerged, and placental mammals could not make their way there. So in Australia marsupials not merely survived but branched out into many shapes and sizes. Some took to the trees, like the phalangers; some burrowed underground, like the wombats; some hopped about the plains like kangaroos. And each of these specialized forms developed in Australia by the marsupials corresponds, sometimes with a striking similarity, to a form developed elsewhere by the placentals.

Thus marsupial mice look just like placental mice and have similar functions and habits; the same with moles; the wombat is very like a badger; some of the gliders—the phalangers—with their folding membranes resemble squirrels; native cats match the wildcat of Europe and Asia; the koala was called a bear because it looks just like one, in miniature; the Tasmanian "tiger" is—apart from its stripes—the image of the wolf, and so on. Only the kangaroo tribe seems to lack a placental opposite number; elsewhere no big mammals hop. But ecologically they take the place of ungulates—deer, sheep, cattle and goats. Australia had no ungulates until man introduced them.

Once the placentals were introduced, most of them proceeded to push out the marsupials, telescoping into a century or so an evolutionary process that elsewhere had extended over millions of years. The pushing out seems to operate partly by superior powers of foraging. Rabbits, for instance, proved better foragers than rat kangaroos, foxes better than native cats, dingoes better than the native carnivores such as the marsupial "wolf" and the Tasmanian "devil," and so on. And so, of course with active human aid, the placental is ousting the marsupial.

After a gestation period averaging only thirty-three days, the infant kangaroo is launched into the world as a soft, blind, naked, utterly helpless creature, less than one inch long and weighing between 750 and 900 milligrams—roughly one-thirtieth of an ounce, or the equal in weight of half a dozen small safety matches. The only parts to be at all developed are the forelegs and clawed hands with which the embryo clings to its mother's fur and drags itself through a thick, rough forest of hairs from the mouth of the vagina into the pouch. This it must accomplish within four minutes, or it is unlikely to survive. Formerly the mother was believed to help by licking a path ahead of it through her own fur, but when at last the birth of a red kangaroo was witnessed by scientists, this was found to be another myth. The embryo must struggle unaided to the pouch and there attach itself to one of the teats; once in position, it does not leave until at least 190 days have elapsed, and then only for short periods. Gradually these periods lengthen, until the joey leaves for good some 235 days after birth, to hop along beside his mother and continue to suckle for another ten months or so. No wonder that, even under reasonably good conditions, half the joeys die before they reach maturity and four out of every five in times of drought, when the mother's milk dries up and they die of starvation.

Hard times bring into play a wonderful mechanism for limiting the population. Normally a doe comes into season within twenty-four hours —sometimes an hour or so—of giving birth. She is immediately mated. Then an odd thing happens—or rather, as was remarked of Australian disasters, does not happen: the fertile egg stays quiescent, and the usual process of growth into an embryo is suspended. This is known as "delayed implantation," and it is brought to an end about a month before the joey leaves the pouch for good by the falling off of the mother's milk supply. Not, be it noted, by the weaning of the joey, who goes on suckling on a reduced scale *after* it has left its comfortable quarters, but at the stage when that accommodation falls vacant by reason of joey number one's departure.

Then joey number two, at that stage an embryo biding its time in the womb, resumes its growth; and so exact is the timing that normally it is born within *one day* of the permanent vacating of the pouch by joey number one, then about eight months old. The mother will then have a baby in the pouch and a self-propelled, partially weaned offspring hopping along beside her. If she is shot, both joeys will die too.

In times of drought the doe fails to come into season immediately after giving birth; not until she has weaned her joey will oestrus occur and the doe be mated. So instead of producing one joey every eight or nine months, the next birth will be delayed until, with any luck, rain will have fallen, and the young will get a better chance to survive. This "delayed oestrus" is an extraordinary example of a specialized mechanism evolved to enable a species to meet the challenge of its environment. The controlling factor seems to be effects resulting from starvation on the pituitary gland. The red kangaroo has it, and several kinds of wallaby, but not, strangely enough, the grey. Combined with a heavy loss of joeys during lean times, it enables kangaroos to survive droughts without damaging their delicate environment. This is more than can be said for sheep, controlled not by nature but by man, and as a rule left in large numbers on drought-stricken pastures in the hope that rain will fall in time to save them. If it does not, they die in thousands, but not before they have eaten every bit of vegetation down to the roots and then with their sharp, hard hoofs harmed the grass roots and trampled what little soil there was into dust. Then winds blow away the dust, leaving bare stretches of rock and hard clay pans that never can recover, however much rain may fall.

[7]

Driving over the bare, drought-inflicted sheep runs, with names like Gumpoplar and Bootera, we saw scarcely any kangaroos; but as they are nocturnal animals, this was to be expected. Researchers do their field work in the dark. They are out four nights a week, searching with a powerful spotlight for yellow plastic collars. In fifteen months Peter Bailey "recovered" 160 marked kangaroos, about forty of them dead ones whose collars were returned. This is a high mortality—one in four—in so short a time, especially as by no means all the collars from deceased 'roos are likely to have been recovered. The researchers intend soon to fix to each of their trapped macropods a transistor radio, no larger than a sixpence, that will emit continuous signals to show not only where the animal is, but what it is doing—resting, feeding, travelling, or sleeping. For animals there will be no more private lives.

If macropods are reticent here, birds are resplendent to the point of being gaudy. A flock of green budgerigars darts in and out of a mulga's graceful branches like a shower of emerald spray; a flight of slim, long-tailed grass parrots swoops by; the splendid crested bronze-wing pigeon struts in the sand; numerous apostle birds, members of the crow family who share territories and even nests, chatter noisily. They build their nests of mud, in trees; when there is no water, there can be no mud, so they cannot build—another neat and simple mechanism to adjust a population to the habitat's capacity to sustain it. This enormous plain seems to go on forever and does go on to blend into the great central desert. So flat is it that a rocky ridge a few hundred feet above the general elevation rises like a spine of mountain, and from its crest you can see the rim of the horizon all around you, as from a ship at sea.

The "range" we made for, the Vancannia, was littered with loose quartzite rocks, some of them liver-red, and speckled with withered saltbushes from which a flock of pink sheep—pink with dust—seemed able to pick a living. A wedge-tailed eagle tore at a carcass under a rock. Superb birds, these "wedgies," with a wing span of six to seven feet, and with wicked talons, garnet eyes and the proud gait of all eagles. This bird had a pheasant-gold head, neck and shoulders that betrayed his imma-turity: "wedgies" darken with age and look almost black when they are six or seven. Sheepmen accuse them of destroying lambs and regard them as vermin; the Western Australian Government pays a bounty on their beaks. Birdmen say that, as a general rule, they devour only weak-lings or lambs already dead. The carcass we passed was of a euro that had probably been shot.

All day we saw one living macropod, another euro sheltering in a creek under a coolibah tree. It had a sharp, pointed little face and looked at us appealingly. To have shot it would have been child's play, but we shared peaceably the peace of a creek lined with gums and acacias that threw a dark tracery of shadow over the red sand. Such gentle shade is like a bandage over aching eyes. After the glitter of quartz, the dryness and stark sunlight, the pitiless and gritty tones and heat, there is a sudden transformation, a kindliness. Birds pipe and chatter among drooping leaves. The euro sat under his tree and we under ours, not wishing to molest each other.

Our creek was dry. Australian watercourses, unlike those elsewhere, instead of uniting to converge into a single river, spread out like the fingers of a hand to dissipate themselves in rocks and sand. If you follow a creek, it is more likely to lead you farther into the wilderness than to a river. This must have confused the explorers. You think of them with awe. How could they have summoned strength and faith to keep on day after day, week after week, through the heat and bareness and the sheer emptiness? They needed a myth to pursue. African explorers had fabulous kingdoms like Prester John's; for Australians, there was that great inland sea. But there turned out to be nothing, just vanishing creeks where even the shade of coolibahs and river gums became an agonizing memory.

We paid a call on the owners of the creek and the pink sheep. They lived in a grove of oranges and lemons, apples and pears, and of oleander shrubs and roses and flowers, sustained by irrigation. All around their small oasis lay the drought-gripped desert. Their reservoirs were shrinking, even the tawny mulgas withering; half their sheep had already been moved away. Now the grazier's problem is to find somewhere to move them to. Throughout western New South Wales thousands of sheep are dying of starvation; before the drought broke, four million were to perish in this terrible fashion and another three million to go as walking skeletons to abattoirs. If the explorers needed faith and courage, so in equal measure do the men and women who have settled where they camped and must live with conditions that destroyed Burke and Wills and Leichhardt and many others. They must watch their pastures shrivel, their waters dwindle, their sheep die; they must endure cyclones that unroof their houses, rasping winds that stifle them in dust, flies and monotony and extremes of heat, and there is nothing they can do but stick it out.

> The rock says "Endure".
> The wind says "Pursue".
> The sun says "I will suck your bones
> And afterwards bury you."

No one could survive here without the virtues of patience and endurance. These breed a wry fatalism that is the hallmark of the outback Australian.

The mistress of this house tumbled out of a cigarette tin onto the kitchen table a heap of gem stones—uncut emeralds, agates, beryl, rose crystal, other delicately coloured stones. She had picked them up on a property they had owned in Western Australia. There had been minerals everywhere, she said. Every time you rode across one of the ten-thousand-acre paddocks the glint of a gem might catch your eye; under the spinifex might lie deposits of ironstone worth millions of dollars. Here is the other side of the Australian coin. Drought may kill your livestock, cyclones destroy your home, and you may go out next morning to discover the richest gold mine in the world. Next year there will be a bonanza wool clip; somewhere, still, there awaits that great inland sea.

[8]

As we bumped across the plain with its hopbush and mulga scrub, we passed many piles of bones picked clean by scavengers and bleached by sun. " 'Roo shooters," Peter Bailey said. Their camp was a dilapidated homemade caravan and a tent ringed by empty beer cans. From the caravan emerged a nut-brown, hairy-chested, curly-headed giant with a week's growth of stubble, the tattooed torso of a fairground weight lifter, and a friendly smile. This was Jim, formerly a rabbit trapper, now a shooter or 'roos.

Six nights a week, he told us, he is out in his battered truck with its mounted spotlight, which he manipulates with one hand while he steers with the other. The beam mesmerizes the animal, which he topples over with his high-velocity .22 rifle. Sometimes he employs the hip shot to avoid damaging the skin; he then dispatches the disabled creature, eviscerates it and cuts off feet and fore parts. When the night's work is done, he returns to collect the "butts," or hind parts, which he transports to his mobile chiller. To make a living he needs a "take" of forty 'roos a night—thirty is the bare minimum, seventy to eighty a good bag. When he and his mate have accumulated a chiller-full, they radio for a truck to collect the "take," which is conveyed to Broken Hill, processed, and sent to Adelaide. These processing firms provide the mobile chillers and pay shooters like Jim an average of about three cents a pound. In New South Wales alone there are over sixty of such chilling plants, each supporting a dozen or so teams of professional shooters.

I visited a couple of the chilling plants in Broken Hill. One of the two operates eleven mobile chillers, whose positions are charted on a map; they keep in touch by radio with each team. Their best shooter reckons to get three thousand pounds of meat most nights, which works out at around one hundred animals. (About seventy red 'roos go to a ton of processed meat.) This firm also deals in rabbits, and one of its teams sends in twelve thousand pairs a week. The second plant I saw was a smaller, one-man business. The owner, aided by three employees, was busy boning the butts, chopping them up, and packing the meat into large plastic bags; these were to be deep-frozen and dispatched to Adelaide to be minced and marketed as pet food. This operator has eight chillers in the bush at present and processes between one thousand and fifteen hundred 'roos a week; the best of the meat goes for human consumption, packed into sixty-pound cartons ready to be exported. The conditions under which the carcasses are shot and handled in the bush would scarcely satisfy a meat inspector, and those who dislike the whole business often draw attention to the danger of an outbreak of infection such as that caused by the bacillus salmonella. Japan now takes the bulk of the exported meat. Over eleven million pounds of 'roo flesh were sent overseas last year.

Once a shooter's nightly "take" drops below the thirty mark or thereabouts, he moves on. So he always leaves a residue and as 'roos are fast breeders, it is claimed by non-alarmists that the population will soon build up again and that the danger of extermination has been much exaggerated.

This leaves out of account natural disasters such as drought. If the population falls below what biologists call the critical level, a "population crash" may occur. Over a century ago the naturalist John Gould wrote: "In the stockmen and keepers aided by their fleet, powerful and well-trained dogs, the red kangaroo finds an enemy which at once drives it from all newly occupied districts and will lead to its entire extirpation unless some law be enacted for the protection of this noble animal." Except in Victoria and Tasmania, no such law has been enacted. "We do not know yet what *is* the critical level of any Australian species," Professor Marshall has written. We do know what happens when it is passed. The last pair of rabbit bandicoots, or bilbies, in New South Wales, once so common as to be a popular pet, was shot in 1919. The Toolache wallaby, whose pelts were marketed in Melbourne by the thousand, is now extinct. The world has said good-by to the freckled marsupial mouse. Probably there are no more night parrots; the magnificent Australian bustard or plains turkey has vanished from Victoria, creature after creature has retreated to a fragment of its former habitat. It is surprising how quickly a species can dwindle once its numbers fall below the critical level. In 1871 a single nesting area of the passenger pigeon, in Wisconsin, was estimated to contain 136 *million* breeding birds. The last of these pigeons died in a Cincinnati zoo in 1914. It would be tedious to add more examples.

What about kangaroos? Can they really support so heavy an annual "cropping" when bad times come? Is the critical level being approached? Or even reached?

I asked Jim's opinion. He smiled and rubbed a big, horny hand over a furry chest. "Me and my mate'll be moving on next week. About cleaned up here. They know in Broken Hill where there's plenty more. Finish altogether?" He shook his curly head and drawled emphatically, "Never! Get a few storms of rain and you'll find plenty. They follow the rain. No tucker for them here now, but they'll come back with the wet." This was echoed next day by a girl in White Cliffs, a ghost town that once served a cluster of opal mines. She was the daughter of another 'roo shooter and had been reared in a caravan, always on the move. The family had never known a settled mode of life and, so far as she was concerned, never wanted one. They had a truck, plenty of meat, as much clothing as a hot climate calls for and few worries, little discipline—what more could anybody need? "Dad'll always find 'roos," she said. " 'Roos and rabbits."

The scientific view is rather less confident. Recently a flaw has appeared in the comfortable theory that 'roo shooters, by moving on when the "take" falls below a certain level, will always leave a safe breeding residue. Step by step the slaughter of kanagroos is becoming "industrialized"; that is, money-makers in cities are taking over control of operators in the bush like Jim and his mates. Capital investment, forward contracts, companies, dividends—all the apparatus of modern industry has begun to rear its superstructure on a foundation of dead kangaroos.

Already in New South Wales there are half a dozen men with big money invested in the "industry," and this gives it a momentum that is carrying it beyond the stage where "cropping" is controlled by the ease of "harvesting"—that is, where Jim moves on when he cannot any longer slay thirty or forty 'roos a night. Shooters may be kept at work even when their nightly bag falls to next to nothing, in order to hold teams together until richer areas can be found; efficiency will be sharpened by the use of aircraft and better equipment. There is a sinister analogy between this situation and that which arose when big financial interests took over the hunting of whales. Formerly the blue whale frequented the southern seas in countless millions; today this mighty creature, the largest of the mammals, is all but extinct. Once the factory ship, the helicopter and big business displaced the rowboat, the lookout in the crow's-nest and Captain Ahab, the large whales were doomed; and it is possible that a similar fate may lie in store for the larger macropods. But Jim is not worrying; there will always be 'roos.

[9]

Next day I left Tero Creek and flew back to Broken Hill over the abandoned opal mines at White Cliffs. From up aloft they have the appearance of round, white pustules clustering on flesh of pinkish grey. Each pustule is a circular hole, thirty or forty feet deep, dug by hand from limestone rock about seventy years ago. The amount of sheer gut-busting, backbreaking toil in blistering heat summoned from those diggers by the hope of riches beggars the imagination. At one time over three thousand men worked the diggings with pick and shovel—and worked them out.

Our Cessna paused at White Cliffs long enough to allow us to whirl in a dilapidated pickup van, amid a cloud of fine dust, to the diggings, which looked as totally barren as the crater-pitted surface of the moon. A noise like the grinding of a monster's teeth guided us to a large excavator, which was sucking into its mechanical maw a stream of rock from an abandoned mine, crushing it, and regurgitating heaps of rubble. A mahogany-coloured giant bestrode the machinery, and others on their feet greeted us with flashing white smiles. They were Italians: seven brown and burly optimists who had clubbed together to hire the excavator and their luck in the abandoned workings.

How different is their lot from that of their predecessors in the fly-blown, blistering-hot humpies that once clustered at the foot of these rocks! Those dwellings lacked comfort, sanitation, water, almost everything but dust and thirst, sweat and flies; here, in an old mine gallery, these Italians have made themselves an entrancing grotto, dark and cool and pleasant, like a palace of goblins. Glare and heat and dust have been replaced by a solacing twilight. The Italians have colour-washed in soft pastel shades the rough, crumbly walls and roof of the galleries, installed two enormous refrigerators in one cave and the latest in electric cookers in another; in a third, a trestle table covered with a gay check cloth and set with knives and forks, unchipped plates and pottery mugs and flagons of chianti in their straw jackets. There is no litter, no empty beer cans, no detritus of cigarette stubs and ice-cream cartons; everything is clean, swept and tidy. Latins have made a home where most Anglo-Saxons would be content to pitch a camp.

On the way back to Broken Hill the air taxi landed on twenty-six air strips, at each of which someone waited to collect the weekly mail, to welcome a visitor, or just to pass the time of day with the pilot. A few minutes only at each stop, and we took off again into the bumpy heat and watched a puff of ashen dust move away from the air strip as the jeep, pickup, or truck that would have met us sped back to the homestead with mail, groceries and news. The sun was going down redly behind a hard and merciless horizon, and it was time for a chilled beer.

SEVEN ᵐᵐᵐᵐ

The Murray, Fruit and Wine

The mallee country has a ten-inch rainfall in a good year, five inches in a poorish year, and none at all in a bad one. Mallee consists of several kinds of dwarf eucalypt with large, gnarled roots that make excellent firewood and that have been adapted through the ages to sustain life almost without moisture in a hot, fine-grained sand almost devoid of humus. There are millions and millions of acres of mallee with a fauna and a flora of its own. These bent, spindly trees bind and shelter the earth's fragile skin of loose sand. If you remove them, the hot gales that sweep across the plains peel off the skin to leave a stony skeleton. Yet it was to the mallee that soldier settlers were invited after World War I to take up land for mixed farming in blocks of 640 acres—one square mile.

A resolve to limit the acreage any one individual may own or lease is a thread that runs through all Australian land legislation. It has done untold harm. It goes against the grain of land and climate. The only men who knew how to live in balance with this dry country were the aborigines. They did not ration themselves to one square mile or to one hundred. They roamed about over thousands of square miles, and when the wallabies and goannas, the roots and berries and nardoo seeds and frogs grew short in one direction, they followed another, so they did no harm. But in this transplanted society a desire for social justice and equality tugs in one direction, the needs of the land in another; ideology is at war with ecology, and something has to give way. Ideology has pulled the stronger hitherto. Men of action, such as politicians, seldom listen when men of contemplation, such as scientists, tell them things they do not want to hear. So they have carved the mallee into blocks of one square mile and expected families to live on it, and families have been ruined.

Along the Murray, where water has turned wilderness into a garden, governments have put a ten-acre limit. The Murray is the country's greatest river system and the fourth largest in the world, reckoned by navigable length. You could proceed in a modest vessel well over three thousand miles from an unimpressive estuary in the Great Australian Bight towards the source of the Murrumbidgee or the Darling.

Nile, Amazon, Mississippi—and then the Murray, which lacks the myths, the mystery, the fabled greatness of those others. No Isis and Osiris, no Thebes and pyramids and Temples of the Kings; no Moses in a basket of rushes and exiled Israelites; no viperous jungles, buried cities soaked in sacrificial blood, no deathly darts blown by silent-footed Indians—not even any rollicking riverboats, mint-julep-drinking colonels, coal-black mammies, or crumbling levees. No gods and no evil, the stuff of legends; nothing but sluggish water (there are no cataracts) subservient to engineers, sultanas and raisins hygenically packaged, festival queens. A democratic river system ignoring mysteries; a prosaic watercourse baring itself to the skies.

Yet it has had its dramas and terrors; rather it is the storytellers that have been lacking. There have been great floods. People still remember those of 1956 when the swollen river submerged orchards and homesteads, drowned sheep and cattle, and threatened to engulf the riverine towns. Men on tractors converged to work night and day with ferocious energy to raise the levees and succeeded with literally a couple of inches to spare. The still-remembered saga is commemorated not by some great epic drama, or even by a nursery tale of a plucky lad who stuck fingers into a crack, but by a small facsimile of a Ferguson tractor, unobtrusively mounted on plinth in Wentworth, where the Murray and the Darling converge. It was these agile tractors, people said, that saved the day and so deserved the monument, which was unveiled, with suitable publicity, by the managing director of the firm.

[2]

Wentworth has older legends, and ghosts if people were attuned to them. It started as a convict settlement, and the stout brick walls of the jail, built to endure, are now a tourist attraction. After the convicts came the overlanders, droving mobs of cattle from eastern New South Wales to establish settlements. These were harried by the blacks, who speared many of the settlers until subdued by a mounted expedition sent from Adelaide. Then came an age of paddle steamers that towed wool-laden barges to the sea; sheep were brought in by the hundred thousand and began to wreck soil formerly protected by mallee scrub. A woodcutting industry sprang up to supply the paddle steamers; kangaroos were hunted down; fish blasted from the rivers. Civilization had arrived. Wentworth mustered six hotels and Bourke thirty-two. Australian towns assess their importance by the number of their pubs, like the horsepower of a car.

After a five-year drought in the eighties had killed the sheep, rabbits took over. The land's surface, it was said, heaved and rippled like the flanks of a panting animal, packed obscenely with rabbits. They finished the work the sheep had begun. And they did create legends, uniquely Australian in their wry humour: a whole town was said to have been swept away by a tide of rabbits ten miles wide and ten feet deep, leaving a solitary human survivor.

About twenty miles up the Murray from Wentworth was a sheep run called Mildura whose first owners had planted a few vines. When drought and rabbits had turned the run into a wilderness, it was bought by two Canadians whom the Melbourne politician Alfred Deacon had invited to inspect the Murray with a view to irrigation. These brothers, George and W. B. Chaffey, were men of vision who had planned, laid out and successfully launched the first irrigated settlements in California.

The potentialties of the Murray, meandering through an immeasurable waste of scrub, so excited their imaginations that they sold out in California and came impetuously to Melbourne. In 1886 the Victoria Government offered to lease them a quarter of a million acres on condition that they divided the land into blocks for settlers, installed irrigation works, cleared all vermin, built an agricultural college and established an industry to grow, can and dry fruit. This was an excellent bargain for the state, but press and people turned against it and drowned the unfortunate brothers under a torrent of vituperation. Scheming Yankee marauders come to grab hundreds of thousands of acres of good Victorian land. The State Parliament refused to ratify the agreement, and South Australia, always jealous of its richer neighbour, snapped up the bewildered Chaffeys and their visionary yet practical scheme. In 1887 it leased them a quarter of a million acres downstream near the present site of Renmark. The Victorians then recanted, and the brothers got their quarter-million acres round Mildura too. So started one of the great irrigations projects of the world.

The Chaffeys were as hard-working, efficient and tough as the pumps they designed and had specially built in England and which went on pumping for over seventy years. These protean brothers introduced citrus and wines, pruned olives and figs, built houses, laid out blocks and whole towns. They were teetotallers and banned the sale of alcohol. Yet all their energy and vision foundered on lack of markets, dishonest nurseymen who sold the settlers bad stock, salt that rose from the subsoil to kill the vines, and above all on a disastrous financial crash that closed the banks in 1893. The Murray settlers streamed away to seek any kind of work, anywhere; rabbits moved in; the pumps were stopped. Mildura failed to raise $600 needed to restart them. The Murray Irrigation Trust went bankrupt and the brothers lost every penny and the fruit of eight years' toil. George Chaffey had to borrow the cost of his fare back to California. Then he proceeded to irrigate more desert, which became the rich Imperial Valley, full of orchards and thriving families.

W. B. Chaffey stayed on the Murray. "I sold everything to buy bread," he afterwards wrote—even his horse and buggy. One of his sons won a bicycle in a lottery and he borrowed it to get to work. At night, after the day's labour as a hired hand, he replanted with new stock the ninety acres he had managed to keep. "I didn't get straight until 1919 and had the devil's own game." Meanwhile he talked those who had stayed to struggle on into supporting a co-operative to sell their processed fruit. So was born the Australian Dried Fruits Association, today one of the most powerful and efficient co-operative marketing organizations in the world.

The story of W. B. Chaffey ended happily, if ironically. Abandoning temperance, he founded at Merbein a distillery which became one of the largest exporters of spirits in the country. So he prospered, gained a C.M.G., was unanimously elected first mayor of Mildura, and died in 1926, universally honoured. In Mildura's main street stands a handsome statue whose inscription salutes him as "the moving spirit and for many years President of the Dried Fruits Association, which in time of stress saved these settlements from extinction." The added comment, "He laboured for the common good," probably comes closer to the truth than most obituary encomiums.

[3]

Mediterranean soils produced the vine and now Mediterranean people are following it to the heart of Australia. Round Mildura the irrigated land is squared off into rectangular blocks, and many of the blockies, as the owners are called, are Greeks or Italians. Although Latins do not yet predominate, there are more Italian-born than British-born migrants in the district, and now the Greeks are moving in.

Stopping at random by the roadside, I joined a family in tugging from the vines fat bunches of tiny pale-green grapes that would turn into currants. Although no doubt a dawn-to-dusk stint in the broiling sun would pall, few forms of harvesting can be more enjoyable for an hour or so. You eat all you want, and the little grapes are sweet and juicy and fall with a satisfying, gentle plop into a bucket which soon fills. There is something bacchanalian about the scene—a hint of fawns, a whisper of the pipes of Pan and of silenic laughter.

These migrants turned out not to be Greeks or Italians but Central Europeans. For twelve years the husband, a Yugoslav, had worked as a builder's labourer and the wife, an Austrian, in a fruit-packing factory, and both had saved every penny. The wife was fair and thin and handsome in a bony way, her hair scraped back from an intelligent face, her arms brawny. As her fingers deftly stripped the vines she smiled and said, "Always we have wanted land, our own place. This is why we come to Australia. Now I shall have a goat, a pit, some choox, even perhaps a cow. We shall make our own wine. I do not like to live in the town." She looked blissfully happy. Her husband still drew his wages and worked on their block in his spare time, as the forty-hour week allows. The place had been in a run-down condition. "That is why we could but it—the price was low." Salinity had killed many of the vines; efficient drainage is the only cure for this—at a cost of $300 an acre. "We shall do it acre by acre," said the Yugoslav, just as they were building a house brick by brick in the Australian fashion, helped, also in that fashion, by their mates who give time and skill for nothing, so long as it is for a mate and not a boss. Their two healthy, sun-browned daughters spoke, looked, felt and were pure Australians.

"That family will make a go of it," said the blockie I was with. "They live on soupbones. At night they rig up spotlights to get on with the building. They came with nothing, and I reckon they paid sixteen thousand dollars for the place. In a few years, you'll see, they'll be buying up a neighbour. But they'll still drive around in an old bone-rattling pickup and eat bacon rind and goat's milk."

John, the blockie, spoke with a blend of grudging admiration and stifled resentment that I found common among the Australian-born. In part this attitude expresses the resentment felt by all communities of creatures, whether human or animal, against foreigners who encroach upon their territory. It is like the robin's song or the lyrebird's dance, though much less graceful. And in part I think it springs from guilt. In Australian minds the puritan tradition is embedded. People genuflect to the virtues of hard work, frugality and self-denial while engaged in gambling, drinking, or idling on the nearest beach. Here are these New Australians who really *do* work and save, not just think they ought to, and so clamber up the ladder of worldly success.

"We were afraid," said John, "that they would lower our standard of living. They'll accept conditions we won't." John had established for his family enviable standards in a comfortable and well-found home, replete with all the usual appliances, very efficiently run by an attractive wife and frequented by two well-behaved, hard-working, sport-loving, God-fearing sons with clean, short hair and excellent manners. And in this family the puritan tradition was no dummy; no one drank or smoked, and there was grace before meals.

John was honest with his fears as well as in his dealings. "I think we were wrong," he said, "about standards of living. When the migrants find their feet, they improve their own standards. I've an Italian neighbour and he's a good bloke."

He took me to see the neighbour and a smiling wife with a couple of healthy toddlers at foot and a *bambino* in her arms. This migrant had been followed to Australia by four brothers and two sisters, she by her entire family. After ten years as a factory worker, her father became a half-sharer on a nearby block. Half-sharing is a system that enables a man with little capital to get a start. The blockie provides land, vines and equipment, the newcomer the labour; no one pays rent or draws wages, and the two have the profits. In a few years, if all goes well, the half-sharer will have saved enough to make the down payment on a block of his own.

[4]

In all this the blockie will be helped by "the Shed," which acts to many as father and mother, tutor and banker, confessor and friend; it is the local co-operative, linked to the all-powerful Dried Fruits Board, but semi-independent. The basic function of the Shed is to receive, grade, pack and dispatch towards various markets the currants, sultanas and raisins into which sunshine has transformed the grapes, but it also keeps the blockies' accounts, advances their working capital, pays their irrigation dues, sends experts to advise them, provides fuel and sprays and tools, and carries them on credit through bad seasons and ill luck.

Without the Shed's help many of these Italians, Greeks and Central Europeans, whose English is rudimentary and whose grasp of the business side of fruitgrowing generally nil, would fail. Successful blockies invest money in their local co-operatives, and citizens like John sit on their boards without payment. It is these men who contribute the practical advice and experience on which newcomers draw. Loyalty to the Shed is deep and strong. Here the co-operative movement is not just a cog in the economic machinery but also a social ideal and almost a religious belief. This is the way you help your neighbour as well as profiting yourself. In the image of the Good Shepherd, the Shed guides without abusing, shelters without patronage, befriends without self-interest. All this arises from the need to sell sultanas, but in these Murray settlements the sun-shrivelled grape is not merely a crop; it is a way of life as well.

Where else does a whole community own the hotels? For ten cents each citizen acquires, for life, a share and a say in a concern whose profits are returned in the shape of improvements to schools and hospitals, the provision of playing fields and youth clubs, and in other desirable ways. No one may sell his share or give it away. This positively fierce community spirit is especially noticeable in Barmera, which was born of a soldier settlement scheme after World War I.

"The key to Barmera," said the secretary of the Community Center, "is that it's an ex-servicemen's town. It started in the 1920's when the South Australian Government gave out land to ex-soldiers and put in the irrigation works. The comradeship the men had formed in war was carried over into peacetime. Everyone helped each other." Here is mateship in action, a rare example of practical socialism combined with individual ownership of property. In Barmera there is a splendid modern hotel, air-conditioned, up-to-date, which was launched, developed and is now owned by a community smaller than that of most English market towns—3,500 people in the whole district. Everyone has a vote in the appointment of a board of management. Overlooking Lake Bonney stands a new children's clinic, a meetinghouse for the Country Women's

Association, a sports ground and a center for Boy Scouts—all built out of profits which have siphoned nearly half a million dollars into community benefits. There can be few more prosperous little townships, despite the bleak surroundings of the mallee, a shade temperature (when I was there) of 111° F., and a fall in prices which has halved the income of the surrounding blockies.

Tourists now support Barmera. They come to see the grape picking and the wineries—nearby, at Berri, is the largest, they are told, in the Southern Hemisphere—and to shoot duck, to water-ski, fish and swim. Lake Bonney is called after one of the minor but more engaging explorers who came upon it while droving cattle from Melbourne to Adelaide and made friends with the natives by playing the flute. The lake then was "perfectly alive with myriads of live fowl in motion upon its surface, screaming and cackling with alarm at the novel sound"—that sound being, of course, the bang of a gun. The blacks, also numerous, called the region Cobdogla, meaning land of plenty, because of all the fish, the wildfowl, and many kangaroos and a bed of mussels.

The mallee scrub that straggles to the lake's shores proved no land of plenty to the first settlers. These mallee eucalypts have a number of slender grey trunks that spring from each root, and branch out into the shape of an umbrella; their feathery foliage is somber in tone, and they stand amid white chalk-like rubble, wind-polished stones, and bluebush about a foot high. A grey and somber landscape under a hard blue sky; all absolutely flat, absolutely dry. Here and there wind has blown sand right over the fences, so that only the top strand of wire shows through.

Life in the mallee is hard still, though nothing like as hard as it has been within living memory. A man called Jack, not much above sixty, told me of how, as a lad of sixteen, he came here from London under a scheme organized by Sir Henry Newman Barwell, premier of South Australia. Arriving after dark, he was led by his German employer to a lean-to shed full of chaff which was to be his bedding. The sound of a handle being turned brought to his urban mind the picture of a gramophone; he stumbled through the darkness to find Mrs. Schmidt sitting on a mallee stump with a baby in one arm, churning butter with the other, a lantern at her feet. Before dawn next morning he was out chopping mallee, and for dinner he got a boiled turnip and a small hunk of rancid kangaroo meat. With hands raw and bleeding and sun-blistered shoulders, at sunset he knocked off. "What are you doing? Something wrong?" Schmidt inquired when he reached the shack. "We don't finish till dark. But as you're here, fetch the cows, and I'll show you how to milk them." Jack exhibited his raw hands. "The milk will do them good." For the duration of three years' apprenticeship he drew the equivalent of forty cents a week.

Jack showed me his contract with Schmidt. He undertook to live an honest, sober and upright life, not to smoke, and to obey his master; Schmidt undertook to treat him fairly and give him time off every Sunday to attend a place of worship. "That I never got, not in all those three years," Jack recalled. "I never once went into town." When his apprenticeship was up, he went to Adelaide and brought a motorcycle. Later he became a blockie, raised a family, and retired in affluence to a house in which he and his wife had incorporated all the luxuries they so often dreamed about during their struggles. An air-conditioning plant, a Deepfreeze, the kitchen agleam with stainless steel and Formica, a laundry with the very latest in washing machines, and a bedroom in which everything is mauve—candlewick bedspreads, the shade of a bedside light supported by two Dresden courtiers in crinoline and knee breeches, a flowery wallpaper, even a pot of African violets on a kidney-shaped dressing table with mauve muslin frills. After a hard and comfortless life the pot of gold has come to light at the end of the rainbow. Old Schmidt is still alive. "I see him in the street occasionally. We nod but don't speak."

[5]

Nine out of ten of the sales or leases negotiated by a land agent I met in Renmark were to non-British migrants. Most of these were Greeks, and most Greeks grow vegetables. In a shed surrounded by tomato plants two plump toddlers were playing among a pile of melons while their mother was out gathering triambles and trombones, kinds of pumpkin. A slender, classically profiled girl, she had come to Adelaide six years before as a nursing aide and saved the money for the fare of her betrothed. Together they went fruit picking until they had enough put by for the down payment on a sixteen-acre block. Three sisters have followed her to South Australia. A handsome, piratical-looking young man with curly hair, white teeth and a leather-coloured torso, who might have stepped from an Italian painting, appeared like some young god in a halo of dust, driving a lorry. This was the husband, come to take the tomatoes and trombones to a packing shed where women of all ages, from small schoolgirls to stout grannies, were grading and packing, while older children minded babies among a litter of sacks, boxes, baskets and overripe tomatoes.

"Our Australian people wouldn't come at that," said my native-born companion, looking askance at the toddlers parked among the melons. "I wouldn't see my wife on the block. A woman's job is to look after her children and her man. The way these migrants treat their women sticks in my gullet." He told me that one day he was walking across his block with a Greek neighbour when they came upon a fallen fence post, which he offered to the neighbour to burn. The Greek's wife was walking just behind; at a word from her husband she picked up the post and carried it on her shoulder. "The women are just beasts of burden," said the Old Australian. "And these Greeks, they're flocking to Australia, but they're taking no part in community life. They won't go to meetings. They won't do their stint of voluntary work."

I never ceased to be amazed at the amount of voluntary work the men and women of these small communities undertake after a full day's toil. It is rare for the more public-spirited to have an evening free. In Barmera I listed twenty voluntary organizations, not counting national bodies, like Rotary and Apex.* It is the family that binds the Latins, not a masculine ideal of comradeship.

"This is my little paradise on earth." So said a German migrant, spare and brown and hard like all these people of the sun, who dismounted from his tractor to offer us an iced drink on the veranda of his squat little wooden house, home-built and hedged in by vines and fruit trees. Every inch of his twenty-three acres was put to use: there was no room even for a garden.

"A mixed salad," he said of his output: vines for currants, for sultanas and for wine; citrus; apricots and peaches for the Shed, where his French wife works by day, helping on the block at evenings and at

---

* Here is the list: the Hospital Auxiliary, Show Society, Country Women's Association, Mothers and Babies Health Association, Kindergarten Welfare, Ambulance Committee, Marching Girls Association, Church of Christ Guild, St. Joseph's Welfare Club, Congregational Guild, Church of England Guild, School Committee, School Welfare Fund, Boy Scouts, Girl Guides, Good Neighbour Council, Girls Life Brigade, Kindergarten Mothers Club, Homes for the Aged. When not engaged in good works, the community grew $1,000,000 worth of vegetables, 12,000 tons of citrus and 4,000 tons of tomatoes for the juice factory, 3,300 tons of dried fruit and about 24,000 tons of fresh grapes for the winery. All this in a district of 3,500 people where for weeks on end the summer temperature exceeds 110°F. in the shade.

weekends. Packing stations offer almost the only paid employment for women. At one I visited everyone I spoke to was Italian, Greek, Polish, or Yugoslav but for a solitary English migrant, daughter of a painter from Bath. This energetic German has won prizes for the improvements he has made and for the quality of his products; starting without capital, he has achieved an income of around $6,000 a year. Unlike the Latins, he and his wife take an active part in the life of the community. "Everything I do here is for the future," he said.

[6]

To harvest all these grapes and oranges, these pears and apricots, seasonal pickers come from all over Australia. Some work round the year and over half the continent, from cane cutting in northern Queensland down to apple picking in Tasmania. A good worker can make up to $10 a day, perhaps a bit more if things are right, but many earn less. The employer provides accommodation but not keep.

In Mildura I watched the arrival of a trainload of about three hundred pickers from Melbourne, each of whom had received a free ticket from the Department of Labour in exchange for a promise to stay at least three weeks. There emerged as varied a collection of people as you could hope to see, each clutching a cheap little suitcase, a bulging shopping bag, or just a paper holder. One man had nothing at all: a lean, cadaverous individual with a thick bush of black hair on his chin and none whatever on his scalp. He came, I was told, every year, with no possessions, not even a hat, vowed apparently to silence; officials believed him to be a Hungarian ex-monk. In a remarkably short time everyone had vanished by bus or car with his new boss. My host collected two Austrians from Mount Isa, in Queensland, where the lead and silver mines were paralyzed by a prolonged strike. They had come by car and were enjoying a combination of holiday with open-air work that enabled them to keep up payments on their homes, where they had left their families. Already installed in a caravan on the block was a young German couple who had been on the move for two years, seeing Australia and earning up to $100 a week between them towards a future place of their own. "We are in no hurry," the young man said. "Where else in the world can you go where you please and find always work with good money? We shall become Australians." The caravan was spick and span. Their employer commented, "Germans and Italians are the best migrants. The British? Apt to grizzle."

[7]

The town clerk was immaculate in a neat dark suit, a tie and collar, polished shoes. Except for the sun tan which is the Australian uniform, he might have modelled for a civil servant anywhere. He even had a black homburg hat. "Next time you see me," he remarked cryptically, "I shall look different."

Next time he was on a tractor and stripped to the waist, his hair stiff with dust, hauling a trailer-load of oranges. He and a colleague in the Town Hall, both middle-aged men with families, between them bought a fifty-acre block in a run-down condition and, bit by bit, are restoring it on borrowed capital and in their off-duty time. Their first task was to grub out a lot of dead or dying orange trees and to put in pipe drains, and now they are replanting with superior citrus and mean to work up to 7,000 trees. About a year ago overproduction brought the price of oranges plummeting down. This has slowed but not deranged their plants to increase the output to a point that will enable both of them to hang their hats on an office peg for the last time. "I love to get my fingers in the dirt," said the health inspector. His wife deeps their rambling wooden house, set down on dusty flats in a bend of the river. She also milks the cow, feeds the chooks, grows vegetables bottles fruit, cares for three teen-age children and finds time for the innumerable other ploys which keep Australian countrywomen out of mischief.

Citrus is a clean, crisp-smelling, eye-pleasing crop. Its growers take their smoke in the shade with a flask of tea, and dream of the future. A neighbour looks in with a gift of melons and takes away a jug of cream. On a weekend afternoon, the mercury well up in the hundreds, the town clerk tied the cow, a wonderful cow who supplies milk for twelve or thirteen people and three calves, to the tractor and led her to a neighbour's bull. He drank a cold beer on the veranda while the bull performed his function; sometime or other he would help the bull's owner to haul crates to the Shed, or his wife would send across a cockerel. Here in this relaxed, easygoing, almost tropical atmosphere there is no fuss or hurry, yet much gets quietly done. Like a hidden mainspring that keeps the watch ticking, a sense of purpose lies concealed—"it's our own place." "Everything we do is for the future."

Between mates money seldom changes hands. Sometimes you get the impression that mateship is a stronger bond than marriage. Are the wives equally content? We discussed this over sherry on the rocks on the veranda before our tea, at nine o'clock, of rabbit stew and peaches. The health inspector's wife smiled a trifle wryly. "It's a man's country." I had heard that phrase so often by now. She added, "The men don't help you. But they have their own work to do." And she had grown up in the mallee where water for the washing up was used several times over and then carried out to succour wilting lettuces; here she has plenty of water, and that alone is a source of content.

On Sunday, when the heat had abated, we picnicked by the river on a sandy beach shaded by tall and spreading river gums. It was very peaceful. The shallow, silky river scarcely seems to flow, just to lie there idly between inconspicuous banks, unhurried, unflurried, truly Australian. In Africa you would expect crocodiles, but here is nothing dangerous or vicious, not even crabs. Yabbies there are, a king of crayfish good to eat; everyone kept telling me about the goodness of yabbies, but I never encountered them. Big Murray cod tempt anglers but nowadays are rare. Only birds broke the silence. Two kookaburras cackled in a tree. They are bold and handsome birds with strong, coarse beaks and a voracious appetite—a species of kingfisher, very different from the darting, delicate small bird of English streams. Parrots let out their screeches, and a skein of spoonbill ibis skimmed silently by.

There was a cold chicken supper with an iced Barossa reisling, dry and grapy, from vineyards down the river. Not the least among Australian blessings are these excellent and extremely cheap light table wines. The talk was local, easy, and undemanding; no world issue reared its ugly head. The partners spoke of their approaching holiday. Every year they disappear for a fortnight in a cabin cruiser on the river, leaving behind their wives and families and orange trees and their civic cares. "We chug along, stop and fish an hour or two, chug along, stop and have a beer, chug along, stop and cook a bite of lunch. Then snooze an hour or two. Chug along, stop and fish, maybe we pull out something for our tea, maybe not. Chug along, a game of cribbage, have our tea. Read a bit, talk a bit, have a beer, go to bed." No sound but that of birds and lapping water; no problems, just quiet and stars and trees. They take their rods, a case of beer, a few crime stories, some cigars. They know it won't rain. For a fortnight a year these mates and partners journey to the Land of Cockayne.

EIGHT 〰〰

Adelaide

Farther down the Murray lies a valley famous for its vineyards. Some of the Barossa wines could keep company with the finest from the valleys of the Moselle or the Rhine, but they do not travel, or are not allowed to; the Australians very wisely drink them all.

The skill is German. One of the original directors of the South Australian Company which founded Adelaide, George Fyfe Angas, in 1838 established there a group of Lutherans from Brandenburg who had rejected attempts made by the King of Prussia to unite the Lutheran and the Reformed churches. Like the Pilgrim Fathers before them, they chose exile rather than obedience to a secular authority and took their skills and industry with them to a new land. So here are their descendants, in the fourth or fifth generation, still making the best wine in Australia—though possibly growers in the Hunter Valley, in New South Wales, might challenge that—and living God-fearing, industrious, frugal and group-conscious lives.

Wine making in this wide, gentle valley remains very much a family affair, and German names predominate. Few regions of Australia are so closely settled, so neat and tidy, and have so European a feel about them. From each village, ringed by vineyards and planted with trees, modestly arises the plain spire of a wooden chapel whose interior is spick and span, polished, well-tended and austere. The congregations are small but devoted. Each has its own pastor. Six families, no more, support the chapel to which my hosts, Mr. and Mrs. Cyril Henschke, belong, providing for their pastor a house, a car, electricity and the basic minimum wage, plus a good deal of produce; for though these families live modestly, they do not lack their cows and sheep, their hens and vegetables. It is ironic that these abstemious Lutherans should derive their living from the fermented grape. But the pastors do not deny themselves a glass of hock or claret. "There's nothing wrong with wine itself," one of them observed. "It's the use to which men put it that can be sinful. It rests with man to use it wisely." And that these Lutherans do; a community more law-abiding, sober and socially virtuous would be hard to find.

In this one district there are five denominations of the Lutheran faith, divided by doctrinal differences which to outsiders scarcely seem significant. For the best part of a century each congregation recruited its pastors in Germany and kept alive the German tongue, customs and traditions. Now the tongue has all but surrendered, and in 1921 the denominations formed the United Lutheran Protestant Church of Australia, known as Velka, which has done much to knit the communities together.

There is a settled feeling here, an atmosphere of tradition, to be sensed elsewhere only in parts of Tasmania. The century-old stone walls of the Henschkes' cellars are thick, deep, and attached to the homestead in the old European fashion, not set apart as a modern office is, or a factory. To reach them you need only to walk a few paces across a small courtyard. All around are trees and creepers and a garden full of flowers.

In the evening, under a tree on the lawn, we sipped a delicious white wine and nibbled bits of cheese, while my host's conversation darted like a dragonfly about the subjects which attracted his quick, versatile and ingenious mind: the chemistry of wine making (did I know that the only difference between the substance which imparts flavour and that which imparts colour is the position of a single hydrogen atom at one end of a very large and complex carbon chain?), the markings of a butterfly he had just caught; the difference between a hawk and an eagle; the progress of an orbiting satellite he was keeping under observation through his telescope; the merits and demerits of certain sculptors— sculpture is among his hobbies; his wife paints; his two schoolboy sons play the organ. The house is solid, rather dark, modest, practical, equipped with heavy German furniture inherited from a father who lived to be ninety and sired twelve children. Cyril Henschke's sons belong to the fifth generation to have owned these cellars.

[2]

Wine making is at once a creative art and a scientific process, and a good wine maker must possess a certain kind of character. He must have meticulous regard for detail, great patience, curiosity, intelligence,

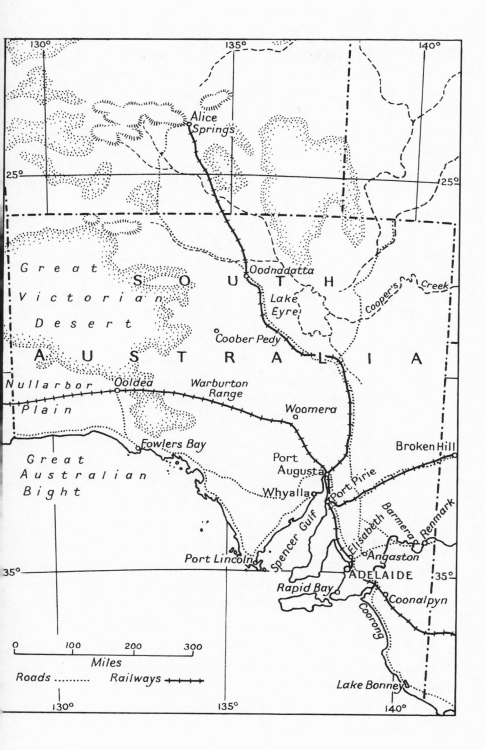

a taste for experiment, imagination, businss acumen and, above all, a tireless love of the trade. The life is exacting. It has, of course, its slack times, but during the vintage everything works up to a crescendo of highly strung activity which continues round the clock. At this time a small mistake can spoil a whole year's work. And judgments are tricky, relating to natural processes not yet fully understood and never quite the same from season to season.

The big underground tanks and the vats and presses had just been scoured and cleansed, and two men were on their knees scraping every fleck of scale from the floor on which the grapes of the new vintage would be deposited. One was a jovial, burly, curly-headed giant of German origin, whose hands, so thick and clumsy looking, wielded the scraper with an artist's deftness and delicacy; the other, no less meaty, a seventeen-year-old son who, so he said, eats a pound of steak and four eggs every morning for breakfast. Wine making is a family affair for men as well as masters; sons follow their fathers, and the skill is in their blood. In the cool darkness of these deep vaults 150,000 bottles are maturing, plus the contents of rows and rows of big casks made of oak imported from Europe. Minute traces of the tannin in the oak imparts body by some process that remains a mystery. The light, grapy table wine produced in these cellars is an aristocrat. The ordinary beverage is fortified by alcohol derived from crushed and fermented skins and forms the bulk of the output of the famous wineries along this valley— Yalumba, Penfold, Seppel, Grampe. Here mass production has been superimposed on traditional skills.

A few English immigrants got in among the Germans at the start of the Barossa vineyards, among them one called Samuel Smith who left his native Dorset, where he worked in a brewery, because his religious principles forbade him to labour, as he was required to do on the Sabbath. He came first to the Angas family as a gardener, saved $600 and took up a grant of land, and his sons started a winery. Now this establishment can store three million gallons, handles two thousand tons of grapes a week during the vintage, and sends its Yalumba wines all over the world. Samuel Smith's genial and hospitable descendants, the Hill-Smiths, inhabit a panelled mansion full of tiger skins and heads of animals slain in India; they breed successful race horses, are connoisseurs of wine and food and modern paintings (I admire particularly the imaginative work of a South Australian, Jacqueline Hick), and themselves paint romantic landscapes. An artistic outlet of some kind seems a necessity with wine makers, whose lives can be as tensed up as a violin string. Descendants of the Angas family also live in this valley, where the founder's sons and grandsons built for themselves handsome country seats standing in parks adorned by red gums with twirling boles and spreading foliage. Rolling countryside, posts and rails, solid stone barns, browsing sheep and cattle, terraced gardens, even yew hedges—another paradise on earth, another English dream realized at last in the antipodes.

Angaston, a neat and prosperous country town, lies less than forty miles from Adelaide, which the first Angas helped to establish in what was then a grassed and wooded plain alive with wallabies. Our modern taste for wildlife would have astonished these pioneers, one of whom remarked on "wallabies disgusting to our eyes, like enormous rats."

[3]

The true founder of Adelaide was Colonel William Light. To Australians he is naturally a famous figure, but although he was an Englishman he is so much less well-known in Britain, and such an attractive and interesting man, that perhaps a digression to glance at his career may be forgiven.

His father, Captain Francis Light, R.N., also founded a city—Penang. Both were bastards: the father, of a Suffolk squire and a servant girl; the son, of the sea captain and a half-caste of Portuguese and Malayan origin. In 1792 this Captain Francis Light sent his eldest son William, then aged six, to England to be educated under the care of old family friends at Theberton Hall. Years later William was to give the name of Theberton to the cottage that he built in Adelaide.

Young William Light entered the Navy at the age of thirteen. Later he bought a cornetcy in the 4th Dragoons and, in the Peninsular War, took part in forty-five actions without sustaining a scratch, although he once galloped the length of the enemy lines "in blue undress" to discover the disposition of the French forces and report to Wellington. "I have never met with a more zealous, intrepid or intelligent officer," wrote Sir Benjamin D'Urban. All his superiors recommended him for promotion; through no fault of his own he found himself on half pay at the equivalent of $5 a week. Wandering disconsolately round Europe with a sketchbook, he produced a series of Sicilian impressions good enough to be redrawn by Peter de Wint. Despite his poverty and several misfortunes, including a ball through the leg in a skirmish at Corunna, he married an illegitimate daughter of the Duke of Richmond and fitted out a cutter called *Gulnare*.

In 1830 Egypt's pasha, Mohammed Ali, was recruiting foreign mercenaries for a nonexistent navy. William Light accepted the command of a nonexistent battleship and returned to England to recruit sailors, leaving in Cairo a headstrong bride of outstanding beauty who wore a white turban with a purple tassel and gold-braided trousers; she smoked a pipe, shot birds, navigated a yacht and spoke, according to Lady Franklin, "as if accustomed that all things should yield to her." An old flame called Captain Bowen certainly did. She bore him a child, and in 1834 she and her husband were separated. William took up with Maria Gandy, a labourer's daughter who must have been a remarkable woman. She went with him to Australia, shared all his privations, nursed him devotedly, and subsequently died of the same turbercular infection.

Mohammed Ali's navy was born when the battleship *Nile* was launched in a British dockyard; "The largest vessel," proudly claimed *The Times,* "hitherto constructed in this or any other country," of 908 tons burden, with two steam engines which "work up to a power of full 260 horses pulling together." William Light took her to Alexandria, shipping as passenger Capt. John Hindmarsh, R.N., who hoped to take command of the Pasha's fleet; but the appointment went to a Frenchman.

Meanwhile the liberal philanthropist Edward Gibbon Wakefield, while serving a sentence in Newgate jail for abducting an heiress, had hatched the notion of a new kind of colony to be founded not by convicts and scallywags but by decent, free and law-abiding members of society, who would transplant themselves as a community equally balanced between young and old, male and female, masters and men. In a new land they would establish a microcosm of their own civilized society, leaving behind its vices and taking only its virtues with them. Self-government would be the goal. Wakefield founded the National Colonization Society and pressed his scheme with such effect that Parliament appointed a Colonization Committee, with Rowland Hill of penny-postage fame as secretary, to translate these ideals into practice in the newly created Colony of South Australia. Hindmarsh was appointed governor, and he offered Light the position of surveyor-general at a salary of $800 a year.

Although by now a man of fifty and in indifferent health, Light jumped at the opportunity. His task was to select, survey and apportion land to the settlers, each of whom was to be invited to buy, for $2 an acre, up to 134 acres in the "country districts," plus one acre in the proposed township for every eighty acres he took up in the bush. The intention was to prevent squatters and speculators from pre-empting vast areas of the interior, as was happening in New South Wales.

Light fitted up the brig *Rapid,* 162 tons, and on May 1, 1836, set sail with three officers, a crew of thirteen, his Maria Gandy, seven "persons of a superior class" who paid their own fares, and seventeen labourers. One of the officers described Light as "a real worthy old fellow as ready to join in our jokes as anyone, a most talented and indefatigable officer, and universally beloved." His instructions were detailed. As well as selecting land for settlers, he was to pick a site for the capital and lay it out. It was to have a "commodious and safe harbour," fertile land all round, fresh water, ample building material close at hand, good drainage, and should be sited "some distance from the limits of the Colony, as a means of avoiding interference from without"—in other words, from the convict settlements of New South Wales and Van Diemen's Land. On August 17, 1836, Light and his party landed in Rapid Bay and made a camp "consisting of four tents, with the Ensign flying and a glorious fire, in as beautiful a valley as was ever made by nature's hands"—a valley which put Woodforde, the surgeon (who had so disliked the wallabies), in mind of the orchards of Devonshire, despite the "dreadfully annoying" flies.

Not long afterwards Governor Hindmarsh arrived in H.M.S. *Buffalo* with more immigrants, a number of pigs and some savage dogs which bit everyone they could get their teeth into. And on December 28, 1836, some two hundred people gathered under a gum tree to hear Hindmarsh proclaim the first free Colony of Australia, while "a dozen or so of drunken marines from H.M.S. *Buffalo* discharged several muskets" and a banquet of salt pork and "an indifferent ham" was served in the open, accompanied by rum which kept the celebrations going all night. Three days later Light's choice of a site for the capital was agreed on and, at the request of King William, called after the Queen.

[4]

In the bush Light's task was daunting. He had scarcely any staff, no transport and poor rations, and jealous colleagues on Hindmarsh's staff intrigued against him. Cash was short, and the labourers lost no time in implanting in this new land the habits of the old. "All the men doing no work and the greater part drunk," a young surveyor recorded in his diary. With rum at less than ten cents a bottle, it was "a very general thing to get scarcely any work done on a Monday." And there was a strike over the tea ration. It was three weeks overdue, while the governor was said to be hoarding ten chests and "damning and swearing that they did not want tea and must go without."

In the bush Light and his small party toiled and sweated, endured tempests and agues, were tormented by flies and, in the leader's case, by insomnia. He worked with such prodigious energy that in less than two months he and his team surveyed 1,142 acres of the new township and marked it out in sections which were auctioned for the equivalent of between $20 and $40 each. In fifteen months they surveyed for settlement a further 150,000 acres of bush.

Yet Light's superiors, far from congratulating him, carped and criticized. "To find by every ship from England," Light protested to Rowland Hill, "a long list of censures passed by the Commissioners on my proceedings, is more than my feelings can stand." It was all very well for them to pen censorious dispatches from a London office, unable even to imagine Light and his men "trudging along the bank of this river carrying my theodolite on my own shoulders, with very often only two men to help me who were employed with the chain, and obliged to tread the same ground over and over placing my flags etc." And all the time he was failing in health. "I am harassed in mind," Light wrote to Wakefield, "beyond all you can conceive. My hours awake are full of distressing thoughts, and when I doze, I can't call it sleep . . . I have spent a laborious life altogether. I have suffered much in fatigue and privations. I have run through many perils. I have, thank God, always acted conscientiously . . . and now on the wane of my life, to find my conduct, my character, called in question. By whom, by Mr. Rowland Hill and vulgar men. My God, I cannot stand this." He resigned. The whole staff of the Survey Department then followed suit, refusing to serve under a deputy who had successfully intrigued in London to oust Light and to succeed him.

Light was penniless and in debt. He sold his sketches, went into partnership in a land agency and eked out a living in a reed and mud cottage, nursed by his Maria. Then fire destroyed his dwelling and all his possessions—his unsold drawings, a journal kept for thirty years, his instruments, clothing, everything. He was broken. "I have now no strength and am waning fast." It was 110° F. in the shade; all was dust and flies. The surgeon who had come out with him in the *Rapid* sat by his side and moistened his tongue with a brandy-soaked feather. He died in 1839 at the age of fifty-four. The Adelaide Corporation voted a sum equal to $20 a year "to be expended in Colonial wine and biscuit that the citizens may drink to the memory of Colonel Light."

His memorial is the layout of the core of Adelaide. The city now sprawls over the surrounding countryside in the manner of all contemporary cities. But there is still the ring of park land that was his original idea. Was Light the begetter of the Green Belt? An obscure retired official of the East India Company published a book* in 1830 suggesting that "a park surround every town like a belt one mile in width." Light probably read it. The author also envisaged two main streets "intended for the wealthy" with their "fashionable equipages" and fine clothes.

So Adelaide became the first modern city to have a ring of park lands half a mile wide all round it. The river Torrens runs through the middle. The park land is full of flowering trees and grass kept green by sprinklers and gives Adelaide most of the character it possesses. Nearly all the rest of Light's design has gone. The settlers built where they pleased and as they pleased, and the ordered dignity envisaged by Light, no less than by L'Enfant and Haussmann, never came to birth.

Two years before the death of its founder a proud citizen extolled "the style of our living and the tone of our society"; you might stumble over a sow with young in the dark, or "congregations of empty bottles," but would also encounter "neatly, and in some cases elegantly, spread dinner tables—well cooked dishes—champagne, hock, claret and maraschino—the presence of some well dressed and well bred women—and the soothing strains of a piano." The first race meeting was attended by eight hundred people but by only ten participating horses.

My own memories of the South Australian capital also center on racing. I was taken to see trotters and pacers, which on hot summer evenings attract citizens in thousands to an open-air stadium to relax in shirt sleeves with the family, bet on the tote and watch the handsome, shiny horses in the floodlit arena throwing out their forelegs as if churning the air. After the first hour or so spectators seem to paddle ankle-

* T. J. Maslon, "A Friend of Australia, or a Plan for Exploring the Interior and for Carrying on a Survey of the Whole Continent." This is referred to in Robin Boyd's *Australia's Home.*

deep in empty plastic cups and ice-cream cartons. Nothing alcoholic may be sold in South Australia after six o'clock, but you may bring your own beer, and soon empty cans join the plastic cups; anything no longer wanted is just chucked away. This does not make for tidiness, but no one minds. The atmosphere is easygoing, good-natured, sweaty-hot. On the way back to the car parks in the muggy darkness people bought cooked crayfish to take home to supper.

[5]

The practice of selecting large areas of bush and laying out on them large modern cities—town planning in the grand manner—is still followed in South Australia. In 1836 there was Adelaide, called after one Queen; in 1953 there was Elizabeth, called after another.

Twelve years ago the site was pastureland and bush. About 6,000 acres were picked out by the South Australian Housing Trust, a state-financed but independent body that annually builds about 40 per cent of the state's houses, to become a modern garden city accommodating at least 50,000 people. The basis is the neighbourhood unit of six or seven thousand citizens grouped together in a semi-independent community, each with its shopping mall, its schools and churches, its doctors and tradesmen, its parking places and clubs. (Elizabeth has an astonishing number of such clubs and societies. I counted in a brochure no less than seventy-seven, embracing everything from archery and bowls to creative writing, pistol shooting, Old Tyme dancing, ballet and Obedience Dogs, and representing the interests of everyone from ratepayers, widows, Lions, Apexists, harmony singers, floral arrangers, model railway addicts, Yorkshiremen and Good Neighbours; this was apart from church-sponsored bodies such as Men's Fellowships, Young Christian Workers, Ladies' Bright Hour, Homemakers, Boys' Brigades and so on.) Another basic principle is the separation of factories from houses, with planned access between the two to minimize traffic jams and the risks of getting run over. So also is the home separated from the shop. There are walkways for pedestrians to balance highways for cars.

All this is to be found in Britain's New Towns, but there are several differences. To a British eye the most obvious is the great diversity in architectural style. It would not be true to say that every single one of Elizabeth's eight or ten thousand new houses is different, as there are about forty basic patterns, but no two of like design have been put next to each other or even in the same street. Though every single house may *be* the same in its fundamentals, answering the same needs for the same kind of people, each one *looks* different.

How can it be possible, you wonder, to ring so many changes on the basic design of a single-storied house with either three or four bedrooms and a sitting room, kitchen and usual offices? The answer, I suppose, is that all human fingers look much alike and serve like purposes, yet we are assured that no two are identical. And probably every stone on the seashore, if you examined it closely enough, would reveal a tiny independence from every other stone, yet the same forces shaped them all.

This resolve to set an individual signature on each separate home has resulted in what Robin Boyd has dubbed Featurism: "the subordination of the essential whole and the accentuation of selected separate features."* Out of the window, with its featurist leaded panes or inset stained-glass panels, goes the unifying idea, in comes a riot of fidgety little gimmicks to plead for attention. And all this protesting by the Australian home, this spraying of sickly mauves and sunset pinks and muddy yellows on to panels of precast concrete, of a roof appropriate to Alpine snow standing next to one designed for Arabian deserts, this juxtaposition of baroque corrugated-iron turrets with "contemporary" plate glass and weird geometrical patterns—all this, in Mr. Boyd's opinion, is an evasion. An evasion of issues, of the frightening insecurity of the country—"a nervous architectural chattering avoiding any mention of the landscape"—and of committal to any principle or design; a nonconformism born not so much of sturdy independence as of fear of the forthright.

The volume of human ingenuity devoted to disguising and torturing a few simple materials like brick, concrete, wood and iron, and to embellishing with incongruous detail a straightforward rectangular pattern, never ceases to amaze—but at the same time it can be rather touching. Everyone is trying so hard. What are they trying to do? Nothing unpleasant, certainly, except of course aesthetically. Nothing brutal, cruel, anti-social, or unkind. They are trying to make a comfortable, hygienic, cozy home for the wife and kids, where everyone can lead a decent, self-respecting life. Some Europeans sneer at this, recoiling from the attendant mediocrity. Like much of the Australian landscape it is flat and, I suppose, dull. But in a world where violence, beastliness and man's

---

* Featurism is treated at length in Boyd's indispensable analysis of *The Australian Ugliness,* Pelican Books, 1960.

inhumanity to man are so very rampant, the sneer seems a little cheap. Our choice too often seems to lie between excruciating dullness and excruciating torture.

Urban Australia has become virtually an enormous suburb chopped into 150 x 50 feet plots which accommodate four households to the acre (allowing for roads) arranged round the rim of a continent.* It has become a nation of homeowners spreading their installments over thirty years, paying the rates, procreating children in cream emulsion-painted wall-to-wall carpeted bedrooms with candlewick bedspreads, getting by during their forty hours of working for the boss with as little drain as possible upon energies reserved for ferocious toil in their own homes and gardens, or possibly on squares of land reserved for sports and games. What can be so annoying to its critics is that so many people really *like* this way of life and would not exchange it for any other. I recall a sun-tanned young man standing in the sunshine on the steps of an office block in, I think, Perth—but it might have been almost anywhere—and saying, "It's too good to last. I've got it all—a good job, my own home just the way I planned it, a pretty wife, healthy kids, the garden's coming on nicely, at weekends I go fishing, I enjoy my work. This is what human beings have always wanted, and now I have it and it's wonderful!"

It is often said that Scandinavians find the achievement of plenty linked with mediocrity and a general absence of extremes, so dull that many of them either take to drink or commit suicide. Australians are more apt to commit smugness. If there should be dimly heard at the three-course feast (soup, steak and fruit salad)—or perhaps not *at* the feast, but on the outskirts—the rattle of a distant skeleton, they turn up the telly, get a beer from the fridge and keep their fingers crossed.

> The creepered wall stands up to hide
> The gathering multitudes outside
>   Whose glances hunger worsens;
> Concealing from their wretchedness
> Our metaphysical distress,
>   Our kindness to ten persons.

---

* This was the size, plus ten feet subsequently knocked off the frontage, that was laid down by Captain Arthur Phillip around 1790 in order "ever to prevent more than one house being built on the allotment." It was adopted throughout Australia and has been stuck to, more or less, ever since.

Substitute in these lines of Auden's, published in 1936, privet hedge, perhaps, for creepered wall, and you have a pretty fair statement of the frame of mind of the man with crossed fingers.

> And now on path on which we move
> But shows already traces of
> Intentions not our own . . .

It is to this underlying unease that Robin Boyd traces the root of Featurism—nervousness not only about the chances of survival in this down-lined nest under the eaves of Asia, but about the vastness and implacability and mystery of a country too big and too empty for people most of whom originated in the close-packed urban stews of a small, crowded, tamed and ordered island. So the newcomers first turned their backs upon it, looking seawards, and then tried to obliterate it by cutting down the native trees and shrubs and substituting English ones where possible and blotting out the fauna. Now they are littering the scene with wires, pipes, signs, masts, roads, hoardings, pylons, neon lights—everything that is artificial and therefore safe, not indigenous and therefore menacing.

"The most beautiful things I saw here," wrote an English woman visitor to the early Tasmania, "were the hawthorn hedges; it seemed like being on the right side of the earth again."* And complaining in 1822 of "the eternal eucalypt," Barron Fields observed: "New South Wales is a perpetual flower-garden, but there is not a single scene in it of which a painter could made a landscape without greatly disguising the character of the trees." There is Featurism in a nutshell—you must "greatly disguise the character of the trees," or of the house, the street, even the room. At all costs the plain, bare outline must be softened or broken. And it is all done with love and with the owner's hands and time and skill.

To most British migrants Featurism is sheer heaven. Only comparative stringency at home, and the grip of borough surveyors and planning officers, curbs to some extent Britain's own native Featurism. Here it takes the bit between its teeth, kicks up its heels and goes. Polyvinyl tiles in different colours, Venetian blinds with each louvre painted a different pastel shade, mock-Tudor beams and stucco walls, ornamental ironwork

---

* This nervousness at finding oneself no longer "on the right side of the earth" has been shared by many later visitors from the Northern Hemisphere, for instance, D. H. Lawrence in *Kangaroo:* "It gave Somers an uneasy feeling, the northward travelling of the climbing sun: as if everything had gone wrong."

above the porch, imitation carriage lanterns, built-in aquariums floodlit in lurid colours, gnomes on the lawn—it is all very satisfying and greatly admired.

Elizabeth is a city of migrants. Two out of every three of its householders have come from Europe, the great majority from Britain. In proportion to its population South Australia is absorbing migrants faster than any other state. There is no pressure to economize in land, so the average density in Elizabeth is less than two families to the acre. One-fifth of the area has been reserved for playing fields and parks, and every factory, school and shopping mall is surrounded by open spaces.

Elizabeth is a strung-out place with no tall, grouped buildings to give it presence, and it has been laid out on the assumption that every family will own at least one car. In the state as a whole there is already one car to every four people, and the ratio is expected soon to rise to one in three. Everyone who secures a new house gets thrown in with it an electric cooker, water-heating apparatus, a laundry with an electric copper boiler and even a rotary clothes hoist—the modern version of a clothesline—in the yard, and six flowering shrubs. In a very short time that yard becomes green with water-sprinkled grass and gay with shrubs and roses. I saw no empty beer cans, old tires and chucked-out newspapers.

Are migrants happy in this suburban paradise? Yes, on the whole. Of course there are failures and wingers. Some have trouble keeping up the weekly payments of $8 to $10. But pay is good and jobs plentiful. The young complain of evening dullness and the six-o'clock closing rule for pubs. After that there is nothing much to do except visit each other's homes and watch television. Elizabeth has no heart pulsating with urban life, no thronged streets, few restaurants and cafés. It is a temple to the home, and people must feed upon their own resources. Often these resources are narrow. The family is all.

[6]

Southeast of Adelaide the Murray ends its journey, more than 3,500 miles from its farthest source, in a salt lake, Alexandria, screened by a maze of spits, peninsulas, creeks and inlets from an ocean that receives it unobtrusively. Parallel with the shore there runs a fifty-mile-long spit of sand forming the seaward wall of a long, narrow, salt-water inlet called The Coorong. It has a wild and wind-swept look and the kind of wiry, sparse, tenacious creeping grasses that you find on saltings.

It was here that I made the acquaintance of wombats: thick-furred, lumbering, barrel-shaped creatures that waddle rather than run or walk and have the poor eyesight usual among burrowing beasts. They have peculiar rootless teeth that grow throughout their lives without wearing down, and enable them to chew the tough roots and herbage on which they live. Because of this ability to chew almost anything, many pastoralists condemn them as destroyers of fence-posts, and have persuaded the Victorian Government to pay a bounty of ten shillings a scalp. On the other hand, wombats may well be territorial in habit; if this is so, many are being needlessly sacrificed.

There are two kinds of wombat: *Vombatus hirsutus,* native to a fairly narrow strip along the coast of New South Wales and Victoria, and the hairy-nosed *Lasiorhinus latifrons,* found only in South Australia. A gap of about 200 miles separates their habitats. The pair I saw were of the hairy-nosed variety and had come from the Nullarbor plain, six or seven hundred miles away; and their owner, Bob Hawkes, a dedicated wildlife lover, hopes to breed them in this alien environment in order to discover whether they will adapt themselves to another habitat. Like most creatures, wombats will have to do a good deal of adapting if they are to survive. The situation here is all too familiar. South Australia has national parks—nearly half a million acres of them, or roughly 0.2 per cent of the state's area, divided into twenty-six reserves, one only four acres in extent; and exactly one park ranger to patrol the lot, plus one field officer to supervise them, in a state more than four times as large as the United Kingdom. "Many of our wildlife reserves," observes the commissioners' latest report, "previously surrounded by large areas of undeveloped land, are rapidly becoming hemmed in by development."

Is it, when you get down to the harsh facts of life, really possible to combine development with wildlife conservation? That is the larger question Mr. Bob Hawkes is trying to answer. He started with 6,000 acres of mallee scrub, a sandy soil virtually devoid of humus, and a carrying capacity of one sheep to fifteen or twenty acres; a flock of about four hundred, therefore, was all his property could have been expected to support. So he set to work to replace the scrub by nutritious grasses. Tractor-drawn heavy chains felled the mallee, and chisel plow tore up the soil; superphosphate was spread by air, mineral deficiencies corrected, the seed of grass and clover sown. Then came fences, then sheep. All this involved a heavy capital outlay on soil so poor that, for over a century, no land-hungry settler and no well-heeled company had thought it worth touching. Yet in less than five years Bob Hawkes had 5,000 sheep grazing on the developed part of the property, which works out at one and a quarter sheep to the acre. He intends to build this up to about 9,000.

Can space be spared for wildlife when everything is fenced, plowed and reseeded? Most of the larger marsupials, it is regretfully conceded, must go. There is a lake on the property surrounded by a belt of vegetation, and this is to remain: tea trees* by the water's edge, then a shrub they call honeysuckle bush, then eucalypts of several kinds, and then mallee. This will provide sanctuary for waterfowl and smaller marsupials, and a few wallabies, with any luck, should survive.

It is the birds that are the glory of the place and, while their habitat must change, these changes should not be too drastic, or the birds too unadaptable, for a balance to be struck. There is a wealth of parrots, including a small flock of a species of grass parrot hitherto believed to be extinct everywhere except in one part of Tasmania. The discovery and identification of these birds was a red-letter day in Mr. Hawkes's life; he trapped five specimens and hopes they will breed in his aviary. He overfed them to begin with, and they put on weight; knowing, as a stockman, that fat animals are often shy breeders, he cut down their rations and awaits results next spring.

His aviary dazzles the eye. The parrots, apparently engaged in a perpetual tussle to outdo each other in gaudiness of plumage, resort to every device to pile on colour after brilliant colour; some species, not content with a single livery, indulge in two, one for the female and another for the male. Thus the female of the Princess of Wales, from Central Australia, is predominantly red and blue with a pink throat and grey beak; in the male green predominates, and he has red underwings and an orange beak.

Here are colonies of Cloncurry ringnecks, rosellas, a rare Eclectus parrot from New Guinea, the Indian wryneck, scarlet-chested grass par-

---

* These are no relation to the true tea bush, a camelia, but are myrtles, belonging to a genus *Leptospermum* of which about thirty species grow in Australia. They were named tea trees by Captain Cook, who made an infusion from the aromatic leaves of one of them, *L. scoparium,* or manuka. Like the eucalypts, they are most confusing; they can be waist-high, rather untidy shrubs, or they can be trees forty or fifty feet tall with slender trunks and spreading branches; they can grow in coastal bogs, on sandy heaths, on granite rocks and on mountains up to 5,000 feet. They thrive especially in the coastal regions. The name tea tree is sometimes applied to a related genus, *Melaleuca,* and this is even more confusing because it has over a hundred species, all but one of which are found only in Australia.

rots and, still among the most handsome despite, or perhaps because of, their chromatic restraint, the Major Mitchell cockatoo with his pure white plumage and soft, sunset-glowing breast. Peaceful doves twinkle from treetops; blue wrens wag their tails sideways by the lake; galahs sweep over like gusts of rose petals; white silky bantams peck around the door, and a herd of shaggy Highland cattle stands knee-deep in the lake, apparently quite at home in circumstances about as far removed as they could be from the misty greyness of their native habitat. Another paradise on earth, though with devils trying to get in. One is there already in the shape of the rabbit, which is just about kept under by scattering poisoned carrots from the air. Rabbits, foxes, dingoes—that is the trinity of devils, and all were introduced by man. They formed no part of nature's design for Australia.

NINE 〰〰〰

Melbourne

No city in the world can once have been more solidly and quintessentially Victorian than Melbourne. Founded half a century later than Sydney, in the year before the Queen's accession, it missed even the tail end of the Georgian tradition. There was no Greenway, no Macquarie, no Rum Corps and convict settlements and harsh brutalities; from the first it was respectable and prosperous. One of its twin founders was a well-to-do Tasmanian pastoralist, John Batman, who, with three white companions and six aborigines, sailed from Launceston to Port Phillip, as the new settlement was at first called, and acquired from the local blacks about 600,000 acres in exchange for a quantity of blankets, knives and tomahawks. The other was John Pascoe Fawkner, a convict's son who had been a bookseller in Launceston and conveyed to the site of the future Melbourne a schooner-load of fruit trees, seeds and implements, as well as the necessary blankets and tomahawks. Soon he opened there a nonalcoholic hotel advertising as its principal attraction access to a good encyclopedia; later he started the first newspaper in Victoria and one of the first libraries, and finally he became a member of the Legislative Council.

Surveyors from Sydney laid out a gridiron city without a spark of imagination and no nonsense about green belts or making use of natural features. Merchants and pastoralists flocked from Tasmania and New South Wales to public land auctions; in ten years the population had reached five thousand and the government had received the equivalent of $1,000,000 from sales of land. Within fifteen years of Batman's and Fawkner's landfall, the state of Victoria hived off from New South Wales.

Then came the big event: the gold discoveries of 1851. Melbourne more or less exploded. Builders toiled incessantly, masonry sprouted, suburbs mushroomed outwards yet failed to keep pace; at the height of the boom over 115,000 people were living in tents and humpies made of sacking, despite an eightfold increase in the number of houses.

Fortunes made on the gold fields were lavished on mansions to enshrine success. It was the age of servants in attics, nurseries on the top floor, ballrooms and spacious dining halls below, large gardens with exotic shrubs, carriages and coachmen, golden fob chains, whiskers, stained glass, coats of armour, wax fruit and "French grotesques" to perch on gables. Everything was faithfully copied from England; there was nothing Australian about it all except a few names like Yarra and Toorak—and verandas, the only major concession made by British settlers to a sunnier clime.

Not that verandas were native to Australia any more than sheep; probably they were introduced by the military architect John Watts, who had served in the West Indies and was appointed to Sydney in 1813. By extending the roof and adding pillars, a veranda was born; in a two-storied house it supported a balcony. Given a balcony, you needed something to prevent you from falling off, and so there came into being the cast-iron balustrades, accompanied by overhanging friezes and brackets and by supporting pillars, that must once have been, and to some extent remain, the pride and glory of Melbourne and Sydney and certain country towns.

[2]

To drive through some of the older streets of Melbourne or Sydney is agonizing; every few yards you want to stop and stare and prowl. The sunlight, striking at an angle the white stucco front of a narrow, terraced house, imprints on the inner wall in black and white the pattern of the balustrade's grille. Slender iron pillars hold aloft a balcony surrounding a hotel to form a shady arcade over the street. For those with time to search, all sorts of bits and pieces reveal themselves: friezes that depend from the verandas, brackets linking frieze to pillar, spandrels and finials; I had no idea so much survived in such variety. Far more, of course, does not. A great wealth of decoration, rich and solid as a Christmas cake, has gone forever. Worse still, more will go.

If anyone could save such cast iron as remains, it would be Dr. Graeme Robertson, a distinguished Melbourne neurologist. His study and photography of decorative cast-iron work has been a lifetime's hobby that has changed the notions of his fellow Australians about their

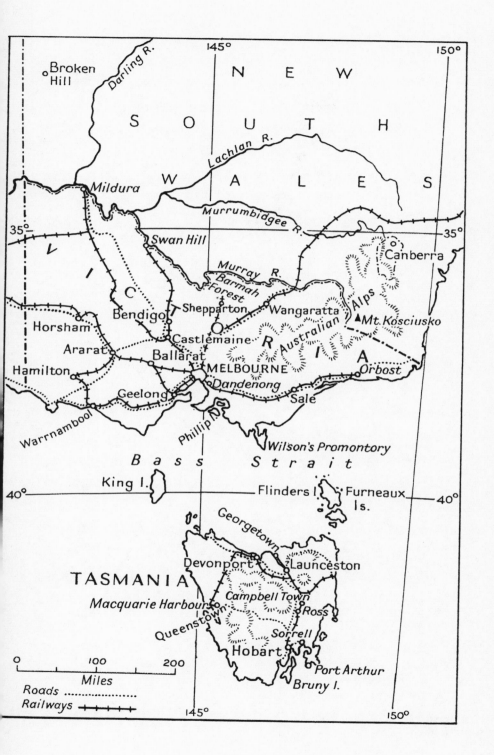

Broken Hill

Darling R.

NEW SOUTH

Mildura

35°

Swan Hill

WALES

Lachlan R.

Murrumbidgee R.

35°

Murray R.

Barmah Forest

Canberra

Shepparton

Wangaratta

Australian Alps

▲ Mt. Kosciusko

Bendigo

Castlemaine

Horsham

Ballarat

Ararat

MELBOURNE

Orbost

Hamilton

Dandenong

Geelong

Sale

Warrnambool

Phillip I.

Wilson's Promontory

B a s s   S t r a i t

King I.

40°

Flinders I.

Furneaux Is.

40°

Georgetown

TASMANIA

Devonport

Launceston

Campbell Town

Macquarie Harbour

Ross

Queenstown

Sorrell

Hobart

Port Arthur

Bruny I.

0   100   200

Miles

Roads ....

Railways ++++++

145°

150°

architectural heritage. Ruskin called decorative cast iron "cold, clumsy and vulgar," a judgment for many years endorsed by Australians, who for the first half of this century despised it as cumbrous, old-fashioned stuff, on a par with horse drays and chamber pots and paraffin lamps; and as, unlike the lamps and chamber pots, it had a scrap value, off it went to make way for more fashionable materials such as plastics and veneers.

To suggest that Dr. Graeme Robertson altered this opinion single-handed would be an overstatement; the rehabilitation of nineteenth-century artistic achievements has been a world-wide trend. But with his magnificent photographs and scholarly texts* he awoke a pride and interest in the architectural past. Cast-iron balustrades became the fashion, to be sought out when old houses where pulled down and removed to new houses by a new generation to whom things that are old and native are no longer rejected in favour of things that are modern and introduced.

Strictly speaking, of course, the iron work is also exotic. Britain supplied both the idea and the early examples. Her manufacturers exported, indeed, whole houses, churches and schools; there is nothing new about prefabrication. In 1853 a portable church arrived from Bristol to seat seven hundred worshippers, complete with "every device fitting for divine service." It cost $2,000 landed and went up in six weeks. A critic complained that the sun drew the nails and buckled the plates, making the interior like a baker's oven; but it could not have been a failure, since the bishop ordered a second like it, and other congregations followed suit. Houses were being landed in Melbourne at a cost, freight included, of $50 each, and in 1855 Melbourne got a complete prefabricated cast-iron theater. Designed on the lines of Paxton's Crystal Palace, it was 88 feet long, 44 feet wide and 24 feet high, seated seven hundred people, and went up in five weeks. Although its interior "presented a light and exceedingly elegant appearance," the public called it the Iron Pot.

Probably the first cast-iron balustrades, with their decorative accom-

---

* His best-known works are: *Victorian Heritage,* 1960, and *Sydney Lace,* 1962, both published by the Georgian House Melbourne; and, with Edith Craig, *Early Houses of Northern Tasmania.* He has also written and illustrated many articles and advises the separate National Trusts of New South Wales, Victoria and Tasmania, which fight a spirited rear-guard action against the destruction of Australian architectural treasures.

paniments, reached Australia from Britain in the 1830's. They came from small foundries and were cast by craftsmen working to their own designs. After smelting of the native ore began at Mittagong in New South Wales in the late forties, many small local foundries came into being, and it was in these that the bulk of the decorative iron work was cast. At first the local craftsmen copied imported designs and later sometimes incorporated motifs of their own such as kookaburras, emus and cockatoos. Naturally their merit varies; some are rather coarse and dull, but others possess an intricate balance and rhythm that gives great pleasure to the eye. The skill of some of these anonymous craftsmen— none were artists or architects, so far as we know—was of a high order; this was a genuine, creative folk art.

The researches of Dr. Graeme Robertson and others have unearthed the names of over a hundred Australian foundries known to have turned out ornamental castings. After 1870 designs were registered, and before the turn of the century, thirty-two foundries between them registered one hundred and thirteen designs in Victoria, and twenty-two foundries registered designs in New South Wales. All this ended with the financial collapse of 1893, which put a stop to the growth of Melbourne for several years. When a cautious recovery set in, the exuberance had gone, and plainer styles of building were the fashion; no one wanted ornamental iron work. The age of craftsmanship was over and the age of mass production had begun.

[3]

The rich of Melbourne liked their houses to be richly ornamented inside as well as out. To this end they bought paintings. By the late nineteenth and early twentieth centuries a number of painters had outgrown the topographical approach of their colonial predecessors and were recording the native scene with the insight of a native. In the words of one of them—Arthur Streeton—their aim was to "translate some of the great, hidden poetry that I know is here." (One is reminded of Lawrence's "invisible beauty".)

Outside Australia their work is not widely known, if only because Australians bought most of it or enabled their public galleries to do so by presenting them with handsome bequests. The largest of these came from Alfred Felton, who died in 1904 worth a million dollars made from chemicals, fertilizers and bottles. A bachelor and recluse with frugal habits—he was said to breakfast every day off a whiting, take no lunch and, as an occasional and sole indulgence, to smoke a mild cigar —he left half his fortune to the National Gallery of Victoria; by prudent investment the bequest has grown to a round $4 millions and brought to Melbourne a rich selection of the art treasures of the world, there to be displayed, under the vigorous direction of Dr. Eric Westbrook, with taste, intelligence and a refreshing absence of clutter.

The attempts by Australian painters to express the "great hidden poetry" of their native land started with the so-called Heidelberg school. This grew out of the association of four young men who, between 1886 and 1890, lived in tents and improvised shelters and painted out of doors, partly because this was the way they hoped to capture the light, colour and feel of the landscape, and partly because they were too poor to afford anything else. Heidelberg was the name of the district near Melbourne, now a suburb, where they camped. The main instigator of the movement was Tom Roberts, then just on thirty; his principal colleagues were Frederick McCubbin, a baker's assistant; Arthur Streeton, a lithographer's apprentice; and Charles Conder, an English youth who spent only five years in the colony as a budding surveyor but whose influence was contributory to the school.

These young men introduced impressionism into Australia. Roberts studied at London's Royal Academy from 1881 to 1883 and seems to have heard of the French aims and techniques mainly from two Spanish painters he encountered in Granada. These young painters changed the way of looking at, and feeling about, Australia. Hitherto most artists had seen a colony that might be interesting or picturesque, ugly, or downright alarming, but was never on "the right side of the earth"—not quite normal, and best treated "by greatly disguising the character of the trees." With the new school came an urge to participate, to enter in and understand the light and sun and trees and skies and rivers; a desire born of love instead of those lugubrious fears that had prompted writers like Marcus Clarke to see the whole continent as a sort of park around a Castle of Otranto, with forests "funereal, secret, stern," that seemed to "stifle, in their black gorges, a story of sullen despair . . . In the Australian forests no leaves fall. The savage winds shout among rock clefts. From the melancholy gum strips of white bark hang and rustle . . . Great grey kangaroos hop noiselessly over the coarse grass . . . and the mopokes burst out into horrible peals of semi-human laughter."

Against all this the campers-out of Heidelberg revolted. The art historian Dr. Bernard Smith* has suggested that they linked the sun with Australian nationalism as a symbol of this new human enterprise—"an emblem of hope beckoning the European migrant." At any rate, they strove to get the vigour and the magic of it into paint. In 1889 they held an exhibition called the 9 x 5 Impressions, because most of their sketches were made on cigar-box lids of that size. They were greeted with the usual huffings and puffings of critics who could see no virtue in any deviation from conventional Victorian styles; the public, however, bought most of their works.

Conder soon returned to England, leaving the others to pursue that familiar, sad progression from the youthful ferment of the *avant-garde* to middle-aged establishmentarianism. Roberts abandoned his struggle to trap the fleeting moment of the pastoral life in favour of an enormous canvas, which took him two years to complete, of the Opening of the First Commonwealth Parliament by the Duke of Cornwall and York, in his spare time wining and dining with the affluent gentry and at Government House. (That this was not an undiluted snobbery may be surmised from his remark that "you don't usually sell your stuff to people who rent cottages at seven-and-six a week; business, my dear boy, business.") Arthur Streeton, who had so ardently sought the "great warm and loving sun" which had in his youth illuminated girls in "lovely pure muslin, and gold, sweet grass-seeds, and the motherly she-oak"; who had seen in the blasting of rock "a perfect blazing glory of white, orange, cream and blue streaks"—Streeton in his sixties became a knighted oracle inhabiting fashionable Toorak and painting, according to a critic of the *Age*, "with the boom and bustle of arrogant commercialism." He lived on until 1943.

Perhaps because in their youth these men had known what they painted and loved what they had known, their work is known and loved today by innumerable Australians. Reproductions of such famous pictures as "Bailed Up," "The Breakaway" and "Shearing the Rams" by Tom Roberts, McCubbin's "Winter Evening" and "Lost Child," and the more dramatic pictures of those who came after, such as Sir John Longstaff and Sir Hans Heysen (who so mastered the eucalypt that "a generation of Australians came to see the gum as he saw it"), are everywhere. Australians are remarkably faithful to those of their native painters

* See Smith, Dr. Bernard, *Australian Painting, 1788–1960*, Oxford University Press, 1962.

and poets who, by recording the Australian legend, have helped to create it. No one has supplanted in their affections writers such as Banjo Paterson and Henry Lawson. Despite the rise of a lively and creative modern group of poets whose work is widely read, Banjo Paterson, born in 1864, remains far and away the best seller of them all.

[4]

Rivalry between Melbourne and Sydney is a standing national joke. The Sydneysider is presented, or presents himself, as a brash, ebullient, happy-go-lucky, cheeky sort of bloke, bronzed from weekends on his superb but overcrowded beaches, sport-crazy, money-conscious and thoroughly Americanized. Melbournians he affects to despise as stuffed shirts from snob schools like Geelong, Melbourne Grammar and Scotch College, inhabiting what is virtually a morgue. (One of the stock Sydney jokes is of the census taker who inquired: "How many children have you, ma'am?" "Two living and three in Melbourne.") At the same time Melbournians are seen as marblehearted financiers manipulating the country's banking and commercial systems for their own nefarious ends —Jekyll and Hyde characters, in fact.

Melbournians, on the other hand, present themselves as hard-working, feet-on-ground, shrewd, reliable, yet go-ahead citizens, Australian patriots to the marrow, civic-minded, culture-conscious, civilized; to them Sydney folk are a lightweight, flashy, vulgar lot given to governments notorious for insolvency, corruption and demagogism. They take a wry pride in their own conservatism. The managing director of an old Melbourne business told me that his chairman was eighty-seven and there were nineteen share-holding members of the one family, nearly all over sixty, and seventeen of them women.

Melbourne is a busy, bustling city, but most of the people I met seemed to talk in whispers. My hotel was the only one I have ever stayed in which demanded to be paid in advance. Topographically much of the city is dull and flat, and through it meanders the Yarra, which Melbournians will tell you is the only river in the world that runs upside down—it looks so brown and muddy. Yet it runs through some attractive suburbs. In the garden belonging to Ray Parkin, who has written so movingly of his wartime naval experiences, a garden that slopes down to the river, I heard the sweet call of bellbirds (the Bell-miner, one of the enormous honey-eater tribe), the kookaburra's cackle and many other kinds of bird; flowering gums harbour possums, and the ripple of a platypus has been seen in the pool.

These two images of Melbourne and Sydney are comparatively modern; they used to be exactly reversed. In 1884 an English visitor, Francis Adams, was struck by Melbourne's cosmopolitan nature—what he called the "metropolitan tone." "These people live quickly," he wrote, and "have no prejudices." By contrast, "the men and women of Sydney do not live so fast mentally . . . they cling to the past which Melbourne throws away." In Sydney he was aghast at the "appalling strength of British civilisation." Melbourne had touches of London, of New York, of Paris and of its own; but in Sydney he detected "the thumb marks and the great toe marks of the six-fingered, six-toed giant, the British Philistine! . . . The same gloomy dresses, cumbrous on the women, hideous on the men, that we see in England! The same food, the same over-eating and over-drinking and at the same hours!"

Those same hours proved, in the future, to be a great deal more sensible than Melbourne's. In 1915, as a wartime measure, a six-o'clock closing rule was introduced throughout Australia. While most states subsequently repealed this legislation, Victoria and South Australia kept it on for fifty years. The natural Victorian conservatism was reinforced —or so it is commonly believed—by an unholy alliance between churches and breweries, who found that people emerging from factories and offices to load themselves up in the "six-o'clock swill" got through more beer in the single permitted hour than comparable consumers in other states swallowed during the whole evening. It was not until 1966 that the Victorian legislature brought itself to allow its citizens to buy drinks until ten o'clock, and Melbourne said good-by to the six-o'clock swill.

In population both have topped the two-million mark, but Sydney keeps just ahead with an estimated 2,350,000 citizens in mid-1965. Melbourne has for long been the banking and stockbroking center of the Commonwealth and also claims educational pre-eminence. To launch out simultaneously not into one but into two full-blown universities, each of which expects to work up to eight or ten thousand students, suggests a pretty high degree of self-confidence and ambition in a self-made city that was nothing but a waste of bush worth a few tomahawks and blankets within the lifetime of the grandfathers of some of my contemporaries.

[5]

Sydney's Opera House and Melbourne's Cultural Center are like champions nominated in ancient times to contend in single combat on behalf of their armies or nations. Each faithfully reflects the image presented by its capital. The Opera House has more *panache*, originality and publicity, and also a reckless disregard for money; the Cultural Center not only pays as it goes and keeps to its budget but has actually cost slightly less, so far, than the estimates allowed.

Instead of inviting entries to an international competition as Sydney did, and Canberra before it, the sponsors of the Melbourne Center chose as their architect a Melbourne man. I was told that Roy Grounds is the most original architect practicing in Australia. He prefers to invent ideas —"one site, one person, one problem"—rather than to copy the ideas of others and seems to have an almost protean range of styles. His most famous public building is the Academy of Sciences' mushroom-like hall —described as "a miniature Ayers' Rock"—in Canberra, with its copper-sheathed dome; but probably his best work lies in the design of private homes.

The only Roy Grounds house I was able personally to visit was that built for Mr. Claudio Alcorso outside Hobart, overlooking the sea: an open, spacious, lofty house with an Italian feel about its cool, tiled floors and high ceilings, its clever use of inlaid stone and subtly tinted walls; there is a big open fireplace built out, as it were, into the living room. It is original, *sui generis,* and bears the imprint of a single mind. It was Roy Grounds, so Robin Boyd informs us, who first "brought the kitchen into the living room" by abolishing the wall normally separating the two chambers and replacing it by a waist-high counter, an essential element in today's fashionable "open plan." He is fond of open, central court-yards surrounded by house, with a tree or two and shrubs and greenery, ideal for the Australian climate. Much of his domestic work has a touch of the dramatic, perhaps deriving from his apprentice days as a set designer in Hollywood.

Now he is matched against the Dane, Joern Utzon, in gladiatorial combat. Nature is on the side of the Opera House; no bend of the Yarra could challenge that magnificent harbour site. But Melbourne has done its best by allocating for its Cultural Center seven acres in the city's heart with the river close at hand. All that is not covered by concrete will be green with grass and trees and gay with flowers. Underneath it all will be a huge car park, a practical convenience overlooked in Sydney, and also a prudent one, since it is expected to attract an annual revenue of $100,000, which will go some way towards financing the drama, ballet, concerts, art displays, training schools, meetings and exhibitions to be provided at the Center.

A trio of rectangular courts will be the core of the Center: one an art gallery, one a theater, and the third a hall for displays. All will be lit from above, four stories high and served by escalators. So far as anyone can judge from models, there will be a sense of space and grandeur and plenty of elbow room. Above the central court a long, thin, needle-like spire sheathed in copper will draw the eye. Asked why he designed this slim and graceful candle snuffer, Roy Grounds gave the only possible reply: "I looked at the site and wanted this spire. I thought it would look good, that's all." Like most features of the Center, it will also be practical; it is a sheath for the theater tower.

So far the building has proceeded on schedule, with no major mishaps, miscalculations, or occasions to revise the plan, and should be completed by 1970; the Victorian Government is providing from its revenue about $2 million a year—no lotteries. Melbournians are quietly confident that in their native son they have a champion fully equal to the challenge of the Sydneysiders' more widely publicized Dane. The two projects have, of course, no real similarity; site, need, concept and execution are entirely different. But both are bold, imaginative projects to be sustained by commercial cities planted on the rim of an inhospitable continent on the far side of the world, the one as a dumping place for convicts, the other as a gold diggers' camp. Despite its reputation for conservatism, Melbourne has already one of the most original buildings in the country in the shape of the Sydney Myer Music Bowl, something like a giant concrete tent flap lightly pegged over lawns, whose platform, I was told, can be seen by twenty thousand people. Melbourne has always been a music-loving city, and now it is a ballet-loving one as well, and its citizens point out that Sydney will be the first place in the world to have an Opera House without an opera company to go with it.

"Melbourne is a city of stewpans and stockbrokers," Francis Adams wrote in 1885. "They know how to make money, but not how to spend it." They have found out in the last eighty years.

[6]

"Australian professors," I was told, "are different." One of the most different is the head of the Department of Zoology at Monash University.

At his miniature country estate beside the Dandenong Ranges outside Melbourne, I admired a pair of Cape Barren geese who reared four goslings on a small lake that the professor has ringed with a great variety of native trees and shrubs and turned into a bird sanctuary. The geese are large, grey, handsome birds with red legs and yellow bills. Flights of these birds, to be numbered literally in millions, filled the skies above Tasmania, the Furneaux Islands in the Bass Strait and the southern coast of Victoria when the first settlers arrived. Now all those millions have dwindled to a tiny handful. Since 1957 the Animals and Birds Protection Board of Tasmania has carried out an annual aerial count of the survivors. The numbers shrank from 1,616 in 1957 to 943 in 1960, a figure verging on the critical point of no return.

But the Cape Barren goose has its champions, among them Professor Jock Marshall, a champion who, when his passions are aroused, lashes about him with a fine frenzy regardless of whose feelings he offends and whose toes he treads on. He has a lively understanding of the uses of publicity and is about as far removed as it is possible to be from the popular image of the cloistered don.

He is not, of course, the only biologist concerned in the survival of the Cape Barren goose (*Cereopsis novae hollandiae*), but his vigorous airing of its plight has done much to shake public apathy. The Tasmanian Government has forbidden the shooting of adult birds and the robbing of nests. The main breeding grounds lie in the Furneaux group of islands, and it has long been the practice of fishermen and others to take the eggs and young. When Lieutenant Matthew Flinders landed on these islands in 1798 he much enjoyed a dinner of roast Cape Barren goose, and people have been enjoying such meals ever since; there are now very many more people and, as we have seen, very many fewer geese.

Slowly, however, from the danger point to which the numbers sank in 1960, the geese have been building up again. By 1965, the Tasmanian count had crept up to 1,728, and in 1966 it reached 2,946. But Professor Marshall estimates that there may still be less than 5,000 left in the world.

The professor's blunt and forthright tongue became blunter and more forthright than ever when he commented upon the Tasmanian decision to declare an open season on the Cape Barren goose in April, 1964. It was true that the open season only lasted for three days and was confined to three islands and resulted, according to the Animals and Birds Protection Board, in the shooting of no more than 116 birds.

"What about the wounded ones that flew out to sea?" Professor Marshall demanded. "Even if only one hundred and fifty birds were massacred, that's one hundred and fifty too many of a species bloody nearly exterminated. Look at Tasmania's record—they've successfully wiped out their aborigines, their emus and their fur seals." Such salvos naturally wound the Tasmanians, who reply that the Cape Barren goose is no longer, in their view, in danger of extermination and that the only way to ensure its survival is to get public opinion on its side; and public opinion includes the opinion of people who enjoy shooting the bird.

"I've probably killed more animals," Professor Marshall said, "than most people in Australia, for experiments, and I don't give a damn about protecting the individual creature. It's the species I want to protect." Apart from the Cape Barren goose, he is not at all happy about kangaroos. "No one has the least idea whether the red 'roo is approaching the critical level or not. All I do know is that they formerly hopped about in tens of thousands on the grasslands between Sydney and Adelaide. Now they're almost extinct there and the pressure is on farther out, where the habitat is harsher anyway. We're too complacent. Ostriches never stick their faces in the sand; people do."

The situation has its ironies. In Western Australia some graziers have so overstocked their properties that the sheep have killed the grasses; that has let in spinifex. Sheep cannot thrive on spinifex, but certain kinds of kangaroo do. So kangaroos have multiplied and graziers have gone broke. "It's not really funny," said Jock Marshall, "but it makes you believe in God."

What this often angry and always different professor believes in appears to include the right of creatures to survive in a world dominated by man and the possibility that man himself can lead a civilized life. He returned from a twelve years' sojourn in Cambridge and in London, where he was pathologist at St. Bartholomew's Hospital, with one of the finest small private collections of antique furniture and glass I have ever seen, now installed in a renovated old farmhouse on the shores of his miniature lake. One wall of his dining room displays a Russell Drysdale

cartoon. With his own hand—he has only one and considers it ample—
he has bricked in an old well to make a cellar to store wine he has been
laying down for twenty years; he sips it on a sun-filled patio where his
children play and his wife paints. Fruit trees have been planted everywhere; birds come here to breed.

Yet another paradise on earth, here on the edge of the Dandenong
Ranges where the lyrebirds display. Professor Jock Marshall can put on a
display as well as they can and for the same reason—defense of territory, in this case not so much his own as that of certain species of the
animal kingdom. Some of his colleagues deplore what they consider to
be bluster, a liking for publicity and a tendency to overstate the case. He
is certainly no meek and ineffectual don. But in the modern world of
onward-marching technology, battles are seldom won by learned papers
delivered in seminars and scientific conferences. All poses can, on occasion, irritate; but beneath the professor's Wild Colonial Boy there lies a
sensitive, warmhearted and civilized man.

[7]

"Would you prefer penguins and muttonbirds on Phillip Island or an
ibis rookery in one of the last remaining stands of river red gum?" It was
like being offered roast grouse or pheasant if you like both. I chose the
red gums and ibises because they were farther and would enable me to
see more of the state of Victoria; they were about 150 miles to the north
and on the Murray, which divides Victoria from New South Wales.

So at an early hour Graham Pizzey, the naturalist and wildlife photographer who kindly offered me the choice, loaded cameras into his car
and we headed north towards the Barmah forest which stands in a loop
of the Murray. Every year, except in times of drought, this region floods
to a depth of six or seven feet and stays flooded for three months or so.
The red gums (*Eucalyptus cameldulensis*) grow to an enormous stature,
sheltering possums and other creatures in their trunks and branches, and
a great variety of birds. The river oozes through a series of lagoons
richly endowed with waterfowl. It is, in Graham Pizzey's view, a perfect
setting for a national park that would protect many animal species and
also these fine trees. At present they are being ruthlessly logged. With
the trees go the possums, phalangers and other creatures—the old story
of a dwindling habitat.

Two species of ibis, the straw-necked and the white, shared a rookery
harbouring at least a thousand birds. The smell was less attractive than

the birds wading in the shallows, strutting in dried-up swamps, and perching among the whitened branches of dead and dying trees. Here they formed, always it seemed in profile, friezes of beauty combined with queerness and distortion. The colour harmonies were marvellous: all greys and whites, silvers and ivories, with streaks and daubs of black. Their thin curved necks, pencil-thin spidery legs, and long, thin, upward-thrusting bills formed a strange avian calligraphy against a clear blue sky.

With us was an inspector from the department of Wildlife and Fisheries: a quiet, solid, unflurried man dedicated to his job, which is mainly to catch poachers. Winter is an open season for duck, but at other times they are protected. In his last pounce this inspector confiscated three thousand illegally slain birds. Anyone may camp in a state forest anywhere he pleases and take a gun; to save the birds therefore needs constant vigilance. "People will blot anything they see"—tern, coot, plover, duck, the stately black swans, anything. But now the duck shooters of Victoria, numbering about 35,000, have agreed to take out an annual license for a pound a year. This is the first time shooting has been licensed in Australia. The money is to go towards research and buying bits of swamp and marsh for breeding grounds, as the Americans have done so successfully. Conservationists see in this a hopeful portent.

The red gums were magnificent. The bole of one specimen soared as cleanly as a skyscraper for over ninety feet and then spread a wide canopy in which a kookaburra chuckled, self-satisfied as a cream-fed cat and aggressive as a street trader. The kookaburra's voice is generally considered ugly, but in it there is a discordantly melodious note like that of many modern symphonies, carrying a hint of pathos. Kookaburras eat other birds and so are manifestly unpopular and appear too insensitive to know why.

We saw no furred creatures. A year or two ago, the inspector said, the forest had been full of wallabies, but drought had forced them onto the properties of farmers who had shot them all. "One grazier wiped out six hundred in a fortnight and left the carcasses to rot." So no wonder the forest seemed empty and quiet. Would the status of a national park remedy matters? At least it would save the trees. Victoria has seventeen national parks, most of them negligible in size and some tiny; one covers eighty-four acres, another ninety-one. There are two fairish-sized ones, but even these are small by Australian standards. One is Wilson's Promontory, some 120 air miles east of Melbourne. The largest, Wyperfield, is in the dry northwestern portion of the state and consists mainly of mallee scrub. It is of particular importance because it offers a measure of protection to one of the world's most remarkable birds, the mallee fowl.

[8]

These birds, once very common, have been described by Dr. Harry Frith as "in great danger of extermination." This is mainly an outcome of the shrinking of their habitat, which lies in the low-rainfall areas of inland eastern Australia, as techniques of exploiting this type of country advance, and of grazing by sheep who destroy those acacia shrubs on which the birds feed. And in some years foxes have destroyed four out of every five eggs. Graham Pizzey said that of about eleven million acres of mallee country in Victoria and South Australia, some eight million have already been cleared. The process continues, and the birds go with the scrub.

Mallee fowl belong to a family unique to Australia and parts of Southeast Asia, the megapodes. Instead of building a nest and sitting on their eggs, they have evolved a method, so complex and efficient as to seem almost miraculous, of using heat derived partly from the sun and partly from the fermentation of decaying vegetable matter.

Many creatures, such as crocodiles and turtles, let the sun supply the heat needed to incubate their eggs. It seems the lazy animal's way out, but the life of a mallee fowl is far from lazy. The sun's heat fluctuates. Therefore the mallee fowl make compost heaps in which they lay their eggs and use heat combined from the two sources. And throughout the period when the eggs are being incubated, which lasts for six or seven months, they keep the temperature steady, night and day, at 92° F., generally to within a fraction of a degree. And this they do in regions where the temperature of the air may range between the freezing point and well over 100° F.

To keep the temperature steady in the mound in which the eggs are laid needs unremitting toil. This is mainly the task of the male. In autumn he scratches in the sandy soil a hole as much as three feet deep and fifteen or sixteen feet in diameter. Then, in the winter months when there is a certain amount of moisture, he gathers from the surrounding bush all the leaves, twigs and other vegetable matter he can find and scratches it into the mound. He may have to kick it, with his powerful legs, for fifty yards. In this mound he digs a hole about a foot deep; he fills it with a mixture of sand and leaves, covers it with loose soil, and smooths it over. This is the egg chamber. The female takes no part in these activities.

By now it is spring, and fermentation starts in the compost heap surrounding the egg chamber. As soon as the temperature approaches 92° F. the hen begins to lay her goose-sized eggs, which can weigh up to half a pound each. The birds themselves are much smaller than geese, not even as big as a domestic hen; they are speckled, their plumage black and white with some brown.

It is the male again who gets everything ready by uncovering the egg chamber, which may entail removing about a cubic yard of soil. The hen then lays her egg and leaves her spouse to cover it all up again. This process he must repeat every time she lays, which is roughly once a week until she has completed her clutch of, as a rule, between twenty and twenty-five eggs.

This is by no means all the male has to do. He has to keep the temperature steady. He uses his beak as a thermometer, thrusting it at frequent intervals into the mound and withdrawing it full of sand. Probably it is his tongue that does the actual measuring—a tongue that must be every bit as sensitive and accurate as the mercury in a man-made thermometer. In the light of what is happening underground he plans his action, sometimes varying this from day to day.

In spring the compost warms up quickly and, if the mallee fowl were to let nature take her course, the egg chamber would overheat. So every morning, before dawn, the male opens the mound, allows some of the heat to escape, and then refills the cavity with cool sand. Normally this holds the temperature to the right level; but weather, as we all know, is seldom normal. There may be a cold spell, in which case the bird scratches more sand and soil onto the mound so as to thicken the insulating layer and retain the heat. But in midsummer his problem is to keep *out* the heat of the sun. So once more, but for a different reason, in the very early morning he uncovers the egg chamber, lets the soil cool in the night-cooled air, and then scratches it all back.

In autumn he changes his routine. The compost has by then stopped working and the sun is losing its bite; stoking up is necessary. Instead of starting work before dawn, the birds—sometimes the hen will lend a claw—wait until the forenoon to uncover the mound to within a few inches of the eggs and so let the midday sun warm them. In the afternoon everything is covered up again to keep out the cold night air. So work continues throughout most of the year, and when the last egg is hatched, the time has come to start making another mound or to remake an old one. Winter or summer, there is no letup for mallee fowl. Their lives are dedicated to thermostatic engineering, and they know, by some mysterious means, exactly how to cope with every change that can occur in their environment—except those changes wrought by modern man and his tame animals. Ancient man, in the shape of aborigines, did not derange them.

Hatching brings another miracle. The chicks emerge about three feet underground in stifling darkness. They must scratch their way out within a few hours or they suffocate—and a lot do suffocate. Their instinct must instruct them to go up, not sideways. They dig upwards, Dr. Frith has found—it is he who has uncovered these astonishing behaviour patterns of the species *Leipoa ocellata,* meaning spotted egg-leaver—they dig upwards at the rate of a foot an hour. After a short rest on top they run swiftly down the mound and into the bush, completely self-propelled. If surprised, they will fly into a clump of leaves and hang upside down, like a bat. The environment is harsh, and probably most of them die of starvation.

A chick never sees its parents; it is never fed or helped in any way; it owes nothing to an adult—all the knowledge it needs in order to survive, and subsequently to pursue the complex mound technique, is inborn. In my student days it was the fashion to decry instinct and to teach that many aspects of behaviour formerly described as instinctive—that is to say, built into the mechanism of heredity—were actually taught, or resulted from imitating the parents' behaviour, and so were a product of environment. That could not possibly be said of the mallee fowl. Everything must come from the genes.

The chick can fly before it is a day old and for the first fortnight feeds on insects; then it eats the seeds of mallee-scrub acacias. So do sheep. Hence the decline of the bird. It was one of my great regrets that I never saw a mallee fowl in the wild, although I saw their mounds and plenty of brush turkeys, which are also megapodes. (There are three species in Australia, five in the world.) In Victoria a group of farmers has presented to the state an area of mallee scrub to be preserved as a sanctuary, and the Fauna Protection Panel in New South Wales has acquired two small reserves for similar purposes. These are salvage operations on a small scale but better than nothing. In the mallee fowl Australia has something that really is unique.

[9]

As we drove south through rolling, closely settled country, all pad-docked, all brown, with many windmills and few trees save in clumps round homesteads, Graham Pizzey brought me up to date on the rabbit situation. Myxomatosis, successfully introduced in 1950, gave the coun-try a respite for some ten years. That respite is over. The disease, though now endemic and still a factor in control, has lost much of its virulence. Too many rabbits have been bred with an immunity inherited from parents who survived the infection. The emphasis now lies on poisoning with compound 1080, which is sodium fluoro-acetate.

It was in Victoria, near Geelong, that rabbits first took hold, after a pastoralist, Thomas Austin, released some in 1859 to provide sport and poor men's dinners. They spread like wildfire, fanning out at the rate of about seventy miles a year until they had colonized most of Australia. (They covered 1,100 miles from Fowlers Bay in South Australia to Geraldton on the northwestern shore in sixteen years.) So gargantuan were their collective appetites that they reduced the sheep population of western New South Wales by half. One rabbit equals seven to ten sheep in grass consumption, and no one will ever know how many billions of rabbits were rampant in Australia by the turn of the century. Graziers fenced, shot, trapped and poisoned in vain. As a by-product there devel-oped a trade in skins and meat that set a pattern now bedevilling at-tempts to stamp the rabbit out once and for all.

Experts believe that this could be done and that it is being done in New Zealand, which has adopted a "killer policy" and outlawed com-pletely the sale of rabbit skins or meat. Australia has a tribe of rabbit catchers and marketers whose interests naturally are to keep the species alive. Before myxomatosis in some years over 100 million rabbits went for export, and within five years of the outbreak in 1950 some 45 million were still being annually "harvested" for skins and carcasses. Trapping may actually promote the procreation of the rabbit by culling the population, taking apparently more males than females, and check-ing their urge to overcrowd their habitat. Most experts would like to see the rabbit "decommercialized," following New Zealand's successful ex-ample. This goes against the Australian grain. The trapper is a figure of tradition. Trapping is also a useful way to pick up a living—not a bad one, either—by square pegs who fail to fit into round holes. So "de-commercialization" has little support, and rugged individualism is the

Australian News and Information Bureau

The homestead, workshops and station buildings of Victoria River.

Downs alongside the Wickham River in Northern Territory.

Australian News and Information Bureau

Rock-fishermen at Sydney Heads, entrance to Sydney Harbour, New South Wales, perch calmly at the water's edge as foam swirls around their feet.

Flynn's Beach, New South Wales, where Port Macquarie holds its surf carnivals.

Australian News and Information Bureau

A pair of Mallee fowl at work on their mounds.

The Kookaburra, or Laughing Jackass, a member of the Kingfisher family.

Australian News and Information Bureau

Australian News and Information Bureau

The lyrebird about to display on one of its mounds.

Mutton birds awaiting a dawn take-off on a beach of the Great Barrier Reef.

Australian News and Information Bureau

Douglas Baglin Pty. Ltd.

A 'roo shooter setting out in his truck with rifle and spotlight.

Kangaroo with a joey in the pouch.

Australian News and Information Bureau

An Aborigine in the Rawlinson Ranges, Western Australia, carrying home a kangaroo after a food hunting expedition.

Australian News and Information Bureau

Graham Pizzey

The sugar glider.

A platypus in a glass-sided tank at the Healesville Sanctuary, Victoria.

Australian News and Information Bureau

rabbit's best friend. Experts reckon that perhaps two farmers out of three fail to carry out proper control measures on their properties.

These consist of putting down bait, as a rule diced carrots, in shallow furrows, providing two or three "free feeds" to tempt the rabbits, and then mixing in the poison. If properly done, this will bring about a 90 per cent kill or even better. Nowadays the bigger landowners spread the bait by air. Rabbit poisoning has become a regular part of good farming practice, like applying fertilizer or spraying against weeds. But the authorities have no legal power either to compel a landowner to poison his rabbits or to carry out the work themselves as they do in New Zealand. They can only exhort and advise, and so the slack graziers penalize the efficient. Therefore there are still rabbits—a lot in places—and the danger of their building up again to menacing proportions cannot be discounted. In any case they are robbing the sheep and eating out the better grasses, allowing poorer ones and weeds to come in, and preventing the regeneration of shrubs and trees.

New methods of control may, of course, be hit upon, as myxomatosis was hit upon, first by the Brazilian Dr. H. B. Aragão—the virus came from South America—and then by Sir Charles Martin, who experimented with it at Cambridge, and finally by Dame Jean Macnamara, who accomplished the difficult task of transplanting it to Melbourne. Several attempts to spread it among wild rabbits failed until a C.S.I.R.O. team under Francis Ratcliffe, then head of the Wildlife Section, achieved success on the upper Murray; and the virus, carried from host to host by mosquitoes, sped across the continent.

In 1889 the government of New South Wales offered a prize equal to $50,000 for an effective method of rabbit control. They got fourteen hundred entries and a suggestion from Louis Pasteur that chicken cholera might answer. Fearing to introduce one pest to combat another, after some discussion that suggestion was dropped. Later tests showed that chicken cholera does not kill rabbits, so Pasteur would not have won the prize. No one did. The spread of myxomatosis has been described as a "biological miracle." A second miracle seems unlikely.

[10]

On our way back to Melbourne we passed through Bendigo, a notable exception to the rule that most mining towns, especially those whose day is done, are drab, depressing, down-at-heel places. I remember it mainly for white paint, a wide main street, green lawns with trees and flower beds, substantial, ornate Victorian buildings of the Mechanics' Institute type, and several splendid specimens of the square, balcony-enveloped, colonnaded country-town hotel. (I hope Robin Boyd was exaggerating when he described such hostelries as "a two-storey iron veranda wrapped around reluctance, impatience and primitive plumbing.")

Bendigo, called after an English boxer, has managed to avoid the fate of so many places that, launched by the gold rush of 1851, were subsequently left like stranded whales by the ebbing of the golden tide. Now it is a market town serving a prosperous farming area, with a few smallish industries and a substantial population of the retired well-to-do. It has a cared-for look suggesting solid citizens and civic pride and a number of late-Victorian houses built by successful speculators and company directors. Nevertheless it is a ghost town by the standards of its previous glory. In the early 1860's it had thirty Methodist chapels and blossomed a few years later into a town of crowded cafés, German bands, illuminated hotels and a stock exchange where speculators from Melbourne made overnight fortunes. Red carpets were spread and champagne served underground to visiting notables. More than one thousand companies owned mines with names like Extended Rustlers, Golden Square, Job's Gully and The Unfortunate Bolle, and Bendigo became the largest mining town in the country.

Although all these gold booms collapsed, they flooded Australia with immigrants in whom the instinct of the fortune seeker was stronger than the spirit of safety first. They put an end to the transportation system. When a labour shortage led to the arrival of Chinese, they sparked off the White Australia policy. And they reinforced the egalitarian tradition. "Nothing, indeed," wrote an English visitor, "can have a more levelling effect on society than the power of digging for gold." Lord and larrikin are equalized by mud, flies, shovels, blisters and the strike-it-rich fever in the blood. So the digger became a symbol of the sturdy, independent Australian who calls no man sir and treads his own road.

South of Bendigo we stopped to buy some sweets at a little village called Castlemaine, the birthplace of the bushranger Jack Donahoe, who was the Wild Colonial Boy of the famous ballad. Not just *any* sweets: Castlemaine rock, made in a tub in the kitchen of an old iron-roofed cottage to a formula handed down through three generations. The family who still make the rock have firmly rejected take-over bids from several confectionary tycoons. So the legend lives on.

[11]

On the far tip of Phillip Island a small sanctuary has been set aside for the fairy penguin (*Eudyptula minor*), one of the world's smallest penguins and the only one of the tribe to breed in Australia. They nest in burrows in the dunes. As we plodded down to the beach in the dark, well before dawn, we heard high-pitched, plaintive wails coming from the murk, mournful and eerie as the lonely cry of a distant, unseen locomotive in the black immensity of some Midwestern plain. These were the cries of penguins who were gathering in small parties, seldom of more than half a dozen birds, to proceed from their burrows to the foreshore and thence out to sea for the day's fishing. They would not be back until nightfall, when they would regurgitate fish and plankton into the mouths of fat, fluffy chicks waiting hungrily underground.

Penguin Parade, as this routine is called, has become a tourist attraction. As we approached the shore, floodlights sprang to life to illuminate wet sand, creamy lapping wavelets and wiry-stemmed grasses on the dunes and turn everything as starkly black and white as the penguins' plumage. The birds' home-coming at dusk is, understandably, more popular with the public than their dawn take-off; long ranks of coaches then fill the parks, and at weekends viewers in thousands line the ropes which check their surge onto the beach in a human tide that would certainly obliterate the penguins.

At three in the morning the coach park was empty, but Bert West, ringmaster of the parade, had generously turned out to switch on the floodlights. In their beams we watched the little parties gather, thrusting forward and then retracting their heads as if engaged in weighty discussion. When the parties had made up their numbers they waddled purposefully across the sand, their forward stance and short flappers giving them the look of eager busybodies in court dress. Their caricature of the more pompous members of the human race is irresistible. All seemed, like the White Rabbit, to be in a hurry. "They're more dignified," said Bert West, "when they return at night"—a full crop slows their pace. Now they were hungry themselves and anxious to satisfy their even hungrier chicks. When I knelt down to touch their richly shining backs they were quite unperturbed, although the slightest push, you felt, would knock them over. They are less than a foot high.

After a while we turned our attention to the muttonbirds, who were issuing from their burrows and proceeding, not towards the sea, but to the crests of low-lying dunes. Through tussocks in the loose sand we stumbled along pathlets that seemed alive with birds lurching rather than scurrying uphill and paying no attention whatever to us. A half-moon, intermittently obscured by ragged cloud, stood over a sea that could be smelled and heard but seen only as an immense dark presence now and then flecked with silver as moonlight glanced off the curl of a roller. By now the black pulp of night was thinning and you could sense rather than see the approach of dawn that was blunting the prickles of the stars.

We strained our eyes to apprehend the outlines of the sooty, waddling creatures that were springing like an immense brood of hobgoblins from the earth. "Probably there are one million nesting on this stretch of Phillip Island alone," Graham Pizzey said. "And this is just an outpost, not their main ground." Each of the birds had left down its burrow a single chick. Only one—no muttonbird lays more than one egg in a season. If this is lost, there is no remedy, for by the time she has laid it, the male's gonads have withered.

The wing span of these birds, which look about the size of a small gull, is so enormous in relation to their size that when afoot they are clumsy, ungainly and have little control. They are weighted down at the bows with breasts that almost touch the ground and advance in little rushes like toddlers learning to walk or nocturnal creatures blundering about in the daylight. They did not in the least mind the beams of our torches and let us touch them with our fingers. They have grey and black plumage with a lovely sheen and a grey collar. On they went, one after the other, all moving uphill, bird after bird. We reckoned they were going by at the rate of two or three every ten seconds, and this went on for about two hours. For miles the dunes were honeycombed with little paths. How many were afoot as dawn bleached the sky? The mind boggled.

As each bird reached the summit of the dunes a miracle occurred. It spread its wings, launched itself upon the air and immediately became an engine of grace, beauty and control. The wings of petrels, specialized for flights over thousands of miles, have attained perfection. The bird leans upon the air, soars upward without the least apparent effort, and loses its identity in a sky you suddenly perceive to be aboil with black shapes that wheel and dip and swoop and bend and weave above the ocean in a magical pattern of constant motion. You marvel that a bird so clumsy on the ground can move with such masterly precision overhead. No wing brushes another. Each takes a few turns and away it swoops out to sea. As the sky reddened over a pencil-limned horizon, the flights thickened; away went the birds in their hundreds of thousands, black fluttering leaves against a glow of apricot, and against far rugged promontories, winging out to sea. At night they would return to feed their chicks. It is a sight that I am thankful to have seen.

These birds are short-tailed shearwaters, *Puffinus tenuirostris,* petrels of the southern seas. Sailors used to call them yowlers because at certain times they howl as banshees are said to, with a lost, demonic, infernal note. Their popular name arose from their taste; the foremost mutton-bird authority, Dr. Dominic Serventy, has traced its first recorded use to a print in the British Museum annotated between 1788 and 1794 by a Surgeon-General John White. The name is applied to other Australasian petrels; this is the Tasmania muttonbird.

Its main breeding grounds are in the Furneaux group of islands in the Bass Strait, especially on and around Flinders Island. There it is exploited by the descendants of a community of tough mariners, whalers and sealers, who were attracted by accounts of the Bass Strait islands, published in 1802 by Matthew Flinders. They settled there and interbred with the aborigines. These islanders rob the burrows, wring the necks of the young birds, squeeze out of them a valuable oil used to make suntan lotions, pluck them, and salt the flesh for export to the mainland, New Zealand and the United States. For years this "industry" (if that is the right word) was uncontrolled, and so many chicks were killed that fears arose for the survival of the muttonbird. Bert West told me that in his youth "hookers" made a good living by fishing eggs from their tunnels and selling them in Melbourne, where confectioners liked them, especially for Christmas cakes.

The taking of eggs is now illicit, and all forms of mutton-birding are outlawed on the mainland. In the Furneaux Group the season is limited to five weeks from the end of March to early May. Then mutton-birders with their families invade the islands in small boats, camp out and set to work—men, women and children—to kill and process every chick they can lay hands on. They make good money, but the trade is in decline. Ten years ago they were taking between half and three-quarters of a million chicks, last year only about 150,000. The muttonbirds can stand up, experts believe, without danger to this degree of "harvesting," but they face other and more serious threats. One is the islanders' habit of firing the grass to get rid of snakes and to expose the burrows. This also exposes the soil, which winter gales remove, leaving rocky terrain unsuitable or burrows. Some islands have already been deserted by the birds for this reason. Even more serious is encroachment by sheep and cattle. Population grows, farming spreads, muttonbirds depart—the old story.

They depart in any case during the first week in May on an astonishing migration, lasting just under five months, that may take them 20,000 miles. They fly first towards New Zealand and then swing north along the Pacific's western margins to the Bering Sea that touches Alaska and Kamchatka—a flight that spans the globe almost from the Antartic to the Arctic Circle. They then proceed down the eastern side of the Pacific, along the coast of North America, until they veer southwest and head not merely for the land of their birth but for the very place of their birth, the selfsame burrow. Observations that began in 1947 under Dr. Serventy's direction have demonstrated that a pair of birds will generally, although not invariably, return year after year to the same nest.

Those that survive such gruelling migrations are long-lived. Muttonbirds do not begin to breed until they are six or seven. Once the fledglings take flight, they do not touch land again until they are three or four years old. While mature adults go ashore to nest, they stay out at sea. Shearwaters need dry land only as a hatchery.

What is most astonishing is the precision of their routine. From their circumnavigation of the Pacific Ocean they punctually return during the last week in September. October they spend putting the burrows to rights. Early in November they mate and fly out to sea, deserting the burrow while the single egg—a very large one—matures within the female. Then on November 20 or 21—they allow themselves two days' margin—they return to lay. Egg-laying reaches its peak on November 25 and 26 and ends on December 1 or 2.

Year after year they keep to this routine. Variations in climate, in temperature, in food supplies do not appear to change the timetable by a single day. Even latitude scarcely affects it. The schedule is the same today as it was over a century ago when the first records were made. And when you focus on individual birds, the regularity is even more striking. Dr. Serventy and his team have banded thousands of birds. Number 12,378 laid on November 24 for four years running, Number 12,523 on the same day for three consecutive seasons.

How can such constancy be explained? Only by an "astronomical factor," which scientists believe to be the hours of daylight. By some mechanism still obscure, when the hours of daylight reach a certain length—possibly to be measured in fractions of a minute—within the bird some change takes place that sets its breeding apparatus in motion, as a time switch will turn on a light. This must happen long before the birds reach their breeding grounds. One day, no doubt, the mechanism will be revealed, together with the mechanism that controls migration. Here again an astronomical factor is thought to lie at the heart of the enigma. That birds navigate by the stars is now an established fact; just how they do so, still a mystery.

Losses during these migrations must be prodigious. The youngsters suffer most, and mostly on the last lap of the journey when they meet strong southeast trades. So is the ancient principle of the survival of the fittest maintained. In the end, of course, the sea that fed them must take back them all, old and young, weak and strong alike. "For every bird there is this last migration," the Australian poet, A. D. Hope, has written in *The Death of the Birds:*

> She feels it close now, the appointed season:
> The invisible thread is broken as she flies:
> Suddenly, without warning, without reason,
> The guiding spark of instinct winks and dies.
>
> Try as she will, the trackless world delivers
> No way, the wilderness of light no sign,
> The immense and complex map of hills and rivers
> Mocks her small wisdom with its vast design.
>
> And darkness rises from the eastern valley,
> And the winds buffet her with their hungry breath,
> And the great earth, with neither grief nor malice,
> Receives the tiny burden of her death.

TEN ⁓⁓⁓⁓

Tasmania

In Hobart the smell and sparkle of the sea lie all about you. A cross between an English provincial town and a modern seaport, the Tasmanian capital sprawls along the Derwent River's bays, inlets, promontories and cliffs, and at its back arise the heights of Mt. Wellington. The situation is Aegean in splendour, but the gods of Olympus have not migrated to Mt. Wellington. Most of Hobart is a bungaloid sprawl with Featurism rampant; but the surviving Victorian houses have a trim, turrety charm, enhanced by verandas with their accompanying ironwork frills and their neat, cared-for gardens.

Tasmanians are said to be more English than other Australians, whatever that means. It could mean that they are slower, more conventional, their arteries hardened by tradition; or that they live more sensibly and calmly, with less of the time-and-motion rat-racing taken over, people think, from the United States. They have leisure, perhaps, to stand and stare, or at any rate to go fishing. In appearance, I am afraid, it means a certain sloppiness, or at the best an absence of chic.

Although Hobart has lately grown in population, it is not growing as fast as other Australian capitals, and the whole island, which is about two-thirds the size of Ireland, has less than 400,000 souls. Migrants are coming in a trickle, not a flood. The problem is to keep the island's own young. Like nearly all small countries overshadowed by big ones, Tasmania suffers from the gravitational pull of the larger body. Away go the brighter, more ambitious young to Sydney or Melbourne, just like the New Zealanders, or as Canadians are sucked away by the United States and the Irish by Britain.

A few industries have come. Launceston has the largest wool-spinning mills in the Southern Hemisphere; Hobart, an up-to-date silk mill started by two dynamic Italian Alcorso brothers, which prints Chinese

184

fabrics and exports them all over the world, and a modern factory to make confectionery. More or less on the spot where Lieutenant John Bowen, R.N., aged eighteen, landed in 1803 with forty-nine Englishmen, mostly convicts, to found the first settlement in Van Diemen's Land, stands a plant for the electrolytic treatment of zinc.

In the year following Bowen's landing came Lieutenant-Colonel David Collins of the Royal Marines with a batch of convicts sent by Governor King in Sydney, who was seeking a place a long way off to dump the more recalcitrant of his charges. So outcasts from an ancient civilization came to what was then as island of the blessed. The hills were clothed in forest, the rivers full of fish; kangaroos and wallabies loped about the glades, if not unmolested, at least not greatly troubled by the aborigines, who were never numerous. These black men were living in a Stone Age culture, ignorant of the use of iron or other metals; nor did they cover their bodies, other than to decorate them with shells and flowers and possibly the bones of deceased relatives, and they had no permanent dwellings.

These Tasmanians were of a different race from the mainland aborigines, probably a Negrito people who came down from the north either before Tasmania was separated from the mainland at least 20,000 years ago or, more probably, by a sea route which must have taken them over 2,500 miles in primitive bark canoes. Their heads wore wool like Negroes instead of silky hair like most of the mainland blacks. The first white men they saw, in 1772, were French, under the explorer Marich du Fresne; there was a quarrel, and one black was killed. Then came Bligh in the famous *Bounty* with happier results; white and black made amicable contact on the shores of Adventure Bay on Bruny Island, where Bligh's botanist David Nelson planted fruit trees, including the first apples. But when Lieutenant Bowen landed with his convicts there was another affray, and within seventy-three years the last aboriginal Tasmanian was dead.

[2]

Nowadays Australians are understandably ashamed of this episode. What went wrong, initially, was a famine that almost destroyed the Hobart settlement within two years of its foundation. Ships failed to bring provisions, and the local fauna did not suffice. About the time the garrison was celebrating the victory of Trafalgar, more than ten months after it had occurred, the Reverend Bobby Knopwood, the chaplain, recorded in his diary: "Not an ounce of meal, wheat or anything to be served to the military or prisoners—none in the store for anyone." He records the following prices: meal, 8/6* a pound; tobacco "not fit to be made use of" 2/6* an inch; sugar, 5/-* a pound; biscuits 4/-,* and tea 20/-.* "The colony very greatly distressed for everything, and everybody crying out of want of bread. Amidst all this scarcity we have scarcely any vegetables—the potatoes are all in the ground." Even the chaplain's tame pigeons were dying. On Sunday he skipped matins to go fishing and "had very bad success." Governor Collins "complained very much for the loss of kangaroo, none being in the store. It is generally believed that the prisoners, who are in the bush, had taken many of the gentlemen's dogs. This morn, a party of five went into the bush."

The prisoners were in the bush hunting kangaroos, and the governor neither could nor would stop them. In the bush they encountered the aborigines. They were not imbued with the principles of the London Missionary Society of the liberal gentry of Exeter Hall. A black was a savage, and although he was not considered edible, the prisoners could, and did, put him out of business as a competitor for victuals. Moreover, they soon slew most of the macropods, and the aborigines were driven from their hunting grounds into forests to which they were not acclimatized. Probably many did of pneumonia, and others may have caught tuberculosis from the convicts, who abducted aboriginal women. It was not a pretty picture; but semi-starving jailbirds who had survived the rigours of convict ships and the tortures of the triangle were not pretty men. Nor were the aborigines themselves living in a state of innocence. They used their weapons on each other as well as on the animals, and sometimes on white intruders who were not always the aggressors. Their numbers have been put at between two and seven thousand, but this is merely a guess.

In loosing the prisoners into the bush, Governor Collins unleashed a devil. When the time came to round them up, many retreated deeper into a country that might have been created to conceal fugitives. These men were natural predators, and the free settlers who took up land along the Derwent and the Huon valleys became their natural prey. So came into existence the bushrangers, who for the best part of a century plagued the law-abiding citizens and defied enforcers of the law. The aborigines, too, took to spearing white shepherds and clubbing farmers

* Rough equivalents in order: $1, 25 cents, 50 cents, 40 cents, and $2.

to death. An aboriginal convict from New South Wales known as Mosquito became the self-appointed chieftain of a local tribe and led its men in numerous and bloody raids on stockmen's huts and homesteads before he was captured.

The only way to end this sporadic war, the authorities decided, was to settle the surviving blacks in some spot where they could be controlled, protected, and taught useful arts. A drive in which three thousand men took part, organized in 1830 by Governor George Arthur, aimed at corralling them in a peninsula where they could be rounded up. After a costly seven-week campaign the haul consisted of one woman with her child caught asleep under a log. Governor Arthur resigned his problem to a remarkable character called George Robinson, who believed that he could achieve by persuasion what the military had failed to do by force.

Robinson was an evangelist bricklayer bent on saving souls along the docks of Hobart Town and moved by compassion for the aborigines. He offered to make his way inland and talk them into submission. In 1831 he set out on foot with a few native companions, a small supply of oatmeal and no firearms, to penetrate the rugged and then quite unknown western ranges. To everyone's astonishment he not only reappeared intact but brought with him fifty-four aborigines. These intrepid journeys he repeated three times and brought back with him a total of 187 blacks. In 1835, with Robinson in charge, they went to Flinders Island to be converted, educated and turned into virtuous citizens.

Despite all Robinson's humane care the settlement—eventually sited, not without a touch of irony, at Civilisation Point—did not thrive. In death, however, some of the aborigines performed a useful service, if it is true that, as legend has it, a local farmer dug up their bones and shipped them in his wool bales to London, where they sold profitably to hospitals in need of skeletons. The sixteen remnants of the living were moved back to Bruny Island where they thrived even less, and the last known pure-blooded member of the race, a woman called Truganini, died in 1876.

[3]

With the convicts in their yellow jackets came their keepers in red ones. In these colonial outposts the officers did their best to keep up the traditions of their age and class. That is to say, they lived in style with numerous servants, quite often drank themselves under the table, enjoyed their sport with dogs and horses, believed in loyalty, discipline and the divine right of the upper class to rule the lower, suffered from gout and apoplexy, and exhibited that combination of callousness towards extremes of human suffering and sensitive appreciation of beauty which makes men of the eighteenth century a perpetual and insoluble enigma to men of the twentieth.

How it was that a gentleman in elegant cravat and brocaded waistcoat, fresh from his Sheraton table with its cut glass, graceful silver, good wine and polite manners reflecting those of an English manor, could have watched, unmoved, a man's flesh flayed to shreds amid the blood and screams appropriate to the torture chamber is as hard for us to understand as, perhaps, it would have been hard for a patron of Regency arts to understand how a civilized man of our own century could recoil from the hanging of a depraved sex murderer, yet live unmoved amid the hideous products of mass production unrelieved by a glimmer of good taste. Is there some mysterious link between abhorrence of cruelty and aesthetic blindness and conversely between indifference to pain and squalor and the fastidious enjoyment of beauty?

At Port Arthur on the Tasman Peninsula, amid the well-preserved ruins of Australia's largest penal settlement, stand the heavy stone walls of the old penitentiary, roofless and gutted by fire, whose level rows of windows so evidently made for bars seem like the sockets of a monster staring sightlessly towards the sea. It was four stories high, devoid of all grace or decoration, a comb of grim, bare cells that have caged more suffering than most walls; over thirty thousand convicts passed through Port Arthur between its foundation in 1830 and its closure in 1878. Despite the beauties of a site excellently kept with green lawns, flowers, shrubs and some magnificent trees, overlooking a sparkling and indented harbour, the shadows of that blackened ruin darken the spirit. Here a discipline as inflexible as it was cruel is expressed in stone cut and laid by the victims of the system, like men who dig their own graves.

Nearby stands a fountain for the prisoners to drink from as they passed. With fluted walls and on a graceful pedestal, it is as light, harmonious and elegant a structure as the penitentiary walls are harsh and heavy. Yet it took spontaneous shape, without fuss or planning, from the mind, eye and hand of some anonymous prisoner who perhaps had followed a mason's trade in some unknown English village and recalled an ornament he had once seen in a nobleman's garden.

"If we built a drinking fountain nowadays," said my companion, "we'd knock it up from old corrugated iron." But the centrally heated bed-sits of our model penitentiary might be equipped with bedside lights and washbasins. Apparently you cannot have it both ways.

At one time even to mention convicts was considered tactless; Australians wanted to forget this aspect of their past. That is so no longer. To have had a transported ancestor has become more often a matter for pride than for shame. With this change of attitude has come rehabilitation of the convicts themselves. Some historians believe the whole story to have been overdramatized. Many of the transported men and women were guilty—if they were guilty at all—of offenses so trivial that today they would not even be put on probation; others were perhaps condemned for meritorious acts like refusing to truckle to a bullying squire. Nor was their treatment, according to this school of thought, normally half so brutal and degrading as books like *For the Term of His Natural Like* made out. Black spots and patches there were, certainly, such as the settlement for recalcitrants at Macquarie Harbour, where men in chains toiled from dawn to dark hauling heavy logs, often waist-deep in water, lashed if they faltered and flogged to the brink of extinction for the least offense. On Norfolk Island a warder recorded in his journal that a convict called Joe Mansbury received two thousand lashes in three years and reached a point where "his collarbones were quite exposed, looking very much like two polished ivory horns, and only with difficulty could we find another place to flog him."

But the majority were not chained or flogged. Assigned to farmers, tradesmen and other masters, most of whom were reasonably kind, they were employed on useful tasks and often better fed than they had ever been before. All who behaved themselves received in time tickets of leave and could go where they pleased in the Australian Colonies, and some got a free pardon. A few made comfortable fortunes, others at least gained a fair living. So for most, even if they arrived in some discomfort, Australia became a land of opportunity just as it did for those who paid their own fares.

This contention is supported by a study made by George Rude of 325 farm workers and rural craftsmen, mostly from Wiltshire, Hampshire and Gloucestershire, transported in 1831 to Van Diemen's Land for assaults upon threshing machines and for burning ricks in protest against the introduction of the former, which they feared would steal their livelihood. A few, according to Governor Arthur, "died almost immediately from disease induced apparently by despair," but the majority behaved in an exemplary fashion and received free pardons within six years.

By 1842 between twenty-five and thirty owned leases of shops, pubs, farms, or houses; others thrived as butchers, bakers, distillers, bricklayers, shoemakers, and in various other trades. The history of Robert Blake, a Wiltshire shoemaker, may be typical of the more successful. Three years after transportation he married and became in due course the father of nine; within four years he received a free pardon; thirty years after his arrival, then aged fifty-six, he owned a substantial house and farm and seven other houses in the town of Bothwell, and his sons founded a brewery. By no means all these rustic rick-burners were, of course, so fortunate; but none, so far as can be traced, was cruelly treated, and none, when free to do so, returned to his native land.

[4]

In Hobart's art gallery hang two or three rather charming portraits drawn by one of the most interesting convicts ever to reach Van Diemen's Land. This was Thomas Wainewright, a crony of Charles Lamb's, a friend of such men as John Clare, Tom Hood and Charles Macready, and a pupil of Fuseli's. His essays and critiques were regularly published, under such fanciful noms de plume as Janus Weathercock and Egomet Bonmot, in London's literary journals, and his paintings had been hung in the Royal Academy and praised by William Blake. In the Prince Regent's London he was well known as a dandy, wit and generous host, described by Lamb as the "light and warm-as-light hearted Janus." In death he held the interest of such men as Dickens, Lord Lytton and Oscar Wilde. His posthumous fame rests, however, not upon his mannered writings, or even on his elegant portraits, but on a tradition that he poisoned several members of his family to get possession of their money.

He reached Van Diemen's Land in 1837, in a convict ship, transported for life for forging a signature on a power of attorney, a capital crime for which he was not tried until thirteen years after its committal. No charge of poisoning was ever brought against him. Yet it has been universally credited. The most recent of his biographers, Robert Crossland, in *Wainewright in Australia*, riddles the theory with doubt and demonstrates that practically everything subsequently written about Wainewright's behaviour during the ten years he spent in Hobart was untrue.

The legend was of a monster of depravity who tried unsuccessfully to poison several of his companions in Van Diemen's Land, of an opium eater, leacher and sensual beast with "a snake-like expression . . . and the passions of a satyr," according to an interview given to the correspondent of a Melbourne newspaper by the ex-prison doctor twenty years after Wainewright's death. The only living creature, said this Dr. Crooke, for whom the evil poisoner had felt a spark of tenderness was a cat.

The reality was of a meek, inoffensive little man who from the first appears to have suffered from a sickness that killed him within ten years and that his biographer thinks may have been disseminated sclerosis. He must have started in a road gang wearing chains and the yellow dress, with the word "Felon" stamped upon it in several places, and toiling, in the words of the official regulations, at "the heaviest and most degrading labour that can be found in the settlement." Two years later he was transferred to the Colonial Hospital as "an invalid wardsman without pay." Thus he was already showing symptoms of his ailment. Had he been a fit man, he would have received a few pennies a day—semi-invalids got nothing, and their use was therefore an economy.

In the pre-Lister age when the surgeon's filthy knife, plied without anesthetics, almost invariably carried sepsis from one patient to another, the duties of a wardsman must have been nauseating in the extreme. The ailing, sensitive artist carried them out in such a manner as to earn the praise of every doctor and official with whom he came in contact, including that Dr. Crooke, who in 1866 was to speak to a newspaperman (if correctly reported) of Wainewright's "malignancy of character" and "lewdness." In 1844, writing in support of Wainewright's petition for a ticket of leave, Dr. Crooke was of a different opinion. "The Petitioner T.G. Wainewright has been under my notice in this establishment for a period exceeding twelve months. I feel happy to have it in my power to testify as to his unexceptionable good conduct during that time—in addition to an unvarying propriety of demeanour he has rendered me on many occasions important service . . ." The petition failed but succeeded eighteen months later. Within two years the petitioner was dead.

The drawings of the notables of Hobart and their wives and children on which Wainewright's reputation rests exhibit a delicacy, refinement and purity that must astonish the beholder who recalls the grisly circumstances in which they were executed. The portraits of women and girls with corkscrew ringlets, long sloping necks, Grecian features and somewhat bovine expressions have about them more than a touch of the chocolate box, but his male portraits I thought much stronger and more penetrating, fluently executed with considerable technical skill. He must have possessed to a singular degree the capacity to live at once in two different worlds. Perhaps that indirectly supports the belief that he really was a poisoner.

[5]

A character a great deal more typical of the day and age than the sad little convict-painter was the bloodthirsty Mike Howe of Yorkshire. Transported for highway robbery, he even robbed his fellow prisoners of their rations on the voyage to Van Diemen's Land; once in the bush he enforced discipline among his gang, it was said, by cutting off the ears of anyone who answered back. He wrote illiterate screeds to the governor in Hobart, signing himself "Governor of the Ranges," and kept a diary, written in the blood of kangaroos, full of fantasies of power and doom and strangely akin to the screeds "posted" in trees by Mau Mau leaders in Africa who, like Howe, challenged authority, dreamed of glory, and were hunted down in forests by the forces of the law.

A more attractive character was Matthew Brady, a Manchester Irishman whose crime was to forge his master's signature on a check, and who became one of the few convicts bold enough to escape, by a daring feat of seamanship, from Macquarie Harbour on Tasmania's wild west coast. He and his gang raided farms and homesteads all over the island and created yet another legend: that of the gentleman-ruffian, the colonial Robin Hood, brave and saucy, loyal to his mates and courteous to his victims. Once he affixed in prominent positions notices offering twenty-five gallons of rum for the capture of Sir George Arthur. "He did much injury, but also showed much forebearance," was the judgment of a local obituary writer, "and on no occasion was feminine delicacy outraged or insulted."

Now the scenes of his exploits are tourist attractions. Near Launceston tourists are taken to a spot called Brady's Lookout where the bandits are said to have camped before their last raid, when their leader entertained the ladies of the pillaged household with a song of his own composition to which he played his own accompaniment. But shooting followed; Brady was wounded in the leg and a few days later taken by John Batman, the future co-founder of Melbourne. The rank and fashion of Hobart called on him in his cell and sent him cakes, wine and jellies. He received the death sentence, in the words of a reporter, "with unshaken fortitude, bowing easily and respectfully to the judge."

[6]

One of the most pleasing aspects of Tasmania is the prevalence of rivers. The Huon, south of Hobart—it has a tributary called the Snug—is famous for hops and apples, for the soil's generosity and for the sound husbandry of its owners, some of whom belong to families that have farmed the same land for a century.

Hitherto the hops have been harvested by itinerant workers who have returned year after year to the same farms, like the hop pickers of Kent. But now they are beginning to give way to machines. I was shown one such monster but lately arrived from England that, together with a twin, will do the work of about twenty-five families who formerly enjoyed a well-paid, hard-working holiday in fresh air and sunshine. So one more traditional country practice, like harvest and haysel, fades away. The same with apples. Women used to sort, grade and pack them by hand —pleasant work amid the sweet smell of apples, with plenty of companionship and a sense of bustle. Now a machine pops each apple into a cell in a waxed carton—boxes are obsolete—and no human hand touches it until a housewife bears it off from the supermarket 12,000 miles away. "Everything today is size and colour," I was told. "People don't seem to mind about flavour any more. But if there's a single little blemish on the skin, then you're in real trouble."

To achieve unblemished apples these growers have to spray their orchards about sixteen times a season, using turbojets that spurt the liquid into the trees at a pressure equivalent to a sixty-mile-an-hour gale. By now these valleys must be well saturated with chemicals that leave persistent residues. What of the effects on soil bacteria and animals, on birds, bees and butterflies? Little scientific work on this has been done as yet in Australia. The next step will be to mechanize yet one more operation—thinning. A spray withers on their twigs the less desirable fruit, relieving hand and eye of the task.

We stopped by the roadside to pass the time of day with the owner of a thirty-acre orchard who was building, with no help but a sixteen-year-old son, a shed to hold a refrigeration plant. "Hail," he said, "that's the enemy!" Hail in Tasmania confines itself to belts that can be mapped almost as precisely as ranges or rivers. This grower was inside it and last year had lost half his crop. Scientists have devised a rocket that will disperse a storm before it is precipitated, but opinions vary as to its effectiveness; this grower thought that it had probably saved the other half of his crop. The sturdy, thick-limbed and rough-stubbled grandson of a German immigrant, he looked like a tramp but had the sound technical knowledge of a good craftsman. He spoke in a slow drawl with a lift at the end, and with pinched vowels, that reminded me of a hillbilly from Tennessee or Kentucky.

Driving back along a narrow country road between steep hills, we might have been in Devon. Small paddocks full of white clover and fat white sheep; small homesteads close together, small well-tended farms— none of the space and openness and emptiness of so much of mainland Australia. The steep hillsides, once thickly forested, are now thinly wooded with gums, beneath whose pink-and-grey-streaked boles grows a vivid yellow fireweed; and you see heaps of orange-glowing sawdust, the colour of certain toadstools, left by the now abandoned sawmills that used to cut timber for apple boxes. Once the Huon Valley had its Huon pines, finest of the few kinds of native conifer. These were felled so relentlessly that they survive only as vegetable museum pieces, to be classed with the aborigines, emus and fur seals.

[7]

Plenty of eucalypt forest survives, mostly in the western half of the island where everything is wild, rugged and by no means fully explored. The gorges are too precipitous, the peaks too jagged, the rocks too adamant to permit even of browsing sheep, let alone of cultivation, so much of this country remains as unexploited as on the day Tasman sailed under the lee of the western mountains in the *Heemskirk* and the *Zeehaen*.

In the northwest big mineral developments are on foot, but in the southwest there are not even roads. Not only are some of the mountains virtually unscalable and dense with rain forest—the annual rainfall is a hundred inches or more—but in places the explorer is confronted with "horizontal scrub." This is a mat of vegetation made of bent, fallen and interlacing trees and shrubs. It forms a sort of platform, sometimes as much as thirty feet above the ground, covered with moss and creepers, and rotten underneath. The traveller can walk, or lurch rather, over the top but sooner or later is bound to sink down into a vegetable morass which may close behind him like a trap.

Prospectors who have vanished without trace a presumed to have perished in this way, like a swimmer caught in seaweed. There is also a kind of scrub called *Bauera* that forms a barrier of thin branches, up to twenty feet high, so tough and whippy as to defy the sharpest ax; the only way to get across it, explorers have reported, is to roll. When you have fought your way through this sort of country for several hundred miles, and scaled many precipitous peaks, you arrive, if still surviving, at a wild and rocky coast lashed by ferocious breakers and without human settlements. So this wilderness could conceal Tasmanian tigers. These are the marsupial equivalent of wolves—about the size of an Alsatian dog with dark stripes across the back.

Formerly these beasts were common, but they killed sheep and so were hunted down. Whether any now survive is a matter of opinion. Dr. William Bryden, director of the Hobart Museum, has recorded all reported sightings in the last twelve years; they amount to twenty-nine, but some, possibly even all, may have been genuine errors. The animal— not, of course, a tiger, but a thylacine, *thylacynus cynocephalus*—is nocturnal and lives in forests, and the last recorded specimen was killed in 1928. An expedition sent a few years ago by the museum to search the southwestern ranges failed to find a single trace of a thylacine, despite extensive trapping. So no one is prepared to be dogmatic; but both Dr. Bryden and Dr. Eric Guiler, chairman of Tasmania's Animal and Birds Protection Board, seemed to think the balance or probability to be tipped against its survival. And a tough old bushman called Mort Turner, who keeps a small private zoo and knows this rugged country well, said that he had come across no pad mark, kill, or dropping for many years; so he, too, was dubious about its survival. On the other hand, zoologists point out that, on the mainland, several animal species thought to have become extinct have reappeared.

This island has a number of creatures found nowhere else. One is a mountain shrimp, no more than two inches long, that dwells in the cold lakes of the western and central ranges, has a straight back instead of a humped one, and burrows into mud. Its interest lies in its antiquity. Like the coelacanth, it existed in carboniferous times, before mammalian forms of life emerged, and was thought to have been extinct for millenniums until its rediscovery in 1892. It is said to be very shy. At the other extreme, not shy at all, is the Tasmanian devil, something like a marsupial wildcat, also found only in Tasmania. This "devil" (*Sarcophilus harrisii*) has a reputation for savagery that may have been exaggerated; the naturalist Harry Frauca has described it as a very timid beast. "Grab a devil and it will claw and bite, but leave it alone and it will run for its life." Like the tiger, a *méchant animal; quand on l'attaque, il se défend.* I saw Mort Turner pick up several in his zoo and fondle them and they responded with apparent affection. Their fur is thick and black, and in size they are midway between a large cat and a small badger.

Fourteen species of Tasmanian bird are not to be found on the mainland. These include four sorts of parrot, two honey eaters, a dusty robin, and a kind of flightless gallinule called the native hen. These now rare birds live in communities of three or four adults with their young; they defend their territory jointly and together build a nest, incubate their eggs and rear the chicks. Often there is only one female in a group; then all the males will mate with her and never quarrel, though if a non-member approaches they will fight. No dingoes have reached the island, and country gentlemen of bygone days who wanted something for their dogs to hunt besides kangaroos introduced deer instead of foxes.

[8]

I found the guardians of the island's fauna more hopeful than in any of the mainland states. This is because Tasmania is not yet overrun by humans. There is still living space for kangaroos and wallabies, as well as for the smaller marsupials, and the Animals and Birds Protection Board has fairly sharp teeth. Its members, who include sportsmen anxious to maintain good stocks of prey, have put the animals into three categories: open, partially protected, and completely protected. They can move a species from one category to another as they please. Thus they have, they consider, saved the Cape Barren goose, despite the weekend open season in 1964, and restored the position of the black swan, whose numbers had dwindled to a mere two thousand. Also, with government consent, they can declare fauna sanctuaries, and one twenty-fifth of the island is now so classified. If—as they hope—they can win consent to the setting aside, while there is still time, of one million acres of the wild southwest and buy an island that has been devastated by sheep in order to conduct an ecological experiment in regeneration, they will have, Dr. Guiler believes, one of the best wildlife setups in the world. But money is still very short. Tasmania is "on the dole"—that is, in receipt of annual subsidies from the Commonwealth Government.

Tasmania also pursues an enlightened policy in regard to its national parks, not to be confused with fauna sanctuaries. Laws to protect some of the island's natural beauties go back to 1915 when the Scenery Preservation Act was passed. It was many years before the rest of Australia woke up to the need. This act must have been one of the first seeds of national parks to be planted anywhere outside the United States. The Scenery Preservation Board also controls places of historic interest such as Port Arthur and, like the National Trust in Britain, several old houses. There is now a National Trust as well, but this is not controlled or financed by the government. There are eight major national parks, which together occupy about 3½ per cent of the total area of the island.

These are true national parks in that the government owns the land and can therefore, within limits, order what people do in them, and it can keep out cultivators, livestock, or developers. It does not always do so. Caravaners, motorists, campers, hikers and skiers are difficult to control, and bush fires a constant threat. The main trouble is to find enough money to keep up with a rising pressure of demand for roads, huts, camping sites and other amenities, as visitors pour on to the island in a geometrically progressive flood. You encounter coaches everywhere —in lay-bys, at lookout points, by roadside cafés, and hurtling along the twisty roads. Most visitors return to the flatter, browner, harsher, more congested mainland aglow with enthusiasm, but two elderly widows from Sydney whom I met in Alice Springs struck an acid note. There was scarcely a part of the continent they had not seen from coach windows on organized tours, and only Tasmania had fallen short of expectations. I inquired why. "Three weeks, twenty-nine people and— you wouldn't believe it!—never a song."

[9]

The Florentine valley, northwest of Hobart up the Derwent River, contains some of the finest eucalypt forest left in the world. The biggest tree of all, the swamp gum or mountain ash—*Eucalyptus regnans**— survives here probably in greater numbers than anywhere else on earth.

---

* The gum situation is very difficult. Not only do popular names vary from place to place, sometimes there is no agreement on the scientific names either. Nor is there agreement about the number of species. Some say there are 500, some say 700. The *Students Flora of Tasmania* (Winifred Curtis) says 600. The difficulty arises from the ease with which they hybridize. Which is a hybrid and which a species is a matter for perpetual argument.

These were national forests, preserved supposedly for all time; now they are being logged for newsprint. Down come the mountain giants, some of them over 300 feet high, tall as the dome of St. Paul's, some no doubt to be put to good use, but the pulp of others to be adorned with strip cartoons, with eulogies of soft drinks, nylons and carpets, with stale political clichés and accounts of murders, rape, theft, perversion and sports results, and finally to end as trampled litter drifting down a dirty street. There is, of course, a good economic case for this, and nature, everyone insists, will ultimately replace the trees. The newsprint company's concession covers nearly a quarter of a million acres, equal to about half the total area of all the national parks in Tasmania. The company puts in roads, controls fires, pays a handsome royalty and encourages nature to replace the trees they fell.

They do not have to replant with seedlings reared in nurseries; they simply burn everything the loggers leave behind, broadcast seed among the ash, and leave the rest to God. Soon the hillside becomes red with the foliage of saplings, which will add a tall man's stature to their height every year and in thirty years be ready for the saw. So never again shall we see the century-old giants in the concession area, which of course does not cover—at present—their entire habitat.

A few specimens are left for show. "The tallest tree in the Southern Hemisphere," possibly even the tallest hardwood in the world, rises from a platform of leaf mould to a height of 322 feet, with a girth of 42 feet—a circumference nearly twice the length of the whaleboat in which George Bass discovered the strait named after him. The seed of this eucalypt germinated before the first Elizabeth came to the English throne.

A single man could fell it, and does fell others much like it, in a very short time. Everything is mechanized: no ring of axes, no cries of "Timber!", no rough logging camps. An enormous pulp mill we passed, which turns out nearly one-third of all the newsprint needed by all the newspapers of Australia, is fed by eighteen men who actually cut down the trees. For each tree feller there are between thirteen and fourteen followers-up. About fifteen years ago the company employed three times as many men and felled about one-third as much timber. So it goes. As for rough logging camps, the men live with their families in modern houses grouped into a tidy village, complete with amenities like school and church, served by good roads, well placed to go fishing in trout-stocked rivers of a Sunday or run down to the pictures in Hobart of a Saturday night. At work they sit comfortably in cabs and cages, pulling levers or switches; gone forever is the brawny, hard-living, hard-drinking wielder of the ax.

On the banks of the Styx we boiled the billy with a proper observance of tradition. You gather twigs, kindle a fire, set on it a smoke-blackened open can, bring the water slowly to the boil, take it off, add a handful of tea leaves, swing the billy round by its handle, let the leaves settle, and then pour the brown, smoke-flavoured liquid into your mug. To bring a thermos would be much quicker and simpler but not so enjoyable; this is one of the few pieces of genuine native ceremonial left in modern Australia. The tea tastes different, anyway. Then you carefully trample out the ashes, always conscious of the risk of fire.

The river Styx is peat-brown like a scots burn and ripples gently, shadow-dappled, between moss-coated rocks and over smooth boulders. The roadside verges are yellow with the flowers of a Senecio (*S. linearifolius*) as tall as hemlock, which they call fireweed because it springs up after fires. Tree ferns are abundant. With the swamp gums mingle many other kinds of eucalypt, notably a stringybark (*E. obliqua*) known as messmate in Victoria, and another stringybark (*E. delegantensis*) sometimes called Tasmanian oak and sometimes Alpine ash; both are fine timber trees. There are several kinds of so-called peppermint with sweet-smelling leaves.* Gums that shed their bark all the year round in long, dangling strips, like old wallpaper, look untidy to an eye accustomed to deciduous trees, but as you get used to them you appreciate the warm tender colours of the young, fresh bark revealed by the peeling of the old. The boles of bark-shedding eucalypts are always partly clad in new growth. And the discarded bark forms round their feet a spongy carpet that mulches the soil and constantly replenishes it with humus; this link in the balanced ecosystem is broken by the logger's saw.

A peaceful silence permeates the banks of the Styx. Birds are scarce,

---

* Such blanket words as "stringybark" and "peppermint" are, of course, non-botanical and are applied to general groups of eucalypts. *Forest Trees of Australia* (Forestry & Timber Bureau, Canberra) states that there are between forty and fifty species and varieties in the stringyback group, and fifteen species of peppermint; five or six of these grow in Tasmania. Other general groups of gum include boxwoods, ironbarks, "apples," and so on. To make things more difficult, some trees known as pines are really eucalypts, such as the karri pine of Western Australia, and some really are pines, such as the Huon pine of Tasmania. The Tasmanian stringybark *E. obliqua* was the first to be described; it was collected in January, 1777, at Adventure Bay on Bruny Island by David Nelson and William Anderson on Captain Cook's third voyage. The name *Eucalyptus* was first published in 1788 by C. L. Heritier de Brutelle.

or perhaps just invisible and resting; not even a parrot lets out a screech. The fauna is nocturnal and so resting too. The foresters regard it as an enemy. Wallabies nibble off the shoots of young trees, and about three thousand are trapped every year in the concession area; bandicoots, which feed mainly on insects, are diminishing too. These forests are uninhabited by humans and probably always have been; the aborigines shunned such high, cold, wet places. To the north and west lies Mount Field National Park, which has a skiing season and a mountaineering school. This part of Tasmania remains wonderfully wild. For how long? No words and hopes have hitherto held back the tide of mechanized men bent on turning the wilderness into farms and pastures.

Between Launceston and Hobart the Midland Highway runs almost due north and south for 123 miles and was passable to carriages in 1821 when Governor Macquarie drove along it with his family, naming embryonic villages as he went. This antiquity, as things go, gives the country a cared-for, settled look. Pedigree cattle graze in paddocks; there are avenues of poplars; young trees are carefully caged. The number of solid, pleasing, late-Georgian stone farmhouses to be seen from the road is a surprise. Some have big barns of yellow-tinted stone, built by convict labour on land awarded to amy officers or to the younger sons of English country squires, who could acquire up to two thousand acres. Sometimes a number of families clubbed together to apply for adjacent blocks of land and then pooled their resources, ending up with ten- or twelve-thousand-acre properties. With as much convict labour assigned to them as they wanted, virtually free, and the price of wool rising, only persistent gambling, a pretty common failing, could come between them and the fortunes they desired and many of them made.

This part of Tasmania conveys a sense of continuity, conservatism and tradition. There is, for example, the Midland Hunt, whose members pursued kangaroos on horseback in the 1820's, and whose descendants, red coats and all, do so today. Among the hunt's first patrons was the Reverend Bobby Knopwood, who rode his white pony out from Hobart to the meets. He had inherited estates worth nearly a half-million dollars in Suffolk and was said to have lost everything at cards, mainly to the Prince Regent, who fixed him up with a Naval chaplaincy in return. In this capacity he came to Hobart on the staff of Colonel Collins, R.M., in 1804, and there remained, conducting divine service provided the weather was not too inclement or the congregation too sparse, cultivating an excellent garden on Battery Point, dining merrily with the governor and enjoying life in other ways suggested by a letter from an old friend, preserved among his papers, that recalls "the many pleasant hours and cheerful days we have spent together at the King's Head and many other places not forgetting old Mother Millywater and her lovely fair crew."

English names confront you as you drive along the highway: Bridgewater, Melton Mowbray, Oatlands, Tunbridge, Ross; a few Scots ones like Perth and Campbell Town; some fragments of the Orient like Mangalore and Bagdad. Off the road, tree-sheltered mansions perpetuate a Georgian dignity that survived here for twenty years after Victorian fussiness had set in at home.

Most of these mansions have been rebuilt or have fallen down, but enough remain to show how successful were their builders in re-creating English country houses among the gums and wallabies. What an impossibly nostalgic, backward-looking, sentimental race we are! No one even thought of trying to create a new, Australian style of building. A majority of these country houses did not even concede a veranda. The most famous Tasmanian architect is still the convict James Blackburn, a counterpart to Francis Greenway, who built solid English churches in a solid English way. And to all the mansions, or nearly all, were attached solid, nostalgic English names: Rosemount, Longford, Rokeby House, Clarendon, Brickendon, Camelford, Quamby, Malahide, Somercotes, Fernleigh, Dysart House, Pleasant Banks, Montacute. If a name was not exactly Anglo-Saxon, it could at least be European, such as Killymoon, built by an Irish baron called von Steiglitz, a family still prominent in northern Tasmania; or the fantastic Mona Vale, a later pile—1868— with 365 windows, fifty-two rooms, twelve chimneys and seven entrances, which now comes in handy for entertaining royalty. Some are even equipped with ghosts; inmates of Rokeby House between Campbell Town and Cressy are said—I cannot vouch for this—to hear at certain seasons the tinkle of breaking glass, recalling a butler who, as a murderer's knife struck him, dropped his tray. Even the ghost is English, with a suggestion of gleaming silver in the pantry, tea in the housekeeper's room and postprandial port wine.

At Ross, just south of Campbell Town, the highway crosses the Macquarie River by one of the loveliest small bridges I have ever seen. It is just a simple arch in mellowed stone across a smallish river, designed by a country gentleman and completed in 1839 by convicts. But two of the convicts took it on themselves to carve a whole wealth of animals, human faces, and traditional symbols in the greyish-yellow stone above the arches. Their identity remained unknown until an architect, Roy Smith, recently unearthed the names of James Colbeck, convicted for burglary, and Daniel Herbert, a signboard writer. Beyond the fact that both men received conditional pardons as a reward for their work, nothing more is known of them.

They worked in stone; a contemporary craftsman has chosen for his medium a less durable material—shrubs. At St. Peter's Pass, just south of Ross, a roadman has shaped the bushes on the highway verge into a vegetable menagerie. You speed past curly-horned rams, squatting rabbits, elephants with trunks, dogs, pigs, kangaroos, emus, a sitting hen, a crouching duck—every kind of bird and beast clipped from roadside bushes. The local council took their roadman-topiarist to task for wasting ratepayer's money, but the government department in charge of tourism intervened. Not only is he now encouraged in his hobby; he has been presented with a pair of silver clippers with which to pursue it.

All this is sheep country—barish, rolling plains, tawny and dry like many parts of Africa. It is not generous: rainfall is less than twenty inches: water is short; flocks are sparse, but the quality of the wool is high. We came at evening to the sea, spume-rimmed beyond the saltings at the mouth of the Scamander River, cobalt in contrast to the garnet and cornelian of the plains.

A stroll into a soft, drizzly wind bearing hints of marshes introduced me to a kind of heath myrtle whose white flowers, sheltering behind dark leaves, had a sweet and melancholy odour. Past a rusty-roofed wooden shed where a man in an old felt hat was milking by hand a few scruffy Jersey cows, up a hill to look over tidal flats opalescent with the mists of evening . . . Sheep and gums and silence . . . Even the birds were quiet. By the estuary sat a silent man with a rod, motionless beneath an old straw hat, as if carved from stringybark. Then back between a row of squat little bungalows from each and every one of which came a succulent smell of frying steak. The hotel had an attractive "craypot bar" done up like a ship's cabin, but there was no one else in it. The crayfish I ordered, while in itself a fine crustacean, had struck no spark of interest in its cook. I should have gone to the dining room instead and eaten steak, more respectfully treated.

[11]

Launceston is another of those Betjeman towns with which Australia is so well endowed. Victoriana is everywhere. Buildings in alternate layers of cream and liver-red like a Neapolitan ice, their waywardly pitched roofs flounced with ornament and frilled with scrolls; balconies also full of scrollwork; tortured brick, unexpected turrets, multicoloured tiles, heavy colonnades, thick vaulted doorways, potted palms in dark lobbies: an overgrown English country town. The narrowish streets are packed with people, the women mostly wearing gloves.

The town used to be Georgian. Then came a gold rush in the 'sixties, and a tin rush to Mount Bischoff; people grew rich and floridly rebuilt these north-coast towns. Now Launceston itself retains very little of its former symmetry, but all around are Georgian country houses that have been studied and recorded by another of those antiquarian-photographer-doctors in which Australia seems to specialize. To match Melbourne's Dr. Graeme Robertson are Launceston's Dr. Clifford Craig, an eminent neurologist, and his wife Edith who, with Dr. Robertson, have described between two and three hundred old buildings they consider worthy of regard in their splendid *Early Houses of Northern Tasmania*. With a small band of dedicated colleagues, the Craigs have also launched a Tasmanian National Trust which struggles with far too little money to save far too many houses that are going down before the twin despoilers of neglect and development.

The Craigs kindly took me to Franklin House and to Entally, the former run by the National Trust and the latter by the Scenery Preservation Board. Franklin House was put up by a speculative builder who advertised it for sale in 1839 as a "genteel family residence" (and on a bus route—"the coaches pass daily"). It is a plain, unpretentious, flat-fronted, perfectly proportioned small Georgian house. On the first floor a long drawing room is hung with some delightful French prints of Tasmanian scenes engraved in 1841 and furnished with period pieces collected by the Craigs, both locally and in England. The doors, windows and shutters are beautifully made from the teaklike New South Wales cedar, the only species of the genus in Australia, now commercially extinct. And all this was done by convict labour. England must have exported a great many of her best craftsmen in chains.

Entally is more ambitious and its nucleus was built in 1820 by a rich settler from Sydney, Thomas Reibey. The history of the Reibey family reads like a film script and opens with a magistrate's sentence, startling even against the background of English criminal law in the eighteenth century. Mary Haydock, daughter of a retired naval officer in Yorkshire, was in 1792 transported for life at the age of thirteen for stealing a horse. She had gone for a ride on a neighbour's cob, much as a modern teen-ager will take an unlocked car for a spin—except that he is apt to ditch the car while she returned the cob unscathed. On the convict vessel a young lieutenant who saw that she was not a prostitute or hardened criminal came to her rescue, got her assigned to some friends in Sydney, and returned two years later to marry her. This was Thomas Reibey, senior.

Between them Thomas and Mary Reibey built up a prosperous trade in sealskins, whale oil and general merchandise and accumulated property which Mary managed while her husband was at sea. They grew rich, had seven children and built Entally Hall in Sydney before Captain Thomas Reibey died in 1811, aged only thirty-six. In 1818 their eldest son received a grant of land near Launceston, settled there, and built the Van Diemen's Land version of Entally. His eldest son, the third Thomas, entered the Church, became Archdeacon of Launceston, was for a short period Prime Minister of the state and finally became the Speaker of the Legislative Council. He lived in style at Entally, bred racehorses and kept a pack of hounds that hunted a tame stag with a ribbon round his neck. This Thomas Reibey died in 1912, the last of the name.

[12]

If, in writing of this island, men and the works of men of the past appear, quite without intention, to have elbowed out those of the present, this may perhaps tell us something about Tasmania. Its people seem more conscious than the citizens of other states of their history and traditions. Now these—the history and traditions—have become tourist attractions, and tourism brings a measure of prosperity to the island.

By mainland standards the farms are small and intensively cultivated. Driving after dark along this well-favoured, well-watered northern coast between Launceston and Devonport, we saw lights winking on the hillsides as men on tractors worked round the clock to harvest green peas and deliver them at the peak of their condition to wayside threshing stations to be mechanically stripped and shelled. The peas go off to be canned and the haulms go back to the farmer to make into silage for his cattle. It is all mechanized and streamlined and, so far as I could judge, very efficient. And these small seaport towns look prosperous; their streets are crowded and the shops full of people spending money. After dark, girls in tight jeans stroll with their swains and suck ice-cream cones, prams are pushed by window-shopping mothers, men's coatless backs may be glimpsed through the open doors of bars, cigarette cartons and sweet wrappings litter every pavement. The brightness of the shop-fronted streets peters out into a dusky wharfside; the masts of ships are hard against the stars, and you can smell the freshness of the sea.

Next day the sea lay in all innocence below an aircraft that spanned in less than half an hour the strait where so many former voyagers had been storm-tossed, wrecked, lost and rescued in days gone by. To reflect on the contrast between the speed, safety, comfort and luxury of today's air-borne traveller and the hardships, dangers and tests of endurance that faced his predecessor in the days of sail is trite; but as you flip so swiftly, in a sitting posture, over the Bass Strait, it is fitting to spare a thought for the young naval surgeon from Lincolnshire after whom this stormy stretch of sea is named. It was George Bass who first perceived Van Diemen's Land to be an island and not, as opinion then held, a promontory attached to the mainland, and who, late in 1797, set out from Sydney in a whaleboat twenty-eight feet long, with six men, to prove his point.

Storms pressed them back against the mainland coast, then unex-plored, and they got almost to the present site of Melbourne before lack of provisions enforced their return to Sydney. Governor Hunter named the strait after their leader "as a just tribute," in Matthew Flinders' words, "to the extreme dangers and fatigues he had undergone in first entering it in the Whaleboat." On the way George Bass discovered Wilson's Promontory, the most southerly tip both of Australia and of the Great Dividing Range that sweeps in a great crescent for 3,000 miles from Cape York to this southerly peninsula.

Nine months later Bass set out in the little sloop *Norfolk,* only twenty-five tons burden, and with a crew of eight, under the command of his old friend Matthew Flinders, R.N., to prove Tasmania to be an island by sailing round it. So they became its first circumnavigators. On the way they discovered the mouth of the Tamar, which they named Port Dalrymple; this is where Launceston now stands.

Flinders was only twenty-four, Bass three years older and with little time left to live. Invalided as "unserviceable" and put on half pay, he was too restless and enterprising a young man to allow ill-health to put an end to his adventures. In London he and a group of friends bought a brig and sailed her back to Sydney, "deep as she can swim and full as an egg" of trade goods, to make a fortune in the Australian colony they had supposed to be short of supplies. They found the market glutted and their goods unsalable. So off went Bass to the South Seas to buy pigs, salt them down and sell the pork to the New South Wales garrison.

His last voyage was to South America to trade with the Indians and to bring back alpacas and guanacos to cross with the merinos that had already been shipped to Sydney from Cape Town. In February, 1803, the brig *Venus* cleared Sydney Heads, George Bass in command, bound for the Spanish colonies. "Pleasing prospects," the young man wrote, "surround us, which time must give into our hands." He was never reliably heard of again. Rumours drifted back of his capture by the Spaniards and consignment to Peruvian silver mines. They were never confirmed, and Bass's biographer considers it more likely that the *Venus* was lost at sea with all hands.

In his short life Bass made other discoveries besides that of the island status of Tasmania. One was of coal south of Sydney; another, of the anatomy of the wombat, which he was the first to dissect. Wombats were made known when sailors wrecked on Preservation Island in the Furneaux Group brought one back to Sydney, shortly before Bass's visit to the islands in 1798. He belonged to a tradition that has shaped Australia's origins and done much to determine her history: the tradition of the sailor-adventurer, and especially of the sailor in the Royal Navy. Sailors not only discovered the continent, but they also first explored, administered and protected it and its adjacent islands and drew the pattern of the nation it was to become. First, and greatest of all, came Captain Cook, R.N., and his second-in-command, Captain Tobias Furneaux; then Captain Arthur Phillip, R.N., with the First Fleet, to become the first governor; then in succession Governors Hunter, R.N., King, R.N., and Bligh of the *Bounty,* not to mention such questing navigators as Flinders, Bass himself, Commander John Hayes and Captain James Kelly. When they were not in the Navy they were apt to be Royal Marines, like Collins and Arthur in Tasmania.

The Royal Navy has left upon Australia an imprint not only to be traced on maps by innumerable names of men and vessels—so many islands, capes, promontories and passages did Captain Cook discover that he ran out of names of even the most junior of his officers and called Lindeman Island on the Great Barrier Reef after his wine merchant—but in the minds and hearts of Australians. That is why so great a psychological hurt was inflicted when the shield that for a century and a half had kept the continent inviolate buckled at the fall of Singapore.

And it was the United States, not the Royal Navy, that evened the account with the new forces of Asia at the Battle of the Coral Sea. A chapter that began when Cook's *Endeavour* anchored in Botany Bay ended with the sinking of the *Repulse* and *Prince of Wales* off the coast of Malaya.

ELEVEN 〰️

Goldmines in the West

For three hundred miles all but three, the metal tracks run absolutely dead straight across an absolutely dead flat and altogether shadeless and waterless plain: not a creek, not a ridge, not a tree. Low, sparse, unbelievably tenacious clumps of silvery-grey saltbush and bluebush speckle a ground which is coloured lung-pink and strewn with ironstone boulders, known as "gibbers," which are polished smooth as gem stones by the wind.

Everything swelters under an everlasting and relentless sun. No life moves, no creature stirs. Under the boulders, under the dry roots of the saltbush, there are no doubt beetles and spiders, skinks and geckos, goannas and tortoises and other creatures adapted to this dessicated world. There are birds. But no humans, except for families who dwell in railway quarters that are strung along the line like beads, each cluster roughly fifty miles apart. Twelve or fifteen identical corrugated-iron bungalows stand in a row facing the line without a bit of shade and without a speck of individuality. Each has a small fenced-in front yard, a squat roof, a barren outlook. Water comes by pipeline from the Murray for the first three hundred miles or so and then in tanks on the train. This is the Nullarbor Plain.

Imagination quails at the monotony of a woman's life in one of these outposts. The man's job at least takes him out of that square kiln of a dwelling; even if he still has nothing to look at but red grit and dust and boulders, they are different boulders, and he has his mates. But his wife is stuck day after day, week after week, in the square metal box, with a brood made fractious by heat. She cannot grow a plant, take a walk, sit under a tree. Outside the metal screens are milliards of flies, and savage dust storms cover everything with grit. What can there be to talk about? What if you fall out with your neighbour? Quarrel with your husband?

208

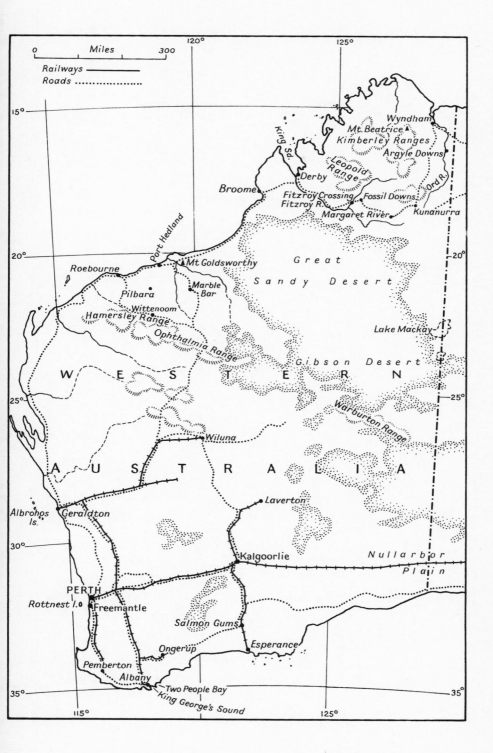

Day after day the same routine, the same sun heat, the same flat horizon, the same food.

I saw the Nullarbor in the utmost comfort from an air-conditioned train which sped from Port Pirie on the Spencer Gulf in South Australia to Kalgoorlie in Western Australia, a distance of 1,100 miles, in about thirty hours. From the observation car you look out, as from a ship's deck, over a level, pink-and-grey and waveless ocean, and you are looking at an old ocean bed. Beneath a limestone crust lies a vast system of caves and cavities, most of which have never been explored. Anything might lurk down the blowholes that sometimes puff out blasts of air and sometimes gulp them in, as if a monster underneath were breathing. That is what the aborigines, who shunned the Nullarbor, believed, and they thought the monster gave rise to dust storms by lashing his tail.

[2]

The Great Australian Bight lies fifty to a hundred miles south of the railway. Between the two, the explorer Edward Eyre tramped about 800 miles from Fowler's Bay, west of Adelaide, to King George Sound where Albany now stands, near the southwestern tip of the continent, without encountering a single spring or river.

I read parts of his agonizing story while cosseted in a luxurious train, constantly tempted by efficient stewards to eat and drink. Eyre set out in blistering midsummer heat with his overseer James Baxter, three native youths, nine pack horses, a foal and six sheep, to reach King George Sound across an unexplored desert. (There had been a small garrison and convict settlement on this sound since 1826.) They left on February 25, 1841, and ninety-seven days later two bedraggled and exhausted survivors managed to attract the attention of a French whaler, not far from where Esperance now stands. On one stage of their journey they had traversed 135 miles of desert without coming upon a single drop of water; the horses had gone five days without a drink and almost without food, being too parched to browse on twigs after the first day. Everything had been jettisoned but one spare shirt each, one bucket, and the minimum of provisions. Dense scrub had prevented them from cutting directly across the desert, so they had plodded along the beach, getting entangled in seaweed, and engaged in a perpetual struggle to prevent their thirst-crazed animals from drinking sea water.

Despite his own misery, Eyre was filled with compassion for the horses which "followed us about like dogs wherever we went, appearing to look to us only for aid." It was, he wrote, "a fearful and heartrending scene to behold the noble animals suffering the extremity of thirst and hunger without having it in our power to relieve them." When the explorers' own meager water supply gave out, they took sponges to the bush in early morning and managed to mop up enough dew to keep them alive; the natives, Eyre had heard, "make use of a large oblong vessel made of bark, which they hold under the branches, whilst they brush them with a little grass." In the next seven days they covered 160 miles before they found water by digging through six feet of sand. They were starving, and even Baxter wanted to turn back.

On the night of April 29, Eyre was minding the horses when he heard a shot; hurrying back to camp, he found Baxter dying from a gunshot wound and two of the aborigines gone with the guns and the remaining stores. Sitting by his comrade's body, hungry and almost naked in a bitter wind, even Eyre all but lost heart. "Ages can never efface the horror of this single night, nor would the wealth of the world ever tempt me to go through similar ones again . . ." He could not even bury poor Baxter, so hard was the ground.

Alone now with the native boy Wylie, on he trudged, both "very weak and worn out, as well as lame, and it was with the greatest difficulty that I could get Wylie to move . . . I myself would gladly have laid down and slept forever. Nothing but a strong sense of duty prevented me . . ." Two days after Baxter's murder he saw some *Banksia* shrubs. "Insignificant as the stunted specimens were, they led me to an inference that I could not be mistaken in"—that King George Sound could not be far away. But it was not for another eighteen days that they shot their first kangaroo. Wylie ate it practically all at one sitting, including the hide, plus a dead penguin he had found on the beach. Succoured by Captain Rossiter of the whaler *Mississippi,* they resumed their walk and reached their goal, ironically enough, through storms so violent that for the last three days they were wading waist-deep in water and shivering with cold.

After reading Eyre's account of this journey, it is hard to believe him guilty of the callousness and brutality of which he was accused some twenty-five years later when, as governor of Jamaica, he was obliged to call out troops to quell a Negro rising. His reputation in Australia, where he became a Protector of Aborigines, and in New Zealand as lieutenant-governor, lay in the contrary direction. Yet for ten years after the Jamaican affair he was hounded by a section of British public opinion, organized and led by John Stuart Mill, Herbert Spencer and T.H. Huxley. From evidence of character it would seem more probable that members of the Eyre Defense Committee, led by Ruskin, Charles Kingsley and Carlyle, were right in describing him as "a good, humane and valiant man."

[3]

Slap in the middle of this enormous baking tin of a desert, where nothing stirs but flies, there is a station called Ooldea. Here the pipeline from the Murray ends. And here one of the most remarkable Australian eccentrics "sat down" for sixteen years to nurse, heal and serve a riffraff collection of sick, destitute, blind and crazy aborigines, living in tents and wurlies, hauling every drop of water in buckets or, subsequently, in a handcart made by a railway ganger. This was Daisy Bates.

Until she was obliged in 1936 by sickness and poverty, at the age of seventy-four, to leave Ooldea, she could be found here, with the thermometer at 110°F. in the shade, meticulously dressed in the costume she had worn in the nineties when, in the Kimberley ranges of Western Australia, as a bride from England she had gone droving in a long-sleeved white blouse with a high collar and ribbon tie, an ankle-length dark skirt, black stockings, and a straw sailor hat with fly veil, plus a dust coat and sunshade when out of doors, and white gloves. From this costume she never deviated despite the heat, flies, dirt and squalor of her incredible physical labours for the lowliest, filthiest and most leprous human derelicts. Once she carried on her back for miles through a violent thunder storm an old homicidal cannibal who had eaten four wives, as well as a good many other humans, and gone mad in a tempest in a Lear-like scene of insane depravity. To sustain her singlehanded mission she sold all her possessions and existed from hand to mouth on fees for articles about the aborigines—she claimed to speak 115 dialects—receiving no penny of government support and herself all but starving; her keep, she said, cost less than two dollars a week, and she once made a pound of tea last for eight weeks and twelve pounds of potatoes for seventeen. She lost her sight for weeks from sand blight but never lost a total confidence in here own divinely sent powers of healing, in the triumph of compassion, and in the glories of the British Empire and the British Crown. The award of a C.B.E. seemed to her full repayment for all her labours.

Daisy Bates did not set out to reform the aborigines but to help them.

She understood, respected and at times almost perversely came to champion their customs and beliefs, even that of cannibalism, which she stated to be a universal practice right into the twenties and thirties. She treated them with their own native remedies, eschewing modern drugs and even antisepsis, in this respect out-Schweitzering Albert Schweitzer. "My system was primitive," she wrote; "so were my patients. I allowed them to live their own lives and die happy." That they would not merely die but die out, she entertained no doubts; civilization would kill them. Yet not an hour of her life, she wrote in her testament, *The Passing of the Aborigines,* had she wasted. "I did what I set out to do—to make their passing easier and to keep the dreaded half-caste menace from our great continent." She lived, in Adelaide, to the age of ninety.

[4]

For years that great belt of desert of which the Nullarbor is the southern extremity forced Western Australia to develop independently, almost as an island, supplied entirely by sea and cut off, landwise, from the rest of the continent. This isolation imbued the state with that distrust of and resentment against the older, wealthier, dominant community that is a common characteristic among islanders who feel themselves to be out on a limb.

Most of the big things that happened in the east did not happen until thirty or forty years later in Western Australia. (A pity some more interesting name could not have been found; they might have stuck to New Holland, the older title.) The gold rush, for instance, that had convulsed Victoria in 1851 did not occur in Kalgoorlie until 1893. Then suddenly a boil of humpies erupted on the plain and soon it sheltered, after a fashion, more people than Perth. There are still men and women alive who can remember those days, and one is Kalgoorlie's mayor, Sir Richard Moore. A sprightly eighty-seven, he limped into his sitting room, when I paid my respects, with an ankle sprained while repainting the roof. This was his twenty-seventh year of uninterrupted office.

He was born, Sir Richard told me, in a small town in Victoria whither his grandfather had come from Devon to ply his trade as blacksmith. Sir Richard's father followed him in the trade and sired fifteen children, including nine boys in a row. Their mother lived to be over eighty and never had a day's illness. The children would flock back from school to find their dinner ready on the table—a good substantial meal, steaming hot; it was their task to clear the table and wash up. Everything was spotlessly clean, their clothes laundered, ears and fingernails inspected daily; Bible reading after tea. "When I left school, I worked for a year with my father in the forge," the Mayor recalled, "and at Christmas he gave me a golden sovereign for the year's wages. I was overjoyed."

But times were lean in Victoria after the economic collapse of the nineties, and in 1903 the Moore family moved out to the western gold fields. People were living still in hessian humpies divided by a single blanket into two "rooms." Heat was intense, flies a constant torment, and everyone lived in a cloud of dust that at intervals became a raging storm. Water had to be piped over three hundred miles from Perth; sanitation was nonexistent, and typhoid broke out several times. "I had it twice," Sir Richard said. "But the worst part was the dust."

Someone had invented the Kalgoorlie cooler, a precursor of the refrigerator. To four posts stuck into the ground you tacked hessian to make a box and on top of this fixed a galvanized tray filled with water. From the tray you hung strips of flannel which kept the hessian moist, cooled the food after a fashion, and excluded some of the blowflies.

Life in a humpy in the dust and heat with her brood can scarcely have been a picnic for Mrs. Moore, accustomed to the comforts of Victoria. But "we were all so busy we hadn't time to scratch ourselves," her son said. Six of the sons became blacksmiths, Richard a carpenter, who learned to make every kind of horse-drawn vehicle—sulkies, buggies, traps, drays, delivery vans. They used local salmon gum for the body, York gum for the hubs, ironbark from Victoria for the spokes, but for the rims, always hickory imported from America; no local timber would do.

Sulkies were made with an eye for looks as well as for utility. An ordinary one cost about $40, but the "king of the road" $60 when open, plus $20 for a hood. It was on tradesmen's vans that the decorative urges of blacksmiths and wheelwrights found their full scope. A really slap-up greengrocer's van had twenty-seven feet of fancy nickel work on it, costing 40 cents a foot. Everything was done with horses, from the proud pacers flashing by with elegant sulkies to the big Clydesdales hauling ore from shaft to battery in heavy drays.

What has become of all those sturdy, hand-built wagons, the decorated sulkies and the gaily painted vans? Broken up, gone for firewood, said Sir Richard; he knows of none that survive. His own shop closed down twenty-five years ago when he retired from carpentry and built himself a home in a tree-lined street, next to a little Methodist chapel.

His family has prospered; one son is a headmaster, one daughter the matron of a hospital. "Those were good days," he said of Kalgoorlie's past. "People helped each other. We were law-abiding and we worked hard. Most of those old stories you hear aren't true. People paid their debts. It was hard on the women, but very few quit; they stuck to their men. You had to fend for yourself in those days."

[5]

Today's miners expect a good deal to be done for them. Recently a batch of Scottish miners called a strike after flying out, with their families, under an agreement providing free transport, rent-free housing for two months, a $2,000 interest-free loan towards buying a house, and wages averaging between $40 and $60 a week. They quit Kalgoorlie in high dudgeon and a blaze of publicity; the pay, they complained, was too low.

"They were exceptions," I was told, and was taken to see a miner and his family nearer to the rule, if there is one. They had come straight from the slums of Glasgow. "We'd been married ten years," said the miner's wife, "and the four kids slept in one room, more like a cupboard, and we had no yard and shared a toilet with four other families. The roof leaked, the wallpaper was peeling; it didn't give you heart to keep it clean. Jim was redundant once for three months and pits were closing down. But here . . ."

Here their house is their own: a large, rambling bungalow and a quarter of an acre for which they paid $1,900, loaned by the company. The house is dilapidated, the garden untended, and most Australians would have been busy with paintbrush and spade, but the Scots were not so energetic or so fussy. "Look at the kiddies." As tanned as any Aussie, they tumbled, crawled, or bounced uninhibitedly about the room. "They can play all day out in the sun. And we've got our own fruit trees— vines, two nectarines and passion fruit. I'd never heard of those before. When we moved in, a neighbour came over with a basket of big juicy peaches—never seen the like. The neighbours have been really kind— asked us to Sunday dinner in their homes, and there's one who offers us a ride in his car at weekends. We haven't got a car yet of our own." There are a few grumbles. "You have to pay here for school uniforms and books and put up a packed lunch. I'm making their uniforms." To balance this, there is a larger family allowance. Costs of living are higher in some directions (bread, eggs, milk) and lower in others (meat, fruit, cigarettes); on average, probably about the same.

The husband is well pleased. "Best lot of mates you could hope for, and good bosses too. At Christmas the company gave a slap-up tea with presents, big boxes of sweets and toys for the kiddies. Nothing like that at home. The money—not as good to start with as I'd expected, but not so bad now. And look at this place! In four years I'll have paid for it and it'll be mine."

The great majority of migrants coming to Western Australia are British. This is not part of a policy; it is because only the British wish to come in any large numbers. Most continental Europeans find all the work and opportunity they ask for closer to their homes. So, indeed, can the British; but we have the British climate. This, I think, is probably the sharpest of the various goads that prod families into leaving home. People are simply fed up with the weather. What about the Dutch, Belgians, Danes, North Germans? They lack sunshine, too, but many fewer emigrate. Perhaps the language checks them, and the necessity to move not merely to a different country but to a different society and way of life. Another powerful motive for emigration is a feeling of frustration engendered by a number of things: by the packed-in, overcrowdedness of everything, from traffic jams and undergrounds to shops and seaside resorts; by a conviction that promotion is too slow, tradition too strong, trade unions too hidebound, new ideas too little welcomed by men at the top; by a belief that the class system is as strong as ever and egalitarian ideals have failed; by a contrary belief that a man willing to work and anxious to make his own way is held back by taxation and the unions; by resentment against coloured immigration; by the housing shortage, and by many other factors.

To what extent the same factors operate in other countries I do not know, but it is a fact that the flow of non-British migrants to Australia has dwindled to a trickle. The Commonwealth Government has opened offices in a number of countries to attract New Australians and to arrange for assisted passages—even, recently, in certain non-European countries such as Israel. For ten or fifteen years after World War II non-English-speaking migrants were queuing to get in. Many were displaced persons left high, dry and stateless by postwar demographic convulsions. Only a comparatively few got to Australia, but most of these turned into first-rate citizens. Such a pair were the Ozerovs, he a Russian, she a French-speaking Alsatian. After years of an existence like a pinball unable to come to rest in any slot, this couple found themselves, with their two children, in a migrants' camp near Perth. Dmitri took a miner's job gladly; in Russia he had been an accounting clerk. Within six years they owned the home in which we sat and sipped hock-and-soda, in the presence of books. Everything was spick and span and beautifully kept—vases of flowers, prints on the walls, polished glasses, and arrangement of shells, paint work fresh and gay. The son is now a civil servant, the daughter a secretary, a third still in school. Both parents, intent on saving money, walk to their places of employment and have no car.

"Australia has been kind to us," Dmitri's wife said. "We have never had regrets—only that we did not see out parents and now they are dead." But there are worries. "The work is hard and soon I shall be fifty," Dmitri observed. "I shan't be fit for the physical labour much longer and I'm too old to study for a diploma. Kalgoorlie is all right for miners, but it's not a growing town. I don't want to move again; we've moved enough, and all this we have made . . ." The garden, like the house, is neat and tidy and well-tended. There are roses. As neither soil nor climate is right for roses, soil has been made from compost and the climate cheated by sprinklers. "But I want to grow a *dark* rose. Every kind I grow turns out to be pink."

[6]

In 1903, just ten years after three Irishmen discovered the reef, twenty thousand men and more worked in these mines. Kalgoorlie was a thriving, bustling place with a stock exchange and thirty-four hotels, the best of them fit to accommodate in worthy style the titled London financiers and the company promoters from Adelaide and Melbourne who came to see the Golden Mile, the richest reef in all Australia. A single company, the Great Boulder—now the largest survivor—has extracted over $200 million worth of metal. But now gold has ceased to glitter. The price was last raised in 1934, and since then the costs of winning it have rocketed. Today there are less than five thousand miners, and numbers continue to decline. A lack of confidence in the future shows in a lack of new buildings and in the shabbiness of the old. But hopes of revival have been kindled by a promising find of nickel at Kambalda, only thirty miles away, and people will assure you that the surface of this highly mineralized state has as yet barely been scratched.

Ghost towns haunt the bush that surrounds Kalgoorlie, telling in the toppled remnants of a brick chimney, or the relics of a rusted tank, a sad story of worker-out reefs and lost fortunes. Even the ghost has vanished in some cases, leaving only saltbush, bluebush, mallee scrub, boulders and sand.

"This was Bulong," said my guide. There was nothing to be seen but scrub parched by an unremitting sun—not a drop of rain had fallen for eight months. "My father was the mayor. He kept a store." I was shown a photograph of Bulong's city fathers with bushy whiskers clad in dark, heavy woollen suits with waistcoats and watch chains and tight, high, stiff collars, stiff-brimmed hats in hand. "Cockeyed bobbies finished it," said the mayor's son. "Cockeyed bobbies?" "Willy-willies." By now I knew what these are: dust devils that whirl across the bush, uprooting everything uprootable in their path. An extra strong one is called a cyclone and removes roofs; lesser fry will sweep up fallen branches, debris and anything left about, whirl it around in a wild embrace, abandon it and prance on its way.

Bulong, in its heyday, was a fair-sized place served by schools, churches, stores, an array of pubs and a Miners' Institute with an imported grand piano. I saw another photograph, a strange one: hundreds of men, possibly thousands, packed shoulder to shoulder and staring fixedly in one direction. There was not a single woman. The men were mostly bearded and wore slouch hats, breeches and loose jackets; some carried picks and shovels. I asked what they were looking at. "The Kanowna magic nugget."

Kanowna was a nearby mining town with fifteen pubs and five churches. Its Roman Catholic Irish priest was fond of his grog. One evening he was sworn to secrecy by several young men and shown a nugget of fantastic size, obviously the harbinger of a strike so rich as to make Kalgoorlie's Golden Mile seem like a teacupful of pebbles. The secret was not to be shared. But rumours spread, everyone was talking about the wonderful nugget, and the priest begged to be allowed to reveal the secret. So a day was appointed. People flocked out from Kalgoorlie, and it was said that between four and six thousand men thronged the street below the balcony of the Criterion Hotel to hear the announcement and to start a new rush. The excited priest stood forth to reveal the secret, describing a spot near a salt lake. On foot, on bicycles, in buggies, the fortune hunters pelted out to start digging. There was no gold. The nugget turned out to be a crudely painted stone. When they had recovered their tempers, the miners held their sides for days, and for years afterwards the story was told in a multitude of bars. The priest became a laughingstock. "It broke his heart," said the mayor of

Bulong's son, who had heard the story from his father. "He disappeared." Now the Criterion Hotel, the street, the whole town has disappeared as well.

[7]

After gold petered out, all this land came into the possession of an English pastoral company. The mayor's son, born in Bulong, leases from it rather more than three-quarters of a million acres, and there is not a drop of natural surface water on the whole run. Underground water, if and when you strike it, is heavily mineralized. So Mr. Barton Jones bought a team of oxen and a scoop and slowly, laboriously, he made dams. Heavy storms filled them, but months or even years went by without heavy storms. Three-quarters of the water, he reckons, was sucked up by the sun and the dams frequently went dry.

Despite all this, Mr. Jones had just about got established, and his wife had borne him seven children, when the depression knocked the bottom out of prices of beef and wool. By cutting timber which he peddled in Kalgoorlie for firewood, eked out by selling homemade butter, life was —if only just—sustained. Gradually, when markets revived, Mr. Barton Jones rebuilt his flocks to a level he believes to be safe for the land, about one sheep to thirty-five or forty acres. Even this, he thinks, may push the land too hard.

"You get a drought and what happens? We're into one now. Half my dams are dry and I'm trucking water from those still holding out." What if those should fail? "Then a lot of sheep will die and I shall truck water from Perth. Even if you can bring enough water in tankers, you cannot bring in food for 20,000 sheep. Why not send the sheep to the food?

"Bathurst bur. It gets into the fleece and ruins the quality. So no sheep can be moved from here without a license, and you can only get a license within six weeks of shearing. So we're shearing now."

Mustering must start a month before the shearing, for some mobs have to be moved fifty miles. Here they muster in radio-directed Land Rovers which either carry motor bikes or draw horse trailers. Four sons, two nephews and the boss run the place between them, with casual help from aborigines.

We watched the shearing teams in the big shed, with its grease-polished timbers, at work with that wonderful dexterity displayed by these professionals, who move from state to state on a contract basis. Shearers get $17 a hundred sheep and should handle about 120 sheep a day. "They're not so quick as they were," I was told. "It's harder to get good men. The youngsters won't take to it. They're off to the cities."

The head classer is the aristocrat of the team. His assistant, a student nearing the completion of a three-year course, said, "I don't like the bush." "Why?" "The isolation." It will be the city for him. The man on the press, a big man strong enough to handle bales weighing three hundred pounds, said he would soon be quitting to get married. "It's no job for a married man." They say many shearers suffer from crook backs. But the contractor was not unduly worried. "If the white boys won't do it, we'll get the natives. They're right enough if they'll stick at it."

[8]

This was my first sight of aborigines in their natural setting and employed on the land, where they preserve a dignity that cities quickly dispel. Some are good horsemen and are well-built and strong. Many are half-bloods, sons of stockmen and station owners; a pure-blood aboriginal stockman is rare.

"They can be good stockmen, but they're unreliable." I heard this opinion, right or wrong, expressed many times. "Just when you want them they'll go walkabout, or else they'll go to town and get drunk and land in jail," said Mr. Jones. "Two of my boys are there now. The grog is their undoing. Although these boys will come back stony broke, they'll hire a taxi for a couple of pounds to get here. They never save a halfpenny, though I pay them twenty-four dollars a week and all found. No, I don't believe they'll change. Education? Well, maybe. But they've no ambition. Sufficient for the day. It's ingrained . . ."

How often have I heard similar generalizations about Africans! Most of them turned out to be untrue. Constantly I found myself hearing echoes of the white man's Africa of twenty, thirty years ago. White Australians may similarly find some of their beliefs in need of revision.

"Ideas have changed already," I was told in Kalgoorlie, where the state government has a branch of its Department of Native Welfare (aboriginal affairs are a state and not a Commonwealth concern). "Or at any rate the policy has. There's been a big change in the last few years."

The old policy, putting it broadly, was to treat the aborigines as wards of the state. A ward is someone who is considered to be in need of protection. This was certainly something the aborigines needed. They were not citizens; they had no vote, and it was an offense for a white Australian to sell them liquor or to cohabit with them. On the positive side, the government accepted responsibility for seeing that they did not starve. Only in the most remote areas could they continue the nomadic hunter's life that was natural to them. Wherever Western man had introduced the settled way of life and the exploitation of nature, as opposed to coexistence with it, the aborigines were stranded. They were succoured mainly by the Christian missions and by the government which established settlements in regions where missions were too few or too poor to do the job.

In such regions there was seldom any useful employment for the blacks, whose skills in any case were useless to a white society. So there grew up the pernicious custom, which still lingers on, of doling out free rations. It was pernicious because it underminded their independence and turned them into pets living on crumbs from the white man's table. Most of them seemed quite contented so to live; apathetic, aimless, day-to-day, without ambition, camping in the crudest of shelters in a squalor which they made no effort to alleviate. This is the way practically all nomads behave when they can no longer be nomadic but find themselves bunched together in static communities. They are not used to it and do not know the rules. Birds who build nests develop habits of cleanliness and tidiness that put most humans to shame. Non-nesting birds have no need to do so. It is the same with mankind.

The wardship policy was based on two propositions: that the blacks belonged to an inferior race incapable of adapting itself to white Australian society, and that they were dying out. Both these propositions no longer stand. Far from dying out, the aborigines are now increasing probably at a faster rate even than the white Australians. And the doctrine of racial inferiority has become, to put it mildly, unfashionable. So the policy of trusteeship has been replaced by that of assimilation. It is now the official intention to do away progressively with all laws and practices that set the aborigines apart from white society and to turn them into fully fledged Australians. There is to be not a multi-racial, but a non-racial, society. This is in line with the general trend of world opinion.

Whatever policy may be, the fact remains that at present most adult blacks lack the education, habit and outlook that would enable them either to enter fully into white society or to be accepted by it. Legislation cannot convert a black fellow skilled at digging for water-storing frogs and catching lizards into a clerk skilled at balancing a ledger—or, these days, more probably dealing with a computer. There must be time, money, patience. And the pace varies, with the problem, in each state.

No one knows precisely how many aborigines there are in Western Australia because such nomads as still exist cannot be counted, and because it is impossible exactly to define an aborigine, since a majority are of mixed blood. The estimate I was given was, in round figures, twenty thousand, but only about three thousand in the huge area known as the Eastern Goldfields, of which Kalgoorlie is the headquarters.

"In this area," I was told at the Native Welfare office," until 1961, we had one man and one man only, and he had no cash, no office staff and practically no transport. Now we have three welfare officers, a married couple with a mobile works unit whose job is to repair and see to houses in the native reserves, and much more money. Way out in the Warburton Range there are mobile patrols in contact with the nomads; most of the natives have come in. They're given food and shelter in transitional camps, and many of them drift down to Laverton, where there's a settlement and they're given some employment. The policy now is that they mustn't be given anything for nothing but must work for their keep. The trouble is to find anything for them to do." At Laverton they make boomerangs for the tourist trade. Is the demand sufficient to keep them busy? "They get big orders from America." So, in these distant sun-parched ranges, the First Australians, as it is now polite to call them, squat in a shelter made of sacking and shape bits of wood into boomerangs to hang, for a while, upon the walls of shelters made of stone or timber in another continent—an activity enriching, one would think, to nobody, either in mind or in body.

The makers of boomerangs may now vote, they may buy liquor, and their women may even become prostitutes if they wish to. Until this change of policy prostitution was reserved for whites and a colour bar observed in brothels. There was an awkward moment when an eminent Asian visitor was turned away from one of the Kalgoorlie houses and had to get a white friend to testify that he was not a native or a Negro. Otherwise the madam would have broken the law. She can admit all comers of all colours now.

[9]

One of the welfare officers took me to a pleasant little park which, he said, had become a sort of unofficial native reservation. It was an oasis of green grass, flowering trees and bougainvillaea trellises in a dusty brown city where a vicious desert glare struck up from the bitumen. "The whites won't come here any longer because they say it's been taken over by the natives who are dirty and carry disease." Family parties were sitting on the grass with babies, baskets, food wrapped in newspapers, and melted ice creams. All were women, who every morning walk in from a small reservation about two miles out of town, half a dozen acres or so, to spend the day here while their children are at school.

These dusky women were enormously fat; their bodies bulged and sagged; their hair was long and lanky and unwashed; their dresses were dirty; they stank and were not prepossessing, yet their wide-browed faces had a certain strength and dignity, and their black eyes held an enigmatic quality, seeming to set up a barrier rather than to open a channel of communication. Were their thoughts of the same shape and pattern as one's own? Impossible to say. They were friendly and had wide, generous smiles.

One family sat amid banana skins and lottery tickets. These were "castes." A youngish woman, fat like her elders, had a white baby and two toddlers of a rather darker hue. Her husband was away shearing, and three older children were at school. How did the children get on? "All right." Did they mix with the whites? "Oh yes. They're treated just the same as whites. They use the swimming pool." This topic was in the news because, at the time, a group of Sydney students was engaged upon a much-publicized "freedom ride," by bus, to campaign against the exclusion of aborigines from swimming pools in some of the smaller towns of New South Wales.

It will be the next generation, children of the women I spoke to in this park, who will, or may, "integrate." A handful have passed through high schools and trained as secretaries, teachers and nurses. The process is bound to be slow. Although in class the children get the same treatment —and I believe they genuinely do—the great majority are handicapped at home by bad housing and by their parents' ignorance. Homework in a humpy, huggermugger with a dozen relatives from grannies to newborn babes, is almost impossible, and there is no one to help you if you get stuck over a sum.

"Castes" have a great advantage over "purebloods" in that English is generally their mother tongue. In the park there was a group of pureblood women, even fatter than the castes, whose English was confined to a few halting and reluctant words. No doubt it was the language difficulty that made them seem, by contrast with the castes, so suspicious and surly. Their older children were in school, but the smaller ones with them spoke a tribal tongue and will have to start their school career by learning English. Inevitably this puts them behind.

A couple of whites were, after all, to be seen in the park. They were young men with flowing locks and tight jeans, playing cards with half a dozen young natives. Empty bottles and cans lay around. "No hopers," said my guide.

[10]

Esperance is well named. The air all but crackles with hope and confidence. It is a wide blue bay on the Indian Ocean rimmed with white sand, the terminus of a railway to Coolgardie that links it with the transcontinental line joining Perth to the eastern states, and the center of an ambitious scheme of agricultural development literally built on sand.

The sand supports a natural vegetation of *Banksia speciosa,* a member of the Protea family with narrow leaves and big, bottle-brush flowers the shape of pineapples, which in colour may be pale yellow, greenish yellow, or a burnt orange, and which blacken as they fade. Where banksia grows nothing much else will, but where the sand is shallower you get plants peculiar to a European eye and with interesting names like munji, chittick, Christmas bush and blackboy, also called the grass tree. This is an odd plant indeed, whose stiff black flower stem sticks up like a poker from a collar of very narrow leaves that look like a tuft of grass; these are mounted on a stubby trunk that contains a valuable resin. The blackboy is apparently a very ancient tree, related to the cycads, which in turn stem from an early branch of the conifer family; one of the Queensland cycads, known as Father Peter, was thought to be three thousand years old.

Inland of the banksia dunes lie millions and millions of acres of mallee scrub, where poverty of soil and rainfall for many years defeated all attempts to grow crops economically or even to graze sheep. Plenty of attempts were made. Soldier settlers were brought in after World War I to open up for wheat the region round Salmon Gums, about sixty miles inland from Esperance; the scheme failed. Then a biggish company leased some land with the intention of starting pine plantations. These failed too; but the manager, Mr. A. D. Helms, discovered that, if you dressed the land with superphosphate, it would yield good crops of lupins and of subterranean clover. These crops were useless commercially, but they proved a point. They were the beginning.

One of the settlers who tried—and failed—to grow wheat near Salmon Gums was Alf Button. He remained convinced that the sand beneath the mallee held a great store of fertility, if you could find the key to unlock it. After the second war he took up a lease near Esperance, cleared some scrub, and sought the advice of professional agronomists who were beginning to think they knew why this land had disappointed so many hopes. Officers of the State Department of Agriculture carried out experiments on his farm while their own research station was taking shape. Alf Button still lives there. He and his wife were gathering firewood when I saw them and wheeling it in an ancient barrow to their cottage in a small orchard they had planted. They were just back from a holiday in England—their first and only one for forty-two years.

"Never been so tired in my life," Alf Button said. "Be good to get back into harness." He had emigrated to Western Australia at the age of seventeen from Staffordshire and still speaks with the broad Midland accent. A stocky, sturdy man, his face is broad and honest as his voice, and tough as if it had been carved from the roots of the mallee. "He doesn't farm just to make the money and crowd on every sheep he can," said the agricultural officer who took me to see the Buttons. "It's more a way of life with him."

The man who found the key that Alf Button and others like him were looking for is Professor Eric Underwood of the University of Western Australia. As long ago as 1932, before he was thirty, Dr. Underwood began to study a cattle sickness known in Kenya as Nakuruitis, in parts of Australia and in Denmark as wasting disease, and by different names elsewhere. At the Rowett Institute near Aberdeen in Scotland it had been ascribed to a lack of iron in the soil and hence in the vegetation eaten by the cattle. Dr. Underwood challenged these conclusions and traced the trouble to a lack of cobalt.

This proved to be a turning point in the science of animal nutrition. Little attention had hitherto been paid to what are called the trace elements: minerals present in the soil in such minute quantities that older techniques of analysis could not measure them but could detect only traces. Infinitesimal as the quantities may be, without them plants and animals cannot thrive. Zinc, copper, iron, iodine and cobalt are among the most important; manganese and molybdenum are also needed; others are coming to light.

Without molybdenum the ability of clover plants to extract and fix nitrogen from the air is impaired. So the grazing animal gets short of nitrogen, cannot build up its body tissues, and wastes away. Millions of acres in the eastern states and in Tasmania lack molybdenum. The quantities needed to put matters right are unbelievably small. One-sixteenth of an ounce to the acre is sufficient, and the effects last for ten years. A *single teaspoonful* to the acre will correct a deficiency of selenium, the latest trace element to come under scrutiny. As for cobalt, it is now being fired by a special gun, in the form of pellets, into the throats of sheep. Without cobalt they cannot make a certain necessary vitamin.

On the Esperance Downs it is zinc and copper that are lacking. This discovery, made primarily by Professor Underwood, links up with studies in South Australia of that state's "Ninety-mile desert," which has similar deficiencies. Formerly this desert, which is larger than Israel, could support sheep at the rate of one to twenty acres at the best. Copper and zinc, spread at the rate of seven pounds to the acre, enable the area to support two sheep to the acre—a fortyfold increase. As it is obviously absurd to go on calling it a desert, the region has been renamed the Coonalpyn Downs.

The same application of the same trace elements round Esperance is having the same effect, only more so because the rainfall is higher and more reliable. On the research station a rate of stocking of four dry sheep to the acre is being successfully maintained, and the experts believe they will do even better. This is on land that fifteen years ago maintained no domestic animals at all. In the area so far developed by the new settlers the numbers of sheep have gone up from nil to well over half a million and should reach two millions in the next five or six years.

The implications of this for the country as a whole are staggering. Professor Underwood has calculated that for every acre at present growing crops, timber, or improved pastures, at least four acres of adequately watered land lie undeveloped—largely, though of course not entirely, for lack of trace elements. This amounts to an area equal to France, the Netherlands, West Germany, Switzerland and Italy combined. The fact is that Australia is very much an underdeveloped continent; and if some of the money being currently bestowed on the underdeveloped countries

of Africa and Asia were to be invested here, while the political returns
might seem less attractive, the returns in terms of output of food for the
hungry would certainly be infinitely greater.

[11]

It costs a lot of money to give this country the full treatment it needs.
You must clear the scrub with chains and tractors, burn it, plow the
land, fallow it, replow, spread fertilizer, plant your crop or your improved pasture grasses, make paddocks and dams and all the rest. Virgin land is cheap enough, but to bring it into use may cost up to $60 an
acre. The state government was therefore well disposed towards an
American syndicate that proposed to transform 1½ million acres into
productive farmland. This ended in the biggest failure of all. The right
technique was known by now, but the Americans tried to take a short
cut: they left out the nine months' fallow. The native vegetation harbours moulds destructive to the capacity of those bacteria which live on
clover roots to fix nitrogen. The purpose of the fallow is to kill these
harmful moulds. So—no fallow, no nitrogen, no payable crops or grazing. In 1957 there was a bad season and the clovers failed. So did the
company. The short cut proved a blind alley, and everyone had to start
again.

Now the Esperance Land and Development Company, also an American concern, is developing, stage by stage, about half a million acres
and holding the other million in reserve. They keep half of all they develop for themselves and must divide the other half into farms, prepare
them for occupation, and offer them for sale. The farms vary in size but
average around 2,000 acres, of which the company develops about one-
third by clearing it, establishing good pastures, making dams, fences and
possibly a woolshed, and generally preparing it for a family to move in.
Anyone who takes up one of these farms needs at least $40,000 in
capital, and there is a very lively demand.

The demand for farms leased directly from the state government is
even livelier because they seem a lot cheaper, and the tenant, not the
landlord, must put in the capital improvements. But whoever puts them
in, they need a lot of money, and Mr. Leo Shier, the Deputy Director of
Agriculture, emphasized that the day of the pioneer with an empty
pocket and a stout heart is over; a substantial bank balance is needed as
well, and the board that selects tenants from a large pool of applicants

will take only those with adequate resources. Even so, a few opportunists with little else but faith, hope and resolution manage to slip through.

One such, whose farm I visited, had been a city architect in Hull. Returning from wartime service in the R.A.F., he found his native city blitzed and drab, cold and murky—he had to defrost his hands under a lukewarm-water tap before working at his drawing board—and future prospects bleak. So off he went to Western Australia and a job in the wheat belt.

"I got bitten by the farming bug," Dennis Marshall said. "One day some blokes got talking in the pub about Esperance and I said I'd like to see it. An old chap who overheard wrote and suggested we go in together and apply for two adjoining blocks. He'd supply machinery and fertilizer; I'd do the work. I agreed, but I never thought we'd get the land. We did, though—that was fairly early in the scheme—two thousand acres for sixty cents an acre spread over thirty years. Nothing on it, of course, only scrub. I got a job surveying and worked the land at night and weekends. I chained, burnt and fallowed seven hundred acres, plowed it, put on super and got in the seed. I knocked up a rough sort of shed for the fertilizer and slept in a corner of it; all the equipment I had of my own was a very ancient van."

After his first crop—a good one—he sent for his fiancée, who was working as a secretary in Oxfordshire. They curtained off a bit of the open-fronted fertilizer shed with a blanket, nailed some planks together for a bedstead, stuffed straw into some sacking for a matress, hitched a lantern to a nail, bought a frying pan and an enamel basin and an old wood-burning stove, and settled in. "I've only one regret," said Ursula Marshall, "that we didn't come here years ago. It's all so clean and open, the dawn's marvellous, the stars are always clear. We do everything together, plan it and see it grow; it's all ours." She has learned to muster sheep and draft them, to dose and dip them and do everything from repairing a fence to changing a tractor wheel. There is no one else to help with 2,500 sheep and 700 acres under the plow.

Also there are three small children and a home in a corner of a greatly superior fertilizer shed, with partitions made of corrugated iron instead of blankets, with a door and windows that open and a floor—there is even a bookshelf holding a set of Dickens they will never have time to read. The old wood-burning stove is still there; a tiger snake spent a week or two behind it not long ago. That warmth attracts snakes is well known, but you would scarcely think even snakes would need to be in search of warmth on the Esperance Downs. All around this iron shed the shadeless white and pale-pink sand quivers like jelly under the pounding heat waves, and in summer the mercury seldom drops below 90°F. Nothing is in sight but dust and flatness. "We love it," said the Marshalls—it is their own. "Once we've worked up to five thousand jumbucks, we'll be home and dry."

Three sheep to the acre, that will mean, on sand that everyone had written off as useless. So vanishes the wilderness, in Western Australia alone at the rate of about one million acres every year. Sooner or later a European visitor, surveying what still *looks* like wilderness, is bound to ask, "But what do the sheep live on? Do they eat sand?" For answer, my guide stopped the car in a bare paddock, got out, and scooped up handfuls of the hot, coarse, sandy particles, which he winnowed in his hands. A number of small, hard-coated burs emerged: seeds of subterranean clover (*Trifolium subterraneum*), rich in nutriments, which the sheep extract by blowing down their nostrils, digging with their sharp hoofs and nuzzling into the ground. They are not stupid creatures, sheep. These seeds lie dormant in the heat of summer, but in winter, when the rain falls, they germinate, and all these plains are rich with green growth.

This wonderful plant is not a native of Australia. It came by accident from Spain or from North Africa about sixty years ago, and once its extraordinary drought-resisting properties were realized, the plant breeders got to work and have bred different strains to suit different conditions. These are now the mainstay of all the new techniques of pasture improvement in the dry-summer and winter-rainfall regions— techniques which are bringing into use enormous slabs of this enormous continent. (A few statistics: Australia is about the same size as the United States minus Alaska. This single state of Western Australia occupies one-third of it and nearly one million square miles—it is almost four times as large as Texas. From one end of the state to the other is farther than from London to Moscow. The southwestern corner, which has a relatively stable, if not generous, rainfall, occupies one-tenth of the state and grows about nine-tenths of its produce. Hence the importance of these Esperance Downs and the mallee scrub lying immediately inland.)

Now and again the unexpected happens in plant breeding as in everything else. The geneticists bred a strain of subterranean clover they called Yarloop, which many of the Esperance settlers adopted. Soon afterwards a mysterious infertility smote the ewes, and crops of lambs declined disastrously. "When my lambing rate fell to twenty-two per cent," one of the settlers told me, "I quit and switched to cattle. They cost me a lot and didn't pay so good. So after a while I wondered if the trouble might have worn itself out. I bought some rams and joined them and got a lamb crop of seventy-five per cent. And then the agri blokes came up with the answer—estrogens."

These are female hormones, and they inhibit the fertility of ewes. Yarloop, to everyone's surprise, proved to harbour one of these estrogens in harmful quantities. Now other strains of subterranean clover, including one with the more attractive name of Bacchus Marsh, have replaced it, and the fertility of the ewes of Esperance has been restored.

[12]

We drove 120 miles due west on bitumen without seeing another car. The emptiness of these roads, once you leave the major cities, and their excellence in relation to the sparsity of population, never ceased to amaze me. Drowsiness, not traffic, is the hazard. Mallee is terribly monotonous and the country dead flat. Here and there we passed a clearing where a corrugated-iron bungalow had been planted in the open with no shade, no garden, no anything but four walls and a roof. We also passed a bush fire that was filling the sky with black smoke dense enough, it looked, to cut with a knife and roaring like a bogged tractor. The ferocity of these bush fires is terrifying. Men are too few and far between to fight them in these parts, and so they sweep savagely on, exterminating every leaf and mouse and beetle in their path, and leaving only scorched and blackened trees and shrubs. Yet, over the millenniums, many eucalypts and acacias have learned to survive.

Beyond Ongerup and Mount Barker suddenly the country changes. It becomes a great deal more settled and kind. The farmsteads are larger and trees have been planted for shade and there are orchards, paddocks with grass in them, Guernsey cows. Here in this clement southwest corner, back of Albany, lie the fattest farms in the state and the finest surviving forest of the best timber in Australia.

These are jarrah and karri. Both are eucalypts (*E. marginata* and *E. diversicolor* respectively) and both have been, and are being, squandered. All day, on and off, we passed new clearings where trees that had been bashed with chains and raked by bulldozers into windrows were being burned or awaited burning. Thousands of tons of firewood must be wasted every year in this manner, presumably because the high cost of transport condemns it; yet in other countries a scarcity of firewood can be as desperate as the dearth of food, and every twig is treasured and hoarded. Or not even twigs—anything that will burn. I recalled two scenes from another continent: black-garbed Egyptian women scurrying from their hovels, each with a basket and shovel, to collect dung dropped by a passing camel; and in Nigeria little donkeys converging through the dust on Kano, carrying, behind their turbaned riders, Guinea-corn stalks to be sold for a few pennies each in the market. The fuel-hungry and the fuel-happy—no one's fault, I suppose.

Farther on, around Pemberton, are state forests where the jarrah and karri are being logged to a scientific plan that provides for regeneration. Jarrahs may live, foresters believe, for a thousand years; they are tall, and karris even taller, tapering up to 250 feet and over. The boles of both are straight as the columns of a temple and a lovely silvery-grey colour with tan showing through where the bark is peeling. Mr. Kelly, kingpin of Pemberton, explained that their clean-boled state is a result of crowding together; grown separately, they would spread instead of towering. Saplings germinate at the rate of hundreds of thousands to the acre and grow up spindly, and then "wolf trees" emerge, form a canopy, and smother weaker trees, until only twenty or twenty-five to the acre remain.

Thus the law of survival of the fittest, enforced century after century, must have eliminated all but the very toughest strains. So hard is the timber that it blunts the strongest saws and nowadays the trees are felled by high explosive. Yet it was here that, after World War I, newcomers from British cities were expected to fell these monsters *by hand* and then, settled in groups of twenty families on hundred-acre blocks, to make a living out of milk and potatoes. They all failed. Formerly these stubborn timbers were much sought after for wharves and mines, but now the demand is all for plywood, veneers and laminated woods and they have fallen out of favour, and so "the largest sawmill in the Southern Hemisphere" is no longer at full stretch.

The Pemberton district also has the largest pear tree not merely in the Southern Hemisphere but, I was assured, in the world. It was planted by the district's first settler, Edward Brockman, who in 1861 built a substantial house of home-burned bricks roofed with jarrah shingles, planted fruit trees, and bred horses for the Indian army. The Brockman family was well-to-do and accustomed to comfort and the best of colonial society, and life for the ladies in this isolated, savage spot, hemmed in by gigantic trees, must have been dreadful. "Nothing ever seemed to be repaired," a visitor recalled. "How could it be with no servants and no neighbours within thirty miles? Mr. B. and his sons look after the cattle and horses from morning till night dressed in rags, and his pretty lady wife does everything that is to be done within the house with only an orphan from the Perth orphanage to help her." Perhaps they bottled pears. It was said that four tons of fruit were picked from this single tree in one season and hauled to Kalgoorlie in a bullock dray.

There was a tribe of aborigines living here then; none survive. But this was not a brutal story of natives shot at sight or given poisoned flour. A shy, friendly people who lived on possums and on nuts of the zamia palm (which are poisonous if eaten fresh but become nutritious after six weeks' burial), they did not molest the settlers' cattle; the whites were anxious only to help them, and a paternal government issued them nice warm blankets. Delighted with this new amenity, the blacks wore the blankets night and day, even when wet; as a result they contracted pneumonia to which they succumbed in droves. The last survivors were moved away in 1912 and the tribe became extinct—literally killed by kindness.

All over Australia are places I never reached but wished I had—Shangri-las, Spanish castles. One such is Two People Bay, close to Albany. Not only is the name engaging, but it was the scene of the rediscovery of the noisy scrubbird which everyone believed to be extinct. It had not been seen since 1899. On Christmas day in 1961 an Albany schoolmaster, Mr. Harley Webster, secured a close enough view of a bird he had been keeping under observation to confirm his hopes and hurried home to telephone to Dr. Dominic Serventy in Perth. Abandoning his family Christmas, Dr. Serventy drove at top speed for 500 miles and endorsed the identification. A movement was set a foot to put aside a small reserve especially for the bird, which probably exists nowhere else. Unfortunately a new township had already been planned on the peninsula it frequents. So interests clashed, and a lively argument arose; but the noisy scrubbird has powerful friends and managed to secure its little bit of territory beside Two People Bay.

TWELVE

Perth

Most cities use the rivers on which they lie primarily as highways and sewers. Perth is the only modern city I can recall that puts first the uses of embellishment, as Venice must once have done. The Swan sweeps generously through it and is spanned by a couple of bridges made with a light hand; by day it sparkles and at night becomes a river of stars. One evening I drove across at sunset, stunned by an improbably dramatic welter of colour; great bands of crimson and of orange swept across the sky and were reflected in the water above a necklace of lights. I gazed enraptured, but the taxi driver merely glanced up and grunted. "An apology for a sunset," he said.

The older part of the city, which has some handsome Victorian edifices, turns its back upon the Swan, and you can jostle your way about crowded and, in the main, too-narrow streets unconscious of its presence; but you have only to walk a block to find yourself on the margin of the wide blue river amid grass and trees. River and buildings are parted by a freeway spanned by footbridges with a gay twirl at either end. Trees and lawns line the freeway, and an aromatic whiff from the peppermint tree sometimes triumphs over traffic smells. There is a purity about the atmosphere, a brilliance in the light, and a sense of gaiety rare in cities and deriving, I would suppose, partly from the mild mediterranean climate, and partly from the banishment of heavy industries to the new center of Kwinana, down the coast a little on the Cockburn Sound.

An enormous refinery led the way in 1952, and other industries followed: rolling mills, cement, bauxite, and plants, some of them no doubt the largest in the Southern Hemisphere, to make fertilizers, paper, lubricating oil and many other things. It is all exceedingly impressive—a huge industrial complex that has sprung to life from nothing within fourteen years. The best part of it, to my mind, is that it draws away from the capital the smoke and grime and noise, and the tangle of power lines and transformers and railway sidings and all the ugliness attendant upon industry. Kwinana has enabled Perth to develop more or less as a garden city and has kept the air clean and fresh. And what a difference it makes! White buildings stay white, the sky and river blue, and subtle aromas from flowering shrubs and flowers and the spicy sap of trees are not obliterated by diesel fumes and sulphuretted hydrogen. Brightness hangs in the air.

Above the north bank of the river there are heights where modern glass-and-concrete towers look at home and command magnificent views over the rest of the city, the winding river and the coastal plain. And here is a thousand-acre park, embracing a botanical garden, where you could be a hundred miles from any city, and where the vegetation, with its birds and beasts, has been kept as it was. In a short walk among the eucalypts I saw the green, blue and yellow parrots known as "twenty-eights," a spinebill honey eater diving into a banksia flower, several wattlebirds, a yellow-tailed hornbill, warblers and wrens and at least a dozen other species, all in about half an hour.

Perth is spreading fastest south of the Swan and into an ebullience of colour, traffic and trees. It really is a place of gardens, creepers and semitropical shrubs. Oleanders were in bloom, bougainvillaeas blazed, frangipanis gave out their cloying scent; scarcely a home was without its bed of brilliant annuals—zinnias, begonias, asters, salvias, salpiglossis. There were great clots of blue and pink hydrangeas, rampaging agapanthus, plate-sized dahlias, climbing daturas and bignonias and morning glories, and roses, roses everywhere. Sprinklers whirl day and night and there is no shortage of water. I suppose there must be garden haters in Perth, or at any rate people indifferent to gardens, but they are submerged. And there must be cold, wet, windy days when the river fails to sparkle, the trees drip, people are bad-tempered, and everything goes wrong. I was there in summer when the sun shone, the gardens blazed, the air sparkled, the views delighted, and people seemed, at any rate on short acquaintance, to be good-natured, happy and kind. There is no doubt that Perth, as a city, has most of the things a city ought to have, and at present it is even about the right size—not quite half a million people, enough to have outgrown provincialism, not enough to have lost identity or made it impossible to get about. You can still drive a car in Perth and find a place to park.

[2]

For years the Western Australians felt neglected and even despised by the Easterners. Cut off by over a thousand miles of desert, the rest of the country did not seem to know or care what went on in Perth. A posting there was regarded by sophisticated Easterners as a kind of exile, and the huge, undeveloped state was starved for funds. Right or wrong, this was the conviction. Traces of it linger on. When I remarked upon the excellence of a highway along which we were speeding, my companion bitterly exclaimed, "Bloody Victorian money!" Then he laughed and added, "Well, no one likes being on the dole." The political history of Western Australia is largely a history first of attempts to keep out of the Federation, then to secede and set up an independent state within what was then the British Empire.

All that belongs to the past. Not that Western Australians have come to love the Easterners, or even to like them any better; it is that Western Australia has "arrived." For this there are many reasons, of which three predominate. First there is the death of Australia as an outpost of Europe, a colony planted on the far side of the earth, and its rebirth as an Asiatic power. "We used to be two and a half thousand miles *away* from the center of things," a West Australian put it. "Now we're two and a half thousand miles nearer." Nearer to markets, for one thing— the big and expanding markets of Asia. That, in itself, is drawing to the west capital, enterprise and skill. You see many Asiatic faces in the streets of Perth, and the university is full of them; all told—not only at the university, but training in various skills—there are about five thousand Asian students in and around the capital.

The second reason for the change is the discovery that Western Australia possesses, beneath its rugged and unpeopled ranges, the largest deposits of iron ore and bauxite, not merely in the Southern Hemisphere, but very likely in the world. These discoveries have coincided with technical developments which will enable the minerals to be economically extracted from their rocks and gorges. Western Australia is about to erupt into the industrial age and send its mineral wealth flowing into Asia. This is one of the most dramatic happenings of modern times.

The third factor is less tangible but catalyzes the other two. For years the ablest West Australians have been drawn away to wider opportunities in the eastern states and overseas. This phase is over. Western

Australia has built up a population large enough to generate its own cultural and technical power and lively enough to hold its own talented sons and daughters. They need no longer emigrate to Melbourne or Adelaide, or to New York or London, to make a name or win a fortune. Self-confidence throbs in all parts of the state and among all sorts of people, from university professors to cattle-station cooks.

Migrants are coming, but not in the numbers Western Australia needs and can absorb. To receive them Perth has two hostels, one under the Commonwealth Government and one under the state. The state hostel takes only British migrants, most of whom arrive by air and find themselves at work within two or three days. Its capacity is just under five hundred people, and only seventy were there on the day of my visit. This is a transit hostel, where people stay for six to eight weeks; in the Commonwealth hostel they can stay for two years.

The shortage of houses is rather less acute in Perth than elsewhere. One of the newcomers I spoke to, a young turner from Stroud, had bought a house within a week of his arrival and raised a mortgage; he would pay $10 a week and the house would be his in thirty years. "The country's all we expected and more," he commented. His wife was having a driving lesson; he was getting a sun tan. What had decided them to emigrate? "England's too crowded; everything's on top of you. Traffic, houses everywhere, no country left. We've got two small boys. What'll it be like by the time they're grown up? Here there's space and opportunity." I heard a Western Australian say, "I can point my nose in any direction and go a thousand miles and still be in my own country."

An attractive girl from Leeds, minding a toddler, added, "England's dead. You can't get anywhere till you're forty. My husband's a carpenter; he's studied at night school and wants to start a business on his own. Not much chance at home, is there? Not without something behind you. Here . . . I've a brother in Sydney—he's made a start already with radio repairs. My parents mean to come out when we've got a house."

Not everyone is satisfied, of course. "The wages aren't what we expected," said a Bristol woman. "My husband can't get the overtime. We're worse off than at home and there's no work here for women. And rents much too high. How do they expect us to save?"

Australians, for their part, criticize a "they" outlook among the British. "They" should provide houses, "they" should subsidize rents, "they" should give the children free books and uniforms and school meals; "they," in fact, should support British migrants in the style to which they are accustomed in a full-blown welfare state. The Australian "they" is not so pervasive and generous a benefactor. In Australia "they" do not provide a house, but "we" do. "We" buy or build it ourselves. This the British, accustomed to a council house at a sub-economic rent, find hard to grasp.

Immigration authorities say that all such points of difference are fully explained to all assisted migrants before they are accepted for the scheme. Despite this, many migrants bring their welfare-state mentality with them. Somewhere, they believe, whatever people say, there must be a "they" with a house to rent. In each state a Housing Commission does partially fulfill the function of a "they." It builds relatively cheap houses, some of which it rents, and some it sells at cost price over a period of years; in this case the tenant, not the Commission, must look after the house. If a tap leaks, he must put in a new washer himself, not ring up the council about it.

The proportion of houses built by the Commission, compared with the number built and sold privately, is low and waiting lists long. So most of the migrants have to pay much higher rents than they are used to. This is their principal complaint.

[3]

The hostels maintained by both state and Commonwealth governments have come in for sharp criticism. Most of them are old army hutments and are pretty crude. Each family has a flat of an appropriate size and is not overcrowded, and all the flats I saw were clean. The camps were well-kept, and the hostel officials I met were helpful, conscientious and keen. On the other hand, living is communal, and families, especially the women, seldom enjoy that. They must share ablution blocks and eat in canteens. The food, as far as I could sample it, was adequate and competently cooked, but institutional. People sit at small tables, not in long rows, and in most of the canteens a real effort has been made to brighten things up with fresh paint and plastic flowers. But the great majority of women long to fry their own bit of fish in their own frying pan, to boil their own potato in their own way. Some buy electric pans, which are forbidden, and cook surreptitious meals, and to this most hostel managers turn a blind eye.

A hostel, after all, is not intended as a permanent home. Some families stay no longer than a couple of weeks, others much longer; the period varies widely from state to state. In New South Wales and in the

Commonwealth hostels the average length of stay is only three weeks short of a full year. It is only fourteen weeks in South Australia. Western Australia comes in between, with an average stay of twenty-eight weeks.

To find a house, or buy a block and build one, is difficult eveywhere. If the hostels were made too comfortable, a lot of families would settle in and make no serious effort to overcome these difficulties. A few families do so as it is. In a hostel their upkeep is subsidized, everything is done for them, and there are few worries, so they install a television, park their car outside the Nissen hut, and settle in more or less for life. A balance must be struck between conditions falling below a standard nowadays considered decent and conditions too encouraging to the lazier and more feckless element.

Roughly two out of every three assisted migrants never go near a hostel at all. They are sponsored by relations or friends already in Austrialia and go directly to them. So far as the authorities are concerned, the migrants fill in the forms, get their $20 assisted passages, embark by plane or ship, and disappear.

Over one million British migrants have gone to Australia since the end of World War II. The total of all migrants is twice this figure. The British proportion has been steadily rising and has now reached about seven out of ten. Of the remaining three, one is Greek and rather less than one Italian; then come Dutch and German, a long way behind.

The great majority of British migrants find Australia to their liking and remain. The authorities reckon that only six out of every hundred migrants of all nationalities go home and that about half of these come back again, doubly disillusioned and obliged, the second time, to pay their own fares. A failure rate of 3 per cent suggests that this is probably the most successful scheme of organized migration conducted anywhere in the world. Credit must be shared between good luck and good management. Good luck because the period has been one of an expanding economy; by and large there have been openings for everyone who came with the intention of working. The one or two bad patches have not been sufficiently bad or prolonged to shake the foundations of the scheme. The rest is good management, in that a postitive effort has been made to settle in the migrants—to "integrate" them, in the jargon of the day. The hub of this effort is the Good Neighbour scheme.

Australia is covered by a network of Good Neighbour Councils manned, and womanned, by unpaid volunteers. Their function is to seek out individual migrants in the area they cover, to make them feel at home and tackle any particular problems that may arise—much as Citizens Advice Bureaus do in Britain. They will arrange English classes for speakers of foreign tongues or simply act as friends and ask Mrs. Mazzotti and Mrs. Theopholus and Mrs. Schmidt to tea. Membership of the councils is drawn from all the other voluntary bodies in which the country so generously abounds—about four hundred of them all told.

I was in Canberra when the annual Citizenship Convention was held. Good Neighbours flocked from every nook and cranny of Australia, imbued with great enthusiasm for the cause. The theme of this particular conference was how to persuade more of the migrants—if possible, all of the migrants—to foreswear their native lands and become naturalized Australian citizens. Most of them do so already, but a sizeable minority keep the passports of their country of origin. Australians attach a particular importance to the status of a citizen, as all people do when they are trying to weave the strands of many nations, tongues, religions and traditions into a single pattern. "We must receive them into the brotherhood of our country," Sir Robert Menzies has said. And they, for their part, in the words of the Minister for Immigration, Mr. Hubert Opperman, must remember that "there is no place for inward-looking enclaves or self-perpetuating minorities here." Australians make them welcome without regard to previous allegiances and classes; migrants in return must renounce former loyalties.

As citizens already, Pommies need swear no oaths. They are priviledged in many ways. Have they given back as good as they have taken? Most Australians, I believe, would say that, on the whole, they have, despite the wingeing of which you hear many complaints. Like their hosts, the British migrants have changed. The modern migrant seldom leaves his country for his country's good—much more likely to his country's detriment. Most British migrants today are young—more than two out of every three are under thirty—enterprising and, above all, skilled. These are the pick of the population, the people everyone wants: the tradesmen and professional men and technicians, prepared to take a chance and yet not reckless; married, and probably with young children; responsible, healthy and above the average in intelligence.

Britain, as we all know, is also a magnet for migrants. Here the colour issue enters in. Setting aside the emotive fact that most immigrants into Britain are black or brown, whereas migrants to Australia are almost all white—not quite all; since 1945 there have been 11,000

Chinese—the fact remains that the proportion of skilled to unskilled is probably reversed. That is, while Australia gets one unskilled man for every three skilled, Britain gets at least three unskilled men, probably more, for every one who has a craft, profession, or trade. In other words, Britain is exchanging mechanics, carpenters, plumbers, electricians and people who can program computers for peasants and labourers, many of whom lack knowledge of the alphabet as well as of slide rule or lathe.

Socially perhaps it is desirable. Britain offers opportunity to Pakistani rice tillers and cutters of Barbadian cane, just as Australia does to British engineers and accountants. To what extent it will help to modernize Britain's economy, increase production, stimulate exports, and advance all those other aims the British people are constantly exhorted to pursue is another matter. Meanwhile Australia is pulling the migrants—white migrants—in. Nearly one Australian in five was born overseas and has arrived since 1945. Whatever becomes of the parents, about the children there are no qualms. They are Aussies to the marrow.

[4]

Everything is huge in Western Australia; it has the broadest deserts, the longest coastline, the wildest ranges, the greatest ore reserves, the largest wheat fields, the tallest trees—and the smallest treasures. In Perth I was shown three trees on a street corner. At the university I saw a little tortoise about six inches long; it is not only small but exceedingly rare and has been given a small reserve all to itself—possibly the only reserve in the world set aside entirely for a tortoise.

In 1953 a schoolboy found a single specimen in a swamp near Perth and brought it to his natural-history teacher. This led to a furore among zoologists, who believed it to belong to a new species, named it, and wrote it up in scientific journals. An American zoologist recalled that in a Viennese museum he had seen a similar specimen. They proved to be the same and to have a name already—the short-necked tortoise, *Pseudemydura umbrina*. The Viennese specimen, collected in 1890, was the only other one known.

Perth zoologists have since discovered that the habitat of this short-necked fresh-water tortoise is limited to three swamps, where it lives a very private life, burrowing down a natural hole or crack to estivate. It is not at all prolific, laying only three or four eggs, has a voracious appetite for the larvae of mosquitoes, and will accept a little chopped raw meat. A young zoologist, Andrew Burbage, has captured eight specimens and stuck to their backs tiny radio transistor sets whose regularly transmitted beeps enable him to chart their movements underground.

The carapace of any tortoise, with its domed and polished surface, is not easily adhered to, and all but two of his tortoises have got rid of their transistor sets. Another difficulty is to provide a battery small enough to fit onto the back of a six-inch tortoise that will store enough current to last for six months. Nor had the captive tortoise I inspected in its tank been co-operative; it has refused to breed and shown no sign of growth for a year.

"There are two small reserves," said the zoologist, "one on clay and one on sand. A public appeal raised six hundred dollars, the government gave two thousand, and the owner parted with the land very cheap. So at least the future of the species is secure." Australian tortoises, short-necked or otherwise, appear always to be looking over one shoulder. Their heads are put on sideways, as it were, and retract at an angle, instead of poking out fore and aft like the European species. They are a more primitive form of tortoise, not having developed the rubbery socket into which their more advanced brethren pull back their flat heads.

The story of the short-necked tortoise underlies a point to which conservationists return again and again: if you want to preserve a species, you can almost forget about the animal itself and concentrate upon its habitat. And it is remarkable how small a change can disturb a habitat. "A cow that merely walks across a pasture can change it," said Dr. Dominic Serventy, head of the C.S.I.R.O.'s wildlife division in Perth. Sheep are the worst culprits; by changing the habitat, they drive out the other creatures—even trap-door spiders, who dwell among the brittle layers of litter shed by mulga trees. This the sheep cut into and destroy with their sharp hoofs, rendering the spiders homeless. Most people would not mind much about spiders, but biologists mind very much indeed when any species goes.

[5]

Eleven miles off the mainland lies a small island called Rottnest which is famous for its quokkas. These are very small wallabies (*Setonix brachyurus*) no larger than hares, and there are only two places where they are known for certain to survive: here on Rottnest, and on Bald Island off the southwest coast near Albany. Formerly they were common on the mainland, but in 1935 there occurred a "population crash" whose cause is not certainly known; it could have been an epidemic, and foxes may have played a part. A lesser "crash" that took place on Rottnest Island in a hot, dry summer (1953–54) has been put down to a protein deficiency in the diet.

Rottnest Island is a kind of open-air laboratory attached to the Zoology Department of the University in Perth, over which presides Professor Harry Waring, who is mainly to be found in a pair of shorts and shirt open to the waist among the marsupials, on which he is one of the world's leading authorities, or clambering about his island like an agile wallaby and known to everyone simply as Harry.

Rottnest Island covers 5,000 acres, and about the same number of quokkas are believed to inhabit it. Since 1917 it has been a nature reserve in which all birds and beasts have been protected, so a balance has been struck between the various species, and between them and their habitat, which has left man out of account. There is no fresh water on the island, and the quokkas have adapted themselves to live on brackish water sucked from the margins of salt lakes and to reduce their intake of liquid to an astonishingly low level. They seem able to manage for months at a time on the minute amounts of moisture they extract from droughted, dehydrated plants and to turn the dry and fibrous herbage into protein much more efficiently than sheep can do, or any other ruminant. And like their relatives, the kangaroos, they can suspend the development of the fertile egg within the womb until the pouch is vacant and so ready to receive the embryo. This is, in effect, a built-in mechanism, regulated by endocrine glands, to adjust the population to the food supply; and it was among these little Rottnest Island quokkas that the story was first fully unravelled by Dr. (now Professor) G. B. Sharman, then working with Professor Waring at the University of Western Australia.

I heard from Francis Ratcliffe a story about the genesis of this outstanding piece of research which illustrates the difficulty of ever nailing down a scientific discovery to a particular individual at a particular place and time. To Dr. Sharman undoubtedly belongs the credit of working out in full this story of delayed implantation and suspended oestrus; but fifteen or twenty years before, Mrs. C. F. H. Jenkins, then working in the Perth Museum, looked after a pygmy possum found with a family of pouch young, all of whom died. Soon afterwards, with no help from any male, the little possum produced another family. Mrs. Jenkins published a short note on this phenomenon which was picked up by Dr. Carl Hartman, an American physiologist, who wrote a paper advancing the suggestion of delayed implantation as a possible explanation. This was never followed up, and Dr. Sharman did not hear of the paper until after he had arrived, quite independently, at the same conclusion and demonstrated its truth among the Rottnest quokkas.

Although the island teams with quokkas, in daylight hours not one is to be seen; somehow they manage to conceal themselves in the low, tussocky grass and low, open heath land that has almost entirely replaced bush and forest formerly described as "impenetrable." Fires destroyed these forests, and quokkas prevented their regeneration by nibbling the shoots. Now the Rottnest Island Board is attempting to revive the native vegetation by fencing small plantations of the once predominant eucalypt, the tuart, and of the local tea tree and the Rottnest pine. The enemy is the wind, which howls about the island with remarkable ferocity; we were almost swept away, and my biological education, so kindly provided by Professor Waring and Dr. David Ride of the Perth Museum, had to be conducted in a series of bellows and even then was partially lost upon the air.

[6]

All animals, birds included, in Western Australia are "protected" unless they are placed upon an open list. This is not quite so favourable to the animals as it sounds, because the open list is large and long, and anything elected to it not merely gets no protection but may be classed as vermin. Some of the listed animals are undoubted pests: foxes and dingoes especially and, in the wild mountain ranges of the northwest, formerly domestic creatures that have listened to the call of the wild— camels, donkeys, pigs and goats. Among the native fauna both the red kangaroo—here called the marloo—and the hills kangaroo, or wallaroo —here called the euro—are under attack. A lot of birds are on the open list, including several lovely parrots—the king, the twenty-eight, the western rosella and the ubiquitous galah—and also the salt-water crocodile, and practically all the snakes.

The protection of animals, curiously enough, comes under the Department of Fisheries, which looks after more than 7,000 square miles of nature reserves. These reserves have been chosen to represent all the important habitats, so that almost every species can find some sanctuary where it will not be molested—or at least on paper it will not, but Mr. Shrugg, one of the members of the department, told me that it has two full-time field officers to supervise an area eighteen times larger than England and Wales. There are also four hundred voluntary wardens, but their powers are limited and their zeal and competence naturally uneven.

"Over a million acres are being cleared each year for cropping," Mr. Shrugg said, "and much larger areas are degenerating from overgrazing by sheep." In such degenerating regions the natural grasses are replaced by the harsh and spiky spinifex (*Triodia spp*). Dr. Charles Gardiner, formerly the state's chief botanist, has said that Australia is creating the biggest desert in the world in the shortest space of time ever known.

Salination is another trouble, not peculiar to Western Australia, but to be found here on a serious scale. Clearing the land raises the water table; salt rises with the water and is precipitated in pans. This discourages the deeper-rooted plants which formerly assisted rain water to percolate the soil. Everything dries up and hardens, and in places land has had to be abandoned. Here is one more example of the unforeseen effects of disturbance to the delicate balance between soil, plants, climate and creatures; you clear bush to plant a crop, apparently an innocent procedure, and end up with salt pans, spinifex and yet another desert on your hands.

The ecosystem, once upset, plays all sorts of unpredictable tricks. Sheep cannot thrive on spinfex, but euros can and do, so in they come in droves. The region most severely overrun is called the Pilbara, in the northwestern part of the state: a barren, rugged, empty quarter covering about 50,000 square miles—nearly twice as large as Tasmania—and still much as nature made it; graziers have merely dotted water points about and put in sheep to manage as best they can in competition with the euros, the wild donkeys and the dingoes. The average rate of stocking in the Pilbara is one sheep to fifty acres or more.

When a number of properties had been wholly abandoned because of spinifex and euros, the C.S.I.R.O. mounted a research project to find out how and why the situation had got out of hand. The first thing they discovered was how wonderfully adapted is the euro to these arid regions of unremitting heat. A batch of euros confined to an area of spinifex without shade or water survived for three of the hottest months of the year. They reduced their need for moisture by lying up during the heat of the day and by eating so little that a minimum of urine was needed to wash the wastes away. And scientists think they may have evolved some "yet undetermined physiological adaptations" to enable them to survive such prolonged dehydration. When they do find water, they will naturally drink, and so the graziers put poison in the troughs. On a station called Talga Talga, where only 2,300 sheep were run on 24,000 acres, poisoning of half the water points killed off about 11,500 euros. So the owner had been carrying at least five euros for every one sheep. To poison armies of kangaroos in this manner is even more wasteful than to slaughter them for pet food; the corpses merely rot. Research has also shown that euros do not travel far; many spend their whole lives within a few hundred yards of their birth place. So if a paddock is restored, they will not come for miles to eat it out. A regeneration program for the Pilbara is now under way. A practice known as deferred rotational grazing will, if carefully followed, restore the spinifex and ultimately the grasses; periodic poisoning of the euros forms part of the routine.

Red kangaroos are also under pressure. There is an "open season" all the year round, and teams of professional shooters operate with mobile freezers as in New South Wales and Queensland, but since no comparable statistics are kept, no one knows the annual toll, which must run into hundreds of thousands. On a single station, 800 miles north of Perth, one team recently "cropped" 27,000 kangaroos at the rate of about 120 a night. Although, a vermin-control officer told me, there has been a "significant decrease" in the state's red kangaroo population, they are not officially considered to be on the danger list. But there is always the risk of a "population crash" such as that which wiped out the mainland quokkas; and, as we have seen, year by year their habitat is shrinking.

Two of the smaller species of marsupial *are* on the danger list: the numbat, or banded anteater, a small, striped creature with a bushy tail, a long snout and a tongue especially adapted to extract termites from timber; and a very small honey mouse. There is also some doubt about the tammar wallaby, now virtually extinct on the mainland but still to be found on the Abrolhos Islands off the coast near Geraldton, and Dr. Serventy has listed five species of bird (night and ground parrots, rufous bristlebird, noisy scrubbird, western whipbird) as in danger of extinction.

While it is easy to admire feathered friends if you live in suburbs with birdbaths or in Europe and winterfeed robins and tits, I daresay few of us would feel the same if the robins towered over us like emus, and eagles with a seven-foot wing span perched on bird baths demanding dead lambs. Apart from anything else, the expense of provisioning these avian giants would very soon ruin us. That is more or less the situation which many Western Australian farmers and graziers believe themselves to be in. So the splendid wedge-tailed eagle has a price of fifty cents on its beak, and up to date some 150,000 have been killed for bonus payments; there is also a bonus on dead emus, which has been paid on about 370,000 birds. Some years ago the outcry against emus by the wheat farmers reached such proportions that the state government enlisted the support of the Commonwealth military forces, and machine-gun detachments arrived, plus two Lewis guns, to do battle with an estimated 20,000 birds.

The plan was to drive the emus up against the fences and shoot them down. But the emus, like the Tasmanian aborigines, refused to be driven; they broke into small parties and ran away in all directions and sustained only about a dozen casualties. There were red faces in Canberra, and the troops were withdrawn. Now the emus are protected in the southwestern portion of the state but still classed as vermin elsewhere. Despite a heavy annual toll, however—20,000 in 1965—they are not considered to be in danger of extermination in the state as a whole.

Even sanctuaries set aside for animals, let alone the animals in them, are not always safe. Conservationist opinion was shocked when the state government granted a concession to mine salt on a small island scheduled as a nature reserve and the sole habitat of one particular subspecies of shearwater. Reserves can be made and unmade at the will of legislators. "Too many people," Dr. Serventy said, "look on reserves merely as potentially vacant land held in cold storage until some 'useful' purpose can be found for it."

A proposal to build swimming pools and an amusement center in the middle of King's Park in Perth, where the central object is to preserve the virgin bush in its natural condition, has been brought three times before the State Parliament and has been three times defeated—so far.

[7]

The people of Perth will tell you that their lives are relaxed and informal and that they disbelieve in rat-racing. Certainly they are remarkably hospitable. Never before have I found myself, within a few hours of my arrival, removed from a hotel to be installed in the comfortable dwelling of a total stranger, who himself moved out to a relative's and left me the run of everything from a well-stocked refrigerator to a radiogram and ironing board. Books, records, pictures and the manuscript of a half-written play were strewn about; flowering shrubs, creepers, trees and climbing roses enclosed the flat in a cocoon of greenery. Three minutes' walk took you to the river's bank, and there were scarcely any traffic noises; on the corner a sort of village shop, kept by Italians, afforded opportunities for gossip.

In the flat people came and went; so did corgies, and a cat for whose benefit hatch holes had been cut in the bottoms of doors. A neighbour looked in with a caged parrot that was off-colour; apparently Tom Hungerford knows a bit about birds. "When I lost my husband, Tom came over and did the garden for me," she said. "He planted all the roses." She was an Englishwoman who had stayed on, after her husband had died, to teach in a technical college.

"There are differences," she said of her pupils, comparing them with girls whom she had taught in Liverpool. "These girls are more independent. They want to find out for themselves. In England you give it to them on a plate; here you give them the plate and tell them to go and find something to put on it. Then they'll respond. If they're bored, they'll fold their arms and get bloody-minded. The least suggestion of superiority is the one thing they won't stand."

Among the people for whom Perth is famous are the sisters Mary and Elizabeth Durack, the first a writer and the second a painter. There is a Durack river in the Kimberleys and Durack Range, both called after their grandfather, the hero of one of those astonishing sagas of men who drove their flocks and herds across a continent to found pastoral empires in the northwest. In *Kings in Grass Castles* Mary Durack has told in vivid detail the story of the barefoot boy from the hills of Galway who emigrated at the age of sixteen and became the master of several million acres of Australian land. When his father died, leaving him in charge of a widowed mother and a family of seven, he went to the gold fields and made a couple of thousand dollars enough to start a small holding near Goulburn in New South Wales. A flock of Irish relatives took up land all round and soon there was a rookery of Duracks, Costellos, Kilfoyles, Skehans and Scanlans, who built two-roomed slab shacks with earth floors and stocked their paddocks from the local pound.

When the Free Selection Acts of the 1860's threw open almost for the taking enormous areas, still mainly unexplored, in the new state of Queensland, he set forth into the unknown with four or five brothers and cousins, a hundred horses and four hundred breeding cattle. The farther northwest they got, the more arid did the country become; the ground was cracked and riven by drought, the cattle tormented by thirst, and when at last they smelled water, they broke into a stampede and crushed and trampled each other to death. All that survived, bogged in mud, had to be shot. Even then the men would not give up but trudged on, still hoping to find water. Their horses collapsed; their own supply of water ran out, and finally they shot their last horse and drank its blood. They would certainly have perished had not a party of aborigines appeared, led them to water, and helped them to get back.

Incredibly Patsy Durack returned to this fearful country on the Cooper and, even more incredibly, took his wife and two babies. He borrowed money to buy more cattle and horses, together with wagons and harness and provisions and six pigs, six milking goats, fourteen laying hens, twelve Muscovy ducks and a boar. Once more they spent three months on the track to Bourke. At Warroo Springs on the Queensland border a Costello baby was born. About 300 miles farther to the northwest they reached a creek shaded by coolibahs and wild oranges, the dwelling-place of countless geese and ducks and other waterfowl. Here at Kyabra, in the channel country of the Cooper, in 1868, they found at last their permanent water. On the banks of the creek they built a house that stood for seventy years, proceeded to select land for other members of the tribe and, bit by bit, to paddock their own and to brand their first calves. Ten years after they had reached the creek, Patsy and his brothers drove two thousand "fats" to distant markets and between them and the Costellos held the leaseholds of eleven million acres, an area almost two-thirds the size of their native Ireland.

Still they were not content. In the pubs and stockmen's quarters of western Queensland talk began to veer towards "the Center" and "the Territory" where lay virgin pastures, unclaimed ranges, water in abundance—still the beckoning vision of that great inland sea.

In 1870 the port of Darwin, then called Palmerston, was opened, and connected two years later with Port Augusta in South Australia by the Overland Telegraph. Overlanders were driving mobs of cattle north and west from Queensland, and speculators were marking out leases on the blank spaces of maps. Even farther west, beyond the Gulf country, beyond the Territory, lay lands of even greater promise; wide and never-failing rivers, ranges rich with the good mitchella and flinders grasses, water in billabongs and creeks—all there for the taking. This was in Western Australia. In 1879 the explorer Alexander Forrest made his way from the west coast through ranges that were to be called the Kimberleys and across still unmapped deserts to the Overland Telegraph and wrote a report which was read by Patsy Durack. The move-on fever worked in his blood until, the ruler of one pastoral empire, he sent his sons to found another in the west.

[8]

When Elizabeth Durack started to sketch aborigines living on her father's station, her family disapproved. "What do you want to draw an ugly old native for? Why don't you draw something pretty, like a flower?"

It would be hard to think of a word less applicable to the outback of Western Australia than pretty. Magnificent and mighty, cruel and terrifying; the kernel of the people is tragic. Something of this Elizabeth Durack manages to convey in deceptively simple and technically accomplished drawings. A dark storm lowers over Broome; a lanky stockman with his face shrouded like an Arab's leans into a storm of burning sand; men ride among droughted mulgas and spindly anthills and worn-out soils; a broken-down, white-haired swagman sits limp-handed on an iron bedstead in a humpy with no companions but crows—such are her subjects. Her portraits of aborigines seem to capture the timeless quietude, the patience and dignity and, again, the tragic kernel within these people who knew how to live with the land without trying to change it—to accept and not to conquer.

Despite a network of efficient airlines, and despite a national broadcasting service, Western Australia still remains, to some extent, an island, and in the arts the islanders are beginning to develop a school of their own. Among the formative influences are the feeling of living on a desert's fringe, the still largely non-urban character of society, the heat and desiccation, and the culture of the aborigines. A spurious reflection of that can be seen everywhere—in bark-painting designs on tablecloths, in tourists' boomerangs and so forth. But here something of the spirit of the native people, their resignation perhaps, has been picked up by the antennae of the artist and passed along the nerves and into the creative brain. It may be that Western Australian artists will filter through to the coming Australian culture is only truly indigenous element.

This trend, if it amounts to that, is also at work among writers. In the novels of Randolph Stow, a young West Australian, the aboriginal characters are complete human beings, not symbols or villains or comics. Yet their outlines are fuzzed by mystery, as the shapes of men of other cultures must always be. Both in painting and in writing the influence from this side of the continent seems to me intensely romantic, and yet underlying it is an awareness of the implacability of nature. In the last century an observer wrote of Australians: "They have in their underside the taint of cruelty." It is the cruelty of acceptance, born of rocks and sand and sun. Jehovah was a god of deserts and cried, "I will repay."

Certainly Australia's human legacy is bloodcurdling. In my ignorance I had assumed Captain Phillip and his jailbirds to have been the first white settlers on Australian shores. But Western Australia has a longer history of contact with Europe and far more atrocious harbingers of Christian civilization. Another Perth writer, Henrietta Drake-Brockman, in her *Voyage to Disaster* has chronicled a story that can make the hair stand on end even today.

[9]

Off the coast of Geraldton, some 250 miles north of Perth, lie the Albrohos Islands, and off these islands lie a number of wrecks of Dutch vessels which, in the seventeenth century, were blown from their course between the Cape of Good Hope and Java to founder on the rocks. Six vessels are known to have perished, and the wrecks of four have been identified, including the *Batavia* which was lost in 1629. The senior official of the East India Company on board was Francisco Pelsaert. With his skipper he took to an open boat, reached Java and returned in a yacht, the *Sardam,* to rescue the survivors who were marooned on two small rocky islands of the Albrohos group.

During his absence a maniac called Jeronimus Cornelisz seized authority, appointed a "council" of cutthroats and proceeded to eliminate the rest of the shipwrecked company. His intention was to seize the vessel he rightly anticipated would come to their rescue, massacre the crew and sail away with his band of henchmen to a life of piracy. So on the islands a Mau Mau-like reign of terror prevailed. Men were seized at night and taken out to sea and drowned; children were strangled while Cornelisz entertained their parents at supper; his gangsters cut the throats of all the sick. One night eighteen men and boys were murdered, another night fifteen women and·boys; children were poisoned, men trying to escape caught and beheaded. The *Batavia* had 268 souls abroad when she struck, and only seventy-four returned to Java in the *Sardam*. The mutineers had murdered 125 of the missing total, and forty or fifty had been drowned while trying to escape.

Jeronimus Cornelisz was at last captured and delivered over to Pelsaert, who tried, tortured and hanged him with six of the ringleaders. Cornelisz had displayed all the symptoms of the paranoiac; he had dressed himself and his band in finery looted from the ship's merchandise, "changing daily into different clothes, silk stockings, garters with gold lace . . . to all his followers whom he could best trust, and who were most willing to murder, he gave clothes made from cloth sewn with two or more bands of gold braid . . . when the most murders had been committed, they shared the women who remained." There was the now familiar ritual of secret oaths and public pledges to follow to the death a leader who "did not any longer like the name of merchant" and called himself the captain-general.

Pelsaert appears to have been a gentle character, deeply shocked, and also puzzled, as many who came after him have been, as to how far men terrorized by an obviously mad usurper can be held responsible for the crimes they have been forced to commit. What of the guilt, for instance, of Jan of Bemmel, a cabin boy, aged eighteen, to whom Cornelisz had said, "Here is my sword; go kill Cornelis Aldersen, cut off his head in order to see if it is sharp enough." Jan of Bemmel "could not compose himself to die, weeping and wailing and begging for grace" at the foot of the gallows; the compassionate Pelsaert thereupon made his youth an excuse to set him down, with Wouter Loos of Maastricht, a soldier, aged about twenty-four, who had "through his innate corruptness let himself be used by the godless, Epicurean villain, Jeronimus Cornelisz, to the murdering of people," on the mainland about fifty miles from the beach they had named "*Batavia*'s graveyard."

Pelsaert was merciful; he was also a Dutch merchant. The two young "death-deserving delinquents" were instructed to look about them, make friends with the natives, and do a little market research so as to "be of some service to the Company" if Dutch ships should return. To this end they were provided with knives, beads, bells and small mirrors to give to the natives and instructed to make friends with chiefs who might take them into their "villages," where the castaways were to "observe with all diligence what material, be it Gold or Silver, happens to be found, and what they esteem as valuable"; and so, if and when ships should come, the natives would be properly anxious "to obtain more of such goods as iron, copper or Nurembergen, of which you will have with you several samples which without doubt will please them greatly."

So came the first white Christians to Australia: two self-confessed murderers. "Above all, keep God in mind," Pelsaert abjured them' "never forget Him; and without doubt He will keep you close in His shadow and will yet vouchsafe, at the last, a good outcome." What was the outcome, good or bad, will never be known—whether Wouter Loos of Maastricht, "captain of a troop of murderers," and Jan Pelgrom de Bye of Bemmel, who sat on the legs of a woman while she was strangled with her own hair, were befriended by the aborigines or, far more likely, perished on what Pelsaert called "the dry, cursed earth" of the South-land. They had, at least, a sporting chance—the first white Australians to take a gamble.

While Pelsaert was engaged in "fishing up" the Company's treasure from the wreck, he observed the presence of "large numbers of Cats, which are creatures of miraculous form, as big as a hare"; they took food with their forepaws like apes or squirrels, and their procreation he considered to be "very Miraculous, yea, worthy to note: under the belly the females have a pouch into which one can put a hand, and in that she has her nipples, where have discovered that in there their Young Grow with the nipple in the mouth, and have found lying some which were only as large as a bean, but found the limbs of the small beast to be entirely in proportion . . ." This is the first known description of a wallaby—no doubt the tammar, still to be found on the islands. The wrecks remain there, too, within reach of skin divers who spend week-ends searching for the bullion that was to purchase spices, gems and indigo. One of these divers blew up a wreck to get at the treasure, destroying valuables like astrolabes and compasses and muskets that would have been priceless to museums, and causing such an outcry that the state government passed a law permitting the finder to claim the value of the bullion in present currency, provided it was "fished up" under proper supervision.

THIRTEEN

The Northwest

The northwest is a strange mixture of the immemorial and the bud-new. Its rocks are ancient beyond measure. The passage of millions and millions of years has worn them down like the stumps of decayed molars; erosions has stripped them of their skin and they are stark and bare. Beneath them immeasurable riches lie concealed. Like the marsupial whose embryo bides its time until the pouch is ready to receive it, these riches have been held back until the world needs them, and now that time has come. The northwest is about to give birth not to a single offspring but to a whole complex of mines, railways, cities and harbours. There is to be a sort of economic spawning. "The biggest thing that's happened to Australia since the gold rush of the eighteen-fifties," said a mining engineer. "Or that's happening anywhere. The gold story will be nothing beside what we are going to see in the next decade."

There is to be not one mining field but probably seven, perhaps more. By 1970 there will be seven brand-new cities, five harbours, several of them capable of handling ships of 65,000 tons, and 600 miles of railway line. At the moment these are mostly in the shape of blueprints and words. Within two years, it is believed, they will be in physical being; the iron-ore rush is on. It is quite a different rush this time, taking place in company board rooms and stock exchanges, on drawing boards and in the offices of consulting engineers; no humpies now, but air-conditioned motels; no camels, wheelbarrows and flat feet, but jet-propelled airliners and private planes.

Much of the capital will be American; Britain has a very small share. In Perth, Mr. Charles Court, the zealous Minister for the development of the northwest, said, "Why won't the British come in? Why isn't London interested? British capital developed Australia, but now the

254

Americans are doing it. The British are afraid to take the risks involved. Yet we're one of the few countries in the world with a stable government and we've never yet defaulted on a debt. What's gone wrong?" With modern techniques, he added, the size and potential of an ore body can be accurately measured, and so the risks of failure are much less than they used to be. The iron ore bodies of the Hamersley Range are of high quality and so astronomical in size as to be virtually limitless; as the world industrializes, no one can see an end to the demand, and these deposits have the great advantage of proximity to a coast well supplied with bays and inlets suitable for harbours and also to the great and expanding Asian markets. What can go wrong?

It all started with Mt. Tom Price. In 1961 this was just a nameless bouldery nob in the Pilbara wilderness, a hundred miles or so west of the blue asbestos mines at Wittenoom. The following year an association formed between Conzinc Riotinto and Kaiser Steel of California found a deposit of hematite ore whose size and quality they could scarcely credit. The more they examined it, the bigger and richer it was seen to be. At a conference of mining engineers held in 1964 it was stated that "the Hamersley Iron Province is one of the great iron ore fields of the world, comparable to those of Brazil, the U.S.S.R. and India. Total indicated and inferred reserves of pistolic limonite-goethite-hematite ore, grading between fifty and sixty per cent iron, amount to six thousand million tons." Yet as late as 1960 the government was still embargoing the export of iron ore on the grounds that Australia barely had sufficient for its own needs!

Now there is a railway being laid from Mt. Tom Price (named after an ex-vice-president of Kaiser Steel) to King Bay in the Dampier Archipelago, where a harbour to be capable of handling vessels of 100,000 tons' burden is to arise, and a town to serve the harbour, and there will be a second town at Mt. Tom Price itself. These towns will not at first be large; modern mining calls for a relatively few technicians, of the type who hold diplomas and wear collars and ties and listen to symphony concerts of an evening in their open-plan lounges, rather than a mob of horny-handed sons of toil.

[2]

Another town like Dampier is to arise at Mt. Goldsworthy, which lies sixty miles due east of Port Hedland, farther up the northwest coast towards Broome. Whisked there in a Cessna over a dead-flat coastal

sand plain streaked and scored by innumerable runnels and pools—
Cyclone Joan had just passed over, depositing about ten inches of rain
in six hours—I looked hopefully for a peak, range, or at least a bouldery
nob, but there was nothing except a low ridge, rising no more than two
or three hundred feet from the barren plain, thinly covered with a little
scrub and spinifex. "Mount Goldsworthy," said my American guide,
and proceeded to show me a vast array of specimens of rock extracted
by diamond drilling from the ridge, which seems to consist almost
wholly of a rich iron ore. Soon there will be galleries and adits, crushing
plants and loading ramps, houses and swimming pools, clubs and
cinemas, with nothing all around but sand and rock and spinifex; a
bleak place, you would think, to work in, but everything will be organized and comfortable and wages, very likely, up to $200 a week.

As in the case of Mt. Tom Price, much of the capital is coming from
the United States. With dollars come Americans, mostly of the
managerial type. Those I spoke to thought better of Australians as
companions when off duty than as colleagues on the job. The somewhat
offhand, casual, "She'll do, mate" attitude of many Aussies irritated these
high-powered engineers accustomed to everyone snapping into it and
dedicating all their energies to the task in hand. Port Hedland, a rather
scruffy, unambitious little seaport, with a single main street and a dilapidated jetty, sweltering in the heat of sand dunes used for refuse dumps,
seemed a long way from San Francisco or Los Angeles.

"No idea of competition," an American complained, speaking of his
Australian colleagues. "Take spare parts. Can you get the simplest part
in Perth? No, sir, you cannot. You send to Sydney, and Sydney hasn't
got it either, or they come up with the wrong one. Do they care? Not
they. She'll be right, mate."

Another took up the point Australians often raise about American
capital. "Who's stopping Australian capital coming in? Why don't they
come north themselves and do their own developing? It's their country.
They sit on their backsides in Sydney and Melbourne and moan about
American capital and technicians. The ball's in their court." He added,
a little ruefully, "*Nice* enough, I grant you. Easygoing, generous, good
guys to drink with and to have on your side in a scrap, I guess. But real
competition would fold them up. And then their steaks . . ."

I was surprised; most Americans enjoy steak and this is the land of
steak par excellence. "But not *this* steak!" said my companion in
shocked tones. "They murder their meat. They don't understand it—

don't bother. They don't *finish* their beef. Cheap?" He shook his head. "Not really. All fat and gristle. There's only one thing cheaper here than in the States and that's a haircut . . . Well, yes, they do chill their beer."

We were enjoying some on the terrace of an outback hotel that had found itself unexpectedly confronted with a wholly new kind of customer bringing sophisticated, international standards to this torpid little seaport that had hitherto served the needs of stockmen from a handful of cattle stations, a few drovers and prospectors passing through, and the crews of small trading vessels that called from time to time to load fats. The temperature was well up in the nineties, the flies sticky, the air heavy and inert. One of the older kind of customer was singing wheezily and smiling happily as he executed a shuffling sort of dance among the tables and chairs. Among the sand dunes bulldozers were levelling the site of a construction camp to consist of prefabricated rabbit hutches that could be bolted together almost in a few hours. Mt. Goldsworthy is expected to disgorge a million tons of ore annually to start with, and this will rise year by year. The consortium of two Californian mining companies and one from Sydney that holds the lease will sell the first seven years' output to a group of Japanese firms.

Looking out across the Indian Ocean, whose tides here rise and fall by thirty feet and more, it was hard to visualize the scenes of mechanized and, no doubt, computer-controlled efficiency that will replace the timeless torpor of the present. Already the outback is on the way to becoming a legend. Certain fundamentals will remain: tides, heat, cyclones, sand and flies. Sprays and air conditioning will keep the flies at bay, but let the least gap in these defenses open and they will percolate slyly through.

It was these creepy-crawly little flies that most impressed the first European to report on this part of Australia, William Dampier; they caused the aborigines, he wrote—"the miserablest People in the world" —to keep their eyes permanently half closed against insects "so troublesome here that no fanning will keep them from coming to one's Face; and without the assistance of both hands to keep them off, they will creep into one's Nostrils, and Mouth too, if the Lips are not shut very close." The natives had "great Bottle noses" and no incisor teeth, "no sort of Cloaths" and no dwellings, and lived precariously on small fish washed up by the tides; they lacked iron to make tools or weapons; the earth afforded "neither Herb, Root, Pulse nor any sort of Grain for them to eat: not any sort of Bird or Beast that they can catch, having no instruments where withal to do so"; they mumbled, and "we could not understand one word that they said." In short, this English adventurer in 1688 thought even less of the inhabitants of northwestern Australia than his American successors nearly three centuries later, although—apart from the flies—for different reasons; it would be nearer the mark to describe modern Australians as the most content rather than as "the miserablest People in the world."

[3]

All these developments are naturally creating a lively new demand for trained technicians and skilled men of various kinds. Australia must look to immigrants to fill the gaps, but demand for skills of this type exceeds supply all over the world. One possible source is at present ruled out. Up and down this sweltering coast, from Wyndham to Roebourne, you hear people say, "Most of this ore is going to Japan— there's our market. Japanese ships are coming in to load it. They even take most of our wool. You can't trade with people and keep them out. This will crack the White Australia policy."

Others disagree just as firmly. "We've nothing against the Japs or other Asians. On the contrary, they're hard workers, efficient, good blokes to do business with. But it would be like busting a dam. One hundred and twenty millions in Indonesia alone! We'd become an Asiatic nation for sure. Better go short of labour for a few years than that."* On two occasions in the past a similar situation led to an influx of coloured labour. In the 1850's Chinese came to the gold fields of Victoria and New South Wales, and in the 1860's and 1870's Kanakas from the South Sea islands were brought to cut Queensland cane. Nearly all the men in both groups were repatriated when their contracts ended. From these experiences the so-called White Australia policy was born.

* It is worth noting that the origins of the White Australia policy lay in respect for the superior merits of the Chinese rather than in a "lesser breeds" attitude towards coloured races. Sir Henry Parkes, one of the policy's originators, stated that the Chinese "are a superior set of people, a nation of an old and deep-rooted civilisation . . . It is because I believe the Chinese to be a powerful race capable of taking a great hold upon the country, and because I want to preserve the type of my own nation . . . that I am and always have been opposed to an influx of Chinese." Ninety years later most Australians would echo this view; and there is little doubt that the Chinese, were they in a similar situation, would pursue the same policy and probably with greater stringency.

Although no one officially uses so unfashionable a term nowadays, this policy has been enforced since the birth of the Commonwealth in 1901. It does not keep out *all* coloured people, who can, and do, get permits to study or to trade; but in general it does debar *permanent* coloured immigrants. Anyone, white or coloured, who has lived in Australia for five consecutive years and not got into trouble can become a citizen, and so can anyone, male or female, who marries an Australian citizen. These provisions open loopholes which have been skillfully used; there is a racket in arranged marriages, and Asian wives have brought in suspiciously large broods of little ones. But the loopholes have not destroyed, or as yet seriously weakened, the policy.

The laws that control immigration do not mention race or colour. Between 1901 and 1958 they empowered the authorities to refuse admission to anyone who failed to pass a dictation test of fifty words in any "prescribed language," which could be Eskimo or Tibetan if the officials so wished. The Migration Act of 1958 substituted a procedure obliging the would-be immigrant to get an entry permit. Whether or not he gets one lies entirely in the discretion of the Minister for Immigration and his officials, and few are granted to Africans or Asians. British subjects in the United Kingdom do not need a permit to enter Australia. As a growing number of British nationals are black or brown, another loophole appears to be opening up, and it will be of interest to see what happens when British subjects born of Jamaican or Pakistani parents themselves at the White Australian door.

At the United Nations and in the eyes of the world Australian spokesmen are well out in front condemning apartheid, supporting African and Asian nationalism, and joining in the general courting of Afro-Asian favours. Nor is this a matter of lip service only. Australia has actively supported the Colombo Plan and other schemes to channel aid to the so-called developing countries. Leaving aside the large and growing sums Australians are spending on their own dependent territories in Papua and New Guinea, between the end of World War II and 1964 they gave away nearly $360 million to Asian and African nations—a tidy sum for a country with so small a population and so much developing of its own that needs doing. Also they have brought Asians and Africans to Australia for education and training and sent forth their own experts to advise and instruct. Businessmen, journalists, television teams—in fact, almost any kind of oriental visitor is genuinely welcome, so long as he does not mean to stay. There is even trade with Red China, whose purchase of a heavy surplus saved the wheat farmers from a price collapse not long ago. And Australians insist that they tolerate no colour bar. The country has been happily free of "incidents" involving prejudiced landladies, resentful mothers, or neo-Fascists. There has been no trouble about integration in schools. So really, people will argue, there is no such thing as a White Australia policy.

At the same time Australia, combing the Western world for immigrants, has admitted as permanent residents only about two thousand Asians in the last twenty years. There can have been few more conspicuous examples of double-talk and sophistry. Most Australians realize this and try to change the conversation. They know they have no ideological leg to stand on and are bringing off a skillful feat of balancing firmly on a nonexistent limb.

Hitherto the African and Asian nations have kept surprisingly quiet about this schizophrenic policy. No one expects this immunity to last. Meanwhile all that can be done is to play down immigration restrictions, play up the happy race relations that exist inside Australia, press on with the education and development of the aborigines, extricate the nation as soon as possible from its position, no longer either fashionable or attractive, as a colonial power in Asia, and keep the fingers crossed.

Internally the policy is coming under fire from two quarters: from employers who want labour, and from liberals who want the brotherhood of man. Japanese contractors are to dredge one of the iron-ore harbours-to-be. They will bring their own skilled labour, and the men, perhaps with their families, will live there for several years. "This may be a major break-through," a director of one of the companies observed. "These out-of-date barriers have got to go." And I heard university students passionately condemn the White Australia policy as "disgusting." Significantly, perhaps, both the director and the students were in Melbourne and not in Western Australia on the Indian Ocean, on whose perimeter 1,500 million black and brown people dwell—or did when this was written; some five millions more will have been added while the book is in the press. It is 1,500 air miles from Wyndham to Djakarta and 1,850 from Wyndham to Melbourne.

The labour on these projects is solidly unionized. It was, in the main, pressure from the trade unions that consolidated the White Australia policy at the turn of the century, and it is the trade unions who defend and hold to it with the greatest determination today.

How much do Asians really *want* to come to Australia? When, in

1876, there was an Australian proposal to offer land in the north to the Japanese for settlement, the Emperor rejected it. No country has been more resolute than Japan in keeping other races out. Until overthrown by Commodore Perry, its Brown Japan policy was maintained with the utmost rigour, and Japan was no more anxious to let its citizens go than to let in other people's.

In the view of immigration-law reformers most Australian fears are out of date; modern migrants are no longer starving coolies and peasants with hoes but very likely skilled electricians and research chemists with university degrees. Australia, they say, should welcome in such useful people and end a policy that damages the nation's image overseas. Supporters of the policy retort that while Japan might export desirable technicians, other Asian nations, notably India and Pakistan, would offload the illiterate and unskilled. Meanwhile the iron ore will continue to be mined and loaded by white men. Initially it is to be treated in Japan, but the major firms and consortiums who have secured the mining concessions have undertaken to establish, within periods stipulated by the state government, integrated iron and steel industries along the coast. So the winning of all this ore will be a step towards the emergence of Australia as one of the great steel-making nations of the world. A massive iron and steel plant is going up at Kwinana near Fremantle; others are planned, and soon West Australians, formerly so poor and so ignored, will become rich and great and even able, in their turn, to condescend towards easterners. It is a heady feeling.

[4]

The Margaret and the Fitzroy rivers were stretches of white sand between two narrow bands of trees, the bush-speckled earth hard as iron. Flying over this kind of country, I wondered how any animal could survive, especially since only five inches of rain had fallen in the last fifteen months. They not only live but thrive so long as there is any vegetation, however dry and spiky. Here in the Kimberleys, a district considerably larger than the British Isles, lies some of the finest cattle country on the continent for this type of ranching. (That word is never used here, being disliked as too American.)

For how long can this type of exploitation of the land continue? It is a way of life, a *mystique*, that is picturesque and at times dramatic but belongs to the past. It is a system that does not even produce good beef. It produces cheap beef, which goes mainly into hamburgers and pies, but not beef of the quality that world markets increasingly demand. It impoverishes the land and has scarcely changed its methods, or lack of them, for a hundred years.

"Never have I seen such richness and variety of hue as in these ranges," wrote the Durack who brought the first cattle to the eastern Kimberleys, "and in the vivid flowers of this northern spring." I saw it droughted. After rain, the green floods back in that miraculous fashion of all dry lands in the tropics, and wildflowers are spilled in waves over the plains. Luxuriance is reborn—or seems to be; this is deceptive. A balance has been lost; good grasses have given way to poorer species, and rivers which so amazed the pioneers by their size and permanency have become dry sand beds or, after storms, raging torrents. "Dry season it's desert. West season it's a lake," wrote Xavier Herbert thirty years ago.

Fossil Downs covers about one million acres. This sounds a lot, but Gogo, more or less next door, has some four million acres. The center is the boss's home with his office and the pedal radio, no longer worked by pedal but by batteries. On one side lies the manager's house, quarters for other men, and sheds for implements and for stores which arrive by the ton; there is a saddle room full of rows of carefully oiled saddles, polished bits, and ropes neatly coiled; a mechanics' workshop, and the cookhouse, to which you are summoned by a bell five times a day.

The station cook is a key figure. He and the manager between them create or destroy morale—some hold that his influence is even greater than the manager's, and his personality is as important as his culinary skill. With a shock of white hair, gentian-blue eyes and a spare, sunburned frame, the personality of the Fossil Downs "cookie" inspired immediate trust and liking. He told us a little of his life, which had been hard. His parents had emigrated from Surrey to a small holding in a group-settlement scheme in the southwest and for years battled against hopeless odds; the children had grown up in poverty, often too hungry or too tired to attend school, which in any case finished with them at thirteen. And in the prime of life polio had crippled him. Yet he was cheerful, well-read and content. "This is my home," he said. "I've a cottage with a garden. And this is the best table in the Kimberleys."

In recent years, on all these big stations, the white labour force has dwindled and most of the stockmen are now aborigines. No one knows just how many blacks the camp holds; they come and go as they please. The men, mostly half-bloods, are lean, hard, lounging horsemen wearing slouch hats, stockmen's heeled boots, tight jeans and low-slung belts; generally a cigarette dangles from a lower lip, and they have an air at once withdrawn and arrogant.

The manager gives out the dry rations, which are free, once a week. They get flour, in addition to bread every day, sugar, salt, tea, and either beans or potatoes, and everyone takes away a cake of soap, a tin of fruit and a packet of chewing tobacco. Some of the women have enormous buttocks where they store fat against lean times, as the Hottentots do. Others are just fat everywhere. The plutocrats of this society are the old, who draw the full Commonwealth pension. But money can mean little here; there is free meat every day and an issue of clothing three times a year, employment for women if they want it in the cookhouse, the vegetable garden and the house, where half a dozen girls report for duty, and in an open-air laundry where everything is done by hand (no washing machines). Once more you are halfway back to feudal times, with a lord of the manor, servants, large dogs, many horses, a lady of the manor dispensing medicines to the sick, and no one turned from the door.

[5]

The nearest neighbours are thirty-six miles away at Gogo, which belongs to descendants of the Samuel Emmanuel of Goulburn in New South Wales from whom Patsy Durack borrowed the money to buy his first pony cart. The Emmanuels shipped their livestock to the newly opened port of Derby, but the Duracks overlanded theirs in one of the greatest feats of droving ever performed. They rode away from western Queensland in four parties with a total of 7,520 cattle, 60 working bullocks and 200 horses, and with four Duracks in charge—Big Johnnie, Galway Jerry, Long Michael and Black Pat. They left in June, 1883, and in September, 1885, Long Michael carved his initials on a baobab tree on the banks of the river Ord below those his cousin, Stumpy Michael, had carved three years before when he had gone on a reconnaissance to find this Promised Land. The trek covered nearly 3,000 miles, cost nearly $150,000, and less than half the cattle survived.

The overlanders were beset by disasters. Drought held them up for months, and both men and cattle sickened and died until it was discovered that the water they were camped beside was poisonously alkaline. They suffered from scurvy and "Barcoo sores," and many of the cattle succumbed to pleuropneumonia or sank in bogs. They were harried by the blacks, who by this time were in a state of open warfare with the drovers; they struck off a cook's head into his baking dish during an attack on another overlanding party a few months before. Later, on the Ord, Big Johnnie was to be speared to death by blacks.

The lush, green swamps and plains of the Northern Territory, with their vast flocks of wildfowl, tropical vegetation and crocodile-haunted rivers, seemed to the Duracks like paradise after droughted Queensland; but there were hidden menaces. On the Roper River, amid plagues of sand flies and mosquitoes, two of the men shot themselves in a delirium caused by malaria. Cattle perished from red water which had been introduced, with the ticks that carried it, from Java. Beyond the Victoria River the Duracks' stores ran out and they dug for roots like the natives, chewed pigweed, and searched for honey. And then at last they came to the baobab tree that had been marked three years before by Stumpy Michael. They called the million acres that they took up round the tree Argyle, and it became a famous station but is owned no longer by Duracks; a grandson, however, retains part of the original run at Auvergne in the Northern Territory.

One night, by the Victoria River, Long Michael aimed his rifle at a shadow emerging from the darkness that encircled his campfire. A voice hailed him just in time, and the shadow proved to be the barefooted, half-starved form of Willie MacDonald, one of three brothers overlanding cattle in the wake of the Duracks from Goulburn. They had met with even greater disasters. The day before the expedition was to leave, their father had been thrown from his horse and killed. In Queensland every one of their beasts had perished in the drought of 1883. The brothers took jobs as stockmen, borrowed what they could, assembled another, smaller mob of cattle, and headed west again. On the Roper River one of the brothers became so ill that another took him home by sea. Willie pushed on alone with two men, a Chinese cook and the surviving cattle. They were attacked by blacks; their stores were looted, and they had reached starvation point when they caught up with the Duracks on the Victoria.

Like the Duracks, Willie MacDonald was heading for a single tree— one even farther on, near the junction of the Fitzroy and Margaret rivers in the western Kimberleys. It had been marked by the explorer Alexander Forrest during his expedition in 1879 which revealed the promise of these well-watered, verdant and possibly auriferous ranges and valleys. Willie MacDonald found the tree on which was carved F (for For-rest) 37 (the thirty-seventh camp) and took up about a million acres round it. This is now Fossil Downs.

The tree with F 37 carved on its trunk has gone, but embedded in the stump is the axle of the wagon that was hauled across the continent from Goulburn, and a plaque has been set up. We started in a Land Rover to see it but proceeded no more than three or four miles. What the day before had been a rock-hard, sandy, quartz-glinting desert was now a vast bog.

[6]

We had gone to sleep in camp beds on the lawn, under a clear sky encrusted by stars. The rain started at about eleven. We moved our beds to the veranda, and soon it was bucketing down. Everyone was elated—Bruce the manager, Annette the daughter of the house and her fiancé John, who had driven over for the weekend from a station about a hundred miles away. They had been waiting for this for the best part of a year, and you could almost hear the thirsty earth gulping it in.

Next morning everything was fresh. Rock pigeons were calling; white cockatoos swooped and squawked round the slaughter yard; smiles were on every face. At the morning radio session the air cackled with reports —three inches here, two point six there, only twenty-nine points else-where, and one man said plaintively, "Everyone's had a storm but me; I must have killed a Chinaman." The postmistress at Fitzroy Crossing was kept busy taking down telegrams. "Get this to Aunt Mary in Perth, will you, Dorothy? She's staying with Anne. 'Nearly two inches everything fine love from all.' Isn't it beaut?"

There was a spate of ordering things for tasks that could at last be resumed—heavy-duty truck batteries, spare parts for tractors, two-and-a-half-inch screws, a flywheel, vegetable seeds, seed potatoes, stores. One voice gave a grocery order that included two large bottles of vanilla essence, which seemed a lot. I learned for the first time that swills of vanilla essence can—if you are not sick—intoxicate you. Station cooks are entitled to order groceries but not drink; no doubt one of them was planning a celebration.

Storm water lay in shallow lakes at Fossil Downs. Horses splashed about—hundreds of semi-wild horses about to be mustered in order to draft out mounts for the impending cattle mustering. Here this annual cattle mustering lasts about six months. The rain would make it much harder, but no one minded—anything was worth enduring for the sake of rain.

The musterers do not life soft lives in any case. They sleep in the open, never mind the storms, are in the saddle at four o'clock and stay there until dark; live on damper—bread without yeast—and on beef salted and carried round in sacking, and on strong, smoky, heavily sugared billycan tea. They are away from the homestead for anything up to five or six weeks at a time before they drive their bellowing, dust-kicking mobs into the drafting yards to be sorted out into fats for the meatworks at Broome, the weaners, calves for branding, breeding heifers to run with stud bulls, and other categories. Then the musterers ride out again. As a rule there is one white man to each team, and the rest are aborigines. A proper stockman must be ready to leap from the saddle, seize a wild bull by the tail and, by a clever knack, throw the beast that weighs over half a ton; then he must rope its thrashing legs, sit on top of it, lash it up and, with some assistance, brand and castrate it on the spot and saw off its horns.

Some beasts escape, and these ranges will have wild bulls in them until they are fully paddocked. There can be no valid breeding policy until this has been done, and there is still a long way to go. Fencing costs $600 a mile or more, and on Fossil Downs the farthest boundary lies eighty miles from the homestead. That is why these properties need capital on a scale only to be provided by companies with almost limitless resources. After deducting for freight, fats three or four years old bring in about $40 each, and there is no other source of income. The beasts depend wholly on the pastures and in times of drought will scarcely "finish" at all.

At Fossil Downs the stockmen were driving mobs of horses into the yards: tough, lanky, thin-flanked beasts, there was nothing coarse about them; they had been bred from thoroughbred sires to be as quick as polo ponies, intelligent, sturdy, fast over short distances and stouthearted over long ones. They have endured much. At Fossil Downs they keep about five hundred, but the count will not be known until all have been mustered and the new foals branded.

Wastage is heavy. There are broken legs and fetlocks and injured backs, but the highest casualties result from a condition known as "walkabout" and caused by a poisonous plant which acts on the liver. One of the plant's popular names is rattle-pod, its scientific one *Crotolaria retusa*. The dazed horse cannot stop walking, as a rule in a straight line; if it encounters any obstacle it will butt its head against the wall or tree instead of going around; finally it topples over and dies. There is no remedy. Scientists are seeking a drug to immunize the animals, but this cannot yet be done on a practical scale.

Each stockman keeps his own horses and picks his own replacements at the annual mustering. In their spurred ankle boots and slouch hats with chin straps and dangling cigarettes, the stockmen sit on the heavy stringybark rails with knees tucked up and broad, ashen faces impassive, looking with narrowed eyes at the fly-teased mob of tossing manes and flicking tails and pawing hoofs in the dust of the yards. When one of the men sees a horse he fancies he will lift a hand or nod his head, and the horse will be his for the season. If two men fancy the same animal, they will sort it out amicably at the end, sometimes by the toss of a coin. Each stockman then breaks in and looks ater the horses he has chosen.

[7]

That night we again moved our beds onto the lawn until, about midnight, we heard drumming on the iron roof and felt the wet on our faces. John had been worrying all day about whether he should get back to his sheep. He had to cross the Margaret, which was still dry; if the river "came down" he would be marooned for days, a week—a month if "the Wet" really set in. At about two A.M. he departed. Bruce escorted him in a jeep across the river bed, which was already six inches under water. Morning came, and there was no Bruce, but, all around us, a flooded plain. The gauge showed nearly three inches, and at our cookhouse breakfast (hunks of steak and fried eggs and potatoes) everyone almost sang.

A few hundred yards from the homestead the road, or track, crossed a shallow creek; I had scarcely noticed it the day before, and now it had become a torrent. "We'll wade over," Annette said. Soon we were swimming. The water was as warm as a tepid bath and brown as liquid toffee. Every runnel on the hills cascaded down to wash what little soil remained from rocks and boulders. No dams, no barriers, no plantations, no terraces, no defense against erosion had been mounted in these King Leopold Ranges. We swam, waded, swam again, squelched knee-deep in warm liquid toffee until we reached the flat bank of the Margaret. It really was a river now—about a hundred yards across, fifteen or twenty feet deep, and carrying down logs and tree trunks. On the far side was a spit of sand and on it a figure, small in the distance, waving. It was Bruce.

A little dinghy was tethered to our bank of the river, and in due course—no one was in a hurry—two lads arrived with an outboard motor which refused to start. After an hour or so of string-pulling they carried the motor back through the swamps to the mechanic, while Bruce sat on the bank patiently and no doubt hungrily, having missed his breakfast. After another hour or so the lads returned, but the motor still jibbed. Yet another hour or so, and Annette suggested rowing. The idea was welcomed with enthusiasm. The boys got into the dinghy and one of them dropped an oar, which disappeared at a spanking pace down the river. Bruce had got up but sat down again, having missed by now the first smoke-oh, with its heaped plates of cakes, jam rolls and thickly buttered scones.

Perhaps the fuel was at fault? One of the boys went back and returned an hour later with another can. They drained the engine, put in the new fuel and pulled the cord. The motor spluttered once or twice and died. Bruce sat down again, farther back, as the water was still rising with ominous mutterings.

Perhaps an oar could be improvised? Boughs were cut from trees and some carpentry assayed, but it was not successful. By now Bruce had missed his dinner. We all returned for ours, taking the motor for another overhaul, but further examination revealed no fault; so after dinner back it went. We waved to Bruce, who stood up. The cord was pulled and nothing happened. Everyone pulled in turn until the time came to go back for the afternoon smoke-oh. "Poor old Bruce," we said.

Time passed; the sun went red and orange and sank behind a flat horizon. Still no Bruce. At last, when dusk fell and Bruce looked like spending a wet and hungry night, the boys got the boat across the river with one oar and a pole. Bruce was ferried over safe and sound and not at all bad-tempered. "It's Sunday," he said. "I'm looking forward to my tea." Not a cross word had passed all day.

Next morning on the radio the air was again full of rain-gauge readings. Hope was springing up like the pigweed that would fuzz the red sand in a few days; this could be the real thing—the Wet. The land would then become a sponge, and visitors such as myself immobilized for weeks. Pleasant as this would be in so hospitable a home and at the best table in the Kimberleys, it would derange plans, and over the radio an air taxi was summoned from Derby.

The jeep taking us to the station's airstrip left deep traces in the sand that filled at once with water. Everything sparkled; birds swooped and squawked. You felt a surge of growth and energy. The air was saturated with moisture and warmth. In the Kimberleys they say "You plant your seed and jump clear," and you could understand what it meant. It looked as if a seaplane would be more suitable than a Cessna, but the airstrip had been well chosen, and one end, if not the other, was above water. We drove a mob of horses off and pegged out a sheet while another storm gathered darkly in the west. Water spurted from beneath the wheels of the Cessna when it landed, but it did not sink. "She'll do," said the pilot.

Soon the sheet, the scampering horses, a pair of steel-grey brolgas stalking with dignity through the wet, and a shining amalgam of land and water lay beneath us, and the solitary cluster of buildings fell out of sight. In a few months Annette would be married, Bruce and the others out mustering in the ranges, only Cookie would be there tending his garden, and in the camp the floppy-breasted, lank-haired, quiet-spoken women with their babies and dogs and fleas; and the big house would be silent and hollow.

We reached Fitzroy Crossing at the same time as the storm. A savage gale brought a grey wall of wet; this was a gale that meant business and seemed to have behind it the driving force of a will to destruction. Rain beat with fury against the windows, and we lurched through an opaque world. The pilot brought his aircraft down in squelching sand. There was a hut about twenty yards away, and I was soaked to the skin before I reached it, while the pilot was tethering his machine to some posts. A truck arrived and we proceeded at a brisk pace through a lake that came to the hubcaps, to a huddle of buildings in the midst of the waters, including a hotel on stilts. A few sad-looking aborigines clustered on the veranda: a couple more sat in silence at the bar, and mosquitoes pinged and midges bit without intermission, while the drumming rain and roaring gale drowned all conversation.

Within an hour the gale had slackened like an orchestra that has reached and passed its crescendo. A curtain lifted; suddenly the sky was blue. Behind long banners of indigo the sun emerged, at first halfheartedly, then with gathering confidence. All was warm again and a radio was bleating like a lost sheep in the empty bar.

[8]

"The Ord" is an irrigation scheme on paper, but on the spot it amounts to a religion. You believe in it or you do not. If you are of the faith, you believe with passion and proselytize with fervour. If you are an infidel, you had best keep away. This is the course wisely adopted by a man regarded more or less as Antichrist, the economist Dr. Bruce Davidson. Formerly a Research Fellow of the University in Perth, he has put a good 2,000 miles between himself and Kununurra, the Ord's headquarters, by transferring to the University of Sydney. With a passion almost equal to that of the believers, Dr. Davidson disbelieves in the potentialities of the Ord and has written a book full of statistics to support his views. "He won't come to Kununurra," said a believer, practically grinding his teeth. "We've invited him to a public debate, but he ducks it. He'd be pulped if he came."

The Ord River Irrigation Project is much more than a scheme to dam the Ord, which in the Dry dwindles to a chain of pools and in the Wet may flow at the rate of one million cubic feet a second, and then to irrigate much of the surrounding plain; it is a symbol of the development of the north. And northern development is an article of faith among most Australians and among all those who live there.

One-third of Australia lies north of the Tropic of Capricorn. In it are some of the last remaining areas of any size in the world that are capable of development and yet still, in the main, empty of people and the works of people. To fill them quickly with both is the essence of the northern faith. Partly this is based on the fear that if Australians do not do so, others will—that is, the Asians—and that Australians will lose their continent by default.

But I do not believe that this is the seed of the faith. The overlanders who came in the wake of the Duracks were not worrying about Asians. They were, of course, intent on making fortunes, but I do not believe that this, either, lay at the heart of the matter.

Both fear of Asians and hope of fortunes were, and are, factors in the story, but in part they are rationalizations. The fact is that any large, unused, unpeopled stretch of country presents a challenge to men of Anglo-Saxon origin. Most people of other traditions do not appear to feel the same urges, and some are more inclined to shun empty spaces; but to the men of northwestern Europe, empty spaces represent some kind of defeat that must be avenged. Does a basic lack of confidence lie at the heart of it—a need to prove manhood, to assert mastery? At any rate, the emotions aroused by the idea of northern development are subrational, or para-rational perhaps; and an Antichrist who writes a book called *The Northern Myth* to prove that there is no crop grown in the north that cannot be more cheaply, efficiently and economically grown south of the Tropic of Capricorn must expect to be stoned. The only thing Dr. Davidson says the north *can* produce economically is beef. His opponents, on the other hand, say the pastoral industry has mined the land, kept empty spaces empty, and is now holding back the whole region.

Dr. Davidson has told Australians that they will throw away their money if they put any more of it into schemes like the Ord. Cotton can be grown here, but yields, he says, are lower and costs are higher than they are on the Murrumbidgee irrigation areas in New South Wales, which could produce all the cotton Australia needs and more. Dr. Davidson has even accused the West Australians of sharp practice in that they have used the Ord scheme as a means of extracting money from the Commonwealth Government. No wonder Kununurra is full of people out for his blood. His own god, they say, is simply economics. If a thing does not pay, it must be jettisoned. It is not a matter, Dr. Davidson retorts, of money but of resources: if you grow subsidized cotton on the Ord, you are wasting skills, energies and machinery that could, and should, be more usefully employed in the south.

As for Asians surging into empty spaces, he has pointed out that what attracts bees is not dust but honey. Wealthy cities and thriving industries are richer prizes than deserts and wilderness. In Kenya the pastoral areas of the highlands remained unpeopled until white settlers showed what could be done with them; then the Africans coveted them and took them over. So the argument continues, and Dr. Davidson from a safe distance shoots with arrows of statistics at schemes soaring on wings of hope.

[9]

The Ord already has a barrier, the Bandicoot Bar diversion dam, which was completed in 1963, and the harvest of its first irrigated crops has been marketed. Up to 30,000 acres are to be irrigated from its stored waters. Some thirty miles upriver is the site chosen for the main dam, which will cost an estimated $40 millions and irrigate about

200,000 acres—mainly on Argyle Downs, the original Durack station. The development under way at present is a pilot scheme.

Almost any crop will grow under irrigation on this black alluvial clay that turns into a sticky, viscous glue when it is wet and bakes into a stubborn, cracked pan when it is dry. There has been a research station here since 1946. (It was started by Kim Durack, a grandson of Patsy.) After experimenting with rice, sugar cane, safflower, peanuts and cotton, the agronomists have plumped for cotton, which has a dual purpose: textile mills want the lint to replace imports, mainly from America, and cotton-seed residues make a high-protein cattle feed. So here is the cotton, neat and orderly in irrigated ranks, where three years ago you could have seen only the coarse spear grass or bamboo grass, baobabs, red-ant hills, bauhinias, ghost gums and eucalypt scrub.

The irrigated area has been chopped into 600-acre blocks. At present settlers do not live there but in Kununurra, where there is a school, a club and a bit of life for their wives. The prefabricated houses are well-equipped but expensive; it costs $2,000 merely to transport each one from Perth. The men may have to travel as much as twenty miles to reach their cotton, and all those I met were anxious to move out to their own blocks; many of them camp in the implement shed which each settler, by the terms of his lease, must erect on his property. The land itself is very cheap—each block is leased for thirty years and the tenant may buy it outright for $2 an acre—but the cost of equipping it is high. Each picking machine costs $20,000, and the heavy tractor needed to pull it on this heavy land costs nearly $6,000. Each settler is warned that he must expect to spend at least $44,000 on machinery and on top of that buy fertilizers, sprays, fencing, and seed and pay the costs of clearing and planting. No poor men need apply.

One of the pioneers is Mr. Arbuckle, whom we found in his shed with his two sons: all three large, strong, hairy-chested, slow-spoken, competent men, toasted by sunshine, hard as ironbark trees—they could model for the outback Aussie with the rugged physique of a man for all weathers. Before coming to the Ord they market-gardened outside Perth, but the Italians, said Mr. Arbuckle, undersold them. Here on the Ord, in two seasons, he and his sons have planted 430 acres of cotton and they are putting in more. What, I asked, are their problems? "Wogs," was the terse reply.

"Cotton is a most attractive food for insects," affirms a bulletin listing twenty "wogs" that attack the plant. Six of these are classed as seri-

The author with a koala bear.

The author with Graham Pizzey with a mutton bird on Phillip Island.

Graham Pizzey

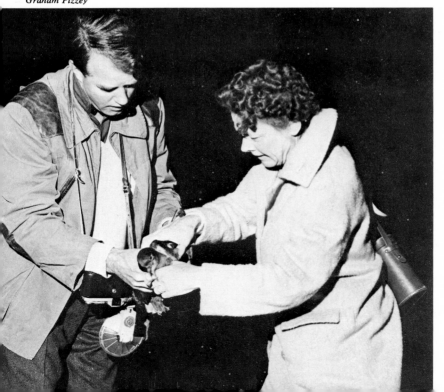

Australian News and Information Bureau

An example of aboriginal "X-ray art" in Arnhem Land.

A copy of aboriginal cave painting at Injaluk, near Oenpelli in Northern Territory.

Australian News and Information Bureau

"Bailed Up!" by Tom Roberts, late 19th century.

"Margaret Olley" by William Dobell.

"The Drover's Wife" by Russell Drysdale.

"Inland Australia" by Sidney Nolan.

ous—the worst, the tobacco cluster grub *Prodenia*. In Egypt it was one of the Biblical Seven Plagues, but it is also native to Australia. A single female of this small nocturnal moth can give birth in a single hatch to up to two thousand voracious little grubs, and she lays a batch of eggs every twenty-eight days. The grubs eat the cotton's leaves to lace. Another moth called *Heliothis,* the climbing cutworm, can also do immense damage.

Whatever may be thought about the dangers of modern chemical sprays, without them scarcely a pound of cotton could be grown on the Ord. In every season the grower must spray, by helicopter, not once but up to sixteen times. Each application will cost $500 or more—one man told me that a single application cost him $3,000. Most of the settlers aim to plant between 300 and 400 acres of cotton, and merely to keep the wogs at bay will cost them between $8,000 and $10,000 a year.

Mr. Arbuckle's cotton plants and the ground around them seethed with *Prodenia* grubs dying from the previous day's application. The newest chemicals penetrate into the sap and, while not harming the plants, kill the grubs that eat the plants. What else they kill may not yet be known—birds, reptiles, small creatures of the soil. Scientists are trying all the time to narrow down the range of their inventions, so that a poison will kill one kind of wog and not another, but there is a limit to this. Some degree of what is so cumbrously called "the contamination of the environment" must be the price we pay for growing crops on a scale now necessary to keep fed, clothed and housed a human population multiplying almost as alarmingly as that of these fecund moths.

The Ord's hothouse atmosphere that drives up the cotton does the same for other plants. One grower told me that twenty-six acres of his crop had been smothered by couch grass, and he had spent six nights a week camped out in his shed and on his tractor, trying to overcome it. He reckoned he worked at least an eighteen-hour day for six days a week. Yet he had not been bred to the land; he was a research scientist from Melbourne, where every morning he had commuted for fifteen miles to spend the day in a laboratory and commuted back to a family of six small children—"the rat race got me down." So when his application for an Ord farm succeeded, the family packed itself and all its goods and furniture into two cars with trailers and overlanded more than 2,000 miles.

There he had been confronted by 400 acres of thick bush and another 200 acres cleared by the Western Australian Government and ready to be planted. With no help except for a few hours at weekends put in by an aborigine, he had planted his crop and cleared another hundred acres. Whatever the economics of growing cotton so far from its markets, and in competition with so many wogs, the output per man must be about the highest in Australia and therefore in the world. Dr. Davidson himself has calculated that in the tropical north there is one worker for every $8,800 worth of produce, against $4,440 per worker, still high by world standards, in the sheep and wheat belts of Victoria.

The only settlers on the Ord with previous experience of cotton are a number of Americans who grew the crop in Arizona until the rising salinity of the soil threatened to put them out of business. They like the Ord. "The wogs? We can handle them, and the scientists may come up with something that will really knock them; the current crop's yield will be better, and the quantity four or five times as large.* About forty farms will be prepared and leased under the pilot scheme; after that everyone must wait for the big dam—if it comes.

The Ord is by no means the only river in this northwestern region that could be used for irrigation; even larger areas could be cultivated on the Fitzroy River system and on the Margaret. There is land and there is water; all that is lacking is a response to the command: "Let there be markets." Also let there be a use for the power that could be cheaply generated hand in hand with irrigation. "The Kimberleys are one of the most underpopulated regions of the world," said a believer. "But things are moving. In 1918 the whole shire had sixty-seven voters. Today there are about forty-five hundred." That does not seem very many in an area considerably larger than the whole of the United Kingdom.

A technical difficulty yet to be overcome is the silting up of dams, present and to come, as a result of erosion. The State Department of Agriculture, allied with the C.S.I.R.O., is attempting to restore about 2,000 square miles of the Ord's catchment area by helping the pastoralists who hold the leases to plant buffel grass and some of the better

---

* If figures quoted by the economist Dr. Rex Patterson, M.P., are sustained, the economics of cotton growing on the Ord are sounder than Dr. Davidson maintains. These costings (March, 1965) show that the Ord farmer needs 850 lbs. of seed cotton per acre to cover his cash costs, and 1,280 lbs. per acre to cover all costs including 6 per cent interest on capital and $4,000 for his own labour. Actual yields in 1964 averaged 1,450 lbs. Experimental yields of up to 4,000 lbs. per acre have been obtained.

native grasses like mitchella and flinders. But little can be done without fencing, and how is that to be paid for? This is the nut on which so many teeth have broken. Then, good pastoralists should feed their animals, especially their breeders, in the dry season, and for this purpose the residues of cotton seed would be ideal. At present, I was told at the research station, *half* the breeders in the Kimberleys, and up to three-quarters of the calves, die from malnutrition and weakness. There is virtually no conservation of fodder, no planting of fodder crops no hay or silage, no rotational grazing, let alone feeding of protein supplements. This remains a primitive form of land use.

There cannot be a quick or easy answer. So much of Australia is undeveloped and hamstrung for lack of money that you can understand a restiveness when people read of the large sums being spent, for example, in New Guinea, mainly for political reasons—at present over $60 millions a year. An expensive university has been created in Port Moresby for a handful of Papuans; there is not even a technical college in Darwin, let alone in Wyndham, Derby, or Broome.

[10]

Some of the wives from Kununurra buy their meat at Ivanhoe, just across the river, which Patsy Durack started for his sons. Much of this land has already been taken, and more will be, for the irrigation scheme. There is poetic justice in this, for it was Kim Durack, born at Ivanhoe, who grew the first crops in the Kimberleys and was the now-forgotten pioneer of the Ord. Beyond the buildings of this dying station—dying to be reborn—the Niggerhead Plains stretch towards the Deception Range, across whose bouldery creeks the Duracks, Costellos and Kilfoyles must have ridden. There are other evocative names: Packsaddle Creek, Mantinea Flats, Cockatoo Springs, Pompey's Pillar, Bandicoot Bar.

It was to Argyle on the Ord that Patsy and his wife repaired when financial disaster struck them down. Patsy had been too sanguine about the gold strikes around Hall's Creek and had neglected his Queensland properties; a general collapse of confidence and prices brought down the chopper. Banks foreclosed, creditors defaulted. Patsy, whose clan had possessed eleven million acres of Queensland, lost everything. "I have only now my old moleskins," he wrote to a son, "my riding saddle and pack and what experience I have at your disposal."

Downcast but not crushed, he and his Mary cultivated a garden and never doubted that their fortunes would revive. But Mary died of malaria, and then Patsy sickened of the Kimberleys. He turned more and more for companionship to his faithful and intelligent native servant, Pumpkin, who had come with him from Cooper's Creek. Patsy's sons kept their stud at Ivanhoe and spread their tentacles into the surrounding ranges until their run extended from the Ord to the Victoria River. The reaction of men with a foothold already in the country, wrote Mary Durack, was "not to sit back and consider how to double the carrying capacity of the land they already held, but to ride forth and double its area." This the younger Duracks did until they owned about seven million acres of these eastern Kimberleys.

Patsy was no longer interested. He and Pumpkin, inseparable companions, spent their last days at Ivanhoe, although it was in Fremantle that Patsy actually died, and Pumpkin wandered off to die alone in the bush at Argyle, where a plaque to his memory stands. Duracks of the next generation were defeated by lack of markets, by the red-water-carrying tick, and by the world depression of the thirties, and all but a remnant of their empire passed into the hands of the pastoral companies. Perhaps all this underlay a sense of sadness that seemed to me to hang over Ivanhoe. A heavy storm broke as we reached Kununurra, lashing about with tropical fury and inundating everything. The Ord became a rushing chocolate torrent—at Ivanhoe it once rose fifty feet in a night—and the floodgates of the barrage were partially opened to release some of the spate. "Raising one gate one foot lets through enough water in one hour to irriate one acre for one year," muttered a believer. "Look at all those cusecs going to waste! All we need is a few . . ." The roaring of the chocolate water drowned his words.

FOURTEEN 〰〰〰

Northern Territory

Cattle mustering had begun at Victoria River Downs and the men were out beyond the paddocks, anywhere up to a hundred miles from the yards. The paddocks round the homestead are tame and domesticated compared with the hills and creeks beyond the fences; but when I rode across a bit of one of them I marvelled that any horse could keep his feet for two minutes, even at the sedate canter which was quite enough for me. The surface is all quartz and ironstone in broken, upended heaps and layers, as if you were to gallop across a precipice lying on its side. The horses' hoofs ring on the rocks and you must keep dodging trunks and low boughs. I saw this country from the air and it is full of queer, shallow craters edged by scarps that look (if this is not too fanciful) like huge petrified *pâté* cases for *vol-au-vents,* and flat-topped hills, strewn with boulders, that might have been shaved off by a razor blade. No grass was to be seen, only scrub, basalt and spinifex. No tracks, of course, no roofs, no fences; this might have been ground thrown out as useless at the time of creation. It is into this country that the stockmen ride at full tilt to head off wild bulls. No wonder each man wears out five or six horses and has to shoe them every day, or even more than once a day; he carries a file to rasp the hoof and shoes them cold. These stockmen must surely be the finest horsemen on earth, in their fashion, though I daresay they would not win prizes for the dressage at Badminton.

The nearest musterers' camp, at Pigeon Hole, can be reached by jeep, and here I met Jim, one of the head stockmen. He is lean, wiry, tough and spare as a thong of leather, and about the same colour, and wears the stockman's uniform: tight jeans and kangaroo-hide ankle boots, a faded cotton shirt open to display a hairy chest, a slouch hat. A pair of clear blue eyes looks out from a walnut-wrinkled face, unshaven; the stub of a hand-rolled cigarette sticks to the lower lip. His surname is Irish. When I addressed him by it he took a step towards me, glared ferociously and growled, "Jim to you!" It was a bad *gaffe;* another bloody pommy trying to teach the Aussies manners. Had I been a man, he might well have laid me flat.

"We're still cattle hunters here, not pastoralists," said the manager, Mr. Bob Miller. Jim had been out since four A.M. hunting scrub bulls. He and his mates, two white jackeroos and four blacks, had just finished roping, castrating and branding them and sawing off their horns. "Lost about twenty," he said. "They keep bustin' out in the hills, and we haven't picked our coachers yet." Coachers are steady-going and reliable cattle, as it were the prefects, who exert a calming influence on the wild scrubs. Jim and his team aim to drive the younger scrubs towards the coachers who, if all goes well, will carry them along more or less peacefully towards the camp and ultimately into one of the yards. Older bulls are not worth the trouble and are shot. On the road to Pigeon Hole we passed several carcasses left to rot where they lay.

Jim has been a stockman all his life and would not change— "Couldn't ever stand a collar and tie." He is in his late forties and a married man; his wife lives in one of the four outstations on the property. Does she mind the isolation? "Not she. Loves the bush. I was away once seven weeks when she was having a baby. No complaints."

A new cook had just arrived at the camp, after a cookless hiatus. "I could of kissed 'im. I threw the lemon essence away and he'll do." Lemon, it seems, will do at a pinch if there is no vanilla. Jim himself is a teetotaller.

Besides the cook, each mustering team carries two tailers whose job is to look after the horses. Around midday they lead a relief batch to some appointed rendezvous with the stockmen and take the exhausted animals back to camp to be treated for sprains and gashes, then hobbled and rested for several days. Now and again a horse breaks a leg or back and has to be shot. They live off the country, such as it is, and get no corn. At Victoria River Downs about two thousand horses are kept. Some stations replenish their supplies by capturing the wild brumbies, but here they breed only from good stallions of proven blood.

[2]

Victoria River Downs is one of the oldest runs in the Northern Territory and the second largest; Alexandria Downs, whose boundaries march with V.R.D.'s, beats it with well over five million acres. Probably

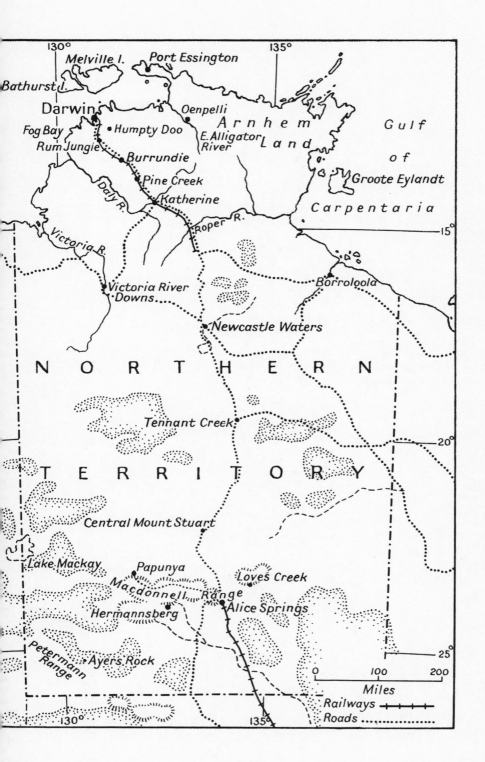

V.R.D. has as many cattle. No one knows just how many there are, but the latest guess is around 70,000 head. It is impossible to be more accurate because less than half the property is paddocked, and beyond the fences cattle live and breed free. The owner of the Humbert River station just across the river told me that he brands between 60 and 65 per cent of his calves and that this is a high percentage for the Northern Territory. The rest "are clearskins" whose males grow up to be scrub bulls.

So long as this state of affairs continues, there can be no significant improvement in the cattle, and therefore no improvement in the quality of the beef, and therefore no better markets and higher prices. Nor can there be improvement to the pastures without control over the numbers and movements of the grazing animals. On the contrary, the cattle concentrate on those species of plant they prefer, and these they overgraze and trample; consequently the better, more nutritious grasses die out and are replaced by coarser and less palatable kinds. So everything comes back to fencing and providing water, which must go hand in had. Fencing at V.R.D. has been let out to contractors at $500 a mile for the labour only; wire and posts are provided by the station, and this brings the total cost to over $600 a mile. In places even power-driven drills can penetrate no more than a few inches into the rock, and men have to excavate with crowbars. The temperature may rise to 170° F. in sun reflected back from rock, so the men's constitutions and their muscles must become as hard as the crowbars they wield.

Over 400 miles of fencing have been erected in the last two or three years and there is still half the run to do; even the boundary fences have not been completed. In addition, between forty-five and fifty bores have been drilled at an average cost of more than $6,000 each, and there are 2,000 miles of road and track to be maintained on the property, which now embraces three and a half million acres—about the same size as Devon, Somerset and Cornwall combined, or two-thirds the size of Israel. In 1907 it covered five million acres, as large as Israel, and when two Melbourne men, Fisher and Lyons, first took possession of the run in the eighties it covered more than eight million acres, about the size of Holland. It has passed through many hands, shedding acres as it went to pay for losses incurred by drought, red-water fever and pleuropneumonia, depradations by aborigines, price collapses and remoteness from markets. There was a time when about one station hand in three perished from accident or disease, and another time when the bounty on a dingo's ears, a matter of four dollars in today's currency, brought in more ready money than a five-year-old bullock delivered at Wyndham.

Now it belongs to a company formed by Mr. L. J. Hooker, a real-estate magnate from the south, and about $2 million have been invested since the change of ownership. Millions more will be needed. A decision has been made to introduce Brahman cattle, a breed evolved in the tropics and believed by many to be more suited to the Top End—the tropical north—than cattle bred to thrive in cold, wet islands in the North Sea. For over a century graziers have gone on importing and breeding the Shorthorns and Herefords their forebears bred before them in the British Isles. And Shorthorns and Herefords have endured much, survived droughts and flood, been overlanded across thousands of miles of desert, and thrived on vegetation their stomachs can never have been intended to deal with. There is nothing wrong with Shorthorns and Herefords, but Zebu breeds, such as the Brahman and its crosses, have certain advantages. Heat and flies bother them less, their temperaments are placid, they are said to convert into protein more efficiently these dry, fibrous grasses and shrubs, and their short hair and folded skins discourage ticks. So at V.R.D. the change is to be made and the war on scrub bulls intensified. Since the Hooker Company took over, more than 10,000 of these bulls have been shot or castrated. But it will be a long time before the last of them can be winkled out of the rugged, rock-strewn ranges and such a measure of control established that every bull calf on the run is mustered and branded and none escape to take shelter, free and entire, in the creeks.

Running a station like V.R.D. is like running a small town. The population includes about two hundred blacks and fifty or sixty whites, and the station has its own post office, a small hospital with a resident nursing sister, and a big store that stocks everything from wrenches to lipstick, tractor tires to children's toys. Provisions come across the continent from Brisbane, 2,250 miles, once a year, in military quantities: thirty-five tons of flour at a time, for example, and twenty-two tons of sugar.

The nearest town is Katherine, population 716, which is 280 miles away along a bumpy road, so there is no running round the corner for a packet of cigarettes. Katherine has a meatworks, and nowadays V.R.D. fats are trucked there in road trains instead of walking, as they used to, down to Wyndham, the nearest seaport, or all the way to the railhead at Mount Isa, more than 1,500 miles. They reach Katherine in a day, but losses may be higher than they were in droving times: about fifteen beasts out of every hundred come to grief through getting crushed or suffocated or badly bruised. If luck was with him, a good drover sometimes handed over more cattle than he started with, thanks to natural increase on the way.

[3]

The native camp, close to the homestead and full of barking dogs, has the squalid appearance of all clusters of temporary dwellings. These are shelters and not homes. The dirty little humpies look as if a good push would knock them down. Sheets of old corrugated iron serve for beds, supported by empty oil drums; a few rags of clothing are flung over bits of string attached to nails in the wall; strips of sacking make the doors; earthen floors are littered with old tins, stale crusts and trampled cigarette packs; a mongrel dog scratches in a corner. Most of the older women look like shapeless bolsters bulging with flock. Their lank hair gives them a bedraggled appearance you do not find among Africans, whose short wool never looks untidy and is often shorn.

A mountainous old woman, squatting under a strip of sacking stretched between posts, had come here on a visit and remained ever since, more immobile than a gorged toad. Would a lorry going in her direction take her home? "No loading for me," she replied cryptically. A withered, ancient man lay in the shade wrapped in filthy blankets, slowly dying of old age. There are three old men here, born on the station, who remember when the camp was attacked by a party of "wild" blacks who speared a station black and carried off some cattle. The station blacks baited the yard with tucker and hid in the bush. After several baitings a large party of "wild" blacks crowded in; the station blacks closed the gates and shot every one. That stockyard has long since vanished, and no one knows whether the old men's story is true; if it is, the date of the episode must have been around 1890.

Today the station blacks are housed, clothed, fed and paid a cash wage of under ten dollars a week—about one-fifth of that paid to white men. But equal pay for blacks and whites in the Northern Territory has been officially decreed and will come into full effect at the end of 1968. A section of the act that controls the pay-fixing machinery for all the major pursuits lays it down that a man who is considered unable to earn the minimum wage may be classified as a "slow worker" and paid less. In an important ruling the Commonwealth Arbitration Commission, the judicial body that fixes the minimum (the "award") wage throughout the country for each industry, upheld the contention of the Northern Territory's pastoralists that a majority of their aboriginal employees do not, as things are, work hard enough or conscientiously enough to be worth as much as a white man; and it may be open to employers to get these chronic "hose-holders," as they are sometimes called, put into this category and so exempted from the full award.

This, of course, would be discrimination, but intended to protect and not to penalize the aborigines. If equal pay were to be brought in by a stroke of the pen, the pastoralists reckon that three blacks out of four would be laid off. No business could afford to quintuple its wage bill overnight, and employers would be compelled by economics to replace most of their amiable but idle blacks by whites who would be more efficient, or at any rate more accustomed to the idea of considering time and skill as marketable commodities, an idea quite foreign to aborigines, as to all nomads in their tribal condition. "These aborigines do not understand the meaning of work in our sense," the Commission bluntly declared; tribal society was not competitive; a prospect of more cash would not spur them on; and no one refuted the employers' evidence that men who could not read, write, or count needed more supervision, in this day and age, than literate stockmen.

So there is to be a compromise: first a breathing space before equal pay comes into effect, then a provision enabling pastoralists to avoid sacking blacks who do not pull their weight, a step that would cause genuine distress to most of them, as well as to the unemployed abos. The numbers involved are small. Only 1,003 adult aborigines—half-bloods were not included, being normally treated as whites—were employed on cattle stations in the Northern Territory in March, 1966, and so affected by the award; and of these about one-quarter, in the Commission's opinion, would receive the full wage in any case, being considered by their employers efficient enough to earn it. As the older abos are replaced by younger men with some education, the difficulty will work itself out. In a few years, probably, unequal pay will have died out, along with many of the other traditions of a pastoral industry now poised on the brink of fundamental changes; and yet, perhaps, behind the future air-conditioned radio-control headquarters staffed by computers, a few bleary-eyed hose-holders may still be found sleeping it off in dilapidated humpies, with mongrel dogs scratching at fleas by their side.

As we walked away from the present camp, we saw some torn-up playing cards lying in the bush. "Nines," my companion explained. "No white man can really get to the bottom of it. They tear up all the court cards and play with the rest. They'll gamble all day. The same boys always win; the rest lose everything." The nursing sister on the station, he added, had made a study of the game, but its rules still eluded her, if indeed it had any. "In the leprosarium there was a man with no fingers on either hand and he always won. How do you explain *that*?" Perhaps he had anointed his palms with frangipani juice, which the blacks believe brings luck.

[4]

The Victoria is a wide, tree-shaded river that flows sometimes sluggishly, sometimes in spate, into the Joseph Bonaparte Gulf between Wyndham and Darwin. Many birds frequent its banks and contribute to the dawn chorus. To identify the contributors was far beyond me, but in *A Territory of Birds* Michael Sharland has done so. It is opened, he writes, by the hesitant notes of the brown Honey eater, followed by the pied butcherbird, whose fluting is not unlike the kind of non-electric doorbell that gives out a chime. There follow on rufus whistlers, bar-shouldered doves, the charming little peaceful doves, other kinds of honey eaters, black-faced wood swallows, pardalotes, kookaburras and many others. But parrots are dominant. You soon get tired of certain species which, at first so striking, as time goes on reveal themselves as vulgar and aggressive birds. I do not, of course, mean the superb lorikeets, flashy as they are, or the glorious rosellas, but I do mean the corellas, which go about in mobs and are terribly noisy, and the sulphur-crested white cockatoos which, like all their kind, screech raucously.

The loveliest bird I saw in the Territory was nesting in a veranda on the Humbert River station. This was the blood finch. The male was wholly scarlet except for a blue patch on the nape of his neck; the female's head was scarlet and her back a lemon-tinted grey. A family of five reposed in a beautifully lined cavity among the ferns of a hanging basket, and the father perched on the arm of my chair.

A big goanna, three or four feet long, scuttled down the Victoria's bank and into the river. With so many aborigines around I was surprised that this giant lizard could survive, but I was told that in the camp few blacks bother nowadays with goannas. "Too much tucker. Too much meat."

Thirty or forty wallabies hopped gaily in front of their long shadows through rocks and scrub. "A pest, I'm afraid," said Mr. Miller with regret. "The men shoot them for sport." The worst of the pests are dingoes, which are poisoned, and Mr. Miller reckoned there might be 30,000 or 40,000 wild donkeys in the hills. In a single year V.R.D. paid out bonuses on 15,000 pairs of donkey's ears. It is a wasteful business, for the carcasses are left to rot in the bush and feed the crows—and the dingoes.

[5]

I spent Anzac Day at "The Katherine." From Broome to Brisbane and Cape York to Albany, this is an occasion that brings out of drawers and cupboards tens of thousands of medals to be pinned to shirts and lapels, while their owners trudge behind a brass band. Pubs are closed until noon; they open then to good purpose, and after that the rules are suspended. Two-up may be played openly in the streets; everyone may get drunk, and millions do. The police stand by, ready to extinguish brawls, but otherwise inactive. Most women stay at home. This is the day of the Returned Servicemen's League which, like the British Legion, but a great deal better supported, has branches in every nook and cranny of the land. On the beaches of Gallipoli, Australia ceased to be a colony and became in spirit an independent nation, and Anzac Day is a celebration of this nationhood, as well as a payment of homage to the dead of two wars.

At The Katherine a couple of dozen men gathered in the darkness for the dawn service. Although the veranda's thermometer would subsequently register over 100° F., it was chilly and everyone wore sweaters. The traditional gathering place is at the war memorial, which is the same in almost every country town and village—a dreadful white plaster soldier standing with his feet apart and his head bowed over a reversed rifle. The Katherine is too small even for a plaster soldier, so the focal point was a little open-sided booth, outside the school, commemorating a corporal killed in an air crash. As the eastern sky began to lighten, a Roman Catholic priest drove up, and we gathered round the booth to listen to a short address, followed by a Salvation Army bugler's somewhat squeaky rendering of the Last Post and the Reveille. Then we dispersed to a welcome cup of hot tea.

After breakfast came the main event of the day, the ex-servicemen's parade. It was a middle-aged parade led by two fat, tubby men in round hats and spectacles, followed by a polyglot assembly; one man was carrying a baby, several were part-bloods, all wore medals. Then came three Boy Scouts with drums and a straggle of Cubs and Brownies. There were no spectators. It was hot by now with harsh, glaring sunshine and a high humidity. Flies and midges were bad. "They tramp in mateship side by side—the Protestant and Roman—They call no biped lord or sir, And touch their hat to no man!"

The parade ended at the school, where the flag was at half-mast and an aircraftsman stood with arms reversed at each corner of the corporal's memorial. We had another short address, "Rock of Ages," "Lead Kindly Light" and the National Anthem. The schoolmaster stepped forward to receive a check for $200 that had been intended for a memorial arch, but as the sum would not run to this, the money was to be spent on books for the school library; this would attract another $200 from the Commonwealth Government, which a memorial arch would not. After a short social interlude everyone drove off, the women to their kitchens and the men to the pubs to perform their duty. He would be a poor fish who did not get a little drunk on Anzac Day.

[6]

Before the days of bitumen and airstrips the heavy monsoonal rains of the Wet marooned everyone in the Top End. No wagon could move with stores; no horse could swim the flooded rivers. If you ran out of tea, you did without, and if you had an accident, you recovered or you died. A local legend relates how Cowboy Collins had his stomach ripped open by a bull. He sewed himself up with a sacking needle threaded with horsehair, mounted a horse and started to ride to The Katherine, but the stitches broke and his insides fell out; so he sewed himself up again and rode on. He survived and still does. I was to have met him, but he was prostrated by sand-blight blindness, a common and extremely painful complaint during the Dry.

"A colourful character," people said. Territorians regard their "characters" as a local product, on a par with beef and buffaloes. Like tall trees, characters need space to develop; people squashed up together in suburbs become monotonous like scrub and mallee. There is plenty of elbow room in the Territory, which would muster eleven people to the square mile if you spread them out. In practice they are mostly bunched together in Darwin at one end of the bitumen and Alice Springs a thousand miles away at the other, with a few strung out along the bitumen in places like The Katherine, Tennant Creek and Newcastle

Waters. England has 570 to the square mile—and about one yard per person if you lined everyone up along the seashore.

A few characters have strayed off the bitumen to settle in places like Borroloola, a forlorn little settlement on a river that meanders into the Gulf of Carpentaria. It was here that a character called Bill Harney began a remarkable career when he was taken into custody for poddy-dodging—branding with your own brand clearskin calves—and stopped overnight in the jail. That night the Wet came down, and he stayed for six months. In the little court house were half a dozen packing cases full of books inexplicably presented to the nonexistent citizens of Borroloola by the Carnegie Foundation. During his months of enforced inactivity Bill Harney browsed among such of the volumes as had not been eaten by termites or moulds, and by the end of the Wet such writers as Herodotus and Plutarch, Dickens and Balzac, La Rochefoucauld and Dostoevski were his familiars, and the idea of taking to the pen himself had been born.

Bill Harney's own version, given in his book *Grief, Gaiety and Aborigines,* is rather different. A former Borroloola policeman called Corporal Power, he relates, secured the library from the Carnegie Trustees in 1919, and Harney knew of its existence through having come across pages of Plutarch's *Lives* in the earth closet of a local pub. When he was passing through Borroloola on legitimate business, he delved into the forgotten packing cases, but there is no suggestion that he stayed to study their contents. He was a nomad, a "bushie," a trepang fisher, a pearler, a drover, a yarn spinner, a sort of outback troubadour, who married a part-blood aboriginal girl. After her death from tuberculosis of the bone he made a home for his two small children in a humpy on the outskirts of The Katherine amid a fringe community of down-and-outs, half-bloods and social outcasts with names like the Bullock-Tosser, the Expert (an expert on sharpening sheep shears), One-spud Gus (an ex-station cook), the Midnight Stockman (who emptied sanitary buckets), and the Student, who lived in a 2,000-gallon tank anchored to an ironwood tree. Here Bill Harney cared for his children, drew the dole, and picked up any odd jobs he could find with the aid of an ancient truck he named "Muscles." Those who most befriended him were the aborigines with whom he had become related—not by marrying one, but by fathering the children who belonged to his wife's tribe; this gave him a claim—only they would not have seen it as a claim—on every member of that tribe and an inalienable place in the community.

His neighbour Ruby, a member of his wife's tribe, had scant regard for Bill Harney as an individual—for one thing, he had offended by failing to send twists of his dead wife's hair to certain relatives, and for another, he possessed the despicable vice of keeping money and possessions to himself instead of sharing everything out—but she and the children were of one spirit, and all that she had they were entitled to share. Of his own people's attitude, Bill Harney comments caustically that while it was the universal custom for white men to keep native gins—they called them studs—and to take pride in the number they could lie with, by legally marrying one he had lost caste in their eyes.

It is a tragic tale; his beloved daughter died when she was nine or ten, the boy at fifteen when he drowned in the pool at Alice Springs while saving the life of a companion. This and others of Bill Harney's books give, I would suppose, as true, vivid and honest a picture as could be found of the bushie's life, and of the aborigines seen from within a community normally closed to all outsiders. The choice of Bill Harney to be their guide by the organizers of the American-Australian Scientific Expedition to Arnhem Land in 1948 is proof that savants as well as readers of popular magazines respected his knowledge of the outback and its native inhabitants.

At The Katherine another character called Timoghy O'Shea kept a pub which has descended to two of his seven daughters. The O'Sheas reached the Top End in a wagon, accompanied by goats and hens, on their way to the gold fields of Western Australia, but by the time they got to Pine Creek, north of The Katherine, a gold rush had started there, so there they stopped, making a shelter for themselves of branches and sacks stiffened with whitewash, and setting up a blacksmith's forge. "To this day I can remember the glowing of the forge," said Mrs. Kearnain, one of the daughters. "No one ever had a happier childhood." Twenty or thirty children would go off together in a bullock dray with aborigines who would show them how to dig for grubs and catch goannas and how to hunt for turtles' eggs in the banks of billabongs. "The blacks seemed to know by instinct where to scoop away the sand or dig into the mud to find a clutch buried two feet underground. The eggs were always ice-cold." And Mrs. Kearnain remembers also how the bush at night twinkled with lights that bobbed about like fireflies; the Chinese were working in their gardens by lantern light after toiling all day in the sun to build a railway from Darwin. And she describes the clay ovens in the bush where they would roast whole pigs.

What happened to all the Chinese? On the railway from Darwin to Burrundie thousands worked for approximately 35 cents a day and many died from fevers, scurvy and bad conditions in the Wet. Some stayed on when their indentures had expired to "scalp the Silurian rock in a most remorseless manner," in the words of an official report, in order to extract illicit gold. Others set up general stores, but the majority went back to China after the passage of the Chinese Immigration Act of 1888, which imposed a limit of one immigrant per 500 tons of shipping and virtually closed the door to the Chinese. Bush reclaimed the gardens where their lanterns had once bobbed and buried the ovens. Some of their descendants can be seen today in Darwin, and in Pine Creek there is Jimmie Ah Toy, who owns a thriving store, grows a lot of sorghum, and has a son who graduated in economics at the University in Adelaide.

[7]

The Wet starts with heavy storms. Rivers rampage, everything is under water; only along the bitumen is wheeled movement possible. Plants can almost be seen to grow. Normally it lasts about four months —December to March—and then comes the Dry. For the four winter months—June to September—the rainfall averages less than one-twentieth of an inch. What a country for village fetes, church bazaars, garden parties, *son et lumière!*

The economy of the region is based on turning native grasses into beef. The soils are poor, the native grasses inefficient, and nature has omitted to evolve a legume that would help to remedy a nitrogen deficiency by extracting this element from the air. So the fattening of cattle on these native pastures is a slow, clumsy affair. The beasts take five years or more to grow to slaughter weight, and their condition seesaws according to the seasons. When the Wet gets into its stride and everything grows, cattle put on weight at first rapidly, then much more slowly. With the arrival of the Dry, they start to shed their gains and go backwards. Experimental cattle have lost, on average, one-fifth of their weight between May and November, and the annual live-weight gain of growing cattle has averaged only about one hundredweight a year. And the rate of stocking on these pastures is no more than four to six beasts to the *square mile*. On this basis little, if anything, can be done to increase the output of beef from the Top End.

To find out what might be done, the C.S.I.R.O. has a research station at The Katherine staffed by young men whose enthusiasm and belief in their work brushes off on to the visitor. They say that *twenty million acres of* bush in The Katherine region alone—an area about four times the size of Wales—has "agricultural potential"—could grow crops, that is, either directly for human consumption, for example peanuts, rice, sorghum, sugar cane and so forth, or to feed animals which in turn feed humans. It is to this that the main inquiry is directed: how to grow forage crops to fatten cattle in the Dry, and how to reconstitute the natural pastures so as to carry far more cattle, which will fatten at a much faster rate, all the year round.

The men conducting these experiments—and scientists lean over backwards to avoid making large claims—describe the possibilities being opened up as "dramatic." Hopes center around three exotic plants: Townsville lucerne, which is neither a lucerne nor a native of Townsville in Queensland, but comes from Central America; the perennial birdwood grass, a relation of the Indian buffel; and bulrush millet.* The great achievement of these plants is to enable beasts that have put on weight quickly in the Wet to hold on to and increase their gains, instead of losing them, in the Dry.

These points cannot, I am afraid, be made without deploying some statistics. The normal stocking rate on these natural pastures works out, at best, at one beast to 120 acres. Cattle grazed on bulrush millet are being stocked at the rate of one beast to every half acre—that is, 240 times higher! In the first six weeks after the onset of the Wet their average daily gain has been just over three pounds, instead of four and a half *ounces*. Instead of losing weight in the Dry, they held and slightly added to their gains. On natural pastures beasts normally make use of less that 5 per cent of the dry matter in the plants; on bulrush millet they have extracted up to 60 per cent. And finally, the productivity of improved pastures sown with birdwood grass and Townsville lucerne has, in one set of experiments, and measured by the weight of beef animals, been multiplied by a factor of about forty-five.

What could this mean to a protein-hungry world? The same area of

---

* Their Latin names are: *Stylosanthes humilia; Cenchrus setigerus;* and *Pennisetum typhoideum*.

land producing forty-five times as much protein—or even more: some put the estimate at sixty times—simply by substituting other plants and managing them properly! If this could be done commercially—and if the protein could be brought to those who need it—our troubles about feeding the hungry would be over. But of course we are a very long way from that. These experiments are new; they may prove overoptimistic; they can only point the way. A long, hard haul lies ahead before they can be translated into practice on any significant scale.

Nearly all these tropical soils lack adequate nitrogen and phosphates. While we may look to natural organisms on the roots of Townsville lucerne to remedy the former, the latter must be imported. Everyone is after phosphates; the cost is high, and a world shortage impends. And no one can say for certain how these exotic plants are going to behave in surroundings new to them. To find out merely by watching them, and by trial and error, would take many years, so the scientists are using complex and subtle apparatus to imitate the conditions of the natural world and to play tricks with them, and with the plants, in order to see what happens if, say, you shorten the hours of daylight, or step up the intensity of the light, or create the condition of a storm. All this can be simulated in cages full of vegetable guinea pigs and housed in a contraption called CERES, the pride of the Plant Industry Division of the C.S.I.R.O.

CERES stands for the Controlled Environment Research Laboratory. It is also called a phytotron, and there are at present only four of this particular kind in the world: in Canberra, in California, in Moscow and in Paris. It consists of a large number of insulated glass cages in which light, temperature, humidity and air flow are regulated with less-than-hair's-breadth accuracy by thermostatic, automatically controlled means. A scientist has only to say, "Let there be light at x degrees of intensity for y hours (or minutes, or seconds); let there be the conditions of an approaching thunderstorm; let there be a sudden drop in temperature; let there be a stiff wind, a hot air current, a whirley, an eclipse of the sun"—anything he pleases—and it happens. In their pots the plants—any kind of plant a scientist pleases—will respond, and its responses will be automatically recorded on charts and graphs. What makes a plant grow or not grow, succumb to or resist disease, transmit or not transmit certain qualities to its progeny, flower and fruit and die—all these mysteries are being laid bare, one by one, within the phytotron and for the first time.

[8]

A C.S.I.R.O. report starts with the words: "Monsoonal northern Australia has had a long history of agricultural failure since the first attempts at European settlement were made 120 years ago." Neither soil nor climate is primarily to blame. The Chinese grew excellent vegetables, and in Darwin a resourceful pair of botanists, Dr. Maurice Holtze and subsequently his son Nicholas, successfully cultivated almost every useful tropical plant that can be named. Things grow; the problem is to grow them economically, and to sell them when they are grown. The Top End is too far away from the consumers, who live on the other side of a desert which is expensive either to cross overland or to get round by sea. So projects to settle small-scale mixed farmers on the land have petered out obscurely in disappointed hopes, and others to establish large-scale plantations have foundered with a fanfare of publicity.

Such a one was Humpty Doo, whose relics are to be seen not far from Darwin in the shape of abandoned paddy fields and a dam favoured by birds. (The Top End has some memorable place names: Humpty Doo, Rum Jungle, Blue Mud Bay, Red Lily Lagoon, Seven Emus.) Here dams were built, irrigation channels dug, fertilizer applied, and rice cultivated with the latest of American techniques. The rice grew, although not so well as had been expected. Difficulties arose that no one had foreseen; costs of production were a great deal higher than those of the Asian peasant with his water buffalo and large, unpaid family of helpers. The project failed. Now Humpty Doo is just one more tombstone in a graveyard of hopes in monsoonal northern Australia.

Yet those twenty million acres in the Katherine area with high "agricultural potential," and millions of unused acres elsewhere, haunt the graveyard still. With at least one-third of the world's people underfed, is it enough merely to ignore all those empty spaces and accept defeat? Is there no way round the obstacles of distant markets and high costs? Many Australians have a shrewd suspicion that, despite all the arguments and economic theories, despite Dr. Davidson's insistence that Asians do not *want* empty spaces, jungles and deserts, despite his convincing proofs that everything which can be grown in the tropics can be grown better elsewhere—despite all this, they suspect that, if you were to ship several hundred thousand Chinese peasants to this monsoonal Top End, in five years' time it would be producing a great deal more than it is producing now, which is virtually (minerals apart) nothing except a limited quantity of indifferent beef.

Perhaps some of the better areas could be split into moderate-sized farms and used to fatten store cattle bred on the big pastoral properties? Or for some form of mixed farming? It would be foolish to forget all the past failures but defeatist to accept them as the last word. What else is technology for, if not to turn such failures into ultimate victories?*

[9]

"Women either fall in love with Darwin or they hate its guts." We sat in an open-air beer garden in the sticky heat—and it really *is* hot in Darwin, there is no doubt about its tropical character; the coldest temperature ever recorded was 50°, and that has become historic—under a notice which read: "Shirts must be worn at all times in this area." They need not be worn in the bar. Leather-coloured men go about in shorts and sandals; coats and jackets are unknown. People dress as they please and do as they please in Darwin. There is a sense of gently standing still because it is too hot and torpid to do otherwise, like an afternoon buffalo drowsing under a tree and waiting for nothing.

Racially this must be the most mixed-up town in Australia. (Unless it

* The failures started with the first European settlement on Melville Island in 1824 (Fort Dundas) abandoned in 1829. The Raffles Bay settlement of 1827 was abandoned in 1829, and that established at Port Essington in 1838 closed down in 1849. On all these settlements vegetables were grown and livestock imported; the latter ran wild when the settlements were closed. In 1863, when the region was taken over by South Australia, a Land Act was passed providing for the sale of 250,000 acres in 160-acre blocks—the yeoman-farmer dream again. The North Australian Company, formed in London, took up half the lots but never developed them and eventually demanded its money back. By 1872 it was plain even to politicians in Adelaide that 160-acre farms near Palmerston had no future, and the size of the blocks on offer was increased to a maximum of 1,280 acres. An agent went to Singapore to recruit Chinese coolies, and the government tried to attract settlers from Mauritius, Reunion and India. In 1876 a missionary in Japan was authorized to invite Japanese settlers, but the suggestion was turned down flat by the Japanese Government. In 1879 a Melbourne company selected 100,000 acres on the Daly River to grow sugar cane. The soil proved unsuitable and the total output of the scheme, abandoned in 1884, was five tons. At various times and places people experimented with coffee, rubber, coconuts, sisal, tobacco, maize, indigo and rice; none of these experiments succeeded. In 1890 the South Australian Government passed another Land Act intended to encourage small mixed farms and in 1908 made provision to advance money, but by 1909 less than 9,500 acres were held under agricultural leases, all of them round Darwin. Every project foundered on shortage of labour, distance from markets, and sheer mismanage-

is Broome, another of the tantalizers that I never reached.) You notice immediately the Chinese, who traditionally keep cafés, restaurants and curio shops and work as bartenders and waiters and physically look large and prosperous. Much of the café-restaurant trade has lately been taken over by the Greeks, who form a close-knit and prolific community with their own churches and a bearded Patriarch. To the Greeks, as to the Chinese, the family is everything. They keep in touch with relatives in Greece largely by photography. Members of a prosperous family— and most seem to be prospering—repair half a dozen times a year to the photographer's studio to celebrate the latest event. A betrothal, a wedding, christening, first communion, birthday, anniversary, first tooth, first menstruation, new pregnancy—almost anything will serve as a pretext. Pregnancy is considered especially photogenic; wives proudly stand in profile before the camera, to enable relatives at home to follow the progress of the happy event, just as they would if they shared the same roof.

For centuries the Indian Ocean has been bringing to rest along this ragged coastline people of many races and kinds. Malays came to gather the trepang—the same as *bêche-de-mer* or sea cucumbers—which lie fatly in the shallows and are eaten with relish. Japanese came to dive for pearls and, later, to persuade the oysters to make them. South Sea Islanders came, and fishermen from West Irian and Papua across the narrow Torres Strait, and ship-jumping seamen; people came from all the world over. No one questioned them or interfered.

The results may be seen in the primary school. Skin colours range from sooty black through every shade of chocolate to pale honey. There are ivory Chinese and much darker, burnt-sienna Chinese; half-Malays with eyes aslant; blond Saxon types with blue eyes and tow-coloured hair; olive-skinned and black-haired Greeks and Italians—a human zoo. Its inmates are peaceable. "There's no trouble," the teachers agreed.

---

ment such as that which occurred on the government's experimental farm at Rum Jungle when, in 1918, all the crops failed because the manager was on leave and nothing was planted until too late in the season. When the Commonwealth Government took over in 1911, there were in force twenty-seven agricultural leases totalling 7,037 acres, one mixed farming permit, and thirty-six acres held under special licenses for market gardening. Between 1911 and 1940 a total of 419 agricultural leases were issued, and in 1957 only fifty-nine of these were still in force. And of those fifty-nine, only nine were occupied by the original lessees or their descendants.

"They all mix; there's no racial feeling." Do people mix at home as well as in school? A young woman teacher smiled. "They can't help it sometimes. My father is English, my mother a part-blood from Broome. I've brothers and sisters darker than I am, and some lighter, and one who looks pure white."

You may do as you please—that is the main thing about Darwin. No one tells you what you ought to think of other people. It may be small, but on one side lies the whole of Australia, and on the other there is Asia—400 miles away, whereas Canberra is about 2,000. You feel this Asian presence, but there is nothing menacing about it. Probably there should be, with fumes spreading from the poison hole of Vietnam, and with Darwin's record as the only city in Australia that was bombed, and seriously bombed, by the Japanese.

Over half the population has arrived here since World War II. Darwin is growing at a faster rate than any other Australian city except Canberra. It is about the size of Newburyport, Massachusetts, at present. The part-blood teacher told me over a milk shake concocted by a Chinese and served by a Greek—they have enormous milk shakes in Darwin, out of double-sized mugs—of her plan to see New Zealand, North America and Europe with four or five other girls and to join forces in London, after two years, with another party who intend to explore South America. In London she hopes to see an international women's hockey match. She plays hockey and netball for the Territory and hurried off for an evening's training, which happily did not preclude outsized chocolate milk shakes. I was lost in admiration for anyone prepared to run in the heat.

There seem to be two Darwins. There is the Darwin that started life as Palmerston in 1869 and quietly stagnated beside its magnificent harbour until the end of World War II. It must have been the sort of place that Conrad wrote about: a small, neglected colonial capital, with administrators, if not actually in white topees at least in white shirts, cooled by punkahs and gin slings, hoisting and lowering flags over Government House; and with sweaty men in bars with rolls of fat and stubbly chins drinking themselves into stupors and keeping, or at any rate frequenting, native girls; with down-and-outers, no-hopers, traders in pearls and merchant seamen. Before the coming of the bitumen the ocean was the only highway for about five months of the year, and this must have created an end-of-the-road, isolated, no-one-cares mentality. Everything had failed—the meatworks, the farms and plantations, the gold fields, the rice and sugar schemes. The aborigines were supposed to be dying out. There is little left of this old Darwin, either physically— new buildings are going up everywhere—or humanly; but traditions are the genes of social heredity and take a long time to lose their force.

The other Darwin is a brand-new tourist resort providing air-conditioned hotels overlooking the sea and equipped with the regulation potted palms, white-coated stewards, cavern-like cocktail bars and floodlit patios, exactly like all expensive hotels from Pasadena to Hawaii, Majorca to Madeira; the same iced drinks, the same sort of frozen food, the same sweet music and the same people, all elderly because few of the young can afford such luxuries. Darwin in the Dry is just about perfect for tourists; there is no climatic treachery—the sun always shines.

One or two of these resplendent hotels belong to a male Cinderella who came to Darwin from some poverty-stricken Aegean island where people live on the smell of goats and by unremitting toil, quick wits, charm and ambition rose to become, it is said, the largest individual taxpayer in Australia. Darwin is full of stories about Michael Paspalis. One, which concerns his early struggles, starts with his housekeeper asking what he would like for dinner. "There's a lamb in the fridge." "I think you had better cut it up yourself, Mr. Paspalis." "It's right—you go ahead." The housekeeper insisted. When Mr. Paspalis sliced into the lamb, out tumbled piles and piles of bank notes. The night before he had stuffed the lamb with his cash takings for safekeeping and then forgotten all about it, so many were his irons in the fire, or lambs in the fridge. Now Darwin has divided into two schools of thought about the happiness of Mr. Paspalis. One believes him to be miserable because his wealth separates him from his people and obliges him to regard with suspicion every suitor to his daughters' hands; the other, that he relishes his riches, the big splash he makes in Sydney, and his invitation to dinner on the royal yacht and to lunch at Buckingham Palace. The Paspalis family was away splashing in Sydney, so I had no chance to form an opinion as to which school, if either, was right.

[10]

The Northern Territory has been directly governed from Canberra since 1911; before that it was run, or not run, from Adelaide. The pattern closely reflects the old British colonial system and, now that the wind of change has blown it all away elsewhere, seems oddly archaic. In fact there is a strong whiff of the coelacanth about the Northern Territory Administration. At the head is the Administrator, whose status differs little from that of an old-style colonial governor; it is true that there is no plumed hat—you simply could not wear a plumed hat in Darwin—but there is a Government House, a flag and a Book.

The Administrator has an area to look after larger than France, Spain and Italy combined, with extremely poor communications and a total of about 50,000 inhabitants. He is responsible for carrying out the Commonwealth's aboriginal policy. (Rather more than one-fifth of the Territory's population consists of pure-blood aborigines.) He is the head of a scattered, undermanned public service. More and more people come to Darwin whom he must brief and entertain. He presides over a Legislative Council consisting at present of eight elected members and nine appointed by the Governor-General, of whom six are senior public servants. This Council is a poor thing with no financial powers—another of Australia's flightless birds. Authority is firmly based in Canberra. If the Northern Territory wants to spend $200 on, say, street lighting in Darwin, it has to get the proposal approved, and the money disgorged, by the Commonwealth Government. There is not even a separate budget for the Territory. No wonder that, seen from the Darwin end, delays are many, frustrations galling, and the whole system out of date.

Since May, 1962, aborigines throughout Australia have enjoyed the right to vote in Commonwealth elections. Voting is compulsory, so they could, and in theory should, be prosecuted if they do not go to the polls. In practice very few have, as yet, the least idea of the meaning of votes, elections, councils and the general apparatus of democracy.* The whole framework of local government, which in other countries has underpinned the democratic structure and trained the people in the democratic method, is lacking, so hitherto the law has held its hand. As yet no aborigine has stood for election to the Legislative Council, and few have been sufficiently "assimilated"—the word that has replaced a more self-confident generation's "civilized"—to do so. There is one in Darwin who has considered it and may come forward at the next election: Mr. Philip Roberts, chairman of an unofficial body, formed late in 1961, called the Northern Territory Council for Aboriginal Rights.

* At the election for the Legislative Council in December, 1962, 1,181 aborigines registered and cast their votes. The total aboriginal population of the Territory was then 18,621.

Founders of bodies to demand rights for coloured people in a white society are apt to be angry young men with fires in their bellies and to be regarded by most whites as Communist-inspired fanatics. It would be hard to see Mr. Roberts in this rôle. He is a quiet, middle-aged man with slightly greying hair and a slow, rather hesitant manner of speech, who works as a specialist clerk in the Medical Department. He came from the Roper River Mission where the Territory's Director of Medical Services chose him as a personal assistant largely because, as Dr. Langsford said, "he's very good at fixing things." His principal lieutenant is Mr. Davis Daniels, a fellow worker in the Medical Department and secretary of the Council for Aboriginal Rights. This embryonic body is groping rather than performing, with very little money; the little that it has comes mostly from white supporters in the south.

What are the Council's aims? "We must prepare the people first"; prepare them, Mr. Roberts said, for the full citizenship they enjoy on paper but not in daily life. Ignorance, lack of education and unawareness hold them back. "They do not understand democracy," said Mr. Daniels. "The first step is to get out amongst them and explain. Tell them how to register, how to vote, what to do. We must hold meetings to explain all these things, and for that we need money. And the government must help us more." Help in what particular ways? "More schools, more higher education, better housing, development in the reserves." What sort of development? Beef production, farming, forestry, but also more industries, new industries. Of what kind? "The government must decide." The money for all this? "We abos have no money. The government has money; they must spend it on development."

Hitherto the education provided by scattered missions starved for funds and short of qualified teachers has been rudimentary in the extreme and centered on the catechism. Men like Philip Roberts and Davis Daniels, who are among its products, look to the government to improve the lot of their people; they do not want to take it on themselves. In our political jargon they are moderates. "Their position," a sympathizer told me, "is very difficult. They are under continual pressure from the more extreme wing, mainly white or white-inspired. The only two white members of their executive committee are avowed Communists. Southern left-wing sympathizers want to use the Aboriginal Council to embarrass the Commonwealth Government. The abo leaders here are cautious and sincere and on a different wave length."

For years distance and neglect have combined to isolate the Territory;

within that isolation a greater isolation has enclosed the aborigines. The areas of contact between them and the society they live in have been the missions, and most of the missions are remote and distant even from the little pinpoints of society that prick the vast hide of the north. It is possible to be a thousand miles from Darwin and still be in the Territory. There are missions on the Gulf of Carpentaria, 500 miles away from Darwin, that can be reached only by sea. In 1966 only three full-blooded aborigines in the whole Territory were in secondary schools.

But change is setting in. When I saw them in Darwin, Mr. Roberts and Mr. Daniels had just returned from a meeting in Canberra of a body called the Federal Council for the Advancement of Aborigines and Torres Strait Islanders, which had passed a number of angry resolutions, including one demanding an immediate payment of $300 million as compensation for land taken by the whites. The days of paternalism are over, and the policy of trying to protect blacks from the evil intentions of whites, mainly making them drunk and seducing their women, which has prevailed for about a century, has been finally scrapped.

[11]

The policy of assimilation, which has replaced that of wardship, dates from 1951 when a young university lecturer from Perth who had specialized in aboriginal affairs became the first Commonwealth Minister for Territories. This gave Mr. Paul Hasluck—now Minister for External Affairs—direction of aboriginal affairs in the Northern Territory, though not in any of the states. For years there has been a movement on foot to amend the constitution so as to give the Commonwealth Government powers to advance directly the status and welfare of aborigines outside the Territory. This has been taken up by the Federal Council for the Advancement of Aborigines and Torres Strait Islanders and by a Member of Parliament, Mr. Wentworth, who introduced a private bill to that effect. But to change the constitution is a cumbrous and chancy business that requires a referendum, and anything touching on states rights is political dynamite.

The assimilation policy is a bow to the inevitable. In the country as a whole there were, in 1966, some 45,000 full-blood aborigines and 70,000 to 80,000 part-bloods. Even though they are increasing—the downward trend was reversed around 1930—in a nation of some twelve millions, their fate is clear. The greater must absorb the less. The official definition of this policy is that "all aborigines and part-aborigines will attain the same manner of living as other Australians, and live as members of a single Australiam community, enjoying the same rights and privileges, accepting the same responsibilities, observing the same customs and influenced by the same beliefs, hopes and loyalties as other Australians."* If special measures have to be taken meanwhile, as of course they have, these are to be regarded as temporary ones, "to protect from ill effects of sudden change" the ex-wards, and tide them over until assimilation is accomplished. When it is, there will of course be no more aborigines but just Aussies, of whatever hue.

No one has consulted the aborigines as to whether they really want to be assimilated, and now that a few are becoming articulate in English, there have been some protesting bleats. They want, the younger and more race-conscious say, to preserve their own culture, or as much of it as they can—something distinctive, something of their own. They do not want, as a community, to disappear. By all means, white Australians agree enthusiastically; let us keep alive the ancient languages, arts and customs. "Assimilation does not mean," said Mr. Hasluck, "the suppression of the aboriginal culture but rather that, for generation after generation, cultural adjustment will take place."

All that is well meant but is, I am afraid, gobbledygook. Culture is a part of the living organism, the blood in the arteries, the sap in the veins. In this case the living organism was a tribe pursuing a nomadic life. In the whole of the Northern Territory and Western Australia combined there may be five hundred nomadic survivors. By the time these words are printed, there may be none at all.

You cannot snip off bits of culture and plant them out in alien soil and expect them to grow. Abos cannot hunt witchety grubs in coffee bars, dig up estivating frogs in car parks, tap mulga roots for water in a General Motors assembly plant, or dance corroborees in the cinema. Even making boomerangs for tourists has a limited future. Painting is the only branch of culture that might, on the face of it, seem to have survival potential. It is now enjoying a boom, and bark paintings have become a major source of income in many settlements and missions, but this has nothing to do with the living culture of a people. The paintings are repetitious and stereotyped, just a way of getting money out of tourists. Bark and cave paintings were a living expression of the people's

* Quoted in *Assimilation in Action,* a statement in the House of Representatives by the Hon. Paul Hasluck, M.P., on August 14, 1963.

faith; that faith was territorial, anchored to rocks and caves, arising from springs and trees.

What has happened to the aborigines is the same as what has happened to so many other species of Australian fauna: the white man has made fundamental changes in the habitat. As with bandicoot and wombat, scrubbird and marsupial mouse, once the habitat goes, so does the species. As individuals, humans are the most adaptable creatures on earth. As individuals they can change their diet, change their climate, change their habits, and survive. But communities cannot; the community disintegrates into individuals who adapt. So assimilation must put an end to aboriginal culture, even if there may still be dark-skinned individuals in the future who will paint and carve, dance and sing. They will sing the new songs of the city, not the old ones of the cave.

FIFTEEN 〜〜〜〜〜

Aborigines

To reach Snake Bay on Melville Island, north of Darwin, takes twenty-two minutes' flying time in a twin-engined Beechcraft. The island is flat, rocky, thickly forested with bloodwoods and stringybarks, and lacks water. A single spring issues from the rock just above a narrow beach washed by the Timore Sea, which looks enticing but for six months of the year must be shunned because of the sea wasp, a poison-secreting jellyfish. It was at this spring that Matthew Flinders replenished his supplies when he made landfall here in 1803 and named the island. Nearby is the site of the first European settlement in northern Australia, made in 1824 by a party from the warship H.M.S. *Tamar* and two other vessels, and consisting of twenty-six soldiers and forty-four convicts. They planted pumpkins, melons, oranges, bananas, limes and other fruits, and imported pigs, goats and water buffaloes, but despite this suffered from scurvy, not to mention sand flies, mosquitoes and the depredations of unfriendly natives; and after five profitless years the settlers withdrew.

Now there is another settlement facing similar obstacles. The long, dry season with its scorching heat kills off most plants unless they can be irrigated, which is costly and difficult. Nowadays there is no need to be self-supporting, and supplies are brought in to feed some 900 people. The rest of the island is uninhabited. Snake Bay is one of fourteen settlements for aborigines maintained by the Welfare Branch of the Northern Territory Administration. These are the places where the practice of assimilation is injected into the bloodstream of aboriginal life.

The starting point is a canteen to which the abo mothers bring their babies three times a day. Under the eye of a nursing sister, plump infants were being stuffed chockablock with scrambled eggs and tomato, followed by pineapple and custard, plus a mug of milk. Two other meals of these dimensions are served every day, with meat at one of them at least; no wonder the babies are as podgy as little bears. Care of these young First Australians starts even earlier, in prenatal clinics; as a result, a population explosion has occurred in all the settlements, and nearly half the residents are under sixteen.

Paternalism may be dead in theory, but in practice a lot of it survives. All the children, of all ages, have free meals in the canteen three times a day. So do many adults; others get a free weekly issue of almost everything they need. Like the birds, they have no cause to gather into barns, for the hand of the Lord scattering corn never fails.

Can this inculcate a sturdy Aussie independence and make-your-own-way mentality? "This is a transitional stage," an official said. "We're doing what we can to get away from the handout pattern. As soon as a man's in full employment he must pay towards his rent and his food. The trouble is to find employment. And it's taken the abos thousands of years to build up their outlook on life; we can't change it overnight."

The Western and the aboriginal outlooks are not merely different, they are contradictory. The good Westerner who plans ahead, husbands his resources and takes thought for the morrow accumulates possessions; his father-figure is a man of property. The nomad turns this upside down. He who accumulates is a villain. In any case there is nothing to accumulate—no houses, no furniture, not even crops or skins. And what could be said of a man who found a well in the desert and kept it secret? Who guzzled on wallaby while others starved? Fair shares among tribesmen is not an ideal; it is the norm. And what an irony that our own society whose religion teaches this ideal should, in the name of progress, so totally extinguish the only human societies on our planet that have achieved it! The tribesmen reproach us, perhaps, with their success.

At any rate, the settlement's intention is to wean the aborigines away from the breast milk of dependence on to a sieved money economy. In this they are hampered not only by the aborigines' reluctance to understand about money but by the difficulty of finding useful tasks. Remoteness from markets puts most settlements out of business before they start. At Snake Bay hopes center on forestry; there are pine plantations, a sawmill and a school of carpentry. At Beswick Creek the Welfare Branch has bought and stocked a station of some 800,000 acres with the object of training native stockmen, and of producing beef. At

Maningrida, in Arnhem Land, a pilot project for a commercial fishery has begun well. But nothing yet has begun to pay.

Minerals offer the brightest hope but depend on the luck of finding them in the right places. A discovery on Groote Eylandt in the Gulf of Carpentaria of what is said to be the richest deposit in the world of manganese has led to the employment of a few young aborigines at the minimum "award" wage of $60 a week. Groote Eylandt forms part of an aboriginal reserve, and there were questions as to whether big mining companies, which would bring in their wake towns and white men and the usual vices, should be allowed in to stay. But if blacks are to be assimilated, those in Arnhem Land could scarcely be left out, and the company is to pay a royalty of 2½ per cent, on top of the normal royalty levied by the government, into a trust fund to be used for the general welfare of the aborigines.

[2]

At least 500 aboriginal languages were spoken in Australia before the white man came. The Melville Islanders spoke a tongue called Tiwi and were different in many ways from the mainland natives. Boomerangs and *didgeridoos* were unknown, spears were of another pattern, and many ceremonies betrayed a Pacific Island influence. Fishing, not hunting, was the life. When an individual died, his relatives cut, decorated and erected burial poles that bore a close resemblance to the totem poles of the South Pacific. Each of the relatives selected for the task would choose with care a bloodwood tree, fell and trim it, and carve and paint the pole with elaborate designs in yellow and red ochre, charcoal, and white clay. In due course the Pukamani rites would follow. The men wore bizarre disguises—false beards of cockatoo plumes stuck with beeswax, strings of wallaby bones, shells, leaves and feathers—in order to confuse the spirits of the dead, who in their loneliness might kidnap any relative they recognized. Dances, shriekings and wailings, mock battles and lamentations went on all night; next day the relatives tidied up the grave, erected the poles, and shaved for the first time since their bereavement.

Today the Pukamani has shrivelled to a halfhearted caper held at the weekend so as not to interfere with working hours. In a clearing among the eucalypts I saw a recent grave surrounded by about a dozen poles which were not painted and only roughly carved. The painting was never the work or professionals; all males of the tribe would sooner or later be called upon to do it. None of this tradition is being handed on to today's schoolboys.

It is in the school that the real break is made between past and future. The Snake Bay children looked bright as buttons, clean and scrubbed; and they put on for our benefit several little mimes, mostly in imitation of wallabies, emus, or domestic fowls. An enthusiastic young woman teacher, full of Anglo-Saxon drive and energy, had them well in hand. "Tell us what you did over Easter." The abo girls giggled and looked coy and said their little pieces shyly and in halting English. "I went with my family to the bush for four days; we killed a turtle on the beach and then we roasted and ate it . . ." "I went into the bush and my father killed three wallabies and they tasted good . . ." "My father took some—some"—she gestured with her fingers—"in a canoe and then we went to a place and hunted for crabs and then we . . ." More gestures. "They hook out the mud crabs with a piece of wire," the teacher explained. "They're beaut." We had some for lunch, and they were.

These children spend their first school year learning English, hygiene, and the basic customs of the society they are about to enter, so they are a year behind white children in the curriculum; but every teacher I spoke to believed there to be no fundamental difference in the mental equipment of white and aboriginal children. The difference lay in what was fed into the mind and what was expected by adult society of the mind, not in the mind itself. But some teachers spoke of a change at adolescence when the intellect seemed to lose its grip instead of strengthening and deeping and wondered whether sex and the initiation ceremonies, which survive in an attenuated and sometimes clandestine form, might dominate the child's energies to the exclusion of everything else.

[3]

The Welfare Branch is trying to move as many families as possible out of their "wurlies" made of branches and sacking into huts made of concrete and aluminum. The simplest model has only one basic room: a bare cube with a concrete floor which must be hard and cold to sleep on. There is no need for a kitchen, since these families are still being communally fed. The cube is enclosed by a veranda under wide aluminum eaves, and extra rooms can be added as the need arises simply by walling in sections of this veranda. A somewhat more ambitious model has two rooms with a part-veranda; later on a kitchen, shower and laundry room can be added, with a passageway between.

These simple forms of housing have been decried as future slums and mass-produced wurlies. Certainly they are no palaces. Leaving aside the question of cost—which cannot be left aside in practice, since the cheapest home built to the white Australian urban pattern costs at least $10,000—here is a psychological factor. If people are asked to leap from one extreme in housing to another in a single bound, they fall. I have seen what happens when a raw African tribesman takes possession of a European home; the house is quickly reduced to a shambles.

You would not expect a peasant who has known no other form of transport than his feet, and the heads and backs of his load-carrying wives, to drive off happily and safely in a new Rolls Royce; there must be wheelbarrows, donkey carts, bicycles and battered trucks in between. Equally the way from wurlies to the three-bedroomed modern home must surely lie in stages. These aluminum cubes mark the first stage, which consists in essence of putting a layer of concrete between earth and people and a sheet of metal between people and the stars.

About 5,000 aborigines are now living in the government's settlements, roughly one in four of the Territory's native population. Though many will take periodic walkabouts, none of these will ever revert to the true nomadic life. Another 6,000 are living at, or in close contact with, the various missions, of which there are thirteen. (Four churches are mainly involved: Lutherans, first in the field; Roman Catholics; Methodists; and Anglicans.) Another 6,500 are believed to be on pastoral properties, and there are a few in the mines. That leaves less than 800 in the towns, perhaps 300 nomads, and rather more than 100 lepers. All children at missions and settlements now attend school. Only on some pastoral properties do a few children slip through the scholastic net, and in a year or two the mesh will be fine enough to bring them all in. Then the break with the past will be complete and final.

[4]

The oldest Roman Catholic mission in the Territory was opened in 1911 and is on Bathurst Island, next to Melville Island and fifty miles or so north of Darwin. Now there is a population explosion here, too, and the schools are packed with youngsters whose future causes anxiety; they will have to venture forth from their sheltered lives, but regular employment is hard to find and many do not want to leave their families.

To recruit enough teachers is another difficulty. The priests and nuns, all white Australians,* are supplemented by lay workers who are fed, housed and clothed, but unpaid, and the supply of idealists prepared to renounce the cash economy has dwindled. A young man who took me round had come to Bathurst Island some years before as a bachelor, but now a wife and three children made altruism seem a luxury he could no longer afford.

He was the president, he told me, of the mission's Local Native Council, set up by the authorities as a microcosm of democracy. Half the members are appointed by the mission and half elected at an open meeting by a show of hands. My guide's first task had been to persuade those qualified to vote to register their names. Despite a positive bombardment of talks, leaflets and films, and even the use of drama—he made a model of a polling booth out of cardboard and cast imaginary votes—very few took any interest, he regretfully said. "I'm afraid they're not ready yet to run their own affairs."

For many years these missions, like missions everywhere, struggled on from hand to mouth, able to continue only because members of the staff, whether or not in Holy Orders, were unpaid. The economic aim was self-sufficiency; the missions grew or caught their own food, kept flocks and herds for meat and milk, canoes for fishing, cut and worked the timber for their buildings. Schools and hospitals were subsidized by the government.

There has been a big change in the last few years. Government money has come pouring in. New schools have gone up, new hospitals and dispensaries, new houses, new everything. While a couple of the councillors were telling me about their work, a new tractor roared past drawing a new trailer full of young men going out to one of the new plantations. The councillors handed me a sheet of paper bearing their latest annual report.

> The Council is pleased to report that the children are now able to use a new infants' dining room and a large girls' school, while a new staff house has been built for the single men who have come to help our people . . . In the last three years, 13,000 trees have been planted to provide cypress pine timber for the people in the future . . . One hundred acres are to be cleared for mixed farming, so far ten men have

---

* The first full-blooded aboriginal nun recently took her vows in Darwin. She is Sister Jeanne Marie, of the Murinbadda tribe.

cleared three acres there, they have planted 91 cashew trees for a start
. . . Pasture improvement is being carried out to build up a first-class
beef herd of 300 head for fresh meat, 100 acres have been mown and
eight bags of Townsville lucerne planted . . .

No one, least of all the Australians themselves, would maintain that
in the past the handling of the native peoples has been either generous or
enlightened. Now there is a real attempt to make up for lost time. The
Director of Welfare, Mr. Harry Giese, told me that when he took up his
appointment in 1954 he had less than $100,000 to spend and a staff of
less than sixty; now he has over $4 millions and a staff of more than
500.

Welfare officers, like police and clergy—and to some extent they are a
mixture of the two—are on call for twenty-four hours of the day and see
nothing unusual in being summoned in the middle of the night, say to
rescue children from a father who has come home fighting drunk and is
beating up his family. Welfare is not just routine; it is a dedication and a
way of life. Many of the officers are young, untried men and women who
can learn the job only by doing it; there is no book of rules. Such officers
deal every day with human beings of a different race and outlook, and
there are many pitfalls—it is easy to patronize or bully, to be too lenient
and starry-eyed, to lose patience, to expect too much, to get discouraged,
to let standards fall too low. On a practical level they may be called
upon to fix an engine, start a co-operative, doctor a baby, muster cattle,
fill in returns, settle a matrimonial quarrel and run a troop of Boy
Scouts, all at the same time.

To inspire this force of scattered individualists with a feeling of unity,
purpose and loyalty demands something of the qualities of a general, a
bishop, an actor and a diplomat. For twelve years Mr. Harry Giese has
directed the service, picked its officers, seen a tenfold increase in its staff
and budget, fought like a tiger for its status and expansion, and impressed upon it the stamp of his strong personality. The next few years
are likely to make even heavier demands on the wisdom, patience and
understanding of the Welfare Branch. Soon the aborigines, unless they
react in a very different fashion from almost all other peoples in their
position, will start to bite the hand that feeds them and show what
others will consider to be intemperance, subversive tendencies and in-
gratitude. If in the long term their future is certain—assimilation equals
disappearance, Pukamanis and *didgeridoos* and boomerangs and all—
they may not go quietly; and there is still a long way to go.

[5]

East of Darwin, towards the Coburg Peninsula, sea and land are interlaced in such a manner that you cannot tell which is which. The sea thrusts its tenacles into swamps; the estuaries of rivers twist and turn like silvery snakes among the mangroves; it is all dead flat, spongy, brilliant green. From the air it looks level as a tennis lawn, but if your aircraft tried to land it would find only mud and tangled vegetation and would quickly sink.

In the Wet this coastal plain is impassable to anything but buffaloes, turtles, crocodiles and other amphibious creatures. The road, which lies back from the sea, is closed for six months and supplies must reach the missions by sea or by air. I went by air to Oenpelli, a mission beyond the East Alligator River in West Arnhem Land, some 300 miles from Darwin by road and half that distance by air.

Arnhem Land is about the same size as Tasmania and an aboriginal reserve whose people, though nearly all have ceased to be nomadic, have not wholly severed the ties between their spirits and the rocks, trees, rivers and caves. They still go walkabout, partly to hunt and partly to visit places held by their tribe to be sacred—a granite outcrop, perhaps, a spring, a rock or cave. Across the billabong at Oenpelli there is a cave containing rock paintings which, while no longer replenished every year as they used to be, remain—for how long?—well preserved. Some are executed in a style of painting peculiar to western Arnhem Land and known as X-ray art, because it depicts not only the external form of the creature—a bird, fish, reptile, or mammal, very seldom a man—but also the skeleton, stomach, heart, liver and lights which the artists know to lie inside the envelope.

These are fluent paintings, all in red and yellow ocher, charcoal and white limestone wash. Often one animal is superimposed upon another, and the result is an intricate web of brush strokes (the brushes are twigs) depicting skeltons and guts, ears and tails and fins. There are also the so-called "Mimi figures," often only three or four inches high, depicting in silhouette troops of scurrying little humans armed with bows and spears. These paintings are thought to be the work of a race now extinct and said by the present aborigines to have been tall, thin magicians who disappeared by blowing on a crevice in the rocks, which opened to receive them; men so brittle they could hunt only in calm weather, for a high wind would snap their limbs.

There is something about cave paintings that is eerie and chilling. You are in the presence of a mystery that can never be solved; however much these queer, aimless-seeming and yet not aimless paintings can be explained and interpreted, they can never be apprehended. You cannot feel as the artists felt or know what they were really after in these amalgams of the physical and spiritual; the message cannot get through. Were these ocher animals intended as spells to aid the hunter? As charms to make the beasts more prolific? Were they connected with the totems to which every individual belonged? A man's totem bound him spiritually to other members of the animal kingdom, as he was bound to them physically by his need of their flesh to sustain his own. How did he regard his totem creature? We can only speculate. The missionaries at Oenpelli did not seem to speculate at all. Their purpose is to replace these ancient beliefs, not to preserve them. Paintings on bark they encourage, for the sale brings in a useful income. They do not frown on the corroboree, provided it is conducted with decorum; the religious significance of these dances has in any case disappeared.

To mount a full-scale corroboree needs time and an occasion, but Silas, one of the English-speaking mission dwellers and a lay preacher, said he would gratify my wish to hear a *didgeridoo*. So I strolled over one evening to the camp, which consisted of a row of wurlies, squalid as these all are, but open to air and sun and used only for sleeping, and not always that; except when it rains, life takes place outside. You cook your dinner over an open fire, squat beside the sandy path, and gossip; children play, dogs hunt fleas, hens scratch, passers-by pause with greetings, meat hangs on trees. A man was gently playing a harmonica; everyone looked contented and fed. In the distance the billabong was white with egrets and aflight with ducks; in the background was a red eroded hillside, coarse green grasses, and forests of eucalypts. The sun was slanting valedictory rays across the billabong onto the red rock palisades where the caves were hidden; the rocks glowed with the burnished colour of a red bull's hide. It was an evening of blue waters, golden light, soft air.

The boom of the *didgeridoo* sounded, distantly at first, then louder—low and throaty, thumplike, something between a grunting and the far-off bellow of a bull. A group approached singing, led by a man clasping the big *didgeridoo*. It was a hollowed-out log with a roughly carved surface, as thick as a man's forearm and about five feet long. A *didgeridoo* has no stops—you just blow. The half-dozen dancers wore loincloths and their bodies were painted in white stripes and rows of dots; one, a greybeard, looked like a black-and-white wasp. They were singing with a gentle, melancholy rhythm in a minor key. The people clapped softly as they passed. The tune was melancholy; *gibba-yerra, gibba-yerra* said the *didgeridoo*.

The wasplike greybeard was carrying a red bundle. The dancers shuffled through the hot sand into the eye of a dying sun, chanting their melancholy song: *gibba-yerra, gibba-yerra,* thump and boom. A clutch of children followed, and slowly a few adults heaved themselves to their feet—there was scarcely a woman who could have weighed less than a hundred and seventy pounds—and shuffled in their wake. Silas either could not or would not interpret the words of the song. "In the past they had a meaning. Now they have none; they are just words." This corroboree was called, in the tongue of the Gunwinggu tribe, the *ingal-labu*—it sounded like that—and was in honour of small children. Why should they be honoured? "It is for the boy's memory." Whether this dance was to lodge in the memory of a living boy, or to commemorate a dead one, I could not ascertain.

We reached an open sandy patch where family parties were sitting on the ground, some with a little cooking fire beside them. Half a dozen women dancers appeared, their bodies also dotted and banded with white clay, to execute a gentle shuffle separate from the men's. It was all curiously dreamy and detached, like a mime under water or seen through heavy glass. There was none of the raw, vibrant, sweaty, coarse and dangerous vigour of an African dance. The *didgeridoo* went on saying *gibba-yerra, gibba-yerra, gibba-yerra.* After a while the greybeard laid the red bundle at the feet of a small boy of four of five years old. "That is for the boy's memory," Silas said again.

A livelier character then appeared: a youngish man who did a jerky, marionette-like *pas seul.* He shook, stamped and postured, clicked his fingers, shot out his arms, all with style and polish and a great deal more energy than anyone else had shown. Distantly it reminded me, at a great many removes, of the *kriss* dances of Indonesia. The women swayed with more spirit but still chanted a melancholy tune.

"That is Justin," Silas said. When Justin stopped his capering and came across to shake hands he proved to be a good-looking, well-built young man with finely cut features, more Malayan than aboriginal, a dashing manner and a gay, carefree smile—a charmer. For centuries Malays came down to Arnhem Land on the northwest monsoon to gather trepang and oyster shells from the coral and left their traces in the blood of the mainland tribes. When I remarked upon the charm of Justin to one of the missionaries, I was brought down to earth. "The worst no-hoper on the station! Draws his rations and never does a stroke of work. Gambling! I've taken off him and destroyed dozens of packs of cards. The others work, and he gets their wages off them in the evening with the cards."

Amid banners of gold and saffron the sun went down; the blue of the lagoon grew steely and then black; a myriad of stars pricked the sky. The corroboree drifted gently on. Women were nursing their babies; it was time to go. I had been invited to another party, to see some colour slides. This time we shut ourselves indoors and took every precaution to keep out the night with its sandflies, mosquitoes and other insects. Drawn by the light, they whirred and pinged against the fine-meshed screens. Aborigines have no bright lights, so their camps attract fewer insects, and to some extent their cooking fires drive them off.

We sat quietly in darkness, watching the slides. Most of these were rather dark too. "Wellington at night; that red dot is the back light of a bus." "An aerial view; not very steady, I'm afraid, because I was being airsick at the time." Then an enormous, hideous mansion in the Scotch baronial style appeared on the screen. "A rich butcher built that for forty thousand dollars and sold it for ten thousand to a man who lives in one room and opens the rest to the public." Someone asked, "What do the public come to see?" "It's a tourist attraction." "Yes, but what attracts them?" "Well, it's a *tourist attraction*." We emerged, sweating gently, into a hot, sticky, syrupy night. From a distance came the deep, throaty, hollow grunt of the *didgeridoo* and, from the billabong, a chorus of frogs and the haunting call of a stone curlew.

[6]

Oenpelli was opened forty years ago by the Church Missionary Society with practically no money and in total isolation, for Arnhem Land, which still has no towns or even villages, then had no airstrip or roads. A little school, a few shacks, a flock of goats and a herd of poor cattle—that was about all there was at Oenpelli until after World War II. Then Commonwealth money started to roll in, and now there are substantial houses, stores, canteens, a hospital, a school with one teacher to every twenty pupils and a white staff of a score or so. Parsons are outnumbered by stockmen, mechanics, bookkeepers and agronomists.

Buffaloes supply the meat at present. There is a "quiet herd" at the station and a "wild" one in the bush, where people combine sport, of a kind, with foraging. These animals are descendants of a few Indian water buffaloes brought to supply the first settlements, which took to the bush when Port Essington on the Coburg Peninsula was closed. Now up to a million may inhabit the swamps and forests of the Top End; and, after many years when they were looked on as pests to be destroyed, people are waking up to their food value.

The missionaries are believers in austerity—no alcohol or tobacco are allowed at Oenpelli—and inclined to look askance at the self-indulgent fecklessness, as they see it, of many aborigines. They took considerable trouble to train a young tractor driver; no sooner was his training complete than he went to Darwin and found a job at $50 a week. "But *we* have to keep his wife and five kids. Too many of these people have no sense of responsibility. They get everything for nothing—subsidized housing, free education, free hospitals, free or subsidized food. Now they're been given the full *rights* of citizens—they can vote and buy alcohol—but what about the obligations? The police don't even prosecute them for crimes for which a white man gets a heavy sentence—such as bigamy and cohabiting with girls under the age of consent. The abos get the best of both worlds."

Another sore point is the growing demand for higher wages on top of the free provision of all the necessities of life. "They don't want to give all that up, far from it, but they want the full award wage as well. We have a Mission Council which meets once a month. The members say: how much did the sale of our bark paintings bring in last year? We tell them. The money's ours, they say; you've no right to keep it back. Last year, we explain, the station bought three new tractors for three thousand dollars each. The bark paintings are a source of income and must go towards the tractors, which pump your water for you, make your electricity and help to provide you with free food. But they won't see it. Give us the money *and* the tractors, they say."

The kinship system is another difficulty. A man's obligations to share everything with his relations, however distant to our way of thinking, shows almost no sign of weakening. "Take Daniel, the tractor driver who went to Darwin. When he comes home for a holiday he isn't two hours on the station before everything's gone—his new trousers, his dandy shirt, his fancy socks, his money—everything. A dozen distant cousins have had the lot and Daniel doesn't dare refuse. So the ambitious have no incentive to rise in the world."

A fear that much of their work may be undone by the pace of events, I think, underlies the missionaries' disgruntlement. Only now are they beginning to deal with the first generation to be born at the Mission: people who, as infants, were, for the first time in history, fed on rations that freed them from malnutrition and given the rudiments of training for a white society. "And it's *their* children who'll be the first to be properly assimilated—children who haven't even yet been born! Assimilation needs several generations; you can't do it all in one. The government is going too fast." How often have I heard the same complaint in Africa! However true, it has become irrelevant; the wheels are moving and the band wagon can only gather speed as it rolls on its way.

I was at Oenpelli over Easter. Would there be painted eggs for the children? I ignorantly inquired. There were disapproving headshakes; Easter was a religious festival, not a pagan feast. The service was evangelical in a restrained fashion. No holy rolling; also no altar, no images, no pulpit, no music or choir. We sat on palm mats while the parson soberly exhorted us to seek salvation. "This is a good opportunity to give yourself to Christ," he told us, without making it very clear what this entailed. Two woman stood up silently, and that was all. The congregation was overwhelmingly female.

Where were the men? "Gone walkabout. Fishing, catching turtles, hunting for goose eggs in the swamps." Even an offer of free rations to those who went to church had failed to find many takers. Tonight they would sup off turtles, barramundi, lizards and the eggs, perferably with chicks in them, of magpie geese; and Justin, I felt sure, would eat the tastiest portion of a lizard caught by someone else.

[7]

Northern lagoons, covered with water lilies and fringed by forest, are famous for their birds and for their beauty. Oenpelli is not unique, but it is unforgettable and has one of the richest fish faunas in the world. When I was there the Wet was ending and the waters falling, but they still submerged the paths around the lagoon, and to reach the opposite side you had to wade up to the armpits. This is no hardship in tepid water and when a scorching sun dries your light clothing in half an hour. Even at first light it is warm. This is the time to watch skeins and flocks flighting across a moon imperceptibly growing paler, and stars melting unobtrusively away as the sky pales behind a black and jagged line of low ranges. There is a thick white coverlet of mist over the water and, in the bush, water squelches underfoot while you push your way through sedgelike, tough-stalked, coarse swamp grasses, waist-high. Everything in this warm, wet climate grows in profusion until the Dry withers it.

Flocks of white cockatoos pass across a white moon, screeching. Busy sounds of birds flapping, moving, feeding and arguing come from the lagoon. Behind the hills the sky turns a warm apricot. Suddenly there are no more stars and then, as suddenly, and with the splendour of a cascade of music that surges from an orchestra when the conductor's baton falls, the sun is over the horizon in full array—"such a big, untamed, proud sun," as Lawrence wrote, "rising up into a sky of such tender delicacy, blue, so blue, and yet so frail that even blue seems too coarse a colour to describe it." Black skeins of geese honk their way across a limpid sky. Egrets like scattered snowflakes cluster on water that has turned a pale topaz blue and is banded by long shadows cast by bloodwoods that are rooted almost on the shores of the lagoon, and whose branches are sometimes loaded with flocks of raucous corellas as if with great bunches of white fruit.

White and black predominate among the birds: the pure white of the big egret with yellow legs and bill, and of the little egret with black ones; the jet black of the head, neck and tail of the handsome pied or magpie goose, and of the head and neck of the white ibis. These plain, black-and-white dinner-jacket markings always make a bird look clean and distinguished. The magpie goose has a curious lump or boss between the base of its bill and the lower part of its forehead.

Once these magpie geese bred in countless millions over most of Australia, including New South Wales and Victoria. It is astonishing that a bird so numerous and wide-ranging should have been expunged from so vast an area in so short a time by such a handful of men. These geese made the fatal error of being good to eat. And now their breeding grounds have dwindled to a narrow strip of swamp and river basin along the subcoastal plain in the extreme north of northern Australia, stretching roughly from the East Alligator River, where Oenpelli is, in the east to the Daly River, just the other side of Darwin, in the west—a mere 200 miles. An estimate made in 1960 by the C.S.I.R.O. put the surviving numbers at about 350,000, and since then they have declined still further. They are protected, but only for six months of the year. This still sounds a lot of birds, but it is not, because this goose (*Anseranas semipalmata*) belongs to what ecologists call a "sensitive species," its rate of increase and the obstacles to its survival being so nicely balanced that a comparatively minor change in the environment, or a disaster like a drought, will topple it over the brink. The greatest threat to its survival is not the gun, or even strychnine, which has often been resorted to, but changes in the water level of swamps and lagoons.

Magpie geese know exactly what they want of their environment, and if these wants are not satisfied, they will not breed. They mate for life, and when they build their nest, which is often shared by two females with a single gander, they require just the right depth of water. If the water falls or rises more than a few inches below or above this optimum, they either seek fresh breeding grounds or do not breed at all. This has happened on a number of occasions, either when drought has reduced the water level or when the building of a dam has heightened it. It is the *depth of water* that mainly controls both food supply and building materials. For food these geese look mainly to wild rice, for nesting materials to a certain rush.

Dr. Frith, who has studied these birds, believes that it is the coming of the rain that, in some still obscure manner connected with hormones, triggers off the breeding cycle. Nesting does not start until the flooded valleys begin to empty. This ensures that, if all goes well, there will be about the right amount of water in the billabongs to produce the right food for the newly hatched goslings. It also ensures that, in times of drought, the geese will not breed at all—just as embryonic kangaroos stay suspended. Almost every non-human species seems to have this built-in system of population control which comes into operation when its food supplies are threatened. Magpie geese lay fairly generous clutches, but so many creatures steal the eggs, ranging from man— aborigines are very fond of goose eggs—to snakes, eagles, crows, dingoes on occasion, water rats and goannas, that only about one egg in five results in a fledged gosling.

These geese are as choosy about their food as about their breeding conditions. They are vegetarians. They start in January with the shoots of young grasses, move on to the seeds of plants that ripen in the Wet, such as wild rice and paspalum, and then, in the Dry, dig with their bills for the bulbs of a certain type of sedge, *Eleocharis*, which sustain them from September until the coming of the next Wet December. This habit of digging for bulbs very nearly dug the grave of the magpie goose. One of their favourite breeding grounds, on the flood plains of the Adelaide River, formed part of an area round Humpty Doo where experimental rice plantations were started in 1953. The geese gathered there in tens of thousands and appeared to be digging up the rice. There was an outcry; drastic measures were used to exterminate the geese—they were even machine-gunned—and the C.S.I.R.O. was called in. Dr. Frith mounted a four-year ecological study which laid bare the habits of the bird and was able, as it turned out, to point the way to a much more effective form of control than poisoning or shooting. Dr. Frith and Mr. S. J. Davies discovered that the geese were not digging for rice at all but for the sedge bulbs, *Eleocharis*. It was true that, when the rice plants came up, the birds did graze the young shoots and poach the ground, and may have done some damage, but they also did good by encouraging the roots to tiller, as British farmers may encourage tillering in winter wheat by turning sheep on to it. The conclusion was that both the numbers of magpie geese involved and the extent of the damage had been greatly exaggerated. There was, however, a risk of greater damage should rice growing spread along these seasonally flooded valleys, as everyone then hoped it would.

The best way to get ride of the geese, the ecologists suggested, would be either to flood or to drain their breeding grounds, so as to change the water level and prevent them from nesting. The birds were reprieved by the collapse of the rice scheme—for the time being. But sooner or later means will almost certainly be found to overcome the obstacles to economic rice growing. As I watched the big, handsome black-and-white birds feeding in the reeds and flighting over the billabong, I reflected how unlikely it was that my grandchildren, should I have any, would be able to enjoy the same experience. They would see egrets probably, ibis, darters, pigeons, plovers, many kinds of duck and of teal, the tiresome corellas, even perhaps the tall, spindly, letharic, rather dull jaribu, the only Australian stork—"a bird," wrote Leach, "that seems to spend much of its time in a state of utter dejection," perhaps because "it has a beak that gives the impression it has been stuck on upside down"—all these and many others they will see at Oenpelli, but not, in all probability, the magpie goose.

The oddest, if not the loveliest, sight on the billabong was a large, blackish bird apparently crucified. Its wings were stretched fully out as if pinned to a board, and its head resembled that of a black snake set on a thin, glossy neck. There it stood on a half-submerged log, absolutely still except for the snakelike flicker of its head. As I splashed towards it, the bird gathered itself together and flew swiftly off, identified by then as the well-named snake-headed darter spreading itself out to dry. The pied cormorant has the same queer habit.

Much more attractive were two pairs of masked plovers, with bright yellow wattles hanging down over black faces and neat, long red legs, that shared a sand pit with me while I basked in the sunshine. They were extremely agitated; presumbably their eggs were somewhere near —one could scarcely speak of a nest, as they lay almost anywhere in sand hollows or under tufts of grass. It is odd how some birds go to an infinity of trouble to make and conceal nests as intricate as filigree, while others just dump the eggs on the ground or on an untidy twig platform. The feckless appear to survive every bit as successfully as the prudent. I suppose it is a matter of habitat. In the Wet this subcoastal plain with its hothouse warmth, its abundant food and its monsoons provides lavishly for its creatures, and even in the Dry there is permanent water. Life is easy and the avian version of a wurlie suffices for a nest. Better to be a masked plover by a billabong, fussing ineffectually about its vulnerable eggs, than a malleee fowl chained to its demanding compost heap for months on end, digging and forever digging away.

[8]

I could have sat for days beside the billabong among the constant avian stir and bustle, but with little sign of the human race. Three small, naked boys splashed by on a crudely constructed raft, armed with homemade fishing rods. How much more did their eyes see than mine? Theirs would be the sharper, but not so sharp as their fathers' had been. A native of a past generation who had sat where I sat on the sand spit would have been aware of another world that lay beneath the crust of the hills, just as he knew of another world of bones and organs beneath a man's flesh to be recorded in his X-ray paintings.

Oenpelli is alive with legends. Here were the hunting grounds of the Nalbidgi people, never seen by human eye, but in cave paintings shown as sticklike creatures with tiny insect heads and headdresses looking like the symbols used in scientific textbooks to represent atoms arranged in chains. Here dwelt the spirit Namgunmal who speared his wife because she disobeyed his orders not to eat the gum of bloodwood trees; a certain termite mound sheltered the harmless monster Nunimunigan who had no axe, no spear, no fire, and lived on gum and honey, and the Pitari who were covered with thick hair like a dog's. Evil spirits called Matjiba would hook unwary travellers with a long stick and cook and eat them, preferring them well done. In a water hole lurked the Lightning Man who hunted among the cabbage palms—no one might damage a cabbage palm for fear of death—and, in the Wet, rode on thunderclouds with axes growing from his hands and knees. A rainbow serpent inhabiting a creek had long whiskers and long teeth and, if he was angry, released hordes of small snakes that entered the bodies of children through their navels.

Every tribe and race had its explanations of such phenomena as fire, death, and the emergence of man. The similarity of approach between these Arnhem Land legends and those of many African tribes is remarkable. Among both peoples death, for example, was unknown until introduced as a punishment for some human or animal failing.* Africans blamed the chameleon, these aborigines the moon-man Alinda, who had two wives and two sons. The sons went fishing while the wives were gathering roots in the forest and returned to say they had caught nothing. But Alinda saw grease on their hands, knew that they had lied to their father, and took them out to sea in his canoe and drowned them. When his wives returned, he told them that the boys had gone hunting; they grew suspicious, pieced together the true story and then, in their anger, burned Alinda to death. Turning himself into a crescent, he climbed a tree and announced to the world that henceforward death would be irrevocable. "I alone, except for three days of every month, I will live forever." So it has been ever since; and the shadows on the moon are the scars on Alinda's body.

The moon is often male, the sun a woman. Every day she walks across the sky with digging sticks; once over the horizon, she turns herself into a wallaby and hops back to her starting point. Sometimes she becomes a turtle. Arnhem Landers considered the Milky Way to be a vast river full of water-lily bulbs which provided food for the star people. Venus and Jupiter had two sons, the stars Lambda and Upsilon, who became friends of the southwest wind; and it is a fact that when these stars grow bright towards the end of April, the southeast wind is at its zenith. The Southern Cross represents a party of hunters who caught a snake; after they had eaten it, their eyes became so bright as to be seen on earth. Orion is a boatload of fishermen, their wives the Pleiades.

* For an account of some of the Arnhem Land legends, see Charles Mountford in the Report of the American-Australian Scientific Expedition to Arnhem Land, 1948. 4 vols. Melbourne University Press.

[9]

On the way back to Darwin we flew low to see water buffaloes clustering in vivid green swamps like fat grey blisters and landed on a bush runway at Munmalary station, where a young couple from New South Wales, John Lord and his wife, are "cropping" buffaloes for a living.

Why exterminate the docile, edible and healthy *Bubalis bubalis,* when on these moist subcoastal plains they thrive better, convert vegetation more economically into protein, and are more resistant to disease, than the domestic cattle that are brought in to replace them? This seems to be such an obvious question that you can only wonder why it was not asked long ago. Perhaps it was, and no one paid attention to the answer.

We found the Lords living with two small, chubby, apricot-coloured sons in a wire cage that keeps out pigs, dingoes and the buffaloes. They found nothing when they came but bush, really thick bush, impenetrable swamps, and billabongs. In the year of their arrival a savage drought dried up the billabongs and buffaloes perished horribly in thousands. They are, Mr. Lord told us, ultra-conservative in their habits; they could have found water within five or six miles if they had gone to look for it, but when the billabong they were accustomed to failed them, they lay down on the caked mud and expired.

Australians, no less than buffaloes, are conservative in habit and do not take readily to buffalo meat although it is juicy, nourishing and clean. The Asians are less prejudiced and buy the crop. Economically buffaloes "kill out" better than the average bullock, they do not lose condition in the Dry, they are resistant to ticks and suffer much less from tuberculosis than domestic cattle do. The main difficulty in cropping them is to get the meat quickly and economically to distant markets. At Munmalary it is frozen, packed in cartons and flown out in DC-3's. And the killing is done with bows and arrows, which seems odd these days; but they are modern weapons made of light, high-alloy steel and nylon fiber and discharge plastic syringes loaded with tranquillizer. The beasts are much more docile, Mr. Lord said, than scrub bulls, yet people come "on safari" with high-powered rifles and bravely slay these meek and inoffensive creatures, returning with trophies and transparencies. The same with crocodiles, whose skins are fetching $2.60 an inch. John Lord displayed the skull of a specimen whose skin had sold for over $140, while the cost of killing it on a dark night had been the value of a couple of cartridges. So probably these big reptiles are doomed.

What, I asked Mrs. Lord, did she find to be the principal drawback to life so isolated that the nearest neighbour is a hundred miles away? "Tourists," she replied. "They roll up off the track at any hour and expect to be shown round and fed and often put up for the night into the bargain. There's no telephone, of course, and everything has to come out from Darwin. We've had to introduce a charge."

[10]

Mr. Don Tulloch, the Wildlife Officer attached to the Agricultural Branch in Darwin, was hoping to show me some pygmy geese on a lagoon at the government's experimental farm at Beatrice Hills, on the Adelaide River and south of the capital. This is a species (*Nettapus pulchellus*) confined to the tropics and once widely distributed, but now shrinking in numbers, throughout the Top End. Magpie geese were dozing in the shade on the margin of the lagoon; Pacific herons, silver grey all over, stood contemplatively by the water's edge; a pair of small pied herons waded about; dapper little jacanas, rufous and white, trod the water lilies with their incredibly thin, brittle legs. But no pygmy geese.

After a prolonged search through glasses, however, a pair of small, agile, unobtrusive birds came to light as they dived and splashed among the roots of fresh-water mangroves: pygmy geese at last. And pygmies they really are, no larger than quite small teals, and not in the least gooselike in appearance. Their black plumage, patched with white, has a greenish tinge and they are quick-moving little birds with great charm.

This is the area where the rice cultivation failed. All that survives is Fogg's dam, a magnet for bird watchers, a few experimental paddy fields and some irrigation channels half obliterated by weeds. It is all flat as a pancake; with the local flair for names, part of it is called Tommy Policeman's plain. We were looking for brolgas. At certain times of year they stalk about in hundreds on these grassy plains: tall, dignified, well-groomed in their steel-grey plumage with that striking roseate band across the base of the bill. They are the only Australian cranes (*Grus rubicundus*) and only to be found in Australia. No one could tell me why they are also called native companions.

The time to see brolgas is when they perform the dance that constitutes their mating display: a spirited yet stately kind of struting to and fro in ranks, and rising up on tiptoe, rather like the displays of African flamingoes. In the Dry, Fogg's Dam attracts birds from miles around, and Mr. Tulloch told me he had seen an estimated two thousand brolgas there. Now we could not find a single one. He thought they must have flown south to Newcastle Waters, between here and Alice Springs, for the nesting season. Why and how the birds en masse pick certain breeding sites in certain seasons remains a mystery, but this is what they do. Brolgas have retreated from many regions where they formerly abounded, and it is only in the north, and in parts of Queensland, that large flocks may still be found.

If we did not, alas, find the handsome grey brolgas, we saw many other kinds of bird. Egrets, large and small, were in their mating plumes, with a graceful fringe of fine white feathers hanging like an old-fashioned petticoat to screen the breast and fluttering over the back. Formerly these plumes were labelled osprey feathers and marketed on such a scale that a single sale in London was estimated to account for 24,000 birds. The cruel part was that breeding birds were shot while their young were in the nests, and so tens of thousands of chicks starved to death. Now these egrets live in peace because modern life and osprey feathers are incompatible.

Whistling eagles circled over; marsh tern abounded; so did black cormorants. We saw the handsome plumed tree duck with a wing fringe of snowy quills; high above the noble white sea eagle glided on his way. There were also jaribu storks, pied cormorants, half a dozen white-headed Burdekin ducks, a shy pair of freckled ducks and a pink-eared duck or two—but far fewer ducks than we ought to have seen. This was the height of the breeding season when all birds on the dam were fully protected by law. But laws are on paper, birds are—or had been—on the lagoon, and the Easter weekend, with its exodus of Darwin "sportsmen," was just over. Among the pandanus palms we found empty cartridge shells by the dozen. The Territory has an enlightened wildlife code but to enforce it only the local policeman, who has an area probably as large as Wales to supervise.

[11]

If the dam was disappointing, the bush was full of songbirds. In the bush a stab of scarlet through the branches, a flash of gold and blue, may be your sole reward; but there is always something unexpected round the next bend. The lemon-breasted flycatcher trills delightfully and has been called the bush canary; there is a weaver finch in blue and yellow like a miniature kingfisher; the mud larks' prosaic name describes their two main attributes: they build nests of mud, like swallows, but in trees, and sing sweetly. They are also known as peewees and as magpie larks, and it has been said that wherever they live, so can man, for they must have water in order to construct their nests.

Brightest of all are the rainbow birds, members of the bee eater tribe and related to kingfishers. Two long pin feathers protrude from the tail; the male has a red collar, wing quills or orange, a back of blue, and his eye is elongated by a black line like an oriental beauty's; nothing can describe him but that hackneyed phrase, an animated jewel. The drabness of the bush and the brilliance of the rainbow bird set each other off like a splendid brooch on a simple garment. This alone was worth coming to see.

So, in their different fashion, were the Bentang cattle at Beatrice Hill, a breed that I had never seen before. Indeed there are few places where they can be seen. Originally they came, it is believed, from Bali and spread from the Coburg Peninsula, where a handful, probably less than a dozen, were left behind when the settlement was abandoned. In colour they are Jersey-grey with white socks and have a most distinctive white, shield-shaped patch over the buttocks. Small, compact, neat and timid, they cluster together and will have no truck with other kinds of cattle. They are not zebus; no one knows their genetic history or can estimate their economic value. The herd slowly building up at Beatrice Hill may be the only one in the world where this attractive breed is being studied in captivity.

Pastorally speaking, this is the land of *laissez faire*. The Beatrice Hill manager waved an arm towards the wide, dead-flat plain which forms the valley of the Adelaide River. "Over half the cattle on that property are clearskins," he said. "There's no paddocking, no bores, no development. The owner just hunts buffaloes. And he has a grazing lease of a thousand square miles."

It is not mere idleness on the part of graziers that is responsible for this inertia. The laws are largely to blame; grazing leases run for *one year*. Clearly nobody in his senses would sink capital in permanent and costly improvements on a property he could only lease from year to year. And on such security, or lack of security, no bank or mortgage company would advance a penny. And these are Commonwealth, not state, laws. I was told that the Administration intends to amend the law so as to enable a grazier to convert a part of his annual lease—a part only—into a thirty-year tenancy; but hitherto a tangle of confused legality has prevented this reform. Even if accomplished, thirty years is a meager term in view of the heavy capital investment needed and the uncertainty of the return.

We stopped on the way back to look at the magnetic anthills, one of the famous sights of the north—in fact, a tourist attraction. Made by termites, they are taller than a man, boulder-grey, four or five feet wide, but only a few inches thick, and look like sarsens; they reminded me of Avebury or Stonehenge. Their peculiarity is that they are invariably aligned north by south. There are theories to account for this but no accepted hypothesis. The most likely theory—or precursor to a theory—seems to be that by pointing north by south they offer the least area of surface to the noonday sun. This seems a bit farfetched; you would suppose there to be more efficient ways of avoiding the midday sun, such as sinking the structure underground instead of building a sky-scraper. However, you cannot probe the motives of termites, or at least the non-biologist cannot; almost as curious as the grey slabs themselves, in places as numerous as tombstones in a graveyard, is the fact that no scientist has as yet found an explanation.

SIXTEEN

Alice Springs

"When one door shuts, another opens." In Alice Springs the door marked "Beef" has been slammed by eight years' almost unmitigated drought—and drought here *is* drought—and the door marked "Tourists" opens wider every year.

What are the tourist attractions? The desert, the great dry heart. Queer, alarming scenery, unlike any other, with a harsh and uncouth kind of beauty; evocations of the Australian legend of the outback with its tough, self-reliant and undaunted people. On the material plane, perpetual sunshine and yet cool nights in modern hotels, motels and tourist camps; plenty of company, plenty of souvenirs, plenty of organized tours.

"The Alice" lies at the foot of the MacDonnell Ranges that, rising from a red sandstone plain, stretch 400 miles from east to west and have peaks well over 4,000 feet high. These hills are full of palisades and gorges; wild and barren, red and eroded, they are flecked with the olive-green of such mulgas as have survived. There is a strange delicacy in the colouring—in the foliage of the mulgas that look as though they had been back-combed, even in the veining of white quartz pebbles and boulders. There are endless flies. What do they live on? The country is lifeless now that the cattle have gone. There is no blood to suck, scarcely any carrion: I did not even see any rabbits. But flies remain.

At Love Creek, fifty miles east of the Alice, is a station comprising 1,500 square miles of the MacDonnell Ranges. For forty years its owners bred horses for the Indian army, horses toughened from birth amid rocks and spinifex, resourceful, and inured to hardship. Then the bottom fell out of the Indian remount trade and Lou Bloomfield, the station's owner, turned to beef for a living and let the horses go wild. Subsequently a demand for horses slowly revived, this time for the home market, and Lou's son Harry Bloomfield caught and broke some of the wild brumbies. Now drought has finished off the brumbies and the cattle also. Love Creek used to carry between 7,000 and 8,000 cattle head, but now there are none—or "only those they couldn't muster." Those they could muster have gone to South Australia where the Broomfields bought a station with two years' keep on it.

The old homestead has been taken over by two brothers, Gil and Doug Green, who have done it up, Australian fashion, with their own hands, built some wooden chalets, and bought a dilapidated but stout-hearted little bus in which they muster their guests every morning for a liver-jolting tour of the ranges, which possess no roads in any usual sense of the word.

[2]

What makes a stay at Love Creek memorable is not only the grandeur and interest of the scenery but the brothers' enthusiasm. The Greens came from the south as timber contractors and fell in love with the Center. They are romantics and see in every stubble-chinned, cigarette-rolling stockman an intrepid bushie with a deep instinctive knowledge of natural lore and a humorous stoicism. "Their hat is their home," said the Greens, and told us stories to illustrate the nature of bushies.

They never winge. When a howling gale was driving a wall of sand before it across a dessicated paddock, a visitor offered his sympathy to a ruined grazier, who replied, "What's wrong? Good weather for windmills." Their powers of observation are exact. A mate afflicted by a boil on the neck that obliged him to hold his head on one side was "like an old crow looking down the neck of a sauce-bottle." They have little use for women. When a woman driver heading in the wrong direction asked the way to Alice Springs, a bushie pointed silently back along the way she had come. "But are you *sure* that's right?" she said. "Keep going if you want to, lady, but better check your petrol if you do—you'll have twenty-three thousand, nine hundred and fifty miles to go."

They are at one with horses. In its heyday the men at Love Creek never spoke of breaking horses but of "gentling" them. The man would put his unbroken colt into a paddock with an old, wise horse and for several days pay it no attention but fondle the old horse and put a bridle and a saddle on and off. The colt would grow curious, then jealous, and keep edging closer. One day the man would stretch out a hand and the colt would sniff his fingers. "When he nudges you, you've got him." But the approach must come from the colt, not from the man. Gil Green said that an old bushie had told him: "The horse must trust you and you must help the horse—never relax in the saddle. Your job is not to give the horse more to do than he has already, but to help him every inch of the way. Then he'll help you. One day your life may depend on that." These horses had to muster other horses, so much swifter, wilder and cleverer than cattle; so they had to be the best.

When Lou Bloomfield brought his bride to Love Creek, he built a place with thick mud walls, a big fireplace and, apparently, no windows; this is now the tourists' sitting room where, of an evening, Gil Green passes round lumps of rocks and discourses on geology. Here in the Center, he says, is possibly the oldest portion of the earth's crust. Millions of years ago layers of sedimentary limestone were laid down on a core of quartz thought to be 1,000 million years older still. The rocks contain fossils of sea-dwelling creatures that became extinct several aeons ago. Some gigantic and prolonged unheaval, or series of unheavals, upended and compressed all these layers of rock and made them perpendicular instead of horizontal. Curiously enough, if you clamber up the steep, jagged hills above the creek, you are immediately reminded of the sea—a savage sea whose mighty swirling waves of ocher and dark olive streaked with white were curling over, and just about to break, when they were frozen into everlasting immobility. You can see how the layers of rock have been tilted up by some fantastic pressure. It is an alarming and grotesque landscape, an abstract landscape, so lifeless, so barren, so silent; an ancient frenzy stilled to monumental calm. On the hilltops nothing stirs.

Below, in the sandy river bed, there was a bush alive with small black-and-white butterflies emerging from cocoons, and galahs and bronze-winged pigeons; and a pademelon vine straggling across the sand, and mulga trees with foliage turning orange-brown from drought; but the tall, white-boled ghost gums that lined the creek thrust their roots deep enough to find moisture. On the surface birds, like men, depend on troughs fed by deep bores. Three wild camels, black in the moonlight, came at night to drink from the trough nearest the homestead, and a dingo howled eerily from the black and silent hills.

[3]

Lou Bloomfield's widow, aged well over eighty, lives in Alice Springs. When, as a bride on her way to Love Creek, she first saw the place there was nothing but a telegraph station, a few shacks and the Stuart

Arms. Once a year her stores arrived on the backs of camels from Oodnadatta, the railhead 300 miles to the south. So when she found her kerosene tins empty because they had been holed by camels bumping them against rocks, she had to make slush lamps out of old baked-bean tins packed three parts full of sand, into which she stuck a wick wrapped in flannel, and poured melted mutton fat. The lamp smoked horribly, and she kept a spoon beside it with which to ladle on more mutton fat.

Everything was homemade. Mrs. Bloomfield brewed her own yeast from dried hops to leaven the bread, but she could never keep her flour free of weevils for a whole year. The meat she salted and hung in calico bags. When native gins—the unmarried girls—came in from the bush she gave each one a cake of soap and taught her how to wash, how to milk a cow and how to wear a dress. None had previously seen a four-walled house, a plate, a cup, or a chair; but they were friendly and wanted to please.

The nearest doctor was in Oodnadatta. When, before his marriage, Lou Bloomfield was gored by a bull, he sent a note to his closest neighbour thirty miles away: "Be glad of a little help if you can come." The neighbour's wife came, too, and washed the wound with a solution of copper and put in 180 horsetail stitches, and the wound healed.

Once a year they put their swag into the buggy and drove to the Alice for the races and a spree. They were good races, Mrs. Bloomfield said, with thoroughbred horses, and at night everyone danced to the light of hurricane lanterns at the Stuart Arms. In those days people did not drink as much as they do now. "We were too busy," she said. "Sometimes Lou was away droving two or three months at a time. I wasn't lonely and never scared of the blacks. We got along together well." When she married, her brother had advised her: "Never hinder Lou. Do what he wants, what he's chosen. Then you'll be happy." She had followed his advice. "It was right," she said.

After her son Harry inherited the property he built another homestead thirty miles away. It is a squat, white house surrounded by a lawn with trellised bougainvillaeas, flowering shrubs, hanging ferns and plants in pots; at the back is a children's playroom, a meat house, a laundry, an aviary. All is spick and span and well loved—and empty. The Bloomfields have migrated to the south in the wake of their surviving cattle, leaving behind little but the contents of the saddle shed. Each saddle is agleam with grease; bits are well-scoured and bright; rows and rows of horseshoes hang on racks; branding irons, heavy packsaddles and big, stiff saddlebags are disposed as if ready for immediate use. But they are no longer needed.

"The Bloomfields will be back," Doug Green confidently predicted. "There've been droughts before, many and often. This country is millions of years old and it'll never be broken. Everything will come back, you'll see. The grass will be so thick you'll lose a dog in it; the creeks will run; the mulgas will regenerate. Never underestimate the power of nature. Now's the time she's having her rest."

I was to hear a different point of view expressed by scientists. Meanwhile the Bloomfields' half-blood stockman has moved over to the tourist camp to take charge of their horses: one door opens when another shuts. And tourists yield better profits than beef: they do not need to be dipped or inoculated, are much more readily mustered, and pay for their keep.

[4]

We drove all day through the eastern MacDonnell Ranges in our rickety bus and saw no blade of grass or tuft of green—just rocks, sand and boulders, all the pale yellowish buff colour of sandpaper, and as abrasive. The wilting mulgas looked gingery in colour, the stunted trees —ironbarks, so-called dogwood, corkwood, witchetties in which the grubs are found—somberly grey and black. It is on the leaves, twigs and seed pods of these trees and shurbs, known collectively as topfeed, that cattle depend in these desert regions, not on grass. Now that so many young trees have been eaten down or killed by sawing off their branches to feed to cattle, the natural cycle of regeneration has been broken, some say for good.

Our destination was a ghost town, Arltunga, where a gold rush which started in 1897 petered out before World War I. Our bus clambered manfully through Tommy's Gap, a precipitous and boulder-bespattered gorge where, in the days of the rush, a twelve-ton boiler had been dragged by a team of fifty horses harnessed three abreast. So steep is the track that in places the men had to cut steps for the animals to get a foothold. The horses dragged this boiler nearly 400 miles, and it is still at Arltunga, like a big black slug lying in the sand amid tumbled walls, blank windows, brick chimneys standing on their own after the houses have gone. A few stones mark the Glencoe Arms that was kept by Sandy MacDonald, who buried a bag of gold dust for safekeeping; a bush fire destroyed his landmarks and, although he dug and dug, he never recovered his hoard; people still come to hunt for it. Race meetings were held outside the town attended by upwards of 1,000 people; there is an old sports ground, a disintegrating jail and a few graves whose headstones, if they had any, have vanished.

We came upon the humpies of the prospectors. Bits of rusty iron sheeting are propped on crooked poles, and half-rotted sacking makes the walls. Or there is a roof made of boughs, a couple of chairs roughly knocked up from mulga poles, an old iron bedstead, and a litter of torn newspapers, empty tins and bottles, rusted buckets and worn-down brooms. Doug Green pointed out a crude contraption made of wood and leather, a homemade blower; in the desert you cannot pan ore by washing it, so you use air instead of water and blow the trash away.

One of the prospectors is eighty-five years old. He pokes about all day among the abandoned workings and rolls himself in a blanket on the cold iron bedstead when darkness falls. During the tourist season the Love Creek bus brings up a few eatables, and now and again the Greens present him with a bottle of brandy; in return he demonstrates the blower to the tourists and regales them with his yarns. He looks the very picture of a down-and-outer in his tattered rat-bag clothes, a hat almost as old as he is, a growth of stubble, and no possessions but his roll of swag. The other day some grazing leases were advertised and applicants required to show assets worth a minimum of $20,000. The old prospector put in for a lease—and qualified. His age was held against him and his application failed, so he will go on prospecting until he dies. And one day Arltunga will finish dying, too; the desert will digest it totally and no trace will remain of men's activities.

On the way home we passed a dead horse, and farther on a dead goanna four feet long. We came to a gorge pimpled by spinifex, like outsized clumps of sea pink made of green porcupine quills, and stopped to set fire to a tuft. Mr. Green wanted to show us how it "exploded." In the gathering darkness we watched orange flames leap, glow and subside; then another bang and more flames, accompanied by a pungent, turpentiny smell. We stamped out the ashes and jolted back to a substantial tea in an annex to the old homestead where Mrs. Bloomfield had made her slush lamps, churned her butter and tried to keep flies off the meat and weevils from the flour.

[5]

Ayers Rock is probably the most photographed boulder in the world: an emperor among tourist attractions. Colour photography and aircraft have made it. The harsh red of the sandstone is dramatic, and Cessnas save you two or three hundred miles of westward jolting through the heat from Alice Springs.

The landscape is dramatic also. It is a flayed landscape. The skin of soil and vegetation has been pared away to reveal the earth's skelton. And what a wild, uncouth, contorted skeleton! The startled air-borne eye sees below hills arranged like bars of Edinburgh rock laid side by side with extraordinary precision, each range with fluted sides, and all spaced out by gorges. Then come lizards: hills kneaded by erosion to look like the humped back of geckos, with legs spread out on either side—rather more legs than are possessed by living lizards, eight or ten on each flank. These hills look chunky and, in a curious way, satisfied, almost smug; their rounded surfaces give them the contour of repletion.

Then we overflew what appeared to be rows of enormous oil drums lying side by side, astonishingly symmetrical. Again erosion; the tricks played by this elemental force have a wayward quality. The wind can be a practical joker. Shadows are sharp as knife blades, totally unfuzzed in this brittle-clear atmosphere. It is a land of no compromise. We flew over the Finke River. It always surprises Europeans to find that a river which on the map looks as important as the Rhone of Danube is, on the ground, merely a stretch of sand, marked by a fringe of coolibahs, red gums or ghost gums. The Finke winds for 1,000 miles, and for at least nine months of the year it is as dry as sandpaper.

On the margin of the Finke is the oldest mission in the north, Hermannsburg, started by the Lutherans in 1877. The most famous of its sons is Albert Namatjira of the Aranda tribe, born near the Finke and trained at the mission to do poker work on mulga wood. A painter called Rex Batterbee showed some work here which so excited the young Aranda that he attached himself to Batterbee as a kind of guide in return for instruction in the technique of water-colour painting.

He became so prolific that he could turn out two or three paintings a day and peddle them at $10 each, which by the standards of his tribe soon made him immensely wealthy; but innumerable relatives moved in to share his bounty, following the tribal custom. Namatjira lived near the Alice amid a mob of hangers-on and took to the bottle. His end was dissolute, sad, and clouded by lawsuits and quarrels. He died in 1959 at the age of fifty-seven, leaving five painting sons and a so-called Aranda school that uses his hard, strong, contrasting colours to portray an angular landscape, but without his simplicity and freshness. Paintings he sold for $10 have since fetched $2,000, and his work has been used on menu cards of Qantas Airways, which constitutes a sort of accolade among Australian painters.

Following our course almost due west, we left behind the crumpled ranges and came to Lake Amadeus, an opague sheet of salt-encrusted liquid glistening with a dozen indefinable colours: peacock blue, the purple of willow herb, muave and lilac, a steely grey, moss green—all shimmering in the sun and opalescent. And then, of all things, scrawled in the lung-pink sandstone below us, came the outline of fishes, flat like flounders on a slab. Why fishes? And fishes startlingly like those in aboriginal paintings. Our aircraft threw the shadow of a moving cross.

I was clasping a handful of twigs, snapped off a tree on the air field for use as a fly whisk, because Ayers Rock is a nature reserve where you may run into trouble for tweaking a leaf off a bush. Without this rule tourists would very soon defoliate such trees as remain. My two companions wore brimmed hats with anti-fly veils. Widows from Sydney, left comfortably off in late middle age, they were so alike I took them to be sisters, even twins; but they were unrelated. Can identical patterns of life in identical circumstances make people not merely think alike but look alike too?

[6]

The discoverer of Ayers Rock, W. B. Gosse, called it "an immense pebble." It is certainly immense. What gives the rock its drama is the flatness of the plain from which it rises to rather over 1,100 feet. The sides are not sheer or even steep, and you can reach the top quite easily, if sweatily, in about two hours. It is very bulky, measuring over five miles round at the base, and very red. The right way to see it is to stay overnight at one of the tourist lodges or motels and watch the sunrise strike and inflame the rock; I could not do this, unfortunately.

Before it became a tourist attraction, Ayers Rock was a religious shrine. People of the local tribe, the Pitjandjaras, came to the caves around its base to worship and to decorate the walls with paintings. These are much more crude and unsophisticated than those to be seen in Arnhem Land. The natives of these arid regions faced a harder struggle for existence in an infinitely harsher habitat and did not develop to the same extent their arts and skills. Here are to be found no bark paintings, no *didgeridoos,* no burial posts, no carved figurines.

For some years Bill Harney, the man from Borroloola, acted as warden at the Rock and made a study of the paintings, legends and customs of the Pitjandjara. Before he left the Rock—he died in 1963—he passed on to his successor, Lance Rust, some of the lore he had accumulated, and Mr. Rust in turn passes on such crumbs as he can to the visitors. He took us first to a cave whose inner wall was crudely decorated with clusters of white circles within circles, symbols of eternity, and with rows of dots that could indicate either a camp or a woman. In places these walls were crudely hatched in red, possibly symoblizing leaves— hence trees, hence fruit, hence fertility. These caves had been used for the circumcision of the gins, Lance Rust told us.

Farther round the Rock were other caves associated with the circumcision of boys. It was forbidden on pain of death for members of one sex to approach areas sacred to the other, and not many years ago a gin was speared after she had picked figs from a tree growing near the entrance to the boys' cave. Now tourists roam in and out at will. On the wall of the boys' cave it is just possible to make out the painted outline of a white pole surmounted by a circle from which many lines radiate outwards. We learned that this represents an uncircumcised boy wearing a headdress of spinifex and cockatoo feathers; the hollow circle suggests an empty head ready to be filled, at circumcision, with the lore of the tribe. All these paintings are fading. When the Rock was a temple of a living faith, they were renewed before every ceremony and so continued from generation to generation.

It would be foolish to compare the customs and beliefs of Australian aborigines with those of any African tribe, on the basis of the few snippets of unco-ordinated information to be picked up by a visitor; but I could not help being struck by many similarities. The all-pervasive belief in magic; the various rituals such as circumcision—including that of girls—with its closely guarded secrets, its passing on of tribal lore and its harsh tests of physical courage; the position of the elders who ruled the tribe and administered justice; the corroboree with the painting of the body, the song and shufflings and thumpings, matched by thousands of *ngomas* all over Africa; the belief in the power and presence of ancestral spirits, and the constant need to placate them with offerings; the use of sorcery to destroy enemies; the conviction that all fortune, good or bad, and all sickness and accident arise from the revenge of offended spirits or from spells woven by an enemy; the power of witch doctors; the close-knit kinship system linking every member of the tribe in blood relationship, and assigning to each man and woman his status in the community and his obligations to everyone else—even down to details like a taboo on the relationship between a man and his mother-in-law so strict that he must avert his eyes when she approaches; the custom of knocking out incisor teeth and cicatrizing arms and chest—all these customs, beliefs and patterns of behaviour are extraordinarily similar.

The explanation, I suppose, must be that in all parts of the world human societies meet the challenge of their environment with social responses that are much the same, and that, despite many obvious differences of geography and climate, the pre-industrial, pre-literate, pre-civilized environment of primitive man had so much in common, in the different continents, that responses to them had to follow much the same pattern; just as (if this is not too fanciful) the environment of middle-class Sydney in the mid-twentieth century had shaped my two widowed companions into beings who, although lacking any genetical tie, not only thought alike and believed alike and followed the same pattern of behaviour but even looked like sisters.

There were, of course, differences as well as similarities between the basic Australian and the basic African social pattern. People who had no cattle and no crops could not, for example, evolve a code of payments and exchanges such as that of bride price, which played so important a part in African tribal life, or of fines for crimes like murder and adultery. Death or mutilation were the only practical sanctions. Lance Rust told us the story of Floppy, an oldish man who attached himself to the aborigines' camp at Ayers Rock. He walked, or waddled, as if on frogman's flappers, dragging his feet, and when the others ate, he sat apart and went round afterwards to scrounge for scraps; sometimes he would be thrown a bone like a dog. He had no friends and no associates. In his youth, Lance Rust had learned, Floppy had been found guilty of adultery and sentenced to be hamstrung, so that he could not chase women any more.

[7]

The aborigines believed that a child was conceived by the entry of a spirit into the mother, often at the moment when her husband performed some specific act like spearing a kangaroo, killing a snake, or digging up a root. As soon as a woman knew herself to be pregnant, the elders would meet, or a family consultation would be held, to decide on the most likely place and moment when the spirit-child had entered the mother; and this would determine the totem of the unborn infant. Every individual had his totem, often several totems, but he did not inherit them so much as derive them from the spirit world at the moment of his conception.

In this lay the bond between an aborigine and the tribal territory where his own spirit had dwelt before it became flesh and where the spirits of his future children waited to enter, at the appropriate moment, a woman who would give them human shape. That is one reason for the walkabout which accords so ill with Western man's enslavement to time and routine. Suddenly the urge may come upon a man or woman to visit the scene of his origin and the habitat of spirits not, at the moment, in possession of a human envelope, or to pay tribute to ancestral spirits linked to the visible world through sacred shrines or such objects as the churinga. These were pieces of wood, or slabs of stone, covered with symbols recording totemic legends. So sacred were they that any woman or child who inadvertently set eyes on one was instantly killed. They were kept in the custody of fully initiated elders and concealed in caves or trees. The powers of the churinga can still be invoked to help overcome an illness or to gain success in a hunt; so off a man will go into the bush to look for one, leaving his employer's horses unshod, the garden half dug, or the mission's next order of tourist boomerangs only half filled.

Every one of the caves, grooves and queer honeycomb formations moulded in Ayers Rock by wind and rain had a history and a meaning to the tribesmen. A deep hole holding permanent water was gouged out by the blood of a hare-totem man who fought to the death with another hare-man in the Dreaming Time—the time of creation—and will discharge a stream of water if the right magic words are shouted; a slab above it is the nose of a warrior struck off by the mother of a man he vanquished in her rage; a cave is her wide-open mouth that mourned her son; and stains on the mineralized rock face opposite were made by a poison that she spat out to keep off intruders. A blackened slab of rock is the body of a man of the sleepy-lizard man totem who was burned to death because he was too mean to share with people of the carpet-snake totem the flesh of an emu he had killed. And so on.

To us [Charles Mountford wrote], "Ayers Rock is a huge monolith; to aborigines, living evidence of the deeds of their heroes of the long distant past. Mutitjilda is not filled with water but with the transformed blood of the dying carpet-snake man; the grey patch on the south cliff of Uluru is not an extensive patch of lichen but metamorphosed smoke from the camp of the greedy sleep-lizard man; the huge semi-detached column of rock on the north-west corner is not an unusual example of exfoliation but a transformed ritual pole that once stood in the centre of the initiation ground of the hare-wallaby men.*

Charles Mountford has summed up the existence of the Pitjandjaro tribe as "a culture where the people are at peace with each other and with the surroundings in which they live." They came to terms with these pitiless surroundings, so intimidating to Europeans, with the aid of only five tools: the spear, the spear thrower, a carrying dish, a digging stick, and grinding stones. The prime object of the cave paintings, as of the song and dance of the corroboree, was to re-create the legends of creation and thus to link the living people of today and their future children with the spirits of the heroes of the ancient Dreaming Time. Living men, to aborigines, are merely vessels through which the tribe's life and unity, created by its heroes, is transmitted and preserved; they are not themselves creators. Creation lies in the past; the sacred duty of the living is to transmit its laws and legends. Is it, perhaps, these opposite notions of the nature of man that have caused the paths of the two kinds of men to diverge—the men we call "primitive" and the men we call "civilized"? The transmitters and the creators? How else can we explain a gulf that puzzles all beholders? "The queer thing is," said Lance Rust, "these natives aren't *stupid;* some of them are very intelligent; they pick up things quickly. Yet in all those centuries they never discovered how to smelt iron, and there was iron all round them. They hunted kangaroos but never thought to wear the skins; they just went on shivering in cold weather. They never built the simplest kind of house. They didn't even link up sex with having babies. It's all a mystery."

The caves of Ayers Rock are used no more for circumcision, the crux and focal point of tribal life. Spirits have given way to tourists, dark mysteries to colour transparencies. Despite ninety years of missionary endeavour, it is not Christianity that has killed the culture of the aborig-

* Mountford, Charles, *Ayers Rock,* Angus & Robertson, Sydney and London, 1965.

ines but the end of the nomadic life and the overpowering presence of a society based upon the use of the superior tool. It is as toolmakers we excel, progressing from the stone-tipped arrow to the space-probing satellite; that is the sum and total of our mastery, that we are very clever at inventing tools. People satisfied with flint-tipped arrows cannot begin to compete.

[8]

The other day Lance Rust saw six stark-naked blacks walk past the cafeteria window at Ayers Rock. First came a man who looked about fifty, with a big bushy beard; then a woman who was a bag of bones; after her, four skinny children with limbs like matchsticks. They wanted food. They ate and ate. Lance Rust named the man Harry, showed him an axe, and made chopping motions with it. Harry had never seen an axe before, or a knife, or a pair of trousers. One day Harry made scratching motions at his beard; Lance shaved it off, and Harry proved to be a young man. They all sat around, ate their rations and got very fat. After three months Harry, who had picked up a little English, said, "I go now," and marched his family off to the nearest settlement. "They'll never go back to the bush," Lance said. "They want our white material goods, our flour and tobacco. They don't want to work for them—they don't understand. They'll be fringe people, hanging around the settlements and missions and expecting to be fed. It's the next generation who may—we hope—understand that they must work for a living."

The government regularly sends out Land Rover patrols to make contact with the nomads and report on the state of the wells. Several hundred miles to the west, by the Petermann Ranges, lies a native reserve covering 45,000 square miles of desert—more than half the size of Britain—that is the hunting ground of the Pinturbi tribe.* I saw a report of a patrol which had gone through this roadless stretch of rock and spinifex, almost without water, that reaches into Western Australia. They patrolled the Wailbri sacred Dreaming area and camped at Desert Oak jump-up, where they found a man, wife and small baby whom they took to the Pupanya settlement. Later they found four young men who

---

* In the Northern Territory there are seventeen aboriginal reserves totalling 60 million acres. Western Australia has 34 million acres of reserve, South Australia 19 million acres and Queensland 6½ million, a grand total of just under 200 million acres.

spoke no English but had English Christian names—Jacky Jambid-jimba, Bob Juburula, Charlie Jambidjimba and Henry Jabangari—"all relations of one called Nosepeg." Prolonged drought, these officers believed, had virtually exterminated the mice, lizards, snakes and frogs that had formerly sustained the Pinturbi. To test this theory, the patrol sent out three young tribesmen experienced in hunting and offered a reward for every trophy they brought back. Their total bag in five days was one small snake, one seven-inch-long lizard and one small goanna, nothing like enough to have sustained the three hunters. Yet this had formerly been known as "good tucker country." Will the snakes and lizards, the frogs and mice and other small creatures build up their numbers again after the drought? No one knows. The Wildlife Officer at Alice Springs feared they might have passed the point of no return.

[9]

Until about 1954 government settlements were simply depots where rations and tobacco were distributed to natives who drifted in from the desert. Some stayed on for the tucker, camping in wurlies, without means of support and without a future—the drifters-in became hangers-on. At the Christian missions there was more sense of purpose but no means to carry out good intentions. Buildings were makeshift and staff minimal, enabled to do little more than preach the Gospels, issue rations and fiddle at the fringes of the people's need for schools, hospitals and practical training. Then came the policy of assimilation, and the Welfare Branch of the Administration moved over to the attack. Money, men, materials came in; new settlements were started, old ones rebuilt and expanded. Some of the missions were taken over and others re-equipped.

It was round successful bore holes that new settlements were made or old ones expanded. The next stage was to make an airstrip, and then real development could begin. Most of the aborigines were living on handouts in squalid wurlies, apparently content to do no work, learn no skills, earn no money, and not even try to keep clean. To revolutionize these habits, it was necessary first to reconstruct their outlook and mentality; and with some exceptions, this was an impossible task among adults already set in their ways. The only real hope lay in getting hold of the children, moulding them to a Western pattern and fitting them to take their place in a white society, and that is now the aim. Even that is not as easy as it sounds, because the parents and grandparents attempt to hold the children and to mould them in the traditional pattern. Out of school, children on the settlements speak their native tongue and not English, their parents shape them, not the white teachers. Many of this halfway generation will be trapped in a bleak halfway house between two cultures.

It is a many-sided, complex task to prepare for assimilation into one of the most self-confident, technologically advanced and competitive branches of the white, Western, neo-Christian culture people so technologically backward, unambitious and non-competitive as this aboriginal race of fossilized nomads. A Japanese observer commented: "The task ahead—to fill in a historical gap of fifty thousand years—is without parallel in the world." It still lies ahead. Except in the south, and relating mainly to half-bloods, assimilation remains a policy on paper and a social aim. Even the preparation for assimilation is only beginning.

It is a lack of the drive to compete with, and triumph over, other people that, I was repeatedly told, holds back the aborigines. Our system works only so long as we all go on acquiring more and more material things. If you lack any wish whatsoever to keep up with the Joneses—if in fact your inclination is to share your washing machine with Mrs. Jones instead of to buy a better one—you simply do not fit in to modern white society. Or so the welfare workers find. So their first task must be to induce in little Harry Pintiburrijala a desire to snatch a toy from little Sammy Warrabulabdgi. Apparently Sam and Harry do not wish to do this when left to themselves. I found the pre-school class the most interesting of many interesting activities I saw at the Amoonguna settlement outside Alice Springs. Its aim is to teach the small children English and to initiate them into the "behaviour patterns" of white children, which differ from those of native children in several important ways.

"If you leave a group of white children alone together," said the teacher, "in ten minutes they'll be scrapping with each other; these native children won't. Generally they'll laugh and play quite contentedly. Most of them pick things up quickly enough, but where they fail is in the powers of concentration, in the follow-through." She thought this might be changed by diet. Some of the children in her class, newcomers to the settlement, had the spindly legs and gingery tint in their hair that is often a sign of malnutrition. Soon this will be a thing of the past.

Do many calories promote ambition? Does malnutrition lead to meekness? It will be instructive to see whether the new entry of plump, glossy, protein-rich children, fed from birth on ample balanced rations, grow up to snatch each other's toys.

Among six officially listed "objectives of a settlement" is "to introduce the concept of 'work' as a worth-while aim in life"—work for its own sake as a moral virtue, not merely as a way to get a roof onto the house or a meal under the belt. This is an uphill struggle. No aborigine has ever thought of work in those terms before, and few, if any, are converted; once more the hope must lie in the children. Young men are being trained as mechanics, carpenters, plumbers and the like, but not, so far, to tradesmen's standards, because they lack the basic education. How low the educational level of most aborigines still remains was brought home by a class I heard conducted for the benefit of hygiene workers drawn from a number of settlements. These men carried responsibility; they were the N.C.O.'s of their communities. They would take charge of stores and were being shown pictures of shovels, wheelbarrows, washbasins, sprays and other objects familiar to us from infancy, but strange to most aborigines. Simple problems were set. "If you have six shovels and four are taken away, how many shovels are left?" The pupils were middle-aged men. "They are accustomed to dependence," said their instructor, "not to thinking for themselves." Or not, at any rate, about shovels. No aborigine has, as yet, qualified as a teacher, and hitherto the few untrained assistants have not proved a conspicuous success. "In their own society it was the elders who gave instruction," said one of the whites. "For young men to do so was against their tradition. They're too passive; they don't assert themselves enough."

The day I left the Alice the forerunner of a fleet of schools-on-wheels pulled in, dusty from a journey of 1,000 miles from Adelaide without bitumen. When unfolded it provides a classroom for forty children, complete with desks and chairs, and it tows a two-roomed caravan fully equipped as a teacher's dwelling. These mobile schools are on their way to isolated stations where children have grown up hitherto beyond the orbit of the educational system. By the end of 1967, the Welfare Branch believes, practically every child in the Territory of the appropriate age will be in school. If only a handful are snatching each other's pens, squabbling and cheeking the teacher, the break-through to assimilation will have begun.

[10]

A tourist attraction just outside the Alice is the Overland Telegraph Station, a substantial stone bungalow built in 1871. The laying of this telegraph is one of Australia's tremendous epics. Adelaide was then the seat of government for the whole of what is now the Northern Territory. Communication between Port Augusta, at the head of the Spencer Gulf north of Adelaide, and the small settlement of Darwin had then to be conducted, if not quite by cleft stick, at least by men on horseback following the desert route discovered by the Scots explorer, John Mc-Douall Stuart. To extend the telegraph line some 1,800 miles to Darwin was an obvious necessity. The British-Australian Telegraph Company agreed to lay a cable between Darwin and Java if South Australia would complete the transcontinental section of the line by January 1, 1872. This gave the South Australians less than eighteen months to span the central desert. Within six weeks of the decision, in August, 1870, a horse-and-bullock caravan had departed from Adelaide of the first stage. Five hundred men erected the line, and only five lost their lives from hazard or accident. Construction parties working from each end joined up at Frews' Pond near Newcastle Waters in August, 1872, and the first messages went through to London. They continued to go through until the cable between Java and Darwin was cut in World War II.

Along much of its path the line followed Stuart's route, which in turn was determined by water. The hardships this man endured are difficult to credit nowadays. He must have been the dour kind of Scot: a prosaic, flat writer, sticking to bare facts, a bit of a martinet, lacking in humour, but a superb bushman, a trusted leader who never lost a man, and absolutely unflinching. His ambition was to be the first to cross the continent from south to north. He made three probing expeditions privately financed by two graziers, William Finke and John Chambers, and in 1860, with only two companions, discovered and named the Mac-Donnell Ranges and found the geographical center of the continent, Central Mt. Stuart. Here he planted a flag, left a dull message in a bottle and wrote: "We then gave three hearty cheers for the flag, the emblem of civil and religious liberty, and may it be a sign to the natives that the dawn of liberty, civilisation and Christianity is about to break upon them." He continued north to Tennant Creek, where the natives greeted the dawn with so little enthusiasm that they ambushed his party at a place called Attack Creek. Prudently he led his two men and eight horses back to his depot at Chambers Creek, where he enlisted reinforcements and started off again with twelve companions, only to be foiled by a failure to find water.

His sixth expedition succeeded. With nine men and forty horses, he found a way across the desert to Newcastle Waters and then along the Roper River and down the Mary to Van Diemen Gulf, where one of his companions, riding ahead, exultantly echoed Xenophon's great cry: "The sea!" Even Stuart was moved to wash his hands and feet in the ocean before the usual flag-planting ceremony, a speech by his second-in-command, William Kekwick, and three cheers for the Queen.

It was the return journey, which took five months, that broke the health of this indomitable man. Drought had descended; well after well was dry. They dug vainly in creeks for meager seepage and, worst of all, suffered from scurvy, beri-beri and sand-blight blindness. Thirst-crazed horses went mad. Stuart was lashed to his saddle. Somewhere about the latitude of Alice Springs he wrote in his journal: "I fear my career is coming to an end . . . The nights are agony and the days are long . . ." He was practically blind. His men made a stretcher and suspended it between two horses and carried him for 500 miles to Chambers Creek. Here he recovered sufficiently to lead six of his bedraggled men through the streets of Adelaide. The South Australian Government voted him a sum equal to $4,000 and gave him 2,000 square miles of land. It was too late; sight and health were gone, and he returned to die in London, some three years later, at the age of fifty. But he had achieved his ambition.

Stuart had reported that his route "could be made nearly a straight line for telegraphic purposes." So it proved. The stations on the line were planted along his route or near it. The springs at the Alice were found by one of the surveyors, who called them after the land surveyor's wife.

Rations for the construction parties arrived on pack horses and camels and on the hoof across great waterless stretches of gibber, spinifex and sand. A famous drover, Arthur Giles, "lifted" 5,000 sheep from the Flinders Ranges in South Australia to the camps along the line practically without casualties but lost about 600 of a second batch from a poison plant, *Gastrolobium grandiflora,* at Devil's Marbles; and at Newcastle Waters he was attacked by a hundred painted warriors. In the wake of the telegraph line came the big cattle stations. A few had already started, and in her small, sentimental, but attractive classic of outback literature, *We of the Never-Never,* Mrs. Aeneas Gunn describes how, anywhere along its length, the line could be tapped in an emergency, or just for a "handshake" with the outside world:

> With the murmuring bush about us, in the space kept always cleared beneath those quivering wires, we stood all dressed in white, first looking up at the operator as he knelt at our feet with his tiny transmitter beside him clicking out our message. And as we stood with our horses' bridles over our arms and the horses nibbling at the sweet grasses, in touch with the world in spite of our isolation, a gorgeous butterfly rested for a brief space on the tiny instrument, with gently swaying purple wings; and away in the great world men were sending telegrams amid clatter and dust, unconscious of that tiny group of bushfolk, or that Nature, who does all things well, can beautify even the sending of a telegram.

This was at the Elsey, a station north of Katherine whither Giles drove many thousand sheep and cattle some 1,800 miles from the Murray, moving his sheep by night across the waterless stretches, and spending fourteen months on the road. The record was achieved in 1861 by Nat Buchanan, who "lifted" 20,000 head of cattle from eastern Queensland in five months. From these exploits there evolved a system of stock routes, mapped and controlled and equipped with water points roughly every sixteen miles, over which the bulk of the Territory's sheep and cattle exports were, until quite recently, overlanded to their markets. Some still are, but the road trains and the beef roads are supplanting them.

The Overland Telegraph Station, known as the Bungalow, has become a national park. The Territory's parks range in size from one of three rods and thirteen perches, which surrounds the grave of John Flynn, the founder of the Flying Doctor Service, to one of 300,000 acres which surrounds Ayers Rock. These are for the benefit of tourists and are quite distinct from wildlife sanctuaries, of which the Territory has about 14,200 square miles; a misleading figure, because a single sanctuary which is sheer desert and has little wildlife of any kind—the Tanami Desert north of Lake Mackay near the Western Australian border—occupies 11,000 square miles, or about five-sixths of the total.

[11]

Everywhere you go in the Center conversation veers towards the drought. When at last it ends, will the country recover? Most of the graziers say "yes," as I had heard at Love Creek. There have been droughts before; there will be droughts again, and in between the trees and bush return. "We should never underestimate the power of nature. The country always comes good after a drought."

Outside Alice Springs, at the research station, I heard pasture experts say "no"—or, at any rate, explain the "no" arguments, for wise experts are never dogmatic. There have been droughts before, followed by regeneration; but now a new, and probably decisive, factor has entered in—the hoofed beast.

Near the southern extremity of the Center, between Broken Hill and Port Augusta, lies an area of some 500 square miles that was set aside in 1925, after years of overgrazing, to see what would happen if all the hoofed beasts, and so far as possible all the rabbits, were kept out. The average rainfall is seven inches, about the same as at Alice Springs, and the dominant vegetation the mulga, the belah (a casuarina), false sandalwood, bullock bush and various small shrubs. Given their chance, would this vegetation recover? If so, how quickly, and in what order? Would any permanent changes result? These were the sort of questions to which botanists addressed themselves at the Koonamore Vegetation Reserve.

For nearly forty years no sheep were allowed there, and many fewer rabbits—it proved impossible to exclude them all. In 1964 the botanists published a dusty answer: "Little or no regeneration of most of the trees and shrub species has occurred." The sheep, in short, had done the vegetation in for good, past the point of no return. There was scarcely a mulga tree under seventy years old, the seedings had been eaten down before they could get established, and almost every other species had been similarly discouraged. This was a dying plant community. Only the low-growing, not particularly nutritious saltbush was struggling to recolonize some of the eaten-out parts of the run. Sheep and rabbits appear to have achieved in half a century what all the droughts and ups and downs of the preceding millenniums failed to do: disrupt, probably for good, an ecosystem that had kept in a perpetual balance vegetation, land, and animal, including primitive man.

Then there is the question of water. Since colonization began, men have been drawing on underground water reserves, tacitly assuming these to be unlimited. But nothing is unlimited here, let alone water. In recent years the water table has been falling, and many bores have run dry. People and their livestock have been, and still are, living on capital accumulated during pluvial cycles that ended perhaps 10,000 years ago. Since then very little has been, as it were, paid into the bank. In western

New South Wales the rate of flow of underground water—if *flow* is the right word for so gradual a movement—is twenty miles in 20,000 years, or just over five feet a year. It will take a long time for water to reach the desert, at that rate, from distant watersheds. Rivers that are dry as bones nearly all the year, like the Finke and Todd, the Cooper and Diamantina, at present merely carry the water away, when rain does fall, instead of conserving it.

Water from deep bores is often brackish, in some cases even saltier than the sea. Although Territorial sheep and cattle develop a considerable tolerance to mineral salts, there are limits. Technically it is a simple matter nowadays to desalinate water, whether from bores or from oceans: already there are in operation perfectly efficient "Solar stills," which do the job without complicated machinery or high running costs, by using energy supplied, free of charge, by the heat of the sun. Their snag is the high cost of installation. But all costs are relative—that is to say, they depend on how much human beings want the object concerned. In the Middle Ages small communities of impoverished peasants who starved in winter on salt beef poured their creative energy into a host of cathedrals, monasteries and churches that absorbed perhaps one-third of their economic resources; today nations devote a similar proportion of their resources to the exploration of space and the making of nuclear weapons, when a tithe of it would feed hungry multitudes who must forget empty bellies as they watch orbiting satellites glide across the sky. "Take what you want, says God, and pay for it"; and that is just what human beings do.

If they wanted, with sufficient fervour, to do so, they could not only pepper their deserts with solar stills but take the salt out of the sea and flood the whole of central Australia, irrigating millions of square miles and feeding everyone who needs to be fed, at least for the time being, until the human population stops exploding, if it ever does. This would cost a lot of money, which the people of the world are not at present prepared to supply. Man, as we are so often reminded, does not live by bread alone, and bread has never had a high priority. Who would not go hungry and be the first to gaze upon the peaks of Jupiter?

Only, I suppose, the incurably effete. As that does not include the Australians, they will no doubt continue to fiddle about with solar stills, deepen dubious boreholes, and hope their livestock will get by on topfeed that will not regenerate. Yet one day, there can be little doubt, they will boil up the ocean and convey its purified waters to the Center, and the call of sea birds will again be heard, fish swim above the Simpson Desert, and trees be reflected in mighty reservoirs. The explorers were seeking that great inland sea a few million years too late and—how long? A century too soon?

[12]   .

The Alice is a curious mixture of the outback rendezvous for drovers, stockmen and prospectors that it used to be and the sophisticated rallying point for bus-borne and air-borne tourists that it is becoming. Its outskirts accommodate the last survivor of the Afghan camel drivers and the newest in air-conditioned, cafeteria-serviced, cocktail-bar-equipped motels; in its main street every other shop seems to offer tea cloths crudely printed in debased aboriginal designs, polished gem stones from the desert, slippers, wallets and purses made of kangaroo hide, prints after Namatjira and his Aranda school, and boomerangs—thousands and thousands of boomerangs. The market must be virtually insatiable. I was told that some of those on sale in the Alice were made in Switzerland but had no opportunity to verify this.

The Alice, like the Top End, also produces characters, and characters are like the mulgas—they are tough, over seventy and gradually dying out. One of the most renowned is Mrs. Jenkins, who lives in a small bungalow called The Ritz and will, if in the right frame of mind, display her collection of black opals, said to be the finest in the world. These were extracted from Lightning Ridge in New South Wales, whither she and her husband migrated from a jeweller's shop in Hobart to make their fortune. This they did, and now Mrs. Jenkins is spending some of it on race horses. The walls of her kitchen are crowded with photographs of horses, sometimes with herself in the saddle, for she was a famous horsewoman in her day. On the table, or on her lap, broods an enormous glossy cat called Horace, who does not so much share The Ritz with her as permit her to share it with him.

The opal collection reposes in a curtained-off alcove that can only be likened, however hackneyed—the comparison to Aladdin's cave—it is so rich and glittering and fabulous, as if tongues and flashes of blue fire had been trapped in these bits of rock, or flights of butterflies with iridescent wings of every shade of blue it is possible for nature to create had been petrified. And there is, too, a slight pantomime flavour about this squat little wooden bungalow, one room hung with original Namatjira paintings and the other with equestrain photographs, about its unexpected Aladdin's cave, and about its short, forthright, blunt-spoken, unpretentious widow with her monster of a cat and her decided opinions, tempting Horace with titbits and brewing tea. I asked her, as many others must have done, whether it was wise to live alone with all those opals. "I've got my gun," she answered, glancing at an object in a corner which looked like part of the armoury of Captain Phillip and the First Fleet. There is also Horace—and Mrs. Jenkins herself, much the most formidable of the three.

[13]

On my last evening at the Alice I went to a hen party. It was a new experience both for me and for many of my fifty or so fellow guests: new, not that they should be dining without their husbands, but that they should be doing so outside their homes and in company.

"It's the first time since I married," one of them said with an air of unbelief in her own audacity, "that I've had a night out on my own, as you might say, without the kids." I asked if her husband was baby-sitting. *"Him?* Not he! He's over there." She nodded towards the bar, where the usual phalanx of white shirts was backed against a world that had women in it. So far as I could see, the couple did not exchange a word, even a wave, all the evening, and there was nothing new in this either. "It started on our wedding night. We stayed in an hotel. 'You go off with the girls,' he said. 'I'm staying with the men.' It was after midnight when he showed up, full of beer. Now we've got four kids. Oh well. He's been a good husband, I suppose." She laughed and fetched another whisky and did not seem to mind.

And what, indeed, had she to mind about? Her man paid the bills, did not ill-treat her, gave her babies—though one might suppose their procreation to be a little perfunctory—and did not chase other women. No doubt this chasing happens sometimes, but for most women it must rank fairly low among the hazards of matrimony. Equally it must be uphill work to be a *femme fatale,* matched against the pubs, two-up and the Returned Servicemen's League.

The art of pleasing men seems to lie more in glossing over or disguising sex than in emphasizing it. Perhaps Diana the huntress, descending from Olympus to take human form, would be best advised to wear shorts, chain-smoke, adopt a crew-cut and concentrate on being a good mate in the Australian rather than the sexual sense of the word. Perhaps that is what the Marching Girls are after with their military drill and

P.T. exercises on playing fields after office hours. For those of riper years there is bowls, for which you wear a plain white skirt, white blouse, white stockings, gym shoes and a white straw or linen hat with brim and ribbon—protective colouring that enables you to mingle almost indistinguishably with the men, whose uniform is the same except for trousers instead of a skirt.

It is odd, this safety first in sex, this persistent streak of puritanism in a breed of males in other ways so bold, so adventurous and so self-indulgent. A Victorian view of sex, almost defunct elsewhere, remains ingrained and predominant. You could not image a fleet of ships setting out from Sydney to retrieve an Australian Helen, not even if she had won the singles at Wimbledon or the Olympic swimming championship, although that would be her best chance. "Too bad," they would say in the pubs, commenting on her abduction, "but there's plenty more sheilas, that's for sure. My shout, mate; Simpson's out for sixty-three . . ." I heard no satisfactory explanation. Most of the women—although I did come across some pockets of resistance—accept their lot, count their blessings and let it go at that. A line from Thomas Gray has been aptly quoted: the "servitude that hugs her chain."

SEVENTEEN ⁙⁙⁙⁙

Tropical Queensland

"Clancy's gone to Queensland droving and we don't know where he are," runs a famous line from one of Banjo Paterson's ballads, and it is easy to understand why no one knew. There is a great deal of Queensland, a great deal of saltbush and spinifex, dust and ranges, dry creek and flooded channel, mallee scrub and brigalow. Cape York thrusts a northern finger almost into New Guinea, and 1,500 miles south the white beaches of the Gold Coast lure holiday-makers from Sydney and Newcastle. Clancy might be anywhere from Burketown on the Gulf to Cooper's Creek, or down near Birdsville on the South Australian border.

He might be droving there today, lifting cattle from the Barkly Table-land in the Top End, south of Borroloola, to Mt. Isa, still the railhead for the western portion of the Territory. No railway spans the 600 miles of saltbush plain and mitchella grass downs between Mt. Isa and the southern terminus of the line from Darwin, or between Mt. Isa and the Alice. But Clancy would not make the blunder committed by an English jackeroo who, droving somewhere in the Gulf country, stopped to quench his thirst at a country pub. The landlord handed him a beer bottle after neatly nipping off the top with his teeth. The Englishman asked for a glass. Looking him up and down, the landlord demanded, "What part of fairyland do *you* come from, mate?"

Mt. Isa constitutes a fairyland of its own, like Broken Hill, only even more so. In the very marrow of this ferocious land, whose rocks would fry an egg in a jiffy, some 18,000 people live in air-conditioned houses on food arriving in a state of pristine freshness from all quarters of the world. Milk comes 1,000 miles in refrigerated trucks: fresh fish is flown daily from the Gulf: beer travels 2,000 miles from Melbourne. Rain may not fall for a year, but lawns are green as Irish pastures and water

350

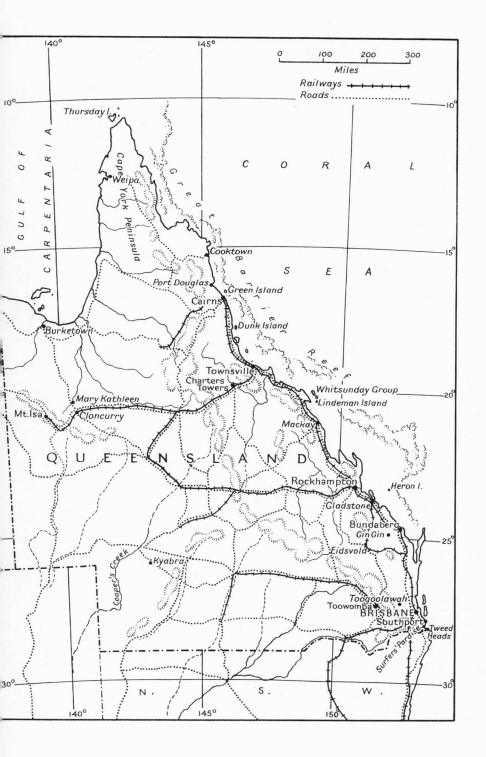

skiing the favourite sport. Swimming pools, open-air cinemas, shopping malls, a racecourse, two cricket ovals, a rodeo ground, goodness knows how many pubs and churches—Mt. Isa offers all they need to men and women of forty different nationalities. The cause of it all is one of the richest deposits in the world of copper, lead, zinc and silver.

The man who started all this, son of a London printer, reached Queensland on a bicycle whose tires were stuffed with grass and drifted round the Gulf country for fifteen years working on stations and shooting wild pigs. Then, on a day in 1923, his pack horse smelled water in the dry bed of the Leichhardt River and sniffed out a water hole, where he camped for the night. Next morning he chipped some rock with his prospector's hammer and thought he recognized sulphide of lead. An assayer in Cloncurry confirmed this and also found traces of silver; so John Campbell Miles and his mate pegged a claim for forty acres, and a lead rush began. Water had to be hauled by horse teams and the ore taken 2,000 miles to Port Kembla in New South Wales for smelting. Gougers gave their claims fancy names like Last Hope, Black Duchess, Ace of Diamonds, Durban Angel, No Tin Lizzie, Collar and Pockets, Edge of Beyond. A humpy town of corrugated iron and hessian sprouted —hot as hades, immersed in flies. The first mission undertaken by the first Flying Doctor was to move a miner with an injured leg from Mt. Isa to Cloncurry, where the service established its initial base in 1927.

Mt. Isa seesawed between fabulous prosperity and total ruin, which in the thirties closed the mines completely and left the town deserted and spent. Prosperity returned on the back of a demand for copper created by World War II, only to be unseated by a slump in postwar copper prices and again restored by a boom in lead. Now, with an output of metal worth about $46 millions a year, Mt. Isa has become the largest mining enterprise in Australia but is still plagued by troubles; costs are high and constantly increasing strikes are frequent and damaging. One of the worst and stupidest had just ended when I passed through; it was not concerned with wages, already fantastically high, but with a struggle for control within the trade union hierarchy. It lasted for several months and cost the country's economy about $2 million a day.

Between Mt. Isa and Cloncurry you fly over an immaculate, slap-up, miniature Mt. Isa, lying cupped amid crag and gorge. Brand-new houses are arranged in echelon formation at an angle from the roads, so as to turn their backs on the prevailing hot and dust-laden winds; all are newly painted, neat, spick and span. Below you lie a cricket oval, a swimming pool, a spacious new shopping mall; the white screen of an open-air cinema stands up like a sail. All roads are of bitumen and lined with newly planted trees, each tree protected by a wire cage.

But there is something odd about it all. No smoke emerges from the tall chimneys; the swimming pool is empty; parking spaces are deserted; no traffic moves along the roads. The whole place is eerily untenanted, like a landlocked *Marie Celeste*. Could you enter one of those pastel-painted, trim and tidy boxes below, surely you would find breakfast half eaten on the table, water boiling in an electric kettle, children's toys on the floor?

This is Mary Kathleen—planned, built and ghosted all within a couple of years. In 1954 an eight-man syndicate, headed by a taxi driver, discovered a mountain of uranium ore and sold its claim for a half million dollars: in that same year the price of uranium collapsed. The mine's owners, Conzinc Riotinto, put the whole place into cold storage in the hope that one day uranium will again be extracted at a profit from these radio active hills. That day has not yet arrived.

[2]

North of Cloncurry, towards the Gulf of Carpentaria, I stayed on a station that by Queensland standards is a mere small holding of 120,000 acres but is relatively well-developed and therefore interesting to compare with, say, Victoria River Downs. Possibly it marks a halfway stage between the *laissez faire* of the past and future methods based on science and aiming at the constant improvement of the land, rather than at its exploitation.

The whole run is paddocked, and there are water points every eight or ten miles; 70 per cent of the calves are branded; no scrub bulls or brumbies remain in creeks and ranges. In fact, there is a stud herd turning out 350 bulls every year. Hitherto these have been shorthorns, but now, as on so many other northern stations, they are to be replaced by the Brahman breed.

Mustering is still done on horses, but from one of several permanent camps equipped with refrigerators; the musterers have ice cream for tea and return most weekends to the homestead, where the missus takes over from the station cook and serves five square meals a day to fifteen or twenty hungry people, including the aboriginal couple employed in house and garden. (White Australians must be the only people in the world who not only do not expect the blacks they employ to do all the so-called menial work for them but do much of it for the blacks—not from a sense of dedication to their less fortunate brothers, but because they do not think the blacks would do it properly. "No one cooks for *my* family," said my hostess, "but me.") A measure of outback feudalism survives; everyone is fed who comes to the table. Every four or five days Rob, the manager, cuts out a beast from the mob of killers, shoots it in the race, hauls the carcass up by winch, flays and eviscerates it and cuts the meat for distribution to everyone employed on the place and for his own table. This is a job he never delegates. "I enjoy eating meat so much," he said, "I thoroughly enjoy preparing it." The nearest shops are fifty miles south in Cloncurry, so it is just as well there is always the best part of a bullock in the deep freeze. To the north the nearest center is Burketown on the Gulf, nearly 250 miles away and a source of stock jokes: they call a brand of rum they sell there the Burketown mosquito net.

Now and again the pastoral company's chairman, or one of its directors from London, pays a state visit in a private aircraft. The chairman brings with him not only his own wine but glasses to drink it from. "It wouldn't taste right out of the wrong-shaped glasses," they explained at the station. No doubt about *his* dwelling in fairyland; he is a baronet and sends a handsomely embossed Christmas card with "former Lord Mayor of London" on it at the appropriate season.

[3]

Rae and Rob are fully in possession of the great Australian secret: how to appear to be doing nothing in particular, and that at the tempo of the Deep South, while, in a mysterious fashion, getting an extraordinary amount of work done. No one ever seems to hurry, fluster, or bluster, or to give an order; people move and speak languidly, as people do in countries of extreme heat; they sprawl with legs apart in wicker chairs, brew tea, turn the transistor set on and off, flap at flies that have found chinks in the screens—you must live always inside a cage; flies cluster in millions as soon as you set foot outside. Dogs lie stretched out and panting slightly or thump their tails gently on the floor; a few hens scratch around the cookhouse; the native boy ambles out to move a sprinkler, scratches his head beneath a tilted hat, ambles back again; horses cluster under a tree, flicking their tails. An engine starts up; a pickup goes by, puffing up dust. Rob comes in which hands smeared with grease, takes a shower, nibbles at a beef sandwich, says something about a turkey's nest and strolls out again.

The turkey's nest turns out to be a round reservoir with earth banks that stores sub-artesian water pumped by windmill and then fed by gravity into troughs. There is no permanent river on the property; all the water comes either from dams or from these bores, some of which descend over 1,000 feet. A bore like this will cost up to $12,000, and about half those sunk turn out to be duds. But the government will pay for dud bores.

A large part of any station manager's life is spent "on the bore run." Every windmill, pump and reservoir must be inspected at least once a week, preferably twice, and if necessary immediately repaired. Rob's bore run was comparatively short, ninety miles; on a large station it can measure several hundred, but then Rob has more bores. If something goes wrong, as it quite often does, you do not ring up for a mechanic; you fix it yourself on the spot, while cattle wait thirstily for their twice-a-day drink under a cloud of flies.

To run a station you have to be master of a lot of trades. Rob's eyes are everywhere. As we drove over a dead-flat plain dotted with thickets of twisty-trunked, untidy little gidyea trees,* he spotted a tilted fence post, took out his tools, straightened the post and strained the wire. Then he put to rights a homemade gate. His eyes were always on the pastures; time this paddock was rested, time those bullocks were moved.

Normally practically the whole year's rain falls in January, February and March—that is, in mid to late summer. A great outburst of growth follows, and the plains are covered in a waist-deep pelt of grass which conserves itself on the stem, as unmown hay, and should last the cattle through the year. My visit was in April, and no more rain was expected before Christmas. But the summer rains had failed. Everything looked brittle and withered; the grass was stunted and scanty, and there was dust everywhere, and an underlying anxiety.

While we boiled the billy and flapped at flies under a clump of gidyeas, Rob discoursed on the pastoral situation in northern Queensland. In essence its problems are the same as those of all commercial enterprises; how to raise output and quality without also raising costs, in so far as you can. This means more meat per acre, which in turn means more beasts per acre and earlier maturing beasts. That spells

* The same as the gidgee: the wattle *Acacia Cambagei*.

greater bulk of grass, which calls for better grasses more efficiently managed, and that in turn calls for more capital. What you have to overcome is a shortage of protein during the long, dry winters when there is no fresh growth. Only the scientists can do this, by breeding drought-tolerant legumes. They are trying hard, and have several in the proving stage that may be winners.

[4]

Rob learned his trade as a stockman on the Elsey station and had, like Clancy, gone to Queensland droving, and down the famous Birdsville track which took cattle from the Top End to their markets in South Australia. He told me how, with two other stockmen, he had lifted a mob of 1,200 cattle from the Elsey, a distance of about 1,400 miles and a six months' journey, averaging nine miles a day. Rob said the stockmen used to sing, whistle, or just talk to the beasts nearly all the time. Cattle are nervous creatures, and any sudden noise will send them stampeding wildly in a mob that may take half a day to turn. The singing and whistling is to let them know where you are and to soothe their nerves. That is the genesis of Australian ballads; stockmen used to make them up as they went along.

Their day started with the dawn, when they "fed the cattle quietly along" for the first mile or two, not pushing them, then "put them together" and moved them till they reached water, generally around noon. Cattle drank and men rested until the bite went out of the sun; then they put the mob together again and moved on. A mile or two from camp they spread the cattle out to feed. It was important, Rob said, to feed into the wind, otherwise the cattle grew restive and obstinate. Sometimes they had to circle round the camp and come in from the far side. "You must get them in full-bellied and content."

Nights were the trickiest time, when the cattle were most apt to panic and a stampede was hardest to check. Dingoes were always on the prowl. The drovers kept their best horses for the night work. The cook's job was to keep a fire burning and the billy on the boil all through the hours of darkness. To sing and whistle to the beasts was even more important in the jumpy nighttime than by day. If a panic started, all you could do was to keep with the stampeding beasts until they halted of their own accord and then turn them.

You got to know the cattle individually, Rob explained. Some emerged as bosses, and the bovine equivalent of a peck order soon formed; those at the bottom took the last turn at the water and got the poorest feed. If the drovers knew their business and the season was right, the cattle did not lose condition; in fact, sometimes they improved. Rob lost only two beasts between the Elsey and Birdsville until the last three days, when twenty-four perished in a quicksands. When the cattle were delivered, Rob and his mates turned round and took the horses back again, averaging thirty miles a day—a ride of nearly 3,000 miles.

By contrast, I watched cattle being loaded into the enormous trucks that nowadays convey them to their markets within twenty-four hours. No one sings or whistles as the beasts are jostled up a ramp into a "prime mover" or into one of the "dogs," as truck and trailers are called, for their short journey to the meatworks. No campfire with a simmering billy under the stars, no dingoes prowling in the moonlight, no wild gallops through the darkness, no battles against drowsiness and fatigue with eyes sore from glare and dust. It is all a lot easier and quicker and presumably more efficient and will soon put the drover into the folk museum along with bushranger, digger and bronco rail.

[5]

It is the manager's task to sort out the cattle in the drafting yards. Perched aloft on a rough-hewn, heavy rail with his feet astride the race, for hours on end he looks down on the backs of cattle as they surge past, head to tail, jostling and shoving, expelling agitated jets of dung, some hanging back to be prodded on by stockmen. Dust hangs above the yards in a golden halo, choking and half blinding beasts and men.

Cattle go through the race at the rate of three or four a minute, and each one presents a decision that cannot be reversed. The boss on his rail looks nonchalant, detached, scarcely attending, but his eyes never stray from the backs of the milling cattle. No one blows a whistle, shouts a command, or makes any noticeable sign of direction, yet everyone knows exactly what to do. Although I never heard Rob speak or saw him make a gesture, the stockman in charge of the gates appears to know by instinct which yard to turn the beast into. I suppose there is some code a stranger cannot immediately detect, as at an auction sale. All the noise comes from the cattle; the men are silent, narrowing their eyes against a powdery dust. Like all jobs calling for speed, judgment and precision, it is mysterious and fascinating to watch. How long before it is all done by computer? Not long, perhaps.

No one shouts an order, but suddenly, without apparent reason, there is a change. Perhaps the boss gives a signal by glancing at his watch. The men turn from the race to light cigarettes and vault the rails into the paddock; the boss descends from his perch and mops his face and neck; the cattle stop their pushing and lunging; it is smoko time. A pickup takes us over to the camp. In an open-sided corrugated-iron shed the tea is already brewed, the cook hands out a batch of freshly baked scones. Everyone relaxes; dust is washed from dry throats. There is not much to be said.

The boss gets up and stretches, washes out his mug at a tap in a rain-water tank outside the shed, strolls over to the pickup; one by one, unhurriedly, the men follow suit. The yards are hotter and dustier than ever as a naked sun stands overhead. Drafting resumes; a break for dinner of steak, fried potatoes, tinned fruit and more tea; more drafting, the yards by now a furnace, the dust of golden fog; afternoon smoko; yards again, the heat abating; everything permeated in a sharp, astringent, nutty cattle smell. The prime mover drawing two dogs packed with beasts head to tail has gone off; batches of immatures have been released to seek water from a trukey's nest and shade in a creek. Five o'clock, and once more the unuttered order, men turning from the rails and Rob hopping from his perch—the rumps of cattle, surely, still passing in procession behind his eyes. Back to the camp for more thick steaks with fried eggs on them, ice cream and more tea, and then a pause to smoke and watch the stars emerge like bright-eyed creatures from their burrows while someone strums on a guitar. Now there will be song perhaps, not to soothe the paddocked cattle, and no longer ballads, but the Beatles' latest hit.

[6]

"For the drover's life has pleasures that the townsfolk never know," wrote Banjo Paterson, ruminating, in the guise of a ledger clerk, on the whereabouts of Clancy of the Overflow.

> And he sees the vision splendid of the sunlit plains extended,
> And at night the wondrous glory of the everlasting stars . . .
> And I somehow rather fancy that I'd like to change with Clancy—

Every townsman fancies this at times, but very few do more than fancy; on the contrary, it is the stockmen who are going to the towns. Australians have become the second most highly urbanized people in the world, second only to Britain. Sixty-five out of every hundred live in cities of not less than 20,000 inhabitants. (In Britain, sixty-nine.) Clancy's gone to Sydney bricking and we don't know where he are.

Perhaps the disregarded women have a say in this. To many of them, the vision splendid from a corrugated-iron box set down on a dusty plain, beleagured by flies, dessicated by heat and left mainly to the undiluted company of small children, may seem too high a price to pay for an uninterrupted view of the wondrous glory of the everlasting stars. Electricity, refrigerators, radios and cars have ameliorated but not fundamentally changed their lot. It is not the hardness of their lives but the monotony and lack of company that palls. It is never work and hardship that destroy humans, but boredom. Psychologists know this but not, as yet, politicians and reformers, and their mistake is proving lethal to us all. The women of the outback know it, and that is why so many of them leave.

There are exceptions, women whom the outback has "hooked." I met one such who, at the age of fifteen, together with a widowed mother, was running a sizeable sheep station. This was in the war, and there were no men, so the two women did everything: mustered, drafted, dosed, lambed, dipped. They lived in the saddle. The sheep prospered; there was a heritage waiting for the sons. In due course the girl married and lived in a shack alone for weeks at a time, generally pregnant, while her husband was away droving or mustering. "I nearly climbed the wall feeling sorry for myself. In spite of that I loved the life and never wanted any other, and it's different now"—different now that they have a good house, reasonable comfort, enough company. She understands the demands and hopes and disappointments of a station, the technicalities few city women grasp. She knows each bore, each creek, every paddock, how to judge a stud bull. Her husband consults her and she talks sense back to him; between them has been built a genuine partnership, rare enough to be remarkable. Possibly a general lack of this has caused a curious dead patch in the heart of a warmhearted people, not a scar, but a blank, reflecting the desert in the geographical center of their land. But perhaps I am being fanciful. To know a country you must live in it, just as to know a person you must live with him.

[7]

There are three Queenslands: the long, moist, tropical coastline that faces on the Coral Sea and stretches 1,600 miles from south of Brisbane to the tip of the Cape York Peninsula and has nearly all the people; a belt of hill, forest and tableland behind it with lakes and rivers, forming part of the Great Dividing Range; and then those enormous scrub-clad plains I flew over, that grow progressively more arid and less scrub-covered until they merge into the great central desert.

Queensland is the youngest of the states, the most varied, and has the greatest wonders, from the polyps, anemones and weird sea creatures of the Great Barrier Reef to giant fruit bats with a five-foot wing span, understandably mistaken by Captain Cook's men for devils, which congregate literally in millions in the forests and live on the nectar of eucalypts and on wild figs and have learned to migrate like birds. Here is the helmeted cassowary that, though flightless, can clear at a bound an eight-foot jump; giant spiders that bark; legless lizards just like little snakes; bearded dragons; the amphibious lungfish, unique to Queensland, that can travel overland and stay underwater for half an hour; and mudskippers that emerge from the sea to dance in mangrove swamps, climb trees in pursuit of insects, make nests in the sand and have retractable eyes on stalks. Another creature unique to Queensland is the golden bowerbird, who builds between two trees a wall of twigs which he decorates with flowers. These he is forever rearranging with his bill to suit his fancy, and no one has been able to suggest any reason for this behaviour except that he has a genuine aesthetic sense, expressed, like that of so many middle-class housewives, through the tasteful arrangement of flowers.

Most Queenslanders come from somewhere else and have the enthusiasm of converts. On the coast of Queensland they have everything, they say—mild winter, constant sunshine, a warm sea, palm-fringed beaches, fresh fish and luscious fruit, plenty of elbowroom, a life to be enjoyed at a leisurely tempo, an expanding economy and a "tourist potential" that is practically unlimited. What is there that they lack? There must be *something*. You rack your brains to find the snag.

You could, I suppose, say there is a lack of cultural life and intellectual stimulus. To travel all the way to Sydney or Melbourne for a cultural fling is very expensive. And can be disappointing too. I met an English couple who had flown several hundred, if not thousand, miles to see *Becket,* a lengthy film that cut across the time for family tea. Many families brought tea with them, these spectators said, well wrapped up in plastic bags and newspapers. "The people in the next seats ate a large chicken and had thermos flasks. I'm afraid even Peter O'Toole couldn't compete."

I am never really convinced by this cultural argument, however. Millions of people who dwell in large industrial cities lack acquaintance with the arts and are immersed in appalling ugliness. Here, even if you cannot get to the ballet, natural beauty surrounds you, and at weekends you can go fossicking in the hills where semiprecious gem stones are plentiful and stumble here and there on the decomposing ruins of a pub or homestead or an abandoned mine.

I have mentioned the places I never reached but always wanted to, the apples on the topmost bough. One such was Cooktown, north of Cairns, where in 1770 Captain Cook beached and repaired the *Endeavour* after she had struck a reef, thus acquainting her master with the existence of the longest string of coral islands in the world. Members of the ship's company, including Joseph Banks, discovered wallabies and fruit bats, ate without ill effects wild fruits of the forest and observed the naked aborigines, who sensibly would not allow their women to approach the sailors and, in Captain Cook's opinion, were "far more happier than we Europeans, being wholly unacquainted not only with the superfluous but the necessary Conveniences so much sought after in Europe", and living therefore

> in a Tranquility which is not disturbed by the Inequality of Conditions. The Earth and Sea of their own accord furnishes them with all things necessary for life; they covet not Magnificent Houses, Household-stuff etc.; they live in a warm and fine Climate and enjoy a very wholesome Air, so that they have very little need of Clothing . . . In short they seemed to set no value upon anything we gave them nor would they ever part with any thing of their own for any one article we could offer them, this is my opinion argues that they think themselves provided with all the necessarys of Life and that they have no superfluities . . .

This seems to sum up very well the condition to which members of the Lapidary club are endeavouring to revert when they take their swag and billy to go fossicking along the Endeavour River.

[8]

The lives of Queensland cane cutters have been made familiar to the world by Ray Lawler's play, *Summer of the Seventeenth Doll*. There can be few harder jobs left in the world than to hack all day in the fierce tropical sunshine and tropical heat at these tough rattans and load them into trolleys. Cutters get burned almost black by the sun and are often blacker still with ash, for normally the cane is fired just before cutting to destroy the dense undergrowth and drive out snakes and rats; coated with ash and sweat, they look like end men in a minstrel show, white showing only round their eyes and mouths. A good cutter can draw $300 a fortnight; the lowest earnings are about $60 a week and the highest up to $200. To achieve this, they will start by moonlight and continue until after dark, and a man will cut and shift in the hours between something like eighteen tons of cane. In a sun temperature of well over 100° this is prodigious and constitutes the highest output in the world.

We called on a cane grower in a big way of business and of the third cane-growing generation, Mr. John Smart, and he showed us the barracks where cutters had their quarters. The same gangs, mainly of Italians, used to come round year after year but come no longer; most of the itinerants have settled down and bought land, and men are being replaced by machines: expensive monsters, costing at least $8,000 apiece, but each will do the work of ten men, and soon the human cutter will be obsolete. Mr. Smart has two machines and ten tractors and employs no more casual labour; everything is mechanized; in a paddock there survives a solitary, pensioned-off horse. Like most Queensland houses, the Smarts' bungalow is raised eight or ten feet above the ground on stilts, but this does not prevent armies of small green frogs from hopping up the steps; in the morning Mrs. Smart has to sweep them out with a broom.

Besides its John Smarts, the backbone of the state, North Queensland has its beatniks and bums. Living is cheap and easy and Social Service payments easier to gather even than prawns from the estuaries and mangoes from trees. "When one bloke meets another at the post office," I was told at a little place up the coast from Cairns, "they both say: 'How's the book coming along?' It's the stock greeting. These blokes draw seven quid* a week on the dole and talk all day about the books they're going to write but never write them, or pictures they're going to paint but never paint them, or they play guitars. On seven pounds* a week in a beach hut they're sitting pretty. Nothing to spend on razor blades, and a pair of shorts are all the clothes they need."

These beatniks knock up little shelters on the beach from mangrove poles and old sacks; this is against the local by laws, and sometimes the authorities have them pulled down. They are up again in a few days. Once the council had them burned. They reappeared a little farther

* $14.00

down the beach. But when December comes with drenching downpours and torrid, steamy midsummer heat, the huts are deserted, like nests. "Now the summer's over these no-hopers will soon be back. There's a couple of guitarists moved in already."

There used to be a colony of artists at Yorkie's Nob, a few miles north of Cairns, but it disintegrated when the pub burned down and Ray Crook moved to Brisbane—Ray Crook has "arrived." There are a few survivors such as Ron Edwards, who likes to paint the ghost towns and deserted pubs around Cooktown, to strum on a guitar, to stroll through an open door onto a sandy beach and into a smooth, lazy, tropical sea, and to experiment with recipes collected on Thursday Island, which has a hotchpotch of races—Polynesian, Melanesian, Japanese, Australoid, Samoan, Malay, Chinese—each with a culinary tradition of its own.

Farther up the beach a couple of young Melbourne potters have taken over a bush-entangled acre, restored a ghost bungalow, built themselves a kiln and settled in to make pots, rear babies, paint pictures, milk a goat and grow most of their own vegetarian diet. The grip of money loosens in this Pacific Arcady.

At Port Douglas, towards Cooktown, I met an English couple who had gone there after World War II to grow pineapples. The fruit grew, but the price collapsed. They made a fresh start with bananas; a cyclone flattened the plantation. So they started a retaurant in a tent and cooked imaginative meals on an old wood stove by the light of a hurricane lamp, endorsing by success Emerson's belief that "if a man make a better mouse-trap than his neighbour, tho' he build his house in the woods, the world will make a beaten path to his door." In time Max and Diana Bowden saved enough money to start a little business making jewelry from the sea shells to be picked up in such great numbers and variety from the beach. At first they designed, made and sold it all themselves, but now there is a factory, exhibits at international fairs and a world-wide business for which nature provides free raw material.

This is a lotus-eating land. "People here are tolerant, easygoing," its inhabitants tell you. "They take you for what you are, not for what you've done or haven't done, or who your parents were, or what sort of school you went to." I was told of a man who bought a wharf at one of the drowsy, dead-beat little harbours along the coast and potters round it in a pair of shorts and gossips with the fishermen; he "gave away" an international reputation as an expert on computers. In Cairns I met Mr. George Welsh, who "gave away" the management of a Melbourne hospital to start a log-cabin restaurant cooled by electrically operated punkahs and festooned with old wagon wheels, packsaddles, horse collars and coach lanterns, where you watch the chef grill your steak or bit of barramundi in the middle of the room. Where else, he asked, but in tropical Queensland can you start the working day with a swim from a palm beach, drive to work with no traffic problem, take your afternoon siesta under a tree and give away your ties and even jackets?

I voiced to this elegant restaurateur a complaint about cheeses. Here is one of the great dairying countries of the world, full of enterprise and also full of Italians, Greeks, Dutch and Germans, and everywhere —really everywhere—nothing but cheddar. And seldom really good cheddar at that. Why no homemade Stiltons, Double Gloucesters and Caerphillies? Where are the local Camemberts, Belle Paeses, Pont l'Evêques, Port Saluts, Gruyères and the ripe Bries? There must be people here who know how to make them; there must be people here who want to eat them. We are told continually that New Australians have civilized the fare of Old Australians, yet there is nothing but mousetrap from Darwin to Melbourne, from Cairns to Perth.

George Welsh shook his head regretfully. "There's no interest in cheeses. No one asks for them. The fact is, customers don't *want* anything different when it comes to food. They're not adventurous." Nor gastronomically creative; so far as I know, there is not a single native Australian dish, unless you count kangaroo-tail soup. Pavlova cake has been suggested, but I scarcely think it would qualify—it was not invented in Australia; and passion fruit is not a native.

[9]

The largest Australian city in the tropics is Townsville, which is rather smaller than Norwalk, Connecticut. This indicates the extent to which people and their works have been, and are, concentrated in the Temperate Zone rather than in the tropics. If the pasture researchers of the C.S.I.R.O. are heeded, this could change dramatically. They are not at one with Dr. Davidson in believing that everything the tropics can produce, the Temperate Zone can produce better. Up to now, they say, the whole approach has been wrong—based on exploitation rather than development. A drastic revision of *ideas,* hence of the practices that flow from them, is needed.

At Townsville a research station has been started to explore the techniques of dealing with tropical pastures. (There is also a University

College opened in 1961 and growing fast towards its destined status as a full-blown university—the first in the tropics.) I had been told at Katherine how the Top End could be revolutionized by the use of new plants and new methods of cattle management. Basically the story is the same in northern Queensland, but there are differences which perhaps justify a résumé—if I have got it right—of the doctrine expounded in Townsville and deriving mainly from a brilliant Welshman, Dr. Jack Griffiths-Davies, who came from the Welsh Plant Breeding Station at Aberystwyth to direct the C.S.I.R.O.'s Division of Tropical Pastures.

Four continents out of five have tropical belts, and in three out of four of these the soils are mainly fertile, rainfall generous, and the potential therefore easy to exploit; "tropical fertility" has become a byword. Only in tropical Australia, with some exceptions, are soils poor and rainfall generally meager and badly distributed. I was told that 95 per cent of all the soils of northern Queensland are short of phosphorous, and most are also deficient in molybdenum. Hence the very low output of indifferent and slow-maturing beef, which is normal throughout the whole of inland tropical Australia.

The orthodox way to tackle a situation of this kind has been to search among the native pasture plants for superior varieties and then set the plant breeder to work to breed up from these selections better strains of plant. This course has been followed elsewhere with spectacular success, and there seemed to be no reason why it should not succeed in tropical Australia. And succeed, to some extent, it may; this approach has not been abandoned, but the emphasis has swung to a new and opposite approach that was formerly a heresy.

This, in brief, is to forget about the native plants and concentrate instead on introducing foreigners—vegetable New Australians, as it were. These foreigners will be selected from the great wealth of plant life to be found in other, and richer, parts of the tropics; they will be acclimatized and then adapted to the new conditions. In particular a hunt for tropical legumes is on: stouthearted legumes not to be defeated by low rainfall, by long, dry seasons, and even by touches of frost. If such a paragon can be developed, and other great improvements made, then in Queensland alone, not counting the rest of northern Australia, some 250,000 square miles—an area five times as great as all the pasture lands of Britain and over thirty times larger than Israel—could achieve a *tenfold* increase in output. And this would only be a start.

Where the right plants do not exist in nature, biologists are quite prepared to invent them. By crossing two strains of a legume found in Mexico they have created a plant they call siratro, which has got off to a flying start. Mixed with Rhodes grass—another foreigner—it has fattened cattle, at the rate of two bullocks an acre, faster and better than native pastures have fattened cattle in all ways similar at the rate of ten acres to the bullock. This is not a tenfold, it is twentyfold increase in the output of the pastures. And then there is our old friend Townsville lucerne, another Mexican. There are twenty-five species in the genus, and so far only two have been used in Australia.

From the world of plants I moved on to the world of birds. In Townsville there is a large swamp which is a center of controversy between those who want to drain it and those who want to leave it as it is—a haunt of birds. One of the two Fauna Officers employed by the Queensland Government, Mr. Lavery, is at work on waterfowl, mainly grey teal, whistling duck and the wonderful brolga, and he has estimated that formerly some 10,000 birds frequented this accessible swamp. In the dry season he has counted upwards of 3,000 brolgas.

About one-third of the swamp has been drained already to enlarge the air field, and this has reduced the bird population by about the same proportion. Should the other two-thirds go? Yes, say the aviation authorities and many of the city fathers; the land is needed for "development"; birds are dangerous to aircraft, swamps encourage mosquitoes and are unhealthy things. The "no's" point out that if you drain all the swamps, you will end up with no waterfowl. This is happening all over Queensland where, Mr. Lavery said, there are practically no swamps and marshy areas left that are not under some form of human use and control. Consequently waterfowl are dwindling, too, and this includes the brolga, that most handsome of cranes.

Does it matter if the waterfowl go? A great many sportsmen think it does; as usual, those who want to kill the birds are the birds' strongest protectors. Now promoters of tourism have joined their side. Birds are becoming powerful tourist attractions; a thousand dancing brolgas within the city boundaries would be a trump card. So the argument continues, and for the moment roughly two-thirds of the birds survive.

EIGHTEEN 〰〰〰

The Great Barrier Reef

There are some things that are simply too much for the imagination, like the Milky Way, eternity and the dimensions of the universe. The Great Barrier Reef is another. The basic facts are plain. It is a chain of more than 3,000 islands, some mere specks a few hundred yards across, but others much larger, strung along the Queensland coast for over 1,200 miles, roughly from the Tropic of Capricorn to the tip of the Cape York Peninsula.

It was discovered in 1770 by Captain Cook, who sailed about two-thirds of the way along it, hugging the coast, before the *Endeavour* (370 tons) struck a reef, and he realized that he had come upon one of the great natural phenomena of the world. Two centuries later, there are still islands that are uncharted and unexplored—indeed, there may be islands that did not exist when Captain Cook arrived, for the reef is largely made of coral, and coral is made by tiny animals called polyps, and polyps are continually at work in numbers quite impossible for the mind to grasp—continuously getting born, living, dying and making new coral. The reef is in a state of continual creation, as one school of thought believes the stars to be. It is the largest deposit of coral in the world and covers an area of over 80,000 square miles.

Two distinct kinds of island form the reef: coral cays and atolls, and the tops of mountains that were formerly part of the mainland and have been turned into islands by the gradual sinking of the continent. These, of course, are ordinary islands, for the most part hilly, and forested in places right down to the sea. Aborigines formerly lived on some of them but have gone, and most of the islands now are uninhabited; less than a dozen have hitherto been recolonized for tourists. The coral islands proper are far from being ordinary; they are very extraordinary islands indeed. Many of the ordinary islands have coral fringes, which are gradually growing, and so have become a combination of the two.

This reef is a tantalizing place to visit because the sights you see are quite impossible to describe or even to memorize. No one can usefully write about colours, shapes and patterns, any more than about music; the words are empty. You can say a blue is deep, an orange glowing, a red is rusty, or a green is emerald, and what does it mean? How can you convey the dreamlike fantasy of an undersea forest of seaweed or garden of anemones, the incredible population of tropical fishes, the coral-encrusted clams? It cannot be done. The wonders that lie under water far exceed in fantasy, in splendour, in richness, in colour, in sheer and startling inventiveness anything to be found on the surface of the globe. It is a savage universe, full of ogres and goblins, and given over to the unremitting efforts of one species to eat another, often by slow and ingenious means.

There is nothing soft and delicate about this universe except the colours, nothing gentle but the slow motion of a waving tentacle. All this beauty is a mask for the implacable, the ruthless, the ferocious purpose to survive. This is a cruel, pitiless and sinister world—a world without love. And what is all the beauty for, the subtle delicacy, the lovely harmonies of colour, the extraordinary shapes and patterns? Who delights in it or who is repelled? What purpose does it serve? Why all the ingenuity, the inventiveness run wild? Surely a coral reef poses more questions than can ever be answered by that magic formula used to explain every phenomenon of the natural world: natural selection.

It was on a coral reef that Darwin first received the Word that was to revolutionize scientific thinking so profoundly; it may be on a coral reef that some later genius will clothe in a respectable theory the sneaking notion, the little niggling worm of doubt, that whispers—for there is no blacker scientific heresy—that the theory of natural selection, while it accounts for a great deal, cannot, in the final reckoning, account for everything.

[2]

Normally I am against an aerial view of earthly things; it tends to create delusions of Olympian detachment. But there is no doubt that to fly over it is much the most exciting and illuminating way to be introduced to coral. There, spread out below, you can see the very birth of atolls. First there is an outer rim of dusky, pinkish brown, something like the colour known as old rose. This rim encloses a lagoon. The contrast between the deep, dark sapphire of the ocean and the pale, hard, opaque turquoise of the shallow lagoon is very striking. The depth of the lagoons varies from a few inches to three or four feet. Through a faintly crinkled film of pale-blue water you can see the pattern of the coral like a mottled lizard's skin, a pattern wildly ramified into loops and twists and lumps and ellipses, craters within craters, just under the sea. Light blue and old rose are the predominant colours.

Down there are the polyps, at their work of creation that has been going on for millions of years and will continue, we must presume, for many millions more. There are reefs as much as *ten thousand feet* deep, built inch on inch by these little animals, each no larger than a peppercorn, and related to the sea anemones. The coral, formed from lime extracted from the sea, is the polyp's outside skeleton; you might compare it to the shell of a stationary snail. Each little depression is the seat of a polyp that has died—if indeed polyps can be said to die, for they multiply by the budding of their cells and so in a sense are immortal.

They also have a sexual phase. Certain polyps develop rudimentary testes which release sperm; when this drifts into the apertures of polyps that have developed equally rudimentary ovaries, minute polyps hatch and enjoy for a few days freedom of movement until they find a suitable place to settle down. This is one way by which polyps colonize new regions; another is by lumps of coral breaking off a reef and being carried to new shores. They are great colonizers but face a constant struggle for existence and are continually being killed by cyclones, direct sunshine, breakers and fresh-water floods.

The existence of coral was known to the Romans and no doubt to others before them, and the red Mediterranean variety has been a valuable article of commerce since pre-Christian times; but how it was formed remained a mystery until a French naturalist, de Peyssonel, in 1727 discovered it to be composed of living animals. His fellow scientists called him a liar, and it was not until 1751 that London's Royal Society published his findings. Coral-forming polyps, it was next found, cannot live below about thirty fathoms—180 feet; the cold kills them. If they can live only in this shallow top layer of the ocean, how then can they have built their structures thousands of feet under water? It was formerly held either that the ocean bed was gradually lifting up the reef or that the corals built only where underlying rocks rose to within 180 feet of the surface.

In 1836 H.M.S. *Beagle* reached the Cocos Islands with young Charles Darwin, aged twenty-seven, on board. After demolishing both of these theories in a few brisk sentences, he advanced one of his own, as revolutionary as it was simple.

> If then the foundations, whence the atoll-building corals sprang, were not formed of sediment, and if they were not lifted up to the required level, they must of necessity have subsided into it; and this at once solves the difficulty. For as mountain after mountain, and island after island, slowly sank beneath the water, fresh bases would be successively afforded for the growth of corals . . . I venture to defy anyone to explain in any other manner, how it is possible that numerous islands should be distributed throughout vast areas—all the islands being low- —all being built of corals, absolutely requiring a foundation within a limited depth from the surface.*

Plenty of scientists took up his challenge to advance other explanations. The obvious way to find out was to sink a bore and see how far down the dead coral extended. An expedition sent by the Royal Society to Funafuti in the South Pacific sank a bore to a depth of 1,114 feet. They struck no rocks, no sediment, only pure coral. To clinch the matter, when the Americans exploded nuclear bombs on Bikini Atoll they took "seismic shots" which traced the coral down to 2,566 feet and failed to find any basement rock 7,000 feet below the surface. From this they estimated that the corals must have been at work in the Mocene Age, between twenty and thirty million years ago. So, more than a century after he advanced his theory, Darwin was proved right.

[3]

I visited both kinds of island, one made of coral and the other of ordinary materials; this was Lindeman, one of the Whitsunday group, uninhabited until Mr. Angus Nicholson arrived in 1923 with a wife and three small children and the disability of having lost his right hand and a part of the arm in a dynamite accident. They found a sort of Robinson Crusoe island, with some pawpaw trees and wild goats left behind by a previous settler who had departed. Mrs. Nicholson used to

* *The Voyage of the Beagle*. Charles Darwin. Everyone's Library, ed. H. Graham Cannon, 1959.

shoot goats to feed the family when her husband was away in his yawl. One day a black cow swam ashore. Floods had swept her down a tributary of the Proserpine River and she had traversed something like eighty miles of sea. She was none the worse and in due course produced a healthy calf.

The island is three miles square and possessed of beaches of pure white sand with no soul to be seen on them and shady places where the roots of trees are almost tickled by the waves. As it is a national park, no wildlife may be molested or destroyed. Paths tidily kept up by the Forestry Department take you through woods of native eucalypts and casuarinas mixed with palms and coconuts, and the handsome so-called umbrella tree which has dark-red flowers and enormous, fleshy leaves radiating outwards from a center like the spokes of a wheel. Birds of sea and shore mingle with those of tropical woodlands, and it would be tedious to list all the species even if I were able to do so, which I certainly am not. But two species come to mind when I recall Lindeman Island. The first is the clumsy, ungainly, rather absurd swamp pheasant, or coucal (*Centropus phasianus*), which runs swiftly on the ground but when it takes to the trees might almost be thought to have got at the grog, so heavily does it plop into the branches. Its long, brown-barred tail is responsible for the name, but it is no relation to the pheasant; it is a kind of cuckoo and the only one among Australia's fourteen species that builds a nest—though I am told there is not much building; the nest is in a tussock and roughly made, with two openings, through one of which it pokes its long tail.

And then there are the rainbow lorikeets (*Trichoglossus moluccanus*). At first I could scarcely believe in them. At certain times of day whole flocks of them swoop swiftly from the trees, screeching their heads off—hideous voices emerge from those gorgeous royal-blue throats and crimson beaks, as if the French and British nobility on the Field of the Cloth of Gold had conversed in strident cockney—to descend upon a bird table beside the swimming pool of the hotel, where water, bread and honey await them. As good Australians, they have exceedingly sweet—not teeth; beaks?—and possess tongues especially adapted to brush nectar from eucalypt and wattle blooms. Their plumage is a harmony of rich, full-bodied blue (head and throat), scarlet and yellow (breast and under tail), and vivid shamrock green (back and wings). When they settle down to bread and honey, packed close as bees and unbelievably radiant, they allow the tourists, almost as numerous and as gaudily clad, to approach with cameras to within ten or fifteen yards. Then, as if at some word of command, suddenly they lift their wings and are gone like a cluster of jewels shot out of a gun.

Another memory of Lindeman Island, more sinister than beautiful, is the nest of the green ant. Many nests, in fact; there are trees gravid with them. They hang down like rust-brown fruit, each the size of a pear. Bravely, I considered—what snakes and spiders are to many, ants are to me; I find them terrifying and abhorrent—I plucked one of the nests and tore it open. Inside was a honeycomb of compartments with wafer-thin, brittle, papery walls.

To make these nests, green ants must use the leaves of only certain kinds of tree, which are never eucalypts. The workers line up along the edge of one leaf, holding on with their hind legs, and grip another leaf with their jaws, and pull the two together. Then other workers take in *their* jaws the grubs of their own species, whose mouths secrete a fluid that, on exposure to air, hardens to form the case of a cocoon. The workers jab the grubs' mouths against the margin first of one leaf, then of the other, thus binding the two with the sticky fluid. So they weave a web between the leaves, using the grubs as a shuttle. Another trick mastered by these workers is to clamber over each other's bodies to form a living chain, five or six ants long, which enables them to grasp a leaf several inches away. The nests at first resemble large buds, but soon the leaves wither to a bronzy colour. The more I looked into the thickets, the more of these nests did I see, reminding me of hanging Chinese lanterns. There must have been thousands.

The bite of these ants, I was told, is most unpleasant; they secrete an acid which was used by aborigines as a cure for colds. The natives steep dozens of nests in water and drink the brew. They also eat the grubs raw and consider them good tucker—good grub, perhaps one should say.

[4]

Of all the numerous coral cays and atolls, only two have been "developed" for tourists. As Darwin observed, all are low and flat and have no fresh water. An atoll has a reef-enclosed lagoon, a cay has not. Heron Island, in the Capricorn Group and at the reef's southern extremity, is a cay and one of the largest—less than half a mile in diameter and practically circular, and nowhere rising more than ten feet above sea level. As you approach the island, it looks like a floating bottle top with a white base and a green cap. The cap is formed mainly by pisonia trees whose seeds were brought from South America entangled in the feathers of sea birds. To ensure this form of distribution, the pisonia seeds are mounted in a sort of cat's-cradle of sticky filaments which adhere to the birds' plumage. The island is packed with noddy terns whose Latin name, *Anoüs stolidus,* means senseless stupid—far too packed, they amount almost to a pest and make the camp smell of guano. At night you are continually stumbling over them in the loose sand and when you flash a torch often find this glaucous tangle smothering their wings—yet another pisonia seed from South America.

As if the noddy terns were not enough, Heron Island is also full of muttonbirds camped out in pairs in holes in the sand, who howl at each other all night. Their howls are remarkably loud, persistent and more like the voices of hyenas than of birds. These apparently are immature muttonbirds, without nests or territories, who are practicing at mating, but unfruitfully—avian teen-agers, more or less, so many *Catchers in the Rye.* I felt sorry for them, but they did not make for restful nights, and altogether there was too much avian life for any but the most dedicated bird lover.

Perhaps I am being unjust; it was only the noddies and muttonbirds that were too much of a good thing. A charming little bar-shouldered dove with a blue-grey head, and plumage as gay and speckled as a pheasant's, pecked round the queer-shaped pandanus palms, whose branching clusters of roots, which grow above and not below the surface, look like pyramids of stacked poles. Dotterels, waders, terns, stilts, oyster catchers and of course innumerable sea gulls frequent the beach; on land there may be visiting quails, silvereyes (related to the tree creepers), the shining-bronze cuckoo and the spangled drongo, whose exciting name is belied by its rather drab appearance, like a starling's, although it is not one, belonging to a family (*Dicruridae*) on its own. The ornithologist Leach calculated that 100,000 birds bred on a single island on the reef, an island considerably smaller than Heron, no more than a hundred acres in extent.

As we approached the island, we saw a group of reef herons feeding, some white and some grey—the bird has two colour phases. At high tide the reefs are naturally submerged, so these herons can visit them only at low tide and often fly considerable distances from the nearest land to reach them. The birds have developed a built-in mechanism to ensure that they will exactly synchronize their flights with the tides, so as to arrive when the reef is exposed. No one knows how this works; but then no one knows how migrants navigate by the stars.

You reach Heron Island in about five hours from the port of Glad-stone. The sea can be rough and the launch small and crowded. There is no jetty, so from the launch you jump into a dinghy which a stalwart young man in bathing trunks tows to an ancient truck standing hub-deep in the pellucid, blue-green water. Hoisted and hauled onto the truck by more stalwart young men, you perch on boxes, or cling to your neigh-bour, while the vehicle jolts across the jagged coral. When you de-bus you are greeted—or at any rate we were—by the howls and shouts of several individuals in fancy dress, one in long plaits made of tow and a hula-hula skirt, another smeared with soot and clasping a spear and bow and arrow to represent an aborigine. This unofficial welcome was de-signed to put us all into the right mood of bonhomie and get-together-ness. As our party consisted mainly of middle-aged or elderly package tourists, somewhat rheumatic and hailing from less matey lands, and as we had all been tossed about for hours and longed mainly for a cup of tea, or even something stronger, I am afraid the well-intentioned gesture misfired. However, we got our tea, and the man with the tow plaits and hula-hula skirt reappeared with a chain of beer-bottle tops round his neck in the guise of mayor and made a speech of welcome we were now more ready to enjoy. That night there was a barbecue with more dress-ing up and get-togetherness, but after that we were left to go our own ways.

[5]

Twice a day, at low tide, the custom was to walk about on the reef and observe what had been uncovered. The going is not easy; you stumble into rock pools, stub your feet on branching corals and feel the coral crunching and sometimes giving way under your feet. The sun is blistering, except when low tide happens to coincide with early morning or late afternoon, and the glare is blinding. An hour or so of this is tiring, but fatigue and discomfort are forgotten as you peer at the aston-ishing world underfoot. Here you may recapture a sense of wonder unknown, perhaps, since childhood. In a few square yards you can see a greater variety of shapes and patterns than the boldest artist could dream of, and there are thousands of square miles of this. No two ramifying branches, no two twigs, or cavities, or caves in miniature, or thumb-sized mountain ranges, are alike. And all this has been created by these myriads of tiny polyps. Why, you ask, in heaven's name, why? All this beauty and inventiveness of design cannot be necessary for mere survival. The object can scarcely be to enrapture tourists or to provide islands for muttonbirds to howl in. The whole thing baffles the mind.

On this particular stretch of reef there are 180 different species of polyp, and each not only shapes its coral skeleton to a different pattern and colour but has a different habit. Some grow around the edges and die in the center, such as a large, round one in pale blue closely crinkled by chestnut ridges. Others grow all over, such as a moss-green one honeycombed by pale-brown ridges. Small clusters of what appear to be green grapes quiver beneath a gently lapping tide; clumps of brilliant scarlet cactus blooms are one inch high; there is a bunch of bright mauve fingers. There is an extraordinary one—but they are all extraordinary—that looks exactly like a beaded purse studded with pearls and flung down on a table with the contents making bulges and hollows; the cinnamon-brown beads are sewn thickly on to green satin. Staghorn or antler corals may be blue, heliotrope, purple, pink, yellow, green or lavender, buff or lemon, or any combination of these. They branch into protuberances which make them look, as their name implies, like the proliferating horns of elks or reindeer. So-called brain corals, looking like lumps of brain flung down in the water, are everywhere; and mushroom corals, which are also correctly named; and dome-shaped porites which may be twenty feet in diameter; clusters of violet spikes that look like petrified buddleias—the tally could continue for pages. Each polyp is equipped with tentacles to entrap its prey, or possibly to shoot it with a tiny barbed and poisoned dart; all are carnivorous and feed only at night. Some tuck into their tissues colonies of algae, tiny plants which use the carbon dioxide that is breathed out by corals during the hours of daylight to synthesize into chlorophyll, the foundation of all life on this planet.

In among the corals there are many other forms of sea life: blood-red or apple-green that withdraw into a crevice as you approach, and soft starfish, patches of vivid green algae, tube worms coloured royal purple corals that wave long, pale-blue hair and attach themselves to other corals or to clams, which they gradually strangle.

And the clams! Sometimes their rough shells are encrusted all over with the pastel-shaded, delicate, waving tentacles of soft corals tinted rose-pink and honey-yellow, powder-blue and dove-grey—and all remorseless and death-dealing. I recall a giant clam whose dark, carmine lips gaped from the coral floor in a crooked smile of unbelievable malevolence; then its thick lips closed, and clenched. There was a clam of a glowing midnight blue I have seen elsewhere only in early medieval altarpieces or in antique mosaics, stylishly set off by coal-black edges. One had a coat of deep velvet green flecked with orange; another, crimson with maroon bands. Some of these giant clams, the world's largest bivalves, weigh between two and three hundredweight.

Among all this, tiny fish dart and forage, gulls and terns sweep and wheel, minute shrimps are active, and the obese, pulpy, repellent sea cucumbers, also known as *bêche-de-mer* and as trepang, lie torpidly. There are thousands of them, and I have no envy for the Chinese custom of eating them. If alarmed, they expel in a turgid jet their entire insides, then settle down and grow a new set. This procedure would certainly dispose of duodenal ulcers, but then no creature seems less likely to contract them. Snapping shrimps might be more ulcer-prone because they are always active. As they move across the sandy sea bed, they make tracks like miniature snowplows and stir up sediment from which gobies, small and slender fish, stationed at the mouths of their burrows, extract their food. Gobies do not appear to do anything for the shrimps in return. But no one knows for sure, so gigantic is the field of the unknown, so tiny the store of garnered knowledge, concerning this marine universe.

[6]

The reefs ends abruptly and drops seventy or eighty feet into the ocean bed, and presumably, in places, to the full 180 feet which is the coral habitat. To explore this region you need to go skin diving, but even by swimming about with goggles you can see a good deal. So we hired a boat and set out well before dawn, accompanied by Julie. Everyone who goes to Heron Island knows Julie, if only because every morning she holds a bird parade. Most of the island's birds know about this, too, and assemble at eleven o'clock for a distribution of scraps of food, while the tourists line up opposite for a distribution of scraps of information.

The only scientific research station for the whole of the Great Barrier Reef is on Heron Island. Considering the degree of scientific ignorance, you might expect to find an academic establishment manned by numerous biologists. Instead, I found a few empty beach huts among the pandanus palms. The former director had left, the new one not arrived, and no one was there to direct except Julie, who augments a very small grant from the C.S.I.R.O. by the sale of photographs and underwater paintings. The Great Barrier Reef Committee, associated with the University of

Queensland, is in charge. The state of Queensland does its best but, despite great resources, it is a poor state and in receipt of Commonwealth bounty. You cannot but wonder why all those lavishly endowed and generous American and international bodies, such as the Ford and Rockefeller and Gulbenkian and many other foundations, appear to take no interest.

Julie looks like a mermaid down to the waist. Clad from head to foot in black tights, with a ballet dancer's graceful figure and long, ash-blond hair streaming over her shoulders, you can well imagine her combing out her locks on a moonlit rock and singing softly to the fishes. She told us, indeed, that fishes follow her around as if seeking to communicate with one of their own kind. With her to guide us, off we went in the boat, anticipating a glorious dawn and a tropic sun to warm our backs, for it was unexpectedly cold as we chugged over the top of the reef. Soon it grew colder instead of warmer. By the time we got beyond the reef and the sky had lightened, a cold wind was blowing a misty half-drizzle in our faces and the sun remained behind a dense black cloud. Could this be the Barrier Reef in the tourist season? Shivering in our swim suits, we huddled under skimpy towels and sucked oranges, wishing we had brought a flask of coffee and thinking more and more gloomily about the forthcoming plunge.

Even Julie seemed reluctant to join the fishes. Our cowardice apart, corals need sunshine; their colours fail to glow in dull light. So, at any rate, we told ourselves; and, shameful to say, the plunge was never taken. Instead we landed on the reef and walked about. Lack of sun had prolonged the feeding period of the corals and they were still active, waving their tentacles if these were wavable, and if not, as in the case of staghorns, in appearance more lively looking and seeming almost to glisten.

To some extent—not of course to the full extent—we were able to make up for our failure by a trip in the glass-bottomed boat. This is a trip every tourist makes and it is enormously rewarding. As soon as the boat is over the reef's edge, a world of sheer fantasy unfolds. Enormous, terrifying caverns yawn below you and their walls are honeycombed with caves. So clear is the water that it seems to sharpen rather than to cloud your vision, so that every stone and shell and clam and coral can be seen in its glowing colours on the white sand. Then comes an abrupt end to the shelf, and down the eye is led to depths where light can never penetrate and eyes are sightless. Here are great clumps of elephant's ears, huge elkhorns, pincushions, ledges, and what look like enormous pancakes stacked layer on layer.

Anything could lurk down there. Fish dart and gleam and vanish into caves. There are shoals of small, quick, electric-blue demoiselles, large parrot fish with peacock-blue scales and yellow stripes, fish bandaged in back and white with golden tails, flat yellow boxfish, surgeonfish trailing behind them a protuberance like a scalpel, big creatures as fugitive as shadows, sharks and stingrays and octopi—goodness knows what else, all preying on others and being preyed upon from birth till death, world without end. And all in these brilliant colours and with no eye to see and enjoy them.

You could drift above that secret, silent world all day. The frenzied, groping arms of coral look like claws turned to stone in the midst of some wild bacchanalian dance. Here surely must be monsters: one-eyed, scaly ogres and creatures half shark and half man; black and coiled sea serpents, and sea Calabans chained in caves. Sonorous words from a half-forgotten childhood poem came thrumming back: *Call her once and come away. This way! This way!* It is no good calling. *And alone dwell for ever the kings of the sea.*

[7]

My last memory of Heron Island is of a mass of baby turtles about three inches long, newly emerged from shells resembling ping-pong balls. These islands are the breeding grounds of the big green turtles (*Chelonia mydas*) that have been so cruelly persecuted because their flesh makes good soup. (Or so they say; I have never tasted any.) Now the harmless turtles are protected everywhere along the reef in theory, but the reef is not policed. They are safe on inhabited islands like Heron, where there used to be a turtle-canning factory. In order to preserve their flesh until a convenient moment came to collect it, the killers, or harvesters, or whatever is the correct word, used to turn the turtles over, thus exposing their unprotected underparts to the scorching sun; the creatures could not right themselves and must have suffered agonies. An even nastier practice was described by Darwin as occurring in the Chagos Archipelago. The natives lit a fire on the back of the living turtle, which caused the shell to curl upwards; then they prized the shell off and returned the turtle to the water. Surprisingly some grew new shells, but these were "too thin to be of service," Darwin wrote, "and the animal always appears languishing and sickly."

You can walk round Heron Island in twenty minutes and, if you do so first thing in the morning, will, at this time of year, come upon tracks across the sand very like small-scale versions of those made by army tanks. These are the tracks of she-turtles returning seawards after prodigious egg-laying feats during the night. First she scoops a hollow in the sand above the tidemark, then she drops into it anywhere up to two hundred round white eggs. As these measure between an inch and an inch and a half in diameter, and the average clutch is 120, her achievement is impressive. Normally she will repeat this three or four times in a season, and seven clutches have been known.

A turtle egg has a poor chance of becoming an adult turtle. Only about half of them hatch. Then these baby turtles must find their way, like mallee-fowl chicks without benefit of parental teaching, to the sea. Some miss the direction; many are picked off by sea birds and ghost crabs, and only a small proportion survives these hazards. Even then they are far from safe from sharks and other predators. However, the reproductive and the death rates of turtles were nicely balanced until the intrusion of the human predator serving commercial markets. Here on the reef the turtles have been reprieved, but that is not the case elsewhere. In most parts of the world the turtles are being exterminated to gratify the greed of soup guzzlers. No wonder she-turtles shed tears as they release their eggs.

The time came for us, like the turtles, to leave Heron Island. At three o'clock in the morning, in pitch-darkness, we found our way across the sandy beach to the ancient truck, to be heaved as before by the stalwart young men onto its platform. The dinghy was hard to locate in the dark, and the stalwart young men had a job to heave us all, including a couple of over eighty, aboard the *Capre II* without a rope ladder. But all was accomplished; huddled on fish boxes, we saw the dawn across a choppy sea and made our landfall at Gladstone.

NINETEEN 〰〰

South of Capricorn

The town of Gladstone, population 8,000, stands on the brink of revolutionary change. You would not know this if you walked along its sun-pickled main street with a pub on each corner, one restaurant, and a general store kept by a respected Chinese called Mr. Lookee. At the bottom of the street is the sea, and at the top the homes, each set in its trees and lawn, a church for each branch of the faith, and the schools.

Most of the houses were built by Mr. Golding, who personally planted nearly all the trees. Mr. Golding is chairman of the Harbour Board and of practically everything else in Gladstone. His grandfather was present at the birth of the town, which took place on a day in 1854 when Captain Maurice O'Connell ran up a flag in the bush overlooking a bay called Port Curtis. Matthew Flinders had so named it and landed there in 1802, but after that it had remained just a stretch of uninhabited bush on a fine, wide bay.

As well as building all the houses and chairing all the boards and committees, Mr. Golding nows all the local history and was interested in my name because H.M.S. *Rattlesnake*, with Thomas Henry Huxley on board, anchored here for about three weeks in 1848. The young biologist, then only twenty-three, might have made some interesting observations in this scientifically virgin territory, but recorded in his journal symptoms of an odd malaise that stifled his intellectual curiosity; instead of collecting specimens, he lay in his cabin reading light novels and Dante's *Inferno* and complaining about the weather. Off Dunk Island he wrote: "Rain! Rain! The ship is intensely miserable. Hot, wet and stinking. One can do nothing but sleep. This wet weather takes away all my energies. I try to pass the time away in thinking, sleeping and novel-reading, which last is a kind of dreaming . . ."

When you consider that at the foot of the gangway lay Dunk Island with its fringing coral and great wealth of birds and of marine creatures, and there in the stuffy cabin lay the great biologist of the future reading a novel he described as "not exactly a first-rate one," you can only wonder what had gone wrong. A few months before, in Sydney, he had become engaged to his future wife and he was tormented by self-doubts and a conviction of his own unworthiness; moreover, he was recuperating from a severe illness. The result was an intellectual blackout. Fortunately he recovered and within four years was elected to the Royal Society. But it seems unlikely that he made observations of any value at Port Curtis, even when it stopped raining.

The settlement of 1854, renamed Gladstone, grew slowly into a small port serving, without undue effort or ambition, as an outlet for the produce of the back country and of a coal mine about a hundred miles inland. It is still a torpid, easygoing little country town where everyone knows everyone else, social life revolves round the church you belong to and the school your children attend, and the *Gladstone Observer* comes out twice a week and is edited, set and printed by the owners, man and wife, in one of those cluttered little office-cum-printing works smelling of wet printer's ink and littered with type and galleys and empty teacups.

Poor Gladstone! The future is about to explode in its dozing main street with all the force of a nuclear-propelled rocket. Strangely enough, the event that is to transform Gladstone is taking place 1,000 miles away. This is the exploitation of one of the largest, if not *the* largest, deposits of bauxite in the world, at Weipa on the Cape York Peninsula. The bauxite is to come down the coast by ship and to be treated at Gladstone, and here is to arise the largest alumina extraction plant in the world.

Mr. Golding took me to see one set of enormous machines scooping an enormous hole out of a hillside to make an enormous reservoir—the plant alone will swallow up 2,000,000 gallons every day, he said—and another set of equally formidable machines making a causeway to link the mainland to an island where the deep-water quays are to be. So a new city will arise, full of new people; Gladstone will grow large and rich and will lose its identity. Everyone will no longer know everyone else, or Mr. Golding personally plant all the trees, or Mr. Lookee supply nearly everyone with groceries, or the *Gladstone Observer* be set by its owner and appear twice a week. But everyone will have a higher standard of living.

The United States is supplying over half the capital for the plant;

Canada and France are each contributing one-fifth; less than one-tenth will be Australian. Once more I was asked, "What's happened to the British? Aren't they interested in us any more?" and once more was unable to suggest an answer. Most of the alumina is expected to go to Japan. Relations between the Japanese and the Gladstonians appear to be excellent. I observed a Japanese vessel in harbour loading coal mechanically, with no human being in sight. There *are* sailors, however. "They behave like gentlemen," I was told. "Which is more than can be said of some of our own people. The Japs put us to shame." The captain gives sake parties on board in an atmosphere that is friendly but correct, and in return Gladstonians entertain the officers. "You can take them home to dinner and they cause no embarrassment," said one of their hosts. "They fit in." Russian vessels also come, to load wheat. I asked how the Russians behaved. "Like bloody foreigners!"

The restaurant where we dined had no license, so my companions and I took along a bottle of Hunter River claret and asked if we might drink it with our evening meal. The waitress looked surprised at the question and gave a rather crushing answer. "Most people bring champagne!"

[2]

Back of Gladstone lies the brigalow. You cannot travel far in central Queensland without hearing the word "brigalow" spoken, as a rule in tones of hope and confidence. Like bauxite, the brigalow is to bring wealth to Queensland—not by coming, however, but by going.

Brigalow is a kind of tree, *Acacia harpophylla*. Like many other trees, it can take on different guises according to the conditions under which it grows. Given root room, it can become a handsome tree sixty or seventy feet high with a straight trunk and silvery-grey foliage, but where it grows in thickets it is spindly and whippy and no more than twelve or fifteen feet high. As a rule, other kinds of tree are mixed in with it: trees with good Australian names like belah, wilga and gidgee, or with made-up ones like yellowwood, sandalwood and bonewood. It spreads by sending suckers up from knobbly roots, like the mallee; so, when cleared, it is a brute for coming back again.

Brigalow is only to be found in eastern Queensland, save for a little in the north of New South Wales, and needs a rainfall of twenty inches or more. By Australian standards this is a high rainfall, so all the brigalow country is potentially valuable. The Tropic of Capricorn roughly bisects it, and from north to south it stretches for about 700 miles, extending inland from 50 to 150 miles. Queensland has about twelve or thirteen million acres of it—an area more than twice the size of Wales—and about half of this remains entirely undeveloped. In a continent so short of land with a respectable rainfall, why should this great belt of country, within easy distance of a coast so well equipped with harbours, have been left undisturbed? The brigalow is like the Hydra; no sooner do you fell one trunk than half a dozen others spring up in its place. Hercules defeated the Hydra by applying a burning brand to the trunk each time he struck off a head. The same treatment was given to the brigalow, but even that did not do the trick; Australia's native vegetation has learned to live with fire.

Another factor that formerly prevented the conquest of the brigalow was the prickly pear. This queer-shaped cactus, which looks like a collection of flat, shiny ears stuck haphazardly together and is covered with spines, was introduced by some misguided soul as a nice ornamental garden plant. By the late twenties it had colonized much of the brigalow country and might well have taken over most of Queensland had it not been for one of the early triumphs of biological control—that is, the control of plant or insect pests by living creatures, generally insects, bacteria or viruses. (Myxomatosis is an example.) The prickly pear is a native of South and Central America, and a natural starting point for research into its control was to find out what prevented it from becoming a serious pest in its native habitat.

Insect predators proved to be the principal answer, in particular a scale insect called *Cactoblastus cactorum* which I remember seeing for the first time near Farnham, where insect predators were bred in what was called a "parasite zoo" and dispatched to every quarter of the world where crops and livestock were suffering loss from pests susceptible to this form of control. *Castoblastus cactorum* fell upon the prickly pear in Queensland so effectively that, over millions of acres, the cactus wilted and died. When, some thirty years later, I drove across the Darling Downs, perhaps the most fertile land in all Australia, I spotted by the roadside two or three miserable, stunted little prickly pear plants, the sickly remnants of an invading army that had formerly sealed off this whole productive region from development, until laid low by a humble and, for once, a virtuous wog.

Now it is the turn of the brigalow, which is being subdued by two modern techniques. One is the use of heavy-duty tractors advancing in pairs through the bush like trawlers, dragging steel cables and heavy chains. The cable, suspended between two tractors about twelve or fifteen feet above the ground, bashes down the trees with a levering action that uproots them; the chain, dragged along the ground, disposes of the undergrowth. Between them, chain and cable shave the landscape as if with a giant's razor, so quickly and expertly that a pair of tractors can deal with thirty-five or forty acres a day. Then all the wrenched-out, battered vegetation is raked into windrows and burned. The other modern technique is the hormone weed killer sprayed from the air, which checks the regeneration of the suckers; then comes the heavy plow to consolidate the conquest.

[3]

At the end of 1962 the Queensland Government, aided by a Commonwealth loan, launched a scheme to develop by these means about four million of the remaining six or seven million acres of brigalow. Although the area was undeveloped, all of it was leased, and the scheme involved repossessing some of the leaseholds, subdividing them, and releasing to new settlers. This is no project for the honest battler with his brawn and axe. Only those who can lay their hands on a sizeable lump of capital may take part in ballots held periodically to allocate available land in blocks of between 5,000 and 10,000 acres—no small holdings this time. One of the settlers, in fact, is a sheep baron from Tasmania who arrived in his own aircraft, bought up extra land and has already cleared 8,000 acres. Another told me that he was investing over $60,-000 and getting 6,000 acres into production.

Some critics say the scheme needs too much capital and is doomed to economic failure; a Commonwealth survey, on the other hand, estimated that a well-managed property should pay well. It is too early yet to say which view is correct. Beef is intended to be the mainstay, raised on improved and managed pastures. To build up a good beef herd takes at least four or five years. Many brigalow settlers are taking a short cut by planting wheat, which brings its rewards within a twelvemonth. Wheat is one of the easiest crops in the world to grow, but also one of the most dangerous, because it leaves the soil exposed to wind and rain at a critical time. Dr. Griffiths-Davies has declared his opinion that "growing wheat on brigalow country will create problems of soil erosion the like of which Queensland has never before seen." Over the years fertility has been accumulated by the roots of the brigalow, which is a legume, and fixes nitrogen from the air. If wheat is grown, these stocks will be exhausted within about ten years. The only way to replenish them, in Dr. Griffiths-Davies' view, is by grazing animals intensively on well-managed pastures. The main reason, he says, that India and China cannot feed their people is because they have neglected the animal; farmers in Europe deploy the animal and by and large have kept most people fed. In Australia "it is vital that the animal is interposed between human beings and the environment."

Not long after I left Queensland, a ferocious dust storm blacked out most of the state for eighteen hours, leaving a deep quilt of dust and suffocating sheep by the thousand. A pilot met the dust 350 miles out to sea, and Brisbane meteorologists calculated that, if evenly spread, it would cover the whole state, all 400 million acres of it, to a depth of one-tenth of an inch. This storm was only one of several. Another pilot flew across the Center from Woomera to Tennant Creek, a distance of about 1,000 miles, without once seeing the ground through the layer of dust beneath his aircraft. To live amid these constantly repeated dust storms can be sheer misery. The dust gets into everything, into the food, into eyes and ears and clothing, and the life of women is a never-ceasing struggle to keep the dry, abrasive particles at bay. Sometimes the lights have to be kept on all day.

This is no new story. Wind erosion, following the destruction of the earth's protective coat of grass and trees, has stripped topsoil from many parts of the world with devastating effect. What will happen when cable, chain and hormone spray have stripped away the brigalow? Nowadays the experts know how to avoid disaster; the question is whether, lured by the prospect of quick returns, people will take their advice, or whether they will continue, as James McAuley put it in *The True Discovery of Australia,* to

> smile
> And sit on their verandas taking tea,
> Watching through the pleasant afternoons
> Flood, fire and cyclone in successive motion
> Complete the work the pioneers began
> Of shifting all the soil into the ocean.

Once the brigalow goes, wildlife goes with it: the wallabies and bandicoots, echidnas and phalangers, and many of the birds. Conservationists have been striving hard to persuade the Queensland Government to set aside part of the area as a nature sanctuary before it is too late. They have secured half-promises, but no more. Before a sanctuary can be officially declared, consent must be given by every branch of government that might be concerned, including the Department of Mines, whose interest in mineral royalties generally eclipses an interest in wildlife. A proposal to reserve 62,000 acres of brigalow nearly came off, but the area might have harboured minerals—any area might—and consent was refused. Another, and a smaller, area was suggested; this time another department raised objections, so hitherto *no* sanctuary has been declared. And every year tractor, chain and cable and the hormone spray strip more of the protective coat of vegetation from these vulnerable Queensland soils.

[4]

I met a young doctor who had been a registrar in a hospital in the north of England where the pay was poor, the smog was horrid, the winds were cold, the equipment antiquated, the work exacting, the prospects of promotion dim; so he decided to go to Australia.

The doctor and his wife were a thorough couple and collected maps and books about Australia, looked places up in the encyclopedia and corresponded with officials at Australia House. They did not fancy a large city; they wanted a smallish town, but not too small: plenty of sunshine, but not quite in the tropics; on the sea for choice; good prospects in a general practice. They sought a pleasant, interesting and not too demanding life and, after a lot of thought and study, hit upon a town of 25,000 inhabitants on the coast of Queensland. They had never met anyone who had been there, nor indeed had they previously heard of it, but it seemed to meet all their requirements. They chose Bundaberg.

Scarcely had they reached this decision than what should they see but an advertisement in the *British Medical Journal* inviting applications for a partnership in a Bundaberg practice. The young registrar landed the job. After building up expectations of an ideal town, an ideal climate and an ideal life, it seemed impossible that they should not have been disappointed. Far from it, they said; Bundaberg was even better than they had hoped. The sun always shone, except for a couple of months during the monsoon season when things were not quite perfect, they agreed; even then, the sun came out between downpours. On wonderfully white beaches they could splash about in a warm sea; the children were healthy as puppies and the colour of dates; for recreation they could fish and sail. Living was cheap; they had fruit in abundance and the most delicious prawns. (I had some: they were.) There was no traffic problem; no one was in a hurry. The pay was excellent and the doctor warm in his praises for the health system, which strikes a compromise between private and public medicine.

There is no National Health Service as such. You choose and pay your own doctor and surgeon; you pay your hospital charges. But almost everyone is insured; the Commonwealth Government subsidizes the fund, and on average, the patient recovers nine-tenths of the cost of being ill. If he cannot pay, his medical benefit association will do so, leaving the patient to refund his share when he can. Sometimes, by a remarkable freak, people even make money by being ill. A man of my acquaintance had appendicitis, went to hospital, rendered an account of all the charges to his medical benefit association and received a check for the full amount plus $32. Naturally this does not often happen, but the fact that it can injects into an otherwise conventional insurance scheme that element of gambling so dear to the Australian heart. No one is financially ruined by falling sick, as he can be in America; the abuses taken for granted in Britain do not prevail; doctors retain their professional freedom and do not complain about their rewards; and the sick get a pretty good service, so far as I could judge.

What is there so special about Bundaberg? Perhaps nothing very much; perhaps other small towns along the coast are equally agreeable. It is not industrialized as Gladstone will become, or vulgarized like Surfers' Paradise. The only industry appears to be making rum, which imparts a pleasant, fruity odour of molasses to that part of the town, on the river, where the large and obviously efficient distillery stands. The girl who set my hair said that she had come to Bundaberg to escape the turmoil and pressure of life in Brisbane. To the people of Sydney and Melbourne, life in Brisbane would seem, I imagine, about as relaxed as Bundaberg seems to fugitives from Brisbane. A current of rat-race escapers appears to flow gently up the coast and into the tropics from the hectic southeast corner where everything is generated in Australia: Melbourne and Sydney to Brisbane, Brisbane to Bundaberg or Yeppoon or Mackay, then, I suppose, on to Cooktown; perhaps refugees from the turmoil of Bundaberg have taken shelter in Cooktown. That is about as far as you can go, unless you take to beachcombing on Thursday Island, or settle on some uninhabited coral reef. But I met no one who wanted to leave Bundaberg.*

For naturalists, I was told by Mr. Harry Frauca, Bundaberg has everything: biologically unexplored country within ten miles; mangrove swamps and river inlets full of crabs and flying foxes and the frogs

* I since have: an acquaintance writes that he and his wife are "leaving Bundaberg for hilly country about 200 miles away where there is still forest so far untouched by the bulldozers and tractors that are spoiling things round here."

which are Mr. Frauca's special concern; little need of clothes and none of heating; fruit in the garden, fish in the sea. When the spirit moves them, into a battered car the Fraucas—he a migrant from Spain, she from France—load their cameras and swag, and off to the bush they go for as long as they feel inclined. This is freedom. "Life here is simple," Mrs. Frauca said, "but it is rich." Only one thing worries them, and that is the rape of their adopted country's wildlife and natural resources. "What the Australians are doing to their country," Harry Frauca sadly said, "is unbelievable."

[5]

The Walla run on the Burnett River is an old-established property, as things go; incorporated into the house is a bit of an original homestead built around 1870. Now it is a typical Queensland station homestead in that life takes place on a wide, encircling veranda, and a great many people turn up for meals; the number matters little, since the Deepfreeze always holds bits of bullock neatly stored in plastic bags. The daughters of the house grill, roast, or fry the meat three times a day. Sometimes they exchange their shorts for skirts, put on sandals and go to Brisbane for a dance or other ploy; they must, I suggested, welcome a bit of chicken or veal for a change? "No, at restaurants we *always* order steak," they said. The eldest daughter has married onto a sheep station, so has nothing but mutton. "You get used to it," they added, "either way."

The dark, stained timbers of the house have been polished to shine like glass. The floorboards of ironbark and spotted gum were hand-sawn sixty or seventy years ago and beautifully laid, and their darkness is restful in a land of brilliant light. There is solid, heavy late-Victorian furniture and silver to match, taking you back to a childhood when widowed aunts dwelt in large, dark houses with a lot of chocolate paint, old maids and possibly a butler who cleaned the silver. Here, I suppose, the daughters do it when they are not inoculating bulls or mustering steers. Their father, Mr. Hugh Innes, has a famous Brahman stud. These Asian cattle, with their long, floppy ears and long, amiable faces, their sloping quarters, their creamy colouring and shiny satin skin, are so quiet and patient, so neat in their movements and so dignified; perhaps it is an accident that they have never been used for the "sports" of baiting and fighting, but it could also be that they would not respond in that violent, tragic manner of other breeds which is needed to satisfy the sadistic instincts of mankind. Mr. Innes is also an expert on birds. So was a previous governor of the state, who used to visit Walla for a weekend's bird watching now and then. I was told a story, certainly untrue, that in order not to disappoint his guest Mr. Innes had been known to station his daughters at strategic points in the bush, instructing them to imitate the call of some rare bird—rare enough to be exciting, but not so rare as to arouse suspicion—when the party approached.

Now drought has shrunk the Burnett River to a shadow of itself. This drought is like a corpse in the house; you feel its presence, and though you may keep off the subject, it is always there. Windmills are motionless, everything is silent and waiting; grass is eaten to the roots, the sinking sun a hard red disc that drops below the sharp, clean line of the horizon. The sugar cane, normally so bright a green, is rusty brown, and this year only irrigated cane will reach the co-operative factory at Gin Gin with its expensive and up-to-date plant. In a few years only irrigated cane is likely to be grown in this part of Queensland, and most of it will be mechanically harvested—two more nails in the coffin of the small man.

The homestead commands a fine view over the valley of the placid river and has a garden full of shady trees and birds. In the evening a bird in a mango tree called persistently—a sad, lonely, piercing squawk. The leaves were black against a dark lavender sky. From the black banks below the garden, where the river faintly gleamed, came an answering call. Try as I might, and close as it was, I could not spot the bird amid the branches and for a fleeting moment wondered whether Pat or Caroline might be having her joke. But later on I saw dark, swooping wings against the lavender sky. It was a nankeen night heron, most handsome of birds, chestnut-plumaged and white-fronted, with a long white plume streaming from the nape of his neck. Every evening he takes off from the same tree to join his mate calling from the river and hunt for food along the muddy banks.

[6]

Eidsvold, like Walla, is an old station, and the walls of the original homestead, made of thick, roughly hewn slabs, are pierced by holes through which the early settlers poked their muskets at marauding blacks. The first Eidsvold squatter took up 100,000 acres and brought in sheep. This is spear-grass country. Spear grass (*Heteropogon contortus*) has sharp, pointed seeds that pierce the fleece and flesh of sheep, which have therefore given way to cattle. After World War I the Queensland Government, in hot pursuit of social justice and equality, split up most of the big runs for closer settlement. Eidsvold's 100,000 acres were reduced to less than 1,500, and small farmers were given leaseholds of 160-acre blocks and told to make a living out of dairy farming.

This advice was misguided. Spear-grass country lacks certain minerals; the grass itself is low in nutriments, and in those days improved pasture plants to replace it had not been bred or even thought of. The best these spear-grass pastures could do was to carry one beast to twenty acres. To make a living out of small-scale dairying was impossible. So the settlers lost their savings, got into debt and finally gave up a hopeless struggle. Bit by bit graziers bought back the derelict land. Gradually Eidsvold built up again to one-third of its former size, but in scattered blocks. Mr. and Mrs. Barney Joyce, its present owners, bought another run on the Burnett, and so the outcome of it all is that a single family has restored the unit to its previous acreage, but instead of being in one piece it is broken into fragments which are more difficult to manage; and in the process quite a lot of other families have gone bankrupt. So much for matching egalitarianism against ecology.

The Joyces were away, but in their absence their nephew, Mr. Anthony Coates, kindly showed me something of the station, which is famous for its Santa Gertrudis cattle introduced from the King ranch in Texas. These cattle are a mixture of three parts Brahman blood to five parts shorthorn and are well adapted to the hot, dry conditions of the north. All the work of the station is done by aborigines, and Mr. Coates does not find them unreliable, unduly drunken, or apt to disappear on walkabouts; but then they are half-bloods born on the run or in the neighbourhood, who would probably be little more at home at corroboree than I should. Their pay is the same as a white man's, and they have much the same virtues and failings.

Even for successful stud breeders the costs of bringing 100,000 rundown acres into a high state of productivity are such that parts of the property are leased to farmers who share both the expense and the returns. Such a one is Mr. David Feez, who farms about 6,000 acres; he provides the labour and equipment and a guarantee to clear so much land each year, while Eidsvold's owners provide land and cattle. Normally the share farmer takes two-thirds of the profits. This year Mr. Feez will take no profits. Singlehanded, he put 1,000 acres under wheat, sorghum, linseed and oats; all have failed. There will be other seasons, said the tough, redheaded, undefeated Mr. Feez; one day rain must fall. If the season is right, so will the profits be.

As we drove through his wilted crops, we came suddenly upon a bougainvillaea bush in full purple blaze among the brigalow and belah trees. Beside it was a crumbled stone wall. Here was a ghost home, a vanished garden. On the 6,000-acre block leased by Mr. Feez there had been twenty-six separate leases and twenty-six homes. All have vanished, and the bush has returned.

We picnicked by a bunyip pool. The bunyip is a creature of hideous mien who snatches bad children from their homes and eats them; this muddy pool, trapped at the bottom of a creek amid a thick stand of eucalypts, was obviously made for bunyips. If you listen long enough, Mr. Coates said, sooner or later you will hear a sort of gasp, almost a human sound, and you might see a ripple. This is not a bunyip but a lungfish coming up for air. Here on the Burnett is the original home of this amphibious fish (*Neouratodus spp*) which retains, as do so many Australian creatures, a number of primitive qualities and has changed little in the last 100 million years. Like those who escaped to Bundaberg, Cairns or Cooktown, the lungfish has kept out of the piscine rat race and gone quietly on inhabiting its muddy pools, heaving itself to the surface every half hour or so for another gulp of air, and able if it must to migrate overland. A fair-sized one will weight forty pounds. I listened for a while but heard no lungfish. In theory they are protected throughout Queensland, but "the boys," Mr. Coates told us—the blacks—cannot resist a little fishing now and then, and lungfish are easy game.

Flights of wood duck wheeled over the pool while we boiled the billy; white cockatoos screeched in the trees; one of the bell magpies gave his wonderfully melodious, liquid call. I got properly confused about these bell magpies, which are also called currawongs and butcherbirds—butcherbirds because some store their prey in trees—and pipers. They are not related to the European magpie, but are what Leach and Morrison call "glorified butcherbirds." They inspired Alfred Russel Wallace to call them "white crows that sing"; they are neither white nor crows, but they do sing. Leach and Morrison list fourteen species of the family *Cracticidae*. The least confusing of the various names, to my mind, is currawong. The naturalist John Gould wrote that "to describe the note of this bird is beyond the power of my pen." It is certainly beyond that of mine.

[7]

"Welcome to Coolyar. Est. 1902, population 875. We Love Them All. Drive Safely." Beyond this roadside notice another plaster soldier on his pedestal with rifle reversed turns his back on empty shops with faded names above cracked, dirty windows. Coolyar is another semi-ghost town.

In midafternoon the heat was paralyzing and the need for moisture imperative. There was the pub, but my companion and I were indubitably females. Queensland is the only state in Australia, and I should not be surprised if it were not the only part of the world, where women are debarred by law, not merely by custom, from entering a public bar. In Brisbane the wives of two university lecturers recently padlocked themselves to the rail of a bar and challenged the police to eject them, while the male customers stood them beers. The police came and sawed off the padlocks, but instead of removing the two young women to the cells, they left them in the bar, remarking as they departed, "Enjoy yourselves, and don't get too tight." There the matter rested when I left Australia, but it was generally thought that sooner or later the Queensland legislators, who are seldom in a hurry, would get around to enabling their wives and daughters to walk legally into a bar.

Defying the laws of Queensland, we slunk into the bar. Four men with weather-beaten faces, all lean, leathery and lined, their hats tilted on the backs of their heads, were talking about cattle. One was praising a bull he was trying to sell for $80. A bull was a bull, we were only women, and they paid us no attention. The publican's wife did not encourage us but equally could scarcely throw us out, and perhaps soft drinks were less criminal than beer.

It was not gold or copper that semi-ghosted Coolyar but hoop pine. Forests of this pine, one of Australia's very few softwoods, had formerly surrounded Coolyar; a sawmill had provided employment and attracted a railway. Then the pines had come to an end, as trees will if no one bothers to replace them. The sawmills had closed. I recalled Harry Frauca's words: "What the Australians are doing to their country . . ." But now the State Forestry Department is repairing some of the damage, and we passed plantations of young pines. We passed also a mob of cattle whose hides were tightly drawn over jutting bones and who were bellowing with hunger, and truckloads of sheep and cattle heading south, presumably for slaughter yards in Brisbane, where sheep were selling for less than fifty cents apiece. Then we came to a small lagoon in a cup among the trees, covered with mauve lilies. Spidery-legged chestnut and white Jacanas flickered on the surface of the leaves; black and white ducks rippled among them; white egrets dozed ankle-deep in the lagoon. A watermark stood high upon the bank above the shrunken surface of the pool. The time was approaching when the ducks would have to move on. For how long would there be water for them to move to? This year tens of thousands, hundreds of thousands, were doomed.

[8]

My visit to Eskdale arose out of a casual conversation with a man I met one evening in Hobart. "I've an aunt in Queensland," he said, "with a station you might like to see . . ." I thought no more about it until I received an invitation from Mrs. White. Of the many remarkable women I met in Australia, none was more remarkable than Mrs. White. When her husband died she took over their station near Toogoolawah to such good purpose that she has since bought two more properties, one twice Eskdale's size. There is no detail of the management she does not supervise, no technicality of the stud breeding she does not direct.

A small, white-haired, fragile-seeming woman of close on seventy, who looks as if she would not say shoo to a mouse, she laid on a dinner party for ten the evening I arrived. And what a dinner! A fine lace tablecloth, finely cut and polished glasses, table napkins folded into boats, for decoration orchids growing out of shells, silver candlesticks . . . The meal began with avocados stuffed with shrimps, went on to steak with all the trimmings, then two frothy kinds of sweet, then a savoury; it must have been cooked by remote control, for there was Mrs. White among her guests, and I saw for myself there was no one in the kitchen. To cap it all, next morning she left the house at four o'clock to fly to Sydney for a business appointment. I still find it hard to believe that, concealed somewhere about the comfortable and rambling house—or perhaps like the bunyip, at the bottom of the swimming pool—there was not a posse of goblins, released at night to scurry round with floor polishers, whip up puddings and arrange flowers, like those stitching mice who came to the rescue of the Tailor of Gloucester.

Mice . . . Pondering later on the determination of so many Australian women—though few quite to the extent of Mrs. White—never to let their standards slide, it came to me suddenly that mice held the clue. At the Eskdale dinner party one of the guests had told me of her start in

Queensland. The daughter of an Anglo-Irish landlord; she had come from Ireland as a bride to a waste of virgin bush in northwestern Queensland. Her husband had knocked up a corrugated-iron shed and there they were, a long way indeed from salmon beats of the Shannon and the Dublin Horse Show—no sanitation, no garden, no water beyond what they hauled in buckets from a creek, no neighbours; just abundant flies, snakes and rodents.

"First," she said, "we had a plague of rats. They went through the place like a revolting cyclone; they ate everything—my shoes, my clothes; they got into the food store, they ate the plants I'd been growing round the house. Literally they made me sick. Well, they went, and then came mice. By that time we had an extra room and were expecting a guest, and I'd made up the bed. The guest was a couple of days late, and when I went to turn down the sheets they'd all been eaten, and there were dead mice inside the bed stinking to high heaven. How I loathed it all! Half the time I was in tears, and then the baby came, and I was scared to death the flies would bring infections, or he'd get bitten by spiders or snakes . . . I stuck it out somehow, and when we got on our feet we took on a manager and moved to another place, and for years I couldn't bring myself to go back. I still feel sick when I think about those mice. . . ."

It is because the corrugated-iron humpy with its flies and mice and earth closet is part of the experience of so many outback women that they are so determined never to revert. It is all too raw and recent to be brushed aside; the cracked cup held too much bitterness. The extra trouble that these undaunted women give themselves amazes those of us more ready for compromise. But then we are not haunted by mice.

TWENTY ﹏﹏

Birds and Beasts

For sheer ugliness, the string of holiday resorts that straggles south of Brisbane from Southport to Tweed Heads on the New South Wales border—the Gold Coast, so-called—would be hard to beat. Beach huts, souvenir shops, motels, bait stalls, filling stations, hot-dog stands, cafés, caravans, dance halls, swimming pools, Bar-B-Q's, choox bars, power cables, advertisements for everything members of an affluent society can possibly need, projected by every means the fertile minds of advertisers can devise—it is all a visual nightmare; but it brings a lot of satisfaction to a lot of people from Sydney and Wollongong, Wagga and Newcastle, and indeed from all over Australia, and a lot of money to Queensland, where the value of tourism, at the present rate of growth, will soon eclipse that of beef or sugar.

Tucked away in all this, there is a sixty-five-acre oasis of woodland and hillside that borders on a small estuary and is preserved as a nature sanctuary by David Fleay—"a slave to animals for thirty years," as his wife described him. He manages his sanctuary without subsidies, grants, or any source of income beyond a very modest admission charge of thirty cents a head, supplemented by his own earnings as a journalist. The press gets abuse for its misdeeds but less often credit for its good ones, such as its support of wildlife conservation, both editorially and, even more important, by paying naturalists to write about it. No doubt this is not done for altruistic reasons, but it has nevertheless enabled many a naturalist to survive as such and to continue his study of wild creatures. Money paid by the Brisbane *Courier-Mail* for Mr. Fleay's weekly contribution goes towards the keep of platypuses, koalas, snakes and possums. It costs the Fleays much more to keep their famous pair of platypuses than it does to keep themselves.

Past the dingo kennels by the entrance—a healthy dingo in his rich,

396

glowing, orangy-yellow pelt with his gingery eyes is a wonderfully alert, attractive dog—the visitor comes to a wooden kiosk, where a bell on the counter will summon one or other of the Fleays from a small back room littered with paper, letters, reference books and all the paraphernalia of a working journalist. Dozens of letters pour in—how do you rear a kangaroo joey? What is the best way to mend a broken wing? I saw a funny-looking bird yesterday (sketch enclosed); will you please identify it? What do parrots eat? Do lizards bite? Each query is time-demanding; the Fleays have no secretary, and deadlines for the delivery of articles approach. Yet there is always time to show round and entertain a genuinely interested visitor.

David Fleay is a tall, kind and gentle man of rising sixty who was born with an affinity for animals and with the timeless patience of the naturalist by instinct rather than by training. He started life as a teacher at Ballarat Grammar School. Animals were always his passion, and his chance came when the Melbourne zoo invited him to start a section devoted entirely to Australian fauna. He went on to direct and reshape the Healesville Sanctuary, where he won international fame as the first and only man—still the only man—to breed the platypus in captivity. A person of independent mind, profound beliefs and complete indifference to the values of the market place, he fell out with the trustees, resigned, and scratched a living for himself and his family until he was able to buy a piece of derelict coast in southern Queensland and start a small sanctuary of his own.

Today, if he were to sell the sixty-five acres he bought before this coast was "developed," he might become a millionaire. Instead, he is worrying about how to pay schoolboys for buckets of earthworms to feed the platypuses, refusing television teams permission to photograph the shyest of his animals because it would upset them, and turning down a large advisory fee from Hollywood because the film's director wanted dingoes organized to chase and kill kangaroos. David Fleay keeps his eyes steadily averted from the main chance and fixed instead upon such objects as a white-breasted sea eagle that has been known to frequent this estuary for twenty-eight years. Mr. Fleay thinks it may live to be a hundred.

He will show you a pair of taipans that entwine themselves around his arms and shoulders and have their venom glands intact. In his time he has milked many snakes for venom and was the first man ever to tackle a taipan, one of the three deadliest snakes in the world. (The other two are the Hammerdryad and the African black mamba.) He dislikes to milk them because, he says it destroys their trust in him. This pair has kept its trust, he is certain—"we helped them out of the egg." He has bred and sent to zoos nineteen taipans. "They attack you only if they're frightened." He handles many other kinds of venomous snake just as freely.

Most impressive of his many birds is the Powerful Own (*Ninox strenua*), a big brown-and-white-dappled bird, the largest owl in Australia. The strength of his talons gave this bird his name; he drove them so hard into his captor's arm that Gould, who first described the species, had great difficulty in prizing them apart. His screech is as formidable as his talons and (according to Morrison) has brought men rushing from their beds to the rescue of women they supposed were being murdered in the bush. David Fleay has five of these owls and is trying to breed them. A secret of breeding, he says, is to provide fresh, *natural* food *ad lib* and not substitutes. A lad drove in a pickup piled high with branches for the koalas, who in these parts insist on three kinds of eucalypt and three only: red gum, scribbly gum and tallowwood. As civilization advances, these become more and more scarce.

[2]

Platypuses are the most exacting animals of all to feed. Each has a daily intake of between five and six hundred earthworms, forty to fifty yabbies (small fresh-water crayfish), and a steamed egg. When the ground is dry and earthworms hard to get at, a pair costs $30 a week to keep—more than an elephant. They will eat half their own weight in food, and sometimes more, every day—every night, rather, for they are nocturnal feeders. But in midafternoon this pair is enticed from its seclusion into open tanks and fed for the visitors' benefit.

Platypuses (*Ornithorhynchus anatinus*), Mr. Fleay said, were paddling about Australian lakes and rivers long before the human species emerged. They are mammals, but only just: they rear their young on milk but have no teats; the milk seeps through an area on the abdomen and the young platypus, which for its first three months is blind and helpless, merely licks off the liquid. As everyone knows, platypuses lay eggs like reptiles but are not reptiles, and, like reptiles, have venomous fangs. These are in the form of spurs on the male's hind leg, and he will—but only under extreme provocation—eject a poison causing his enemies severe pain. Of enemies they have many—foxes, dingoes, snakes, goannas and eagles that eat eggs and young, and above all men, who catch them in fish nets. Probably it is longevity, Mr. Fleay thinks, that enables the species to survive, for they never produce more than two young at a time. So far as anyone knows, they live for about twenty years.

Altogether they seem to be in a biological muddle, with their duck bills and webbed feet and mammary glands and venom. I was surprised at their smallness. Mr. Fleay's female is only about sixteen inches long, and much of this is taken up by the paddle-shaped tail. We watched her weave swiftly about under water with her eyes shut, as if skirting numerous obstacles. One visitor aptly compared her to a small, mobile hot-water bottle with a fur jacket.

Platypuses come in season only once a year for about a fortnight and lay their eggs—three at the most—in nesting chambers at the far end of a tunnel up to forty feet long burrowed into the banks of streams and creeks. These tunnels are intricate structures, and it was partly the difficulty of copying them in a sanctuary that made the breeding of the captive creatures so hard. A Sydney naturalist called Harry Burrell designed and built the first of such structures and coined the name "platypusary" for it. There must be a place for the occupants to lay their eggs, a dry place to sleep, a place to comb their coats, a place to shake out the water, and so on. "You must humour platypuses," Mr. Fleay said. They hate being handled and seek shelter when it rains because the raindrops hurt their sensitive beaks.

It took Mr. Fleay nine years to get a platypus to breed. The task was accomplished to 1943 by a female who had been six years in the Healesville Sanctuary. Her short incubation period is spent curled up with her eggs, not much larger than a sparrow's, in her lap. When he calculated that the young would be about two months old, Mr. Fleay opened the platypusary to find a furious mother guarding a blind, fat, wrinkled creature only nine inches long and quite helpless. Terrified that the disturbance had been premature and would cause the mother to destroy her young, he replaced earth and grass, and it was touch and go for several days; but the maternal instinct triumphed, and the child, a female, was successfully reared.

Others of Mr. Fleay's favourites include two species of quoll, or native cat. Attractive little sharp-nosed, brown-and-cream spotted creatures, smaller than an average cat, to which they are no relation, they are among the few real killers in Australia. They are marsupials and will carry as many as eight tiny joeys in the pouch. Now they are becoming very rare, because of the destruction of the forests in which they dwell.

[3]

In his West Burleigh Sanctuary, David Fleay has paddocks that have been grazed for ten years without intermission by wallabies and kangaroos, and they have done no harm to the pastures. "The native fauna does *not* destroy the habitat," Mr. Fleay said. "Sheep do—men do." Men have certainly destroyed the sand-dune habitat of this stretch of coast, once famed for wildflowers, whose predominant plant is a banksia shrub known as wallum (*Banksia aemula*)—all gnarled and twisted branches and greeny-grey leaves, with a bottle-brush flower and seed pods that have been likened to evil old men with slit eyes. You still see wallum, but thousands of acres of it have been cleared by land developers and have a sad, abandoned look, flat and hot and naked.

When it comes to conservation, Queensland's record is poor. There was the shameful koala story. Now there is concern for the grey kangaroo. I have mentioned the figure of 1,305,011 kangaroos and wallabies "harvested" in Queensland in 1964. The figures over the last ten years are as follows:

1954	218,459
1955	305,616
1956	361,462
1957	631,034
1958	295,820
1959	1,006,919
1960	769,948
1961	471,640
1962	548,771
1963	642,063
1964	1,305,011
Ten-year total:	6,556,743

These included grey and red kangaroos, wallaroos, and whiptail, brush, swamp and sandy wallabies; well over half, in some years two-thirds, were grey kangaroos. In 1960 there were 1,775 registered shooters—mainly men who, in the words of Professor Marshall, "make money by killing anything that hops."

Can the species stand up first to "harvesting" on such a scale and then to this terrible drought? One of the two Fauna Officers employed by the state, Mr. T. Kirkpatrick, is carrying out research. The official belief is that "there is no quantitative evidence that past and current practices have had a detrimental effect on State-wide marsupial populations." The fact that there is no evidence does not mean that evidence does not exist; it may mean that no one has as yet found, or even sought, that evidence.

On paper the Queensland wildlife situation looks healthy. Over the years private individuals have set aside areas as nature reserves—the first to do so were the Archer brothers who started Eidsvold in 1853 and preserved a lake near Rockhampton as a sanctuary for waterfowl—and the government has added others. There are today 661 fauna sanctuaries—many of them islands—totalling some 20,650 square miles, about 3 per cent of the state. These are quite separate from the national parks which are administered by a different department. "It looks much better than it is," Mr. Fleay said. "Whole habitats are left out—the brigalow, for instance. Many of the sanctuaries are in private hands, the owners' powers are limited, and staff to enforce the law is quite inadequate"

The trouble is the usual one—the spread of people; as Mr. Charles Roff, the state's Chief Fauna Officer, has put it, there is "human pressure on the land, heavy pressure, growing pressure." Gone already is a lot of forest, many wildfowl that once flighted over central Queensland, the wildflowers of the wallum. The plains turkey or greater bustard, which is in theory totally protected, is threatened with extinction. "There are feathers by the roadside all the way to Darwin," David Fleay said.

Many people say they would not care to be immensely rich. I would, and then give money to people like David Fleay who struggle with so little help to keep inviolate a few nooks and crannies of an older, quieter, and more secret life. Now a Conservation Foundation has been started to study and co-ordinate the whole setup in Australia, and there is need for at least a dozen such millionaires, since no government, here or elsewhere, has yet recognized that defense against the actual destruction of the habitat by its own citizens has become just as urgent a matter as defense against hypothetical foreign aggressors.

A little way down the coast is the Currumbin bird sanctuary where, every afternoon at four o'clock, thousands of rainbow lorikeets arrive on the wing to accept bread and honey from trays held out to them by thousands of tourists who arrive in coaches from the opposite direction. Both lorikeets and people are punctual, friendly and colourfully clad. Here is a conjunction that brings pleasure to both parties and harm to neither and demonstrates that the interests of humans and of wild creatures can, with imagination and a bit of trouble, be made to coincide.

[4]

There are parts of Australia as dull, monotonous and depressing as anywhere in the world, and there are parts whose beauty is supreme. Into that second category rises Mt. Lamington. If I had seen no other part of the continent, I would have been grateful to have seen this rain-forested mountain on the border of Queensland and New South Wales. I owe my visit to Francis Ratcliffe of the C.S.I.R.O., who wrote so memorably of the place in his *Flying Fox and Drifting Sand,* which today reads as freshly as it did when it was published in 1938. "Whatever else you miss out in Queensland," he said, "don't miss Lamington, and stay at O'Reilly's guesthouse." I took his advice.

Only a few years back I should have got there by pack horse, instead of bowling by car in the utmost comfort along a splendidly graded road. This starts quietly enough from Tamborine through open stands of tall eucalypt; then suddenly you are in a rain forest, where the road must writhe and corkscrew around precipices and crevasses like a demented snake, poised for some distance on a razor's edge with a tremendous drop on one side into a black chasm, and on the other, a slope where trees have thinned out into a park land carpeted in brown. A party of wallabies, the pretty-faced or whiptail, frolicked under the trees. All wallabies are pretty, from near-kangaroos to tiny quokkas, but these have especially appealing, delicate faces. A handsome green-winged pigeon with an opallike green sheen on his back and wings, and white bars on his shoulders, stood in the road until the car almost hit him before taking off. The country is wild, tumbled and magnificent. Gulleys, crests and ridges, green glopes and black jungles; grandeur and tranquillity; evening shadows sharp as knives, a sky blazing with a prodigality of colour—no wonder we arrived benumbed by splendour at the guesthouse the O'Reilly family have created in the middle of the forest, surrounded by the birds and streams and giant trees of the national park.

In the aromatic early morning one of the O'Reilly brothers could be seen milking a Jersey into a bucket in a field or emptying bins onto a

dump in the forest. At four-thirty A.M. Anne O'Reilly lit an old-fashioned wood-burning stove in the kitchen, and a pot of tea stood on the
hob from then on, available to anyone who liked to be about early and,
if he pleased, spear a slice of bread on one of those long-handled toast-
ing forks I have not seen for years and hold it up to the embers. No
other toast is half as good as this; an electric toaster bakes the slice
instead of singeing it quickly on the surface to leave the inside moist and
fresh. Besides, toast should always be slightly burned.

You please yourself at O'Reilly's guesthouse and everyone seems
pleased to see you, including a crimson rosella that sits on the kitchen
window sill, and flocks of fire-browed finches, like rubies on the wing,
that descend at intervals on the bird table, and currawongs that call
melodiously nearly all day, and the brushturkeys, who were so tame I
thought at first they must be domestic turkeys, albeit somewhat small
and slim. Once I realized that these were members of the famous family
of megapodes, the mound builders, together with the mallee fowl and
scrub fowl, I must admit to being rather disillusioned. Here were these
birds with such miraculous habits, constructors of enormous mounds—at
least half a dozen such were to be seen within ten minutes' walk of the
guesthouse—and they had become common scavengers. They haunted
the rubbish dumps. One morning I counted over twenty scratching about
among the eggshells and potato peelings and empty tins. They had shed
all their mystery. However, there they were, in scores, and more or less
on holiday, for at this time of year there is a lull in their building
routine. They have the same built-in temperature-testing mechanism in
their tongues as the mallee fowl; their young have the same astonishing
instinct to dig their way out as soon as they are hatched and fend for
themselves, but they do not make use of solar heat, relying wholly on
the fermentation of compost to incubate their eggs.

Over our large and communal tea Mrs. O'Reilly told us how this
enterprise began when two O'Reilly brothers were eaten out by rabbits
in western New South Wales. All the grass went, the sheep went, everything living went except the rabbits; sick of deserts, the O'Reillys sought
the opposite extreme. On Mt. Lamington they literally hacked a way
into the hills; they even had to cut steps for their pack horses. Seven
male O'Reillys—the two brothers and their sons—set to work on the
trees. They had to clear a space and sow grass seed before they could
bring in so much as a goat and half a dozen hens. In two backbreaking
years they cleared sufficient ground to use a plow they brought up on the

pack horses. Things had just about got going when the blow fell. Mt. Lamington was declared a national park. This did not deprive them of the land they had actually settled on, but it finished their chances of getting more and buttoned them into their holding.

At first this appeared to be a major disaster; but after a while they began to detect advantages. National parks bring people; people want food. O'Reillys could grow it. A market would come to their door. So they built a few extra huts and declared their home a guesthouse. And guests came, still on pack horses, and presumably robust guests; if rain really set in, they might be marooned for a month. On one occasion rain fell for a week without stopping, and all the flour went mouldy. "Amenities," as we know them, did not exist; and, splendid as these mountains are, when shrouded in thick mist and blotted out by perpetual storms, they would be hard to appreciate. But many waters quench neither love nor tourists, and the guesthouse thrived.

[5]

Queensland's Forestry Department, which looks after national parks, has cut paths that twist tactfully about the ridges avoiding all steep climbs and slippery slopes—real old folks' paths; but at least they are paths and not roads, and you do have to walk. And nothing could be more delightful, especially when accompanied by Syd Curtis, the Forestry Officer who supervises the park, and by Gus Kouskos, the warden, who has lived in it for forty years and is on intimate terms, it seems, with every tree, creeper, fern, epiphyte, wildflower, insect, beast and birds. I only wish I could have stored in my mind a sort of microfilm of all the plants and creatures that he named. We plunged into moss-green tunnels whose air seemed thick and viscous as Crême-de-menthe and emerged into dappled light and shade where shafts of sunlight pricked the green canopy. We gazed in silence at views opening suddenly over crest after crest of forest which was like an enormous, billowing, leafy ocean and suffused by a hazy lavender light from the smoke of distant fires.

Despite his close knowledge of the forest birds, Gus Kouskos often paused before identifying a call—it is all bird listening here, not bird watching—with a puzzled look on his face. This is lyrebird country—the Albert lyrebird this time (*Menura alberti*), said to be an even better mimic than the Superb species of the Dandenongs. We heard lyrebirds on and off all day, and the only call which I understood to be indubitably the bird's own was a ringing whistle to wind up a snatch of mimicry.

The most arresting call comes from the whipbird or stockwhip, a kind of shrike or whistler. (Again that confusing multiplicity of names!) It really is just like a snap of a lash, only a whistle rather than a crack. On all sides resounds this shrill and piercing note, made sometimes by a real whipbird but just as often by a lyrebird imitating one. The Lewin honey-eater emits a continual high-pitched, quavering, chattering sort of sound; the lovely oliver whistler comes in with his liquid, gay and thrushlike signature; the friendly grey ground thrush whistles merrily, and then there are the so-called catbirds.

The catbird, also sometimes called the gardener bird, is a close rela-tion of the bowerbirds. (Both satin and regent bowerbirds are found in Lamington Park.) It emits a screeching, not at all melodious note some-thing like a prowling tom's—hence the name. This call is often imitated by lyrebirds. And so is that of the rufous scrubbird, a close relation of the famous noisy Scrubbird of the west, which produces a high-pitched, almost continuous whistle. The rufous scrubbird is a mimic too. Half the birds in the forest seem to be mimics. I still have a memory of Gus, a short, stocky, broad-shouldered man, halting in the path like an alerted pointer with his head on one side while a positive cacophony of sounds came to us from all sides: whistles, whiplashes, cackles, screeches, warbles and twitterings. He was trying to identify a strong, high-pitched whistle repeated several times with a slightly different pitch on each occasion. The possibilities were that it could be (a) a rufous scrubbird *au naturel;* (b) a lyrebird imitating a rufous scrubbird; (c) a bowerbird imitating a lyrebird imitating a rufous scrubbird; (d) a lyrebird imitating a bowerbird imitating a rufous scrubbird; (e) a catbird imitating a bowerbird imitating a lyrebird imitating . . . But I have forgotten the rest. Only an Australian bird man could take all this without succumb-ing to a nervous breakdown. After a while Gus smiled—he had a partic-ularly sweet, gentle smile—and said he thought it was (b)—a lyrebird imitating a rufous scrubbird. I asked how he made that out. "Because the bird was in a hollow," he said.

After this experience I find it hard to believe that nature, or whatever it is that arranges these matters, does not possess a sense of humour, of the practical joking kind; or perhaps the birds have themselves evolved one and do all this to pass the time. Although I am sure pundits can, and do, work out complicated evolutionary reasons, it seems equally hard to believe that birds can derive from all this mimicking any really useful advantage as a means of survival. It is said that mimicking serves to confuse the enemy; but who and what are these birds' enemies? Most lyrebirds, bowerbirds and catbirds live on the ground in thick undergrowth and are pretty secure from sky-borne foes; in any case the raptors hunt by sight, not by ear, nor would they mind whether a lyrebird, a bowerbird, or a scrubbird was to form their dinner. The dangerous enemies are mainly beasts that prowl at night and eat eggs and young, like native cats, feral cats, foxes and sometimes dingoes. The mimicking does not occur at night; even if it did, the predator would merely be assisted by the sound, never mind who made it.

No, surely they do it to amuse themselves, and to play tricks on each other, and to fill a vacuum with sound. They mimic other things besides each other, sounds like saws and crying babies and barking dogs and creaking wheels. I wish that I had heard one imitate the explosive chattering of the kookaburra. But in various places I heard many kookaburras and perhaps some of them *were* lyrebirds, or bowerbirds, or scrubbirds imitating lyrebirds who were imitating kookaburras. The only way to be sure would have been to have taken Gus Kouskos with me all round Australia. He was just as good on plants and trees; and so was Syd Curtis, a forester by training, born and raised in these mountains, whose mother is perhaps the greatest living authority on the region's birds. So I was in good company.

[6]

Never have I seen more majestic trees, more romantic-looking trees, or more sinister trees than those of these McPherson Ranges. Into the majestic class go the hoop pines, here altogether finer, taller, prouder specimens than those I saw near Coolyar; the rose gum, rightly given the specific name of *grandis,* and several other eucalypts; and big, thick-foliaged trees with pleasing but vague names like red almond, saffron heart, bastard crow's ash and brush box. This last, with its pinkish bark, huge girth and towering size, is truly magnificent. The names of trees vary from state to state and are just as confusing as the names of birds, probably even more so, because the appearance of the trees themselves alters with the conditions under which they grow. I saw the brush box elsewhere, for instance in Hyde Park in Sydney, still looking handsome, but less than half the size. For once, it is neither a eucalypt nor an acacia, and its Latin name is musical—*Tristania conferto.*

The romantic tree, and the glory of Lamington, is the antarctic beech.

A tree so old that it was probably alive before the Romans came to Britain, perhaps when the Pharoahs were building pyramids and Homer telling Trojan tales, is a thing to marvel at, and these beeches (*Nothofagus antarctica*) are more magical than, say, Californian sequoias, because they grow in a sort of fairy ring. As the huge tree ages, it throws up from its roots a number of offspring that form a coppice round it, so that each moss-coated, knotted trunk, crumbling with senility, is encircled by a bodyguard of relatively young and vigorous beeches. It is as if the body of some venerable chieftain were to lie in state with his warrior sons around him, defying for all time the common fate of everything that lives and grows. I suppose this process could go on forever and that here is immortality, the tree that never dies.

These antarctic beeches, some of them between two and three thousand years old, are said to be the relics of immense forests that covered much of the Australasian land mass when the climate was a great deal cooler and wetter than it is now. It is something of a miracle that they survive in this one part of southeastern Queensland whose climate is relatively moist and cool, but scarcely comparable to that of the Antarctic. They have their enemies, and among them is the strangler fig.

Like many figs, this is an aerial parasite. A seed or sucker lodges in a crevice or fork of an existing tree and sends down whiplike roots that twist themselves round the trunk of the host, thicken, tighten their grip and, like a vegetable python, gradually strangle it to death. By then the hanging roots have reached the ground, dug in, and converted the fig from a parasite into a large tree standing on its own feet. So far as I could gather, the host has no defense against this form of parasitic attack. If that is so, there seems nothing to prevent the gradual triumph of the fig until it has murdered all its hosts and taken over the whole forest. I do not know whether this has ever happened, and of course it would take thousands of years.

Perhaps some parasite upon the parasite will emerge to keep the balance. Meanwhile, as the strangler fig trees continue to increase, so may the flying foxes who devour their fruit. When the wild figs ripen, great flocks, if that is the right word—mobs perhaps—of these monstrous bats with furry bodies and sharp-featured, foxy faces, assemble to occupy "camps" to which they return season after season. Although they are quite harmless to humans, apart from the damage they inflict on fruit crops, I was glad we did not see any, for they are creatures that make me feel nervous even when I read about them. Francis Ratcliffe, however, grew fond of them during his researches and did not mind their lice running about in his hair.

The other sinister tree abundant on Mt. Lamington is called *Laportea gigas*. Its large, shovel-shaped leaves look innocent enough but are invisibly covered with very fine hairs which secrete an acid. These hairs cause such excruciating pain that they have been known to kill people from shock. The stinging tree *Laportea* is like a gigantic nettle. To venture through this forest off the track must be a nerve-racking experience, far more alarming than the possibility offered by many African forests of bumping into large wild animals. Elephants and rhinos nearly always run away, or you can run away from them, and anyway, you can hear them coming. Stinging trees lurk in utter silence, concealed by creepers and ferns, and it must be all too easy to brush against one without even knowing you have done so until their red-hot needles start torturing you. Give me the savage animal any day, rather than the savage plant.

[7]

As we wound our way along the ridges, crossing many small streams and savouring the smell of moist earth and damp vegetation, I was struck by the absence of any living creatures larger than birds. In an African rain forest we should have seen the tree tops shake and seethe and hear chatterings and squabblings. Monkeys. There are no monkeys in Australia, or even a marsupial version of the race.

But plant life is incredibly rich. Never have I seen so great a variety of ferns: big, floppy tree ferns, epiphytes festooning branches, staghorns and elkhorns all over the place, lacy maidenheads leaning above innumerable little waterfalls. Nor have I ever seen so many waterfalls, each with an attractive aboriginal name like Coomera, Wanungra, or Bithongabel. Most of them are almost miniatures, falling into limpid little pools surrounded by lianas and creepers and set with flowering orchids in the forks of trees. There was a creeper I especially remember with a tiny white, delicate flower like a jasmine that smelled almost as sweet, though more faintly, and explosions of small, reddish, boxlike berries tumbling off another shrub that my companions called lily-pillies. All that these rocky pools lacked was Tarzan. One could almost see that agile individual swinging on a liana into the arms of a dusky beauty in a leopard skin.

We had to be content with blue crustaceans, crawling purposefully about the moist and shaded paths. They were the most decorative crayfish I have ever seen, the subtle blue of an antique Chinese vase, with white bands across the tail and red elbows. We saw dozens. Some walked backwards with their claws outstretched in a formal manner, as if executing a figure in some old-fashioned dance. Far from being filled with old-world courtesy, said my companions, they have testy and aggressive tempers; to prove it, Syd Curtis thrust a stick into the claws of a crayfish and put it back in the pool. "He'll drown that stick for sure," said Mr. Curtis. And drown it he did, good and proper, over and over again. If, as in some science-fiction film, the crayfish could have grown to the stature of a dragon, there is no doubt whatever what he would have done to us.

It may have been a she. We found several crayfish whose broad, rounded tail, shaped like a scoop, was packed with the little threadlike, squirming bodies of her newly hatched young. Predation must be heavy, or the pools and streams would become as full of crayfish as the western plains used to be full of rabbits. They make excellent eating, but everything that lives and grows in any national park is sacrosanct.

Even leeches? Every time we halted I picked dozens off my legs, which were soon covered with blood. But I cannot honestly say that the bites were painful or the creatures difficult to dislodge. No salt was needed, and they caused no subsequent sores. So really the leeches were quite harmless and greatly to be preferred to the merest touch of a stinging tree.

At our farthest lookout point we boiled the billy and gazed for miles and miles over the fertile, wooded valleys of northern New South Wales. This is one of the most favoured farming areas in Australia, with a fair rainfall, plenty of rivers and plenty of trees. Away across the misty valleys, fuzzed by the smoke of bush fires, lay the Pacific on the one hand—the aboriginal name for this spot was Boolamoola, "I see the sea"—and, on the other, the up-sticking thumb of Mt. Warning, so named by Captain Cook, and a queer lump called Mt. Lindsay that put me in mind of a frog rearing up and falling over backwards. Away along the escarpment stretched tier after tier of ridges, hollow after hollow of gorge and valley. Once, said my companions, these mountains were four or five times higher than they are now, and gradually erosion is wearing them down, like aging molars.

[8]

Near Mt. Lamington is Mt. Tamborine, once just as thickly forested as these McPerson Ranges, but now quite closely settled by dairy farmers and fruit growers. Bits and pieces of the forest have been salvaged by half a dozen small national parks—beauty spots and picnic places rather than true parks, the largest only 400 acres in extent and the smallest eighteen.

Judith Wright and her husband, Mr. KcKinney, took me to one of these. It must be an embarrassment to be labelled, as she so often is, as Australia's foremost poet, although gratifying to win a prize, as she has done, for "outstanding contributions to art and culture" awarded by the publishers of the *Encyclopaedia Britannica.* Judith Wright is as ardent a conservationist as she is accomplished a poet, and it was wildlife and how to preserve it that we talked about rather than art and culture. She showed me the piccabean, one of the country's few native palms, and explained why the roots of the black-bean tree, when they strike clay, branch out into a series of buttresses; she pointed out a coiled-up carpet snake and a plant called cunjevoi, wrongly thought to provide an antidote to the stinging tree, as dock to nettle. She told me that on the whole of Mt. Tamborine, once famous for its lyrebirds, only five pairs now survive.

It is from the soil and seasons, the birds she feeds and studies and the animals, and the trees and flowers, that she distills the vision from which her poetry is made. "We have lost the sense," she has written, "of belonging to our environment, and begun to believe that the environment belongs to us." This is *hubris,* and the root of tragedy. And hers is essentially a tragic vision of the world and human destiny, imbued with an archaic sense of fate and, I would think, a non-Australian perplexity.

> Whatever the bird does is right for the bird to do—
> cruel kestrel dividing his hunger in the sky,
> thrush in the trembling dew beginning to sing,
> parrot clinging and quarrelling and veiling his queer eye—
> all these are as birds are and good for birds to do.
> But I am torn and beleageured by my own people.
> The blood that feeds my heart is the blood they gave me,
> and my heart is the house where they gather and fight for dominion—
> all different, all with a wish and a will to save me,

to turn me into the ways of other people.
If I could leave the battleground for the forest of a bird
I could melt the past, the present and the future in one
and find the words that lie behind all these languages.
Then I could fuse my passions into one clear stone
and be simple to myself as the bird is to the bird.

Glossary of Australian Terms

Barcoo: a watercourse; term used mainly in western Queensland and Northern Territory

Barramundi: a fresh water fish

Billabong: an inland water formed by a loop of a river, which can reach the size of large lagoon: a cut-off meander

Billy: a straight-sided metal can with a handle which can be used for brewing tea over an open fire. Derivation: *Bouillon* tins sent to the gold fields and adapted to this and other purposes

Blue flyer: female young of the red kangaroo

Brumby: a horse gone wild

Bunyip: a mythical creature living at the bottom of pools or billabongs, derived from aboriginal legend

Bushie: a man at home in the bush and skilled in bushcraft

Bushrangers: bandits who lived in the bush—originally many were escaped convicts—and preyed on travellers and on lonely homesteads

Centre, the: remote, inland area of Australia

Choox: chickens

Chyack: to tease or taunt someone; to take him down a peg

Clearskins: unbranded cattle

Coacher: steady-going and reliable cattle used as decoys

Cobber: a mate

Cocky: a small farmer; also "cow cocky," a small dairy farmer

Coolibah: a species of eucalypt

Corroboree: ceremonial dance of the aborigines, generally to reenact some traditional legend

413

Crook: a widely used term for anything that fails to work, or for health that has gone wrong

Currawong: a bird of the crow family with a melodious song

Damper: bread made in the bush without yeast

Didgeridoo: long wooden tube or trumpet which gives out a booming sound and plays a part in aborigines' dances

Digger: originally a gold digger, now a Australian soldier

Dingo: native wild dog

Dinkum: genuine

Dogger: man who lives by destroying dingoes, for which scalp bounties are paid in most states

Duff: to steal, used especially of cattle-duffing

Fats: cattle ready for slaughter

Full-bloods: purebred aborigines

Gallah: a kind of parrot, used to describe anyone as a dolt or nitwit

Gibber: large rocks and boulders covering parts of the desert and plains

Gidgee: a stunted kind of acacia, also spelled *gidyea*

Gin: an aboriginal girl

Goanna: large lizard; derived from iguana

Grog: any alcoholic beverage, but mainly beer and spirits

Hose-holder: an idle or gormless non-toiler, technically a "slow worker"

Humpy: a shack

Jackeroo: pupil on a sheep or cattle station

Joey: a baby or immature kangaroo or wallaby

Jumbuck: a sheep

Jump-up: outback (q.v.) road

Kelpie: Australian sheep dog, said to have dingo blood

Larrikin: a tough young man, on the lines of a "ted"

Lubra: a female aborigine

Mallee: thick bush composed of several kinds of eucalypt that branch out from the root to form a number of trunks

Matilda: a bushman's swag (q.v.)

Middy: a medium-sized glass of beer

Muttonbird: one of the shearwaters

Myall: a kind of eucalypt scrub or bush, mainly in Queensland

Nardoo: a desert plant whose seeds were ground by aborigines to make flour

No-hoper: a layabout, ne'er-do-well

Off-sider: mate or assistant, derived from the bullock driver's mate who walked on the off side of the team

Overlander: originally a drover who "lifted" mobs of sheep or cattle long distances to market; now used of anyone who moves himself and his property to another part of the continent

Outback: that part of the continent lying inland of the coastal belt, away from the big cities and fertile land

Plonk: wine

Paddymelon: a small wallaby

Picnic: a shambles

Poof or poofter: a male homosexual

Pommy: an English man or woman

Ratbag: an odd man out, a solitary or eccentric with ideas of his own

Rousabout or roustabout: handy man in a shearing shed, a more or less unskilled assistant

Rozzers: old word for policemen

Run: a property or station, generally large, and as a rule in Queensland

Ringer: originally a champion shearer, now used of anyone who is "in," established, well thought of

Schooner: a large-sized beer

Scrubs: bulls who have gone wild in the ranges

Selection: land picked out for a farm; hence selector, a man who took up virgin land, often under a land-settlement scheme

Sheila: a female

Slab houses: the early buildings made from slabs of timber generally hand-hewn from the bush

Sly grog: liquor sold illegally, originally on the gold fields

Silvertail: a scornful term for the rich and pretentious. You can, however, be rich and socially prominent and "a good bloke," not a silvertail.

Smoke-o: break for tea and snacks in midmorning and midafternoon

Squatter: a large-scale grazier, generally rich

Squattocracy: the community of squatters, equivalent of a combination of aristocracy and plutocracy

Station: a large property on which sheep or cattle are grazed. Smaller ones (say below about 10,000 acres) are just "properties." "Farm" is used only when there is land under the plow.

Stringybark: a kind of eucalypt

Sundowner: itinerant worker or tramp, who turned up at sundown for a night's lodging

Swag: personal possessions carried in a rolled-up bundle by the tramp, seasonal workers and travelers: hence swagman

Top End, the: the northern area of Australia, especially the Northern Territory

Tucker: food

Walkabout, Go: travel, apparently aimlessly over long distances

Whirley or Willy-willy: whirlwind

Bibliography

The following is a list of some of the books I have read or consulted, in whole or in part. It is far from comprehensive or complete.

History and Biography

Blainey, Geoffrey, *A History of Kolan Shire*. Brisbane, University of Queensland Press.

————, *Mines in the Spinifex*. Sydney and London, Angus and Robertson, 1960.

————, *The Rush That Never Ended*. Melbourne, Melbourne University Press, 1963.

Birrell, James, *Walter Burley Griffin*. Brisbane, University of Queensland Press, 1964.

Borrie, W. D., and Packer, D., *Italians and Germans in Australia*. Melbourne, F. W. Cheshire, 1954.

Bowden, Keith, *George Bass, 1771–1803*. Melbourne, Oxford University Press, 1952.

Clark, Manning, *A Short History of Australia*. Mentor, New Australian Library, 1963.

————, ed., *Sources of Australia History,* in World's Classics. Melbourne, Oxford University Press, 1957.

Crossland, Robert, *Wainwright in Australia*. Melbourne, Oxford University Press, 1954.

Darwin, Charles, *The Voyage of the Beagle*. New York, Harper, 1960.

Drake-Brockman, H., *Voyage to Disaster*. Sydney and London, Angus & Robertson, 1964.

Durack, Mary, *Kings in Grass Castles*. London, Constable, 1959.

Dutton, Geoffrey, *Founder of a City*. Melbourne, F. W. Cheshire, 1960.

Ellis, M. H., *Francis Greenway*. Sydney, Shepherd Press, 1949.

————, *John Macarthur*. Sydney and London, Angus & Robertson, 1955.

Fitzpatrick, Kathleen, *Australian Explorers,* in World's Classics. Melbourne, Oxford University Press, 1958.

Flinders, Matthew, *Narrative of His Voyage in the Schooner Francis, 1798.* London, Golden Cockerel Press, 1946.

Hill, Ernestine, *Water into Gold.* Sydney, Robertson & Mullen, 1937.

Huxley, T. H., *Diary of the Voyage of H.M.S. Rattlesnake.* London, Chatto and Windus, 1935.

Joy, William, and Prior, Tom, *The Bushrangers.* Sydney, Shakespeare Head Press, 1963.

Knopwood, Rev. Robert, *Bobby Knopwood and His Times.* Hobart, W. E. Fuller, 1929.

Roberts, Stephen, The *Squatting Age in Australia, 1835–47.* Melbourne, Melbourne University Press, 1935/64.

Rude, George, "Captain Swing and Van Diemen's Land," Vol. 12, No. 1, Tasmanian Historical Research Association, October, 1964.

Sharland, Michael, *Stones of a Century.* Hobart, Odham, Beddowe, and Meredith, 1952.

Shaw, A. G. L., *The Story of Australia.* London, Faber & Faber, 1960.

Wigmore, Lionel, *The Long View: A History of Canberra.* Melbourne, F. W. Cheshire, 1963.

Fauna and Flora

Baner, F. H., "The Eastern Gulf Region," and "Historical Geography of White Settlement in Australia," Divisional Reports Nos. 29/2 and 64/1, Commonwealth Scientific and Industrial Research Organization, Division of Land Research & Regional Survey.

Beatty, Bill, *Unique to Australia.* Sydney and London, Angus & Robertson,

Chisholm, Alexander, *The Romance of the Lyre-Bird.* Sydney and London, Angus & Robertson, 1960.

Curtis, Winifred M., *The Students' Flora of Tasmania.* Hobart, Tasmania Govt. Printer, 1956.

Dakin, W. J., *The Great Barrier Reef,* 2nd edit., revised by Isobel Bennett. Sydney, Ure Smith, 1963.

Frauca, Harry, *The Book of Australian Wildlife.* Melbourne and London, Heinemann, 1965.

Frith, Harold J., *The Mallee-Fowl.* Sydney and London, Angus & Robertson, 1962.

Leach, J. A., *An Australian Bird Book,* revised and rewritten by Philip Crosbie Morrison. Melbourne, Whitcombe & Tombs, 1958.

Marshall, A. J., *Bower Birds.* Melbourne, Oxford University Press, 1954.

——, *The Great Extermination.* Melbourne and London, Heinemann, 1965.

Ratcliffe, Francis, *Flying Fox and Drifting Sand*. Sirius Books, Sydney and London, Angus & Robertson, 1963.

Sharland, Michael, *A Territory of Birds*. Adelaide, Rigby, 1964.

Troughton, Ellis, *Furred Animals of Australia*. Sydney and London, Angus & Robertson, 1951.

Yonge, C. M., *A Year on the Great Barrier Reef*. London, Putnam, 1930.

Art and Literature

Berndt, R. M., ed., *Australian Aboriginal Art*. Sydney, Ure Smith, 1964.

Bonython, Kym, comp., *Modern Australian Painting and Sculpture*. Adelaide, Griffin Press, 1960.

Boyd, Robin, *Australia's Home*. Melbourne, Melbourne University Press Paperback, 1961.

————, *The Australian Ugliness*. Melbourne, Penguin & F. W. Cheshire, 1963.

Herman, Morton, *Georgian Architecture in Australia*. Sydney, Ure Smith, 1963.

Pringle, John, *Australian Accent*. London, Chatto and Windus, 1958.

Rienits, Rex and Thea, *Early Artists of Australia*. Sydney and London, Angus & Robertson, 1963.

Robertson, E. Graeme, *Early Houses of Northern Tasmania*. Melbourne, Georgian House, 1964.

————, *Sydney Lace*. Melbourne, Georgian House, 1962.

————, *Victorian Heritage*. Melbourne, Georgian House, 1960.

Sheppard, Richard, *Cast Iron in Building*. London, Allen & Unwin, 1945.

Simpson, Colin, *Australian Image*. Sydney, Legend Press, 1956.

Slessor, Kenneth, *Poems*. Sirius Books, Sydney and London, Angus & Robertson, 1962.

Smith, Dr. Bernard, *Australian Painting*. Melbourne, Oxford University Press, 1962.

Stewart, Douglas A., *The Birdsville Track and Other Poems*. Sydney and London, Angus & Robertson, 1955.

Ward, Russel, ed., *The Penguin Book of Australian Ballads*. Melbourne, Penguin, 1964.

Wright, Judith, *Five Senses*. Sirius Books, Sydney and London, Angus & Robertson, 1963.

Also:

A Book of Australian Verse. Selected by Judith Wright. Melbourne, Oxford University Press, 1956.

Australian Poets Series: *A. D. Hope*. Sydney and London, Angus & Robertson, 1963.

————: *Douglas Stewart*. Sydney and London, Angus & Robertson, 1963.

————: *James McAuley*. Sydney and London, Angus & Robertson, 1963.

Australian Short Stories. Selected by W. Murdock and H. Drake-Brockman. Melbourne, Oxford University Press, 1951.

Also novels by: Patrick White, George Johnston, Randolph Stow, Hal Porter, Tom Ronan, T. A. G. Hungerford, Frank Clune, Mrs. Aeneas Gunn, Joseph Furphy, Xavier Herbert, Henry Lawson, and many others, ancient and modern.

Aborigines and General

Bates, Daisy, *The Passing of the Aborigines*. Melbourne and London, Heinemann, 1966. (First published 1938.)

Bean, C. E. W., *On the Wool Track*. New York, Scribners, 1947.

Beatty, Bill, *Tasmania*. Melbourne and London, Cassell, 1963.

Coleman, Peter, ed., *Australian Civilisation*. Melbourne, F. W. Cheshire, 1962.

Culotta, Nino, *They're a Weird Mob*. New York, Simon and Schuster, 1962.

Elkin, Adolphus P., *The Aboriginal Australians*. Melbourne, Longmans, 1961.

————, *The Australian Aborigines*, published in co-operation with American Museum of Natural History, New York, Doubleday, 1964.

Flynn, Frank, with Willey, Keith, *The Living Heart*. Sydney, F. P. Leonard, 1964.

Harney, W. E., *Grief, Gaiety and Aborigines*. London, Robert Hale, 1961.

————, *Life Among the Aborigines*. London, Robert Hale, 1957.

Horne, Donald, *The Lucky Country*. Melbourne, Penguin, 1965.

Lauder, Afferbeck, *Let Stalk Stine*. Sydney, Ure Smith, 1965.

McInnes, Colin, *Australia and New Zealand*. LIFE World Library, New York, Time-Life Books, 1965.

Moore, Inglis, ed., *A Book of Australia*. London, Collins, 1961.

Mountford, Charles, *Ayers Rock*. Sydney and London, Angus & Robertson, 1965.

Mountford C. P., ed., Records of the Australian-American Scientific Expedition to Arnhem Land. Melbourne, Melbourne University Press, 1956 to date.

Porter, Hal, *The Watcher on the Cast-Iron Balcony*. London, Faber & Faber, 1963.

Rivett, Kenneth, ed., *Immigration: Control or Colour Bar?* Melbourne, Melbourne University Press, 1962.

Shiels, Helen, ed., *Australian Aboriginal Studies*. Melbourne, Oxford University Press, 1963.

Ward, Russel B., *The Australian Legend*. Melbourne, Oxford University Press, 1960.

Index

Abdulla, Mulla, 104
Aborigines, 103, 157, 211-214, 221-225, 223, 249, 257-258, 262-263, 303-325
  assimilation, 300-302, 340, 341
  education, 299-300, 308, 340-341
  government policies, 221-223, 298-302
  language, 305
  Local Native Council, 308-309
  mission settlements, 307-315
  Northern Territory, 298-302, 338
  number of, 223, 300-301
  Pukamani rites, 305-306, 309
  reserves, 338-341
  Tasmania, 170, 185-187
Adams, Francis, 166, 168
Adelaide, 139-156
  colonization of, 146-148, 149
  parks, 148
Adelaide Corporation, 148
Age (publication), 164
Alcorso, Claudio, 167
Alcorso family, 184-185
Aldersen, Cornelis, 232
Alice Springs, 326-349
  tourism, 326
  water reserves, 345-346
Ambulance Committee, 135
American-Australian Scientific Expedition to Arnhem Land (1948), 289, 230
Anderson, William, 199
Angas, George Fyfe, 139
Angas family, 144
Anglican Church, 135, 307
Animals (publication), 112
Animals and Birds Protection Board of Tasmania, 169-170, 195-196
Antarctic beech trees, 406-408
Antipodeans (art group), 22
Anzac Day, celebration of, 286-287
Apple orchards, 193-194
Aragão, H. B., 177
Aranda tribe, 332
Archibald, J. F., 26
Architecture, 80-83, 88, 149-151, 167
  Australian style, 91
  cast-iron style, 158-162
  featurism, 150-153
  Tasmania, 201-204

420

Arnhem Land, 305, 310-320
  birds, 315-320
  size of, 310
  wildlife, 315-320
Arthur, George, 187, 189-190,
  192
Artists, 104-106, 162-165, 250-
  251, 364
  convict, 190-193
  exhibitions, 22, 164
  Heidelberg art movement, 163-
  164
  9 x 5 Impression exhibit, 164
  Sydney, 19-24
Assimilation in Action (Hasluck),
  300-301
Athenaeum (club), 31
Atolls, 369-371
Auden, W. H., 152
Austin, Thomas, 176
Australia
  colonization, 96, 146-148, 149
  convict, 185-190, 211
  size of, 230
  urbanization in, 359-360
Australian, The (newspaper), 26
Australian ballet, 57
Australian Consolidated Press, 27
Australian Dried Fruits Associa-
  tion, 129
Australian Painting, 1788-1960
  (Smith), 164
Australian Ugliness, The (Boyd),
  150
Australian Women's Weekly, 26
Australia's Home (Boyd), 148
Ayers Rock, 332-338
  cave paintings, 333-338
  discovery of, 333
Ayers Rock (Mountford), 337

Bailed Up (Roberts), 164

Bailey, Peter, 114-116, 118, 121
Bandicoot Bar diversion dam,
  271-272
Bank of New South Wales, 57
Banks, Joseph, 18, 82, 362
Barmera Co-operative Commun-
  ity, 130-136
Barossa vineyards, 139-143
Barrier Daily Truth (newspaper),
  93
Barrier Industrial Council, 94-98
Barwell, Henry Newman, 133
Bass, George, 198
  discoveries of, 205-206
Bastin, Henri, 105
Batavia (shipwreck incident),
  251-253
Bates, Daisy, 213-214
Bathurst, Lord, 87
Batman, John, 157, 192-193
Batterbee, Rex, 332
Battle of the Coral Sea (World
  War II), 207
Baxter, James, 211
Beaches, 363-364
Beagle (ship), 371
Bean, C. E. W., 114
Beatniks, 363-364
Bellona (ship), 83
Bendigo, Australia, 177-178
Bigge, J. T., 89
Bikini Atoll, nuclear bomb test at,
  371
Biological Center, 49-51
Birds, 51-58, 118-119, 155-156,
  285-286, 322-325, 372-374,
  396-411
  Arnhem Land, 315-320
  sanctuaries, 169, 175, 179, 196,
  244-247, 396-402
  for Mallee fowls, 175
  number of, 401

Birds (*continued*)
  Tasmania, 169-175, 179-183, 196
Blackburn, James, 201
Blackman, Charles, 21
Blake, Robert, 190
Blake, William, 190
Bligh, William, 82, 86, 185, 206
Bloomfield, Harry, 327-330
Bloomfield, Lou, 326-330
Bloomfield, Mrs. Lou, 328-330
Boomerangs, 223, 305, 309
Bounty (ship), 185, 206
Bowen, John, 145, 185
Bowerbirds, 52-54, 406
Boy Scouts, 135
Boyd, Arthur, 21
Boyd, Robin, 18, 20, 43, 148, 150-153, 178
Boyden, Stephen, 49-51
Brady, Matthew, 192
Breakaway, The (Roberts), 164
Brigalow trees, 383-387
British-Australian Telegraph Company, 342
British Medical Journal, 387
Brockman, Edward, 232-233
Broken Hill, 92-106
  population, 92
  settlement of, 96
Broken Hill Proprietary Company, 29, 96
Brothels, 223
Brutelle, C. L. Heritier de, 199
Bryden, William, 195
Buchanan, Nat, 344
Buffalo (ship), 146
Bulletin (newspaper), 25, 26-27
Bunn, Alfred, 30
Burbage, Andrew, 242
Button, Alf, 226
Byrne, Sam, 104-105

Camden, Lord, 83
Camels, 102
Canberra, 41-58
  artificial lake, 41-43
  growth of, 41, 44-45
  tourism, 45-46
  wildlife, 51-58
Cape Barren geese, 169-170, 196
  number of, 169
Capre II (ship), 380
Carlyle, Thomas, 213
Cast-iron architecture, 158-162
Cattle industry, 261-264, 274-285, 321, 357-358, 391
  Northern Territory, 277-285, 290-291
  size of, 278-282
Cave paintings, 310-311, 319
  Ayers Rock, 333-338
Chaffey, George, 128-129
Chaffey, W. B., 128
Chambers, John, 342
Chanticleer Mine, 102
Chickens Mine, 102
Chinese immigrants, 178, 240-241, 258, 290
Chinese Immigration Act of 1888, 290
Church of Christ Guild, 135
Church of England Guild, 135
Church Missionary Society, 313-315
Citizenship Convention, 240
Clare, John, 190
Clark, Manning, 47-48
Clarke, Marcus, 163
Cleghorn, Thomas, 22
Climate, 133, 217, 230
  New South Wales, 92
  Sydney, 17-18
Coburn, John, 22
Colbeck, James, 202

Collins, David, 185-189, 200
Commonwealth Arbitration Commission, 283-284
Commonwealth Scientific and Industrial Research Organization (C.S.I.R.O.), 51, 75, 109, 242, 245, 274, 316-318, 365, 377
Division of Tropical Pastures, 366
research experiments, 291-294
Conder, Charles, 163-164
Congregational Guild, 135
Conservation Foundation, 401
Controlled Environment Research Laboratory (CERES), 292
Convicts, 187-190
as artists, 190-193
early colonization of, 187-190, 211
Conzinc Riotinto Company, 95, 255, 354
Cook, Captain James, 109, 155, 199, 206-207, 361, 362, 368, 409
Cook, James
discoveries of, 206
Copper, 226-227, 353
Coral, 370-371, 376
largest deposits of, 368
Cornelisz, Jeronimus, 251-252
Corriedale sheep, 71
Corrugated iron, introduction of, 81
Costello family, 248, 275
Cotton Industry, 272-274
yields, 274
Country Women's Association, 97-98, 132-133, 135
Courier-Mail (newspaper), 24, 396
Court, Charles, 254
Craig, C., 203
Craig, Mrs. C., 203

Crook, Ray, 364
Crooke, Dr., 191
Crossland, Robert, 190
Currumbin sanctuary, 401-402
Curtis, Syd, 404-406, 409
Curtis, Winifred, 197

Daily Telegraph (newspaper), 24, 27
Dampier, William, 257
Daniel (aborigine), 314
Daniels, Davis, 299
Darwin, Australia, 294-300
growth of, 296
tourism, 297
Darwin, Charles, 369, 371, 373, 379
Davidson, Bruce, 260-271, 293, 365
Davies, S. J., 318
Daws, Lawrence, 22
Day Dream Mine, 102
Deacon, Alfred, 128
Death of the Birds, The (Hope), 183
Deferred rotational grazing, meaning of, 246
Denman, Lady, 41
Department of Fisheries, 244
Department of Labour, 136
Department of Mines, 386
Department of Native Welfare, 221, 223
Deserts, 211-214, 241, 326
Dickens, Charles, 190
Dickens, Monica, 37
Didgeridoos, 305, 309, 311-313
Division of Tropical Pastures (C.S.I.R.O.), 366
Dobell, William, 22, 45
Donahoe, Jack, 178
Drake-Brockman, Henrietta, 251

Dried Fruits Board, 131-132
Droughts, 120-121, 128, 344-345, 357, 390
Drydale, Russell, 21, 170-171
Durack, Elizabeth, 248-250
Durack, Jerry, 263-264
Durack, John, 263-264
Durack, Kim, 272, 275
Durack, Mary, 248-250
Durack, Michael, 263-264
Durack, Patsy, 249-250, 263-264
D'Urban, Benjamin, 144

Eagles, beak bounty on, 119, 247
Early Houses of Northern Tasmania (Craig and Robertson), 161, 203
East India Company, 148
Eccles, John, 46
Edwards, Ron, 364
Elizabeth, Australia, 149-153
Elizabeth Farm House, 83-88
Ellis, M. H., 82
Emmanuel, Samuel, 263
Emus, 247
Encyclopaedia Britannica, 410
Endeavour (ship), 207, 362
Esperance, Western Australia, 225-232
Esperance Land and Development Company, 228
Eucalyptus trees, 66-67, 194, 231-232
  kinds of, 199
  number of species, 66-67
Exports, 28-29
  kangaroo, 111, 122
  ore, 258
  rabbits, 176
  wool, 88
Extended Rustlers Mine, 178
Eyre, Edward, 211-213

Eyre Defense Committee, 213

Fairfax, Warwick, 24
Fairweather, Ian, 22
Fairy penguins, 179
Fauna Protection Panel (New South Wales), 111-112, 175
Fawkner, John Pascoe, 157
Featurism (architecture), 150-153
Federal Council for the Advancement of Aborigines and Torres Strait Islanders, 300
Feez, David, 391-392
Felton, Alfred, 162-163
Fields, Barron, 152
Financial crisis of 1893, 162
Finke, William, 342
Fleay, David, 396-402
  background of, 397
Flinders, Matthew, 169, 181, 205-206, 303, 381
Flying Doctor service, the, 98, 107-109
  first mission of, 353
  founded, 344
Flying Fox and Drifting Sand (Ratcliffe), 402
Flynn, John, 344
Forest Trees of Australia, 199
Forestry Department (Queensland), 404
Forrest, Alexander, 250, 264-265
Francis, Black, 80-81
Frauca, Harry, 388-389, 393
French, Leonard, 22
Fresne, Marich du, 185
"Friend of Australia, or a Plan for Exploring the Interior and for Carrying on a Survey of the Whole Continent, A" (Maslon), 148

Frith, Harry, 75, 109, 111-112, 175, 317-318
Fruit industry, 126-138
  data, 135
  harvests, 136
Furneaux, Tobias, 206

Gandy, Maria, 145, 146
Gardiner, Charles, 245
Ghost towns, 102-103, 218-220, 330-331
Giese, Harry, 309
Girl Guides, 135
Girls Life Brigade, 135
Gladstone Observer (newspaper), 382
Glossary of terms, 413-415
Gold, 203, 214, 220, 330
  discoveries of 1851, 157-158, 178
Gold mines, 208-233
  decline of, 218
Golden Square Mine, 178
Good Neighbor Council, 135, 239-240
Gosse, W. B., 333
Gould, John, 35-36, 53, 122, 392
Grass parrots, rarity of, 155
Gray, Thomas, 349
Great Barrier Reef, 361, 368-380
  Darwin at, 369, 371
  discovery of, 206, 368
  size of, 368
Great Barrier Reef Committee, The, 377-378
Green, Doug, 327, 330-331
Green, Gil, 327
Greenway, Francis, 88-90
  death of, 89
Grey, George, 53
Grey kangaroos, 110-111, 118
Grief, Gaiety and Aborigines

(Harney), 288
Griffin, Walter Burley, 42-44
Griffiths-Davies, Jack, 366, 385-386
Grose, Francis, 83
Grounds, Roy, 167-168
Guardian (newspaper), 26
Guiler, Eric, 195
Gulnare (ship), 145
Gum trees, 171, 197-199
  hybrids, 197
  species, 197, 199
Gunn, Mrs. Aeneas, 343-344
Gunwinggu tribe, 312

Hallstrom, Edward, 33
Harding, May, 105-106
Harney, Bill, 288-289, 334
Harry (aborigene), 338
Harte, Professor, 105-106
Hartman, Carl, 244
Hasluck, Paul, 300-301
Hawkes, Bob, 154-155
Haydock, Mary, 203-204
Hayes, John, 206
Healesville Sanctuary, 397, 399
Heemskirk (ship), 194
Heidelberg art movement, 163-164
Helms, A. D., 225-226
Hen Mine, 102
Henschke, Cyril, 139-140
Henschke, Mrs. Cyril, 139-140
Herbert, Daniel, 202
Hermannsburg Mission, 332
Heysen, Hans, 24, 164
Hick, Jacqueline, 143
Hill, Rowland, 145, 147
Hill-Smith family, 143-144
Hindmarsh, John, 145-146
Hobart, Tasmania, 184-185, 195
Hobart Museum, 195

Hodgekinson, Frank, 22
Holford, William, 44
Holtze, Maurice, 293
Hood, Tom, 190
Hooker, L. J., 282
Hope, A. D., 183
Hope (ship), 83
Horne, Donald, 25
Hospital Auxiliary, 135
Howe, Mike, 192
Hudson, William, 59-60
Hungerford, Tom, 248
Hunter, Governor, 205, 206
Hunter (barque), 82
Huxley, Thomas Henry, 213, 381

Ibis birds, 171-172
Immigration, 29-30, 217-218, 238-241, 258-261, 294-296
  Asian, 258-261
  Chinese, 178, 240-241, 258, 290
  laws, 258-259
  policies, 178, 294-295
  rate of, 239
Industry, 121-122, 184-185, 234-235
  development of, 254-255
Innes, Hugh, 389-390
Integration, 224-225
Irrigation, 270-275
  Murray River system, 128-129

Jabangari, Henry, 339
Jambidjimba, Charlie, 339
Jambidjimba, Jacky, 339
Jan (cabin boy), 252
Jeanne Marie, Sister, 308
Jenkins, Mrs., 347-348
Jenkins, Mrs. C. F. H., 243-244
Job's Gully Mine, 178
Joeys, *see* Kangaroos, joeys
John Curtin School of Medical

Research, 46, 49
Johnston, George, 86
Jones, Barton, 220-221
Joyce, Barney, 391
Joyce, Mrs. Barney, 391
Juburula, Bob, 339
Justin (aborigine), 312-313

Kaiser Steel Company, 255
Kangaroo (Lawrence), 28
"Kangaroo Situation, The" (Sharman and Frith), 112
Kangaroos, 51, 75-77, 107-125, 170, 200, 246
  birth cycle, 116-118
  eating habits, 113-114
  extermination, 111-113
  statistics, 400
  joeys, 117-118
  species, 109-111
  number of, 110
  weight, 110, 117
Kearnain, Mrs., 289-290
Kekwick, William, 343
Kelly, John, 206
Kidman, Sidney, 96
Kilfoyle family, 248, 275
Kindergarten Mothers Club, 135
Kindergarten Welfare, 135
King, Philip, 82, 185, 206
Kings in Grass Castles (Durack), 248
Kingsley, Charles, 213
Kipling, Rudyard, 18
Kirkpatrick, T. H., 110
Kmit, Michael, 22
Knopwood, Bobby, 200
Koonamore Vegetation Reserve, 345
Kosciusko State Park, 59-69
  size of, 66
Kouskos, Gus, 404-406

Ladies' Bright Hour (organization), 149
Lake Burley Griffin, 41-43
Lamb, Charles, 190
Land Act, 294
Langsford, Dr., 299
Language, 63-64
  aboriginal, 305
  glossary of terms, 413-415
  Strine, 37-38
Lapidary club, 362
Lavery, Mrs., 367
Lawler, Ray, 362
Lawrence, D. H., 28, 76
Lawson, Henry, 26, 165
Lead mines, 92, 95, 136, 353
Leichhardt, Ludwig, 17
L'Enfant, Pierre, 44
Let Stalk Strine (Morrison), 38
Lewis, Brian, 49
Light, Francis, 144
Light, William, 144-148
  background, 144-145
  death of, 148
Lindsay, Norman, 26
Liquor industry, 129
Local Native Council (aborigine), 308-309
Logging camps, 198-199
Longstaff, John, 24, 164
Loos, Wouter, 252
Lord, John, 321-322
Lord, Mrs. John, 321-322
Lost Child (McCubbin), 164
Low, David, 26
Lucky Country, The (Horne), 25
Lumber industry, 231-232, 393-394
Lutheran Church, 140, 307, 332
Lyrebirds, 54-57, 171, 404-405, 410
  mating habits, 57

Lytton, Lord, 190

Macarthur, James, 87
Macarthur, John, 81-88
Macarthur, Mrs. John, 82-88
Macarthur, William, 87
McAuley, James, 28, 386
McCubbin, Frederick, 24, 163
MacDonald, Willie, 264-265
Macnamara, Jean, 177
Macquarie, Lachlan, 18, 85, 87-88, 200
Macquarie Arms (building), 88
Macready, Charles, 190
Magpie geese, 316-318
Mahomet, Gool, 104
Mallee fowls, 173-175
  sanctuary, 175
Manchester Unity Independent Order of Odd Fellows, 104
Manganese, 227, 305
Marching Girls Association, 135
Marshall, Dennis, 229-230
Marshall, Jock, 53, 122, 169-171
Marsupials, 116-117
Marteniz, Peter, 114-116
Martin, Charles, 177
Maslon, T. J., 148
May, Phil, 26
Melbourne, 157-183
  Cultural Center, 167
  growth of, 157-162
  newspapers, 157
  population, 166
  rivalry with Sydney, 165-166
Melbourne University, 49
Men's Fellowship, 149
Menzies, Robert, 45, 240
Merino sheep, 74
Methodist Church, 307
Migration Act of 1958, 259
Miles, John Campbell, 353

Mill, John Stuart, 213
Miller, Bob, 278, 286
Mine Management Association, 95
Minerals, 226-227, 305, 353, 382
Miners' Institute, 219
Mining industry, 92-106, 216, 218-219, 254, 261, 353-354
decline of, 218
early, 177-178
Mission Council, 314
Missionaries, 307-315
Mississippi (whaler), 212
Mitchell, Major, 156
Mohammed Ali, 145
Monash University, 169
Moore, Richard, 214-216
Moore, Mrs. Richard, 215
Morning Herald (newspaper), 24, 25, 37
Morrison, Alistair, 37-38, 392, 398
Mosquito (aboriginal convict), 187
Mothers and Babies Health Association, 135
Mount Field National Park, 200
Mount Isa, 350-354
Mount Kosciusko, 51
Mount Stromlo observatory, 46
Mt. Tom Price, 255
Mt. Wellington, 184
Mountford, Charles, 320, 337
Muffled Drums (art exhibition), 22
Murdock, Keith, 25
Murdoch, Rupert, 25-26
Murinbadda tribe, 308
Murray Irrigation Trust, 129
Murray river system, 126-138
flood of 1936, 127

irrigation, 128-129
size of, 127, 153
Musicians' club (Broken Hill), 98-99
Muttonbirds, 179-183
migrations, 182-183
Myer Music Bowl, 168
Myxomatosis disease, 176, 177, 384

Namatjira, Albert, 332-333
Nation (newspaper), 27
National Capital Development Commission, 44-45
National Colonization Society, 145
National Gallery of Victoria, 163
National Trust of New South Wales, 90
National Trust (Tasmania), 203
National University, 46-49
Negritos, 185
Nelson, David, 185, 199
New South Wales Corps, 82, 84
Newspapers, 24-27, 157
Nicholson, Angus, 371-372
Nicholson, Mrs. Angus, 371-372
9 x 5 Impressions (art exhibit), 164
Nolan, Sydney, 21, 24
Norfolk (ship), 205
North Australia Company, 294
Northern Myth, The (Davidson), 271
Northern Territory, 277-302
aborigines, 298-302, 338
cattle industry, 277-285, 290-291
government, 297-298
Welfare Branch, 303-309, 340-341
Northern Territory Council for Aboriginal Rights, 298-299

Northwest, the, 254-276
  development of, 254-258
*Note on the Dental Eruption of
  some Macropodinae, A* (Kirkpatrick), 110
Nullarbor Plain, 208-214

O'Connell, Maurice, 381
Olsen, John, 21, 23
O'Malley, King, 45
On the Wool Track (Bean), 114
Opal mines, 105, 123, 124
Opperman, Hubert, 240
Ord River Irrigation Project, 270-274
Ore industry, 95, 254-257
  exports, 258
O'Reilly, Anne, 403-404
O'Reilly family, 402-404
O'Shea, Timoghy, 289
O'Shea family, 289
Overland Telegraph Station
  (Northern Territory), construction of, 342-344
Oxford University, 48
Ozervos, Dmitri, 217-218
Ozervos, Mrs. Dmitri, 217-218

Parkes, Henry, 47, 258
Parkin, Ray, 165-166
Parks, 172-173
  Adelaide, 148
  Queensland, 404-411
  Tasmania, 196-198
  Victoria, 172-173
Parrots, 155-156
  number of species, 65
Paspalis, Michael, 297
Passing of the Aborigines, The
  (Bates), 214
Passmore, John, 21
Pasteur, Louis, 177

Paterson, Banjo, 105, 165, 350, 359
Patterson, Rex, 274
Pelsaert, Francisco, 251-253
Perceval, John, 21
Perth, 234-253
  growth of, 234-237
Perth Museum, 243-244
Phillip, Arthur, 18, 39, 151, 206
Picker, Trevor, 74
Pintiburrijala, Harry, 340
Pitjandjara tribe, 334-338
Pizzey, Graham, 171-176, 180
Platypuses, 397-400
Pollock, Harry, 57-58
Polyps, 368-370
  number of species, 376
Port Arthur penitentiary, 188-189
Prince of Wales (battleship), 207
Pringle, John, 24
Prostitution, 103, 223
Pugh, Clifton, 21
Pukamani rites, 305-306, 309

Queensland, 350-367, 381-395
  beatniks, 363-364
  parks, 404-411
  pubs, 393
  size of, 360-361
Queensland Department of Primary Industries Bulletin, 110
Quokkas, 242-244

Rabbits, 345
  exports, 176
  population, 176-177
Rainfall, 92, 107, 126, 227, 290, 366, 383
Rapid (brig), 146, 147
Raportec, Stanislaus, 21
Rasp, Charles, 96
Rat kangaroos, 110, 117

Ratcliffe, Francis, 177, 243, 402, 407-408
Rattlesnake (ship), 381
Red kangaroos, 110-118, 170, 246, 400-401
Reibey, Archdeacon Thomas, 204
Reibey, Thomas, 203-204
Repulse (battleship), 207
Reserves
  aborigines, 338-341
  wildlife, 241-247
Reservoirs, 65-66, 101, 356
Returned Servicemen's League, 286, 348
Rhizobia bacteria, 78
Ride, David, 244
Roberts, Philip, 299-300
Roberts, Tom, 24, 163-164
Robertson, Graeme, 20, 158-162, 203
Robinson, George, 187
Robinson, Norman, 51-55
Roff, Charles, 401
Roman Catholic Church, 307, 308
Roper River Mission, 299
Rose, William, 22
Rossiter, Captain, 212
Roxburgh, Rachel, 84-85
Rude, George, 189-190
Rum Rebellion of 1807, 86
Ruskin, John, 161, 213
Rust, Lance, 334, 337-338

St. George League's club, 30-31
St. Joseph's Welfare Club, 135
Sardam (yacht), 251-252
Scanlan family, 248
Scenery Preservation Act, 197
Schmidt, Mrs., 133-134
School Welfare Fund, 135
Scrubbirds, rediscovery of, 233

Segregation, 224-225
  of the sexes, 99-100
Serventy, Dominic, 181, 182-183, 233, 242, 247
Sharland, Michael, 285
Sharman, G. B., 112, 243
Shearing the Rams (Roberts), 164
Shed, the, meaning of, 131-132
Sheep industry, 71-91, 102, 202-203, 170, 390-391
  beginning of, 82-83
  changes in, 77
  feed experiments, 77-80
  shearers, 72, 220-221
  Western Australia, 229-231, 245-246
Shier, Leo, 228
Show Society, 135
Silas (lay preacher), 311-313
Silver mines, 92, 95-96, 136, 353
Skehan family, 248
Skiing, 69-70, 200
Slessor, Kenneth, 24, 74-75
Smart, John, 363
Smith, Bernard, 22-23, 164
Smith, Roy, 201-202
Smith, Samuel, 143
Snowy Mountains Hydro-electric Authority, 59-69
  cost of, 69-70
Souter, D. H., 26
South Australian Company, 139
South Australian Housing Trust, 149
Spearfishing, 36
Spencer, Herbert, 213
Spiders, 36
Sports, 31, 36, 101, 148, 200, 350-353
Steel industry, 28-29
Steiglitz, Baron von, 201
Stow, Randolph, 251

Streeton, Arthur, 24, 162, 163-164

Strine (language), 37-38

Strine Association, 38

Strom, Allen, 111

Stuart, John McDouall, 342-343

Students Flora of Tasmania (Curtis), 197

Sturt, Charles, 42, 102

Sturt pea (plant), 101-102

Subterranean clover, 77-78

Sulkies, 215-216

Summer of the Seventeenth Doll (Lawler), 362

Sun (newspaper), 24

Sun-News-Pictorial (newspaper), 24

Superphosphate clover, 77-78

Swann, William, 84

Sydney, 17-40, 158, 165-168
 artists, 19-24
 climate, 17-18
 clubs, 30-33
 newspapers, 24-27
 opera house, 38-40, 167-168
 population, 166
 rivalry with Melbourne, 165-166
 zoo, 33-36

Sydney Lace (Robertson), 161

Tamar (warship), 303

Tanami Desert, 344

Tasman, Abel Janszoon, 194

Tasmania, 184-207
 aborigines, 170, 185-187
 architecture, 201-204
 birds, 169-175, 179-183, 196
 convict settlements, 185-190
 parks, 196-198
 population, 207
 wildlife, 195-197

Tea trees, 155

Territory of Birds, A (Sharland), 285

Thylacine, last recorded specimen of, 195

Tidbinbilla Valley, 41-58
 wildlife, 51-58

Times (Canberra newspaper), 24

Times, The (Adelaide newspaper), 145

Tiwi language, 305

Toolache wallaby, 122

Tortoise reserves, 241-242

Tourism, 60, 133, 192, 332, 342-344
 Alice Springs, 326
 Canberra, 45-46
 Darwin, 297

Toy, Jimmie Ah, 290

True Discovery of Australia, The (McAuley), 386

Truganini (aborigine), 187

Tucker, Albert, 21

Tulloch, Don, 322-323

Turner, Mort, 195-196

Underwood, Eric, 226-227

Unfortunate Bolle, The (mine), 178

Union League, 31

Unions, 93-98

United Lutheran Protestant Church of Australia, 140

University of Birmingham, 47

University College (Canberra), 46

University College (Queensland), 365-366

University of Queensland, 377-378

University of Sidney, 37, 270

University of Western Australia, 226, 243, 270

Uranium, 354
Utzon, Joern, 38, 167

Venus (brig), 206
Verge, John, 81
Victoria
first newspaper in, 157
national parks, 172-173
Victorian Heritage (Robertson), 161
Voyage of the Beagle, The (Darwin), 371
Voyage to Disaster (Drake-Brockman), 251

Wainewright, Thomas, 190-192
Wainewright in Australia (Crossland), 190
Wakefield, Edward Gibbon, 145
Wallabies, 109-112, 122, 200
Wallace, Alfred Russel, 392
Waring, Harry, 243-244
Warrabulabdgi, Sammy, 340
Water-skiing, 101, 350-353
Watson, John, 75, 77-80, 113
Watts, John, 158
Webster, Harley, 233
Welsh, George, 364-365
Welsh Plant Breeding Station, 366
West, Bert, 179
West Burleigh Sanctuary, 400
Westbrook, Eric, 163
Western Australia, 208-233, 234-253
sheep industry, 229-231, 245-246
size of, 230
Whip-tailed wallabies, 109-110
White, Mrs., 394-395
White Australia Policy, 178, 258-261

beginning of, 258-259
Wilde, Oscar, 190
Wildlife, 51-58, 153-156, 396-411
Arnhem Land, 315-320
Canberra, 51-58
reserves, 241-247
for tortoise, 241-242
Tasmania, 195-197
Tidbinbilla Valley, 51-58
William, King, 146
Windsor, Australia, 88-91
Wine industry, 126-138, 139-143
Barossa vineyards, 139-143
data, 135
Wint, Peter de, 144
Winter Evening (McCubbin), 164
Wombats, 153-154
discovery of, 206
types of, 154
Wool industry, 71-91, 102
average production, 77
beginning of, 82-83
exports, 88
mills, 184-185
Woolsheds, 72, 99
World War I, 104
World War II, 206-207
Wren, Christopher, 89
Wright, Frank Lloyd, 42
Wright, Judith, 410-411
Wylie (native boy), 212

Yalumba wines, 143
Young Christian Workers, 149
Young Women's Christian Association (Y.W.C.A.), 97

Zeehaen (ship), 194
Zinc, 226-227, 353
mines, 92, 95

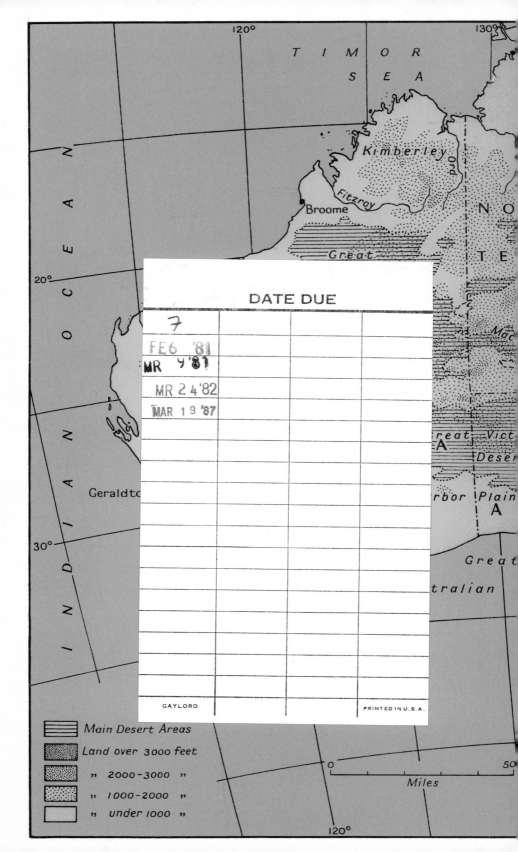

DATE DUE

7			
FE6 '81			
MR 9 '81			
MR 24 '82			
MAR 19 '87			
GAYLORD			PRINTED IN U.S.A.